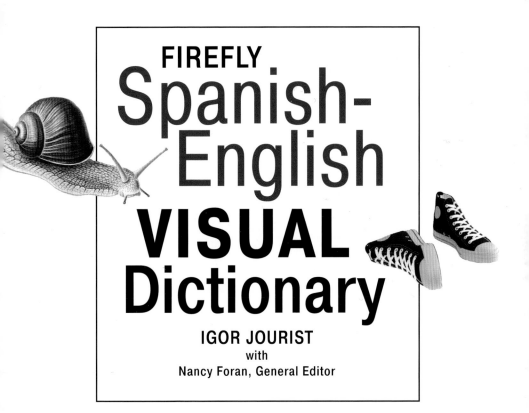

FIREFLY
Spanish-
English
VISUAL
Dictionary

IGOR JOURIST

with
Nancy Foran, General Editor

FIREFLY BOOKS

A FIREFLY BOOK

Published by Firefly Books Ltd. 2015
Illustrations and basic text © 2015 Jourist Verlag GmbH, Hamburg
Text adaptations for this publication © 2015 Firefly Books Ltd.

First printing

Publisher Cataloging-in-Publication Data (U.S.)
Jourist, Igor.
Firefly Spanish-English visual dictionary / Igor Jourist with Nancy Foran, general editor.
[800] pages : color illustrations ; cm.
Includes index. Text in English and Spanish.
Summary: A bilingual reference which presents detailed and accurate
illustrations of thousands of items, from everyday objects to highly specialized equipment.
ISBN-13: 978-1-77085-622-6
1. Picture dictionaries, Spanish. 2. Picture dictionaries, English. 3. Spanish
language – Dictionaries – English. 4. English language – Dictionaries –
Spanish. I. Foran, Nancy, editor. II. Title. III. Spanish-English visual dictionary.
463.21 dc23   PC4640.J576 2015

Library and Archives Canada Cataloguing in Publication
Jourist, Igor, author
Firefly Spanish-English visual dictionary / Igor Jourist ; with Nancy Foran, general editor.
Includes index.
ISBN 978-1-77085-622-6 (bound)
1. Picture dictionaries, Spanish. 2. Picture dictionaries, English.
3. Spanish language–Dictionaries–English. 4. English language–
Dictionaries–Spanish. I. Foran, Nancy, editor
II. Title: Spanish-English visual dictionary.
PC4640.J68 2015   463'.21   C2015-903104-4

Published in the United States by
Firefly Books (U.S.) Inc.
P.O. Box 1338, Ellicott Station
Buffalo, New York 14205

Published in Canada by
Firefly Books Ltd.
50 Staples Avenue, Unit 1
Richmond Hill, Ontario L4B 0A7

Illustrations, terminology and production: Jourist Verlags GmbH, Hamburg

jourist

Cover design: Jacqueline Hope Raynor
Printed in China

LIST OF CHAPTERS
LISTA DE CAPÍTULOS

CONTENTS

LEISURE AND ENTERTAINMENT
OCIO Y ENTRETENIMIENTO   558

OFFICE *OFICINA*   584

TRANSPORTATION
TRANSPORTE   612

HOW TO USE THE DICTIONARY
CÓMO USAR EL DICCIONARIO

Subtheme | *Sub-temas*
The 14 themes are divided into more specific subjects, which group related objects together. | *Los 14 temas se subdividen en asuntos más específicos, en los que se agrupan los objetos relacionados entre sí.*

Indicator
These lines link the vocabulary with the specific part of the illustration that is being identified.
Indicador
Estas líneas unen el vocabulario con la parte específica de la ilustración a la que se refiere.

HOUSEHOLD FURNISHINGS *ARTÍCULOS* ᴹ *DOMÉSTICOS*
Furniture *Muebles* ᴹ

Topic
Some subthemes are divided into topics, which are more specific and more closely related groupings.
Tópico
Algunos sub-temas se subdividen en tópicos, que son agrupaciones aún más específicas y de relación más estrecha.

Sofas
Sofás ᴹ

sectional sofa
sofá ᴹ *seccional*

backrest
respaldo ᴹ

seat cushion
asiento ᴹ *acolchado*

leg
pata ᶠ

arm
brazo ᴹ

Subtopic
Subtopics are the smallest, most specific and most closely related groupings.
Sub-tópico
Los sub-tópicos son las agrupaciones más pequeñas, específicas y de relación más estrecha.

ottoman
otomana ᶠ

loveseat
sofá ᴹ *estrecho*

bench
banco ᴹ *acolchado*

chaise longe
chaiselongue ᶠ

Gender identification
The gender is indicated for every Spanish noun.
Identificación del género
El género de cada nombre en español aparece indicado al lado del mismo.

Object illustration
A detailed illustration of the object being defined; for some illustrations, several parts are identified and defined.
Ilustración del objeto
Una ilustración detallada del objeto que se define. En el caso de algunas ilustraciones, se identifican y definen varias partes del objeto.

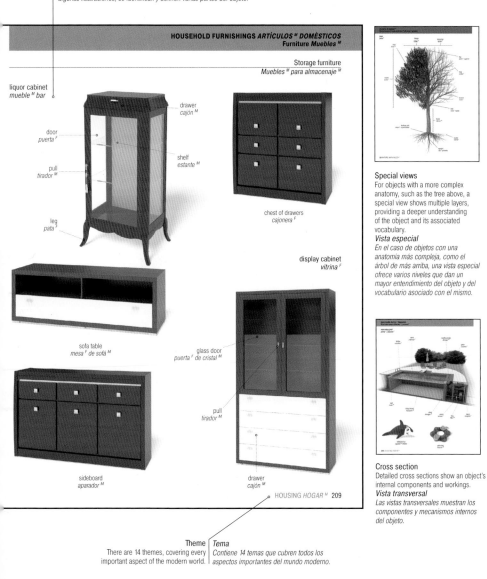

HOUSEHOLD FURNISHINGS *ARTÍCULOS ᴹ DOMÉSTICOS*
Furniture *Muebles ᴹ*

Storage furniture
Muebles ᴹ para almacenaje ᴹ

liquor cabinet
mueble ᴹ bar

drawer
cajón ᴹ

door
puerta ᶠ

shelf
estante ᴹ

pull
tirador ᴹ

leg
pata ᶠ

chest of drawers
cajonera ᶠ

display cabinet
vitrina ᶠ

sofa table
mesa ᶠ de sofá ᴹ

glass door
puerta ᶠ de cristal ᴹ

pull
tirador ᴹ

sideboard
aparador ᴹ

drawer
cajón ᴹ

Special views
For objects with a more complex anatomy, such as the tree above, a special view shows multiple layers, providing a deeper understanding of the object and its associated vocabulary.
Vista especial
En el caso de objetos con una anatomía más compleja, como el árbol de más arriba, una vista especial ofrece varios niveles que dan un mayor entendimiento del objeto y del vocabulario asociado con el mismo.

Cross section
Detailed cross sections show an object's internal components and workings.
Vista transversal
Las vistas transversales muestran los componentes y mecanismos internos del objeto.

Theme | *Tema*
There are 14 themes, covering every important aspect of the modern world. | *Contiene 14 temas que cubren todos los aspectos importantes del mundo moderno.*

NATURE

NATURALEZA

animal cell
célula F animal

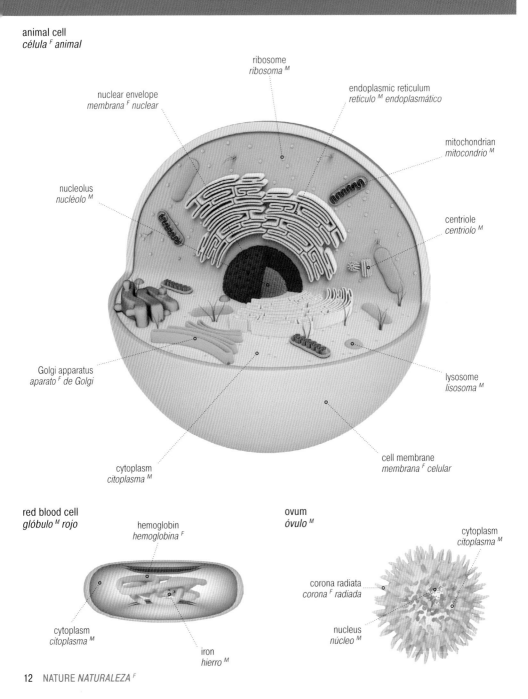

ribosome
ribosoma M

nuclear envelope
membrana F nuclear

endoplasmic reticulum
retículo M endoplasmático

mitochondrian
mitocondrio M

nucleolus
nucléolo M

centriole
centriolo M

Golgi apparatus
aparato F de Golgi

lysosome
lisosoma M

cytoplasm
citoplasma M

cell membrane
membrana F celular

red blood cell
glóbulo M rojo

hemoglobin
hemoglobina F

ovum
óvulo M

cytoplasm
citoplasma M

corona radiata
corona F radiada

cytoplasm
citoplasma M

iron
hierro M

nucleus
núcleo M

Arabian horse
caballo ^M *árabe*

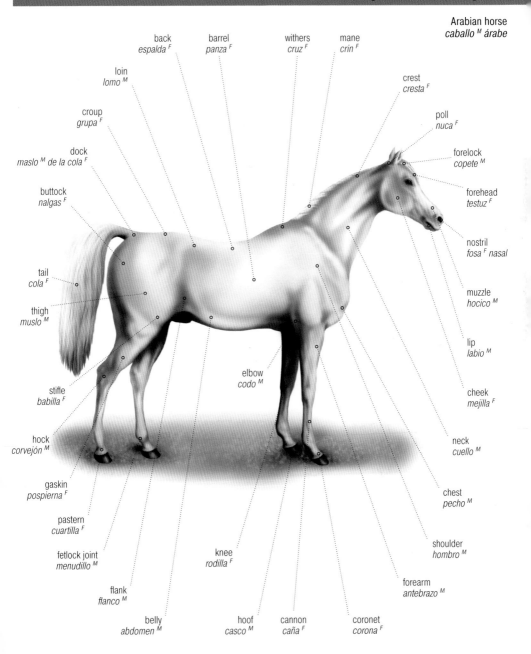

back
espalda ^F

barrel
panza ^F

withers
cruz ^F

mane
crin ^F

loin
lomo ^M

crest
cresta ^F

croup
grupa ^F

poll
nuca ^F

dock
maslo ^M *de la cola* ^F

forelock
copete ^M

buttock
nalgas ^F

forehead
testuz ^F

nostril
fosa ^F *nasal*

tail
cola ^F

muzzle
hocico ^M

thigh
muslo ^M

lip
labio ^M

elbow
codo ^M

cheek
mejilla ^F

stifle
babilla ^F

hock
corvejón ^M

neck
cuello ^M

gaskin
pospierna ^F

chest
pecho ^M

pastern
cuartilla ^F

fetlock joint
menudillo ^M

knee
rodilla ^F

shoulder
hombro ^M

flank
flanco ^M

forearm
antebrazo ^M

belly
abdomen ^M

hoof
casco ^M

cannon
caña ^F

coronet
corona ^F

white-tailed deer
venado ᴹ *de cola* ᶠ *blanca*

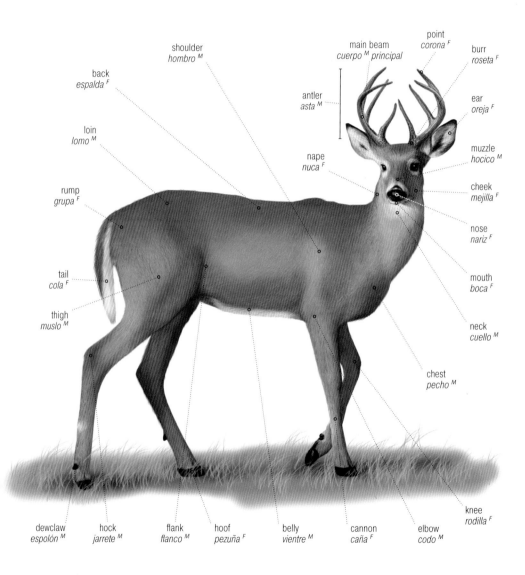

shoulder
hombro ᴹ

back
espalda ᶠ

loin
lomo ᴹ

rump
grupa ᶠ

tail
cola ᶠ

thigh
muslo ᴹ

main beam
cuerpo ᴹ *principal*

point
corona ᶠ

burr
roseta ᶠ

antler
asta ᴹ

ear
oreja ᶠ

nape
nuca ᶠ

muzzle
hocico ᴹ

cheek
mejilla ᶠ

nose
nariz ᶠ

mouth
boca ᶠ

neck
cuello ᴹ

chest
pecho ᴹ

dewclaw
espolón ᴹ

hock
jarrete ᴹ

flank
flanco ᴹ

hoof
pezuña ᶠ

belly
vientre ᴹ

cannon
caña ᶠ

elbow
codo ᴹ

knee
rodilla ᶠ

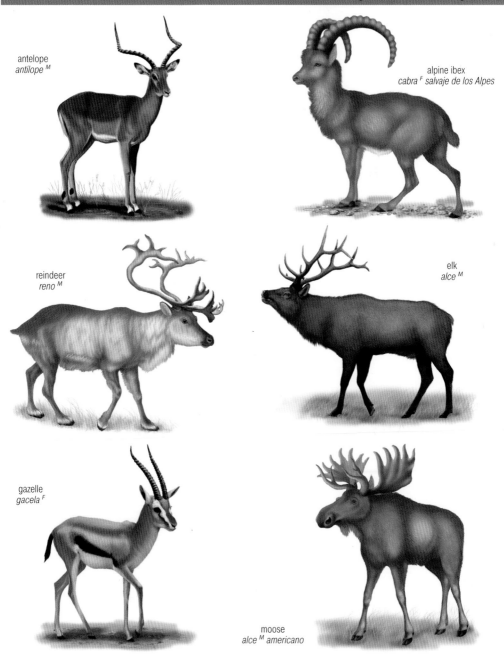

antelope
antílope ^M

alpine ibex
cabra ^F *salvaje de los Alpes*

reindeer
reno ^M

elk
alce ^M

gazelle
gacela ^F

moose
alce ^M *americano*

musk ox
buey ^M almizclero

buffalo
búfalo ^M

bison
bisonte ^M

tapir
tapir ^M / danta ^F

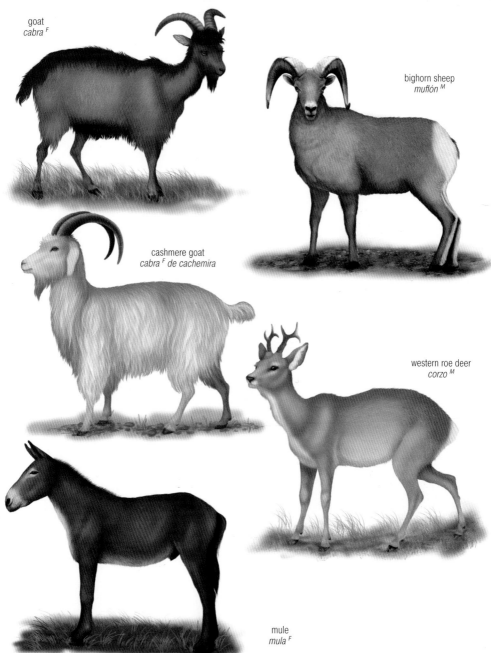

goat
cabra ^F

bighorn sheep
muflón ^M

cashmere goat
cabra ^F *de cachemira*

western roe deer
corzo ^M

mule
mula ^F

rhinoceros
rinoceronte ^M

hippopotamus
hipopótamo ^M

giraffe
jirafa ^F

Asian elephant
elefante ^M *asiático*

dromedary camel
dromedario ᴹ

Bactrian camel
camello ᴹ *bactriano*

llama
llama ᶠ

zebra
cebra ᶠ

cow
vaca ^F

donkey
burro ^M

wild boar
jabalí ^M

pig
cerdo ^M

sheep
oveja ^F

polar bear
oso ᴹ *polar*

black bear
oso ᴹ *negro americano*

giant panda
oso ᴹ *panda*

grizzly bear
oso ᴹ *pardo*

cougar
puma ^M

ear
oreja ^F

chest
pecho ^M

upper arm
parte ^F *superior del brazo* ^M

cheek
mejilla ^F

shoulder
hombro ^M

back
espalda ^F

eye
ojo ^M

elbow
codo ^M

forehead
frente ^F

ribcage
costillas ^F

flank
flanco ^M

stop
depresión ^F *frontonasal*

tail root
raíz ^F *de la cola* ^F

nasal dorsum
dorso ^M *nasal*

buttock
anca ^F

thigh
muslo ^M

whiskers
bigotes ^M

muzzle
hocico ^M

nose
nariz ^F

tail
cola ^F

hind leg
pata ^F *trasera*

paw
pata ^F

hock
jarrete ^M

dewclaw
espolón ^M

belly
vientre ^M

foreleg
pata ^F *delantera*

forearm
antebrazo ^M

digit
dedo ^M

claw
garra ^F

pastern
cuartilla ^F

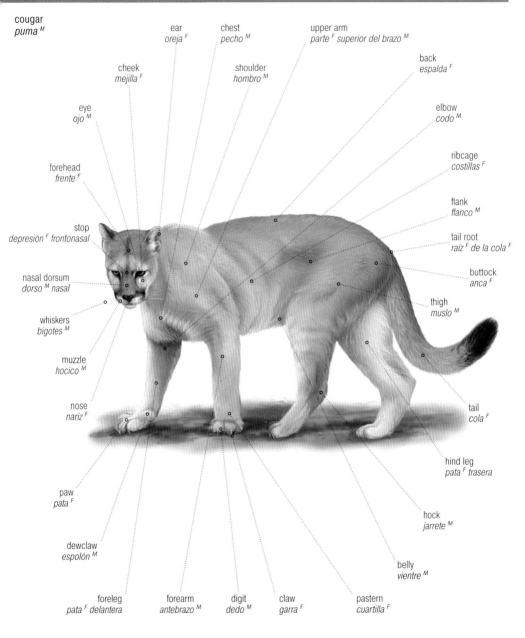

wolf
lobo ^M

cheetah
guepardo ^M

lion
león ^M

jackal
chacal ^M

lynx
lince ^M

spotted hyena
hiena ^F *manchada*

striped hyena
hiena ^F *rayada*

snow leopard
leopardo ^M *de las nieves* ^F

tiger
tigre ^M

jaguar
jaguar ^M

badger
tejón _M_

otter
nutria _F_ _europea_

stoat
armiño _M_

polecat
turón _M_

skunk
mofeta _F_ / _zorrillo_ _M_

racoon
mapache _M_

jungle cat
gato ᴹ *salvaje*

marten
marta ᶠ *europea*

wolverine
glotón ᴹ

wildcat
gato ᴹ *montés*

red fox
zorro ᴹ *rojo*

gray seal
foca ᶠ

fur seal
foca ᴹ *peletera*

walrus
morsa ᶠ

sea lion
león ᴹ *marino*

bulldog
buldog ^M

rottweiler
rottweiler ^M

Siberian husky
husky ^M *siberiano*

collie
collie ^M

dachshund
perro ^M *salchicha* ^F

poodle
caniche ^M

German shepherd
pastor ^M *alemán*

dalmatian
dálmata ^M

golden retriever
golden retriever ^M

Chihuahua
Chihuahua ^M

Labrador retriever
labrador ^M

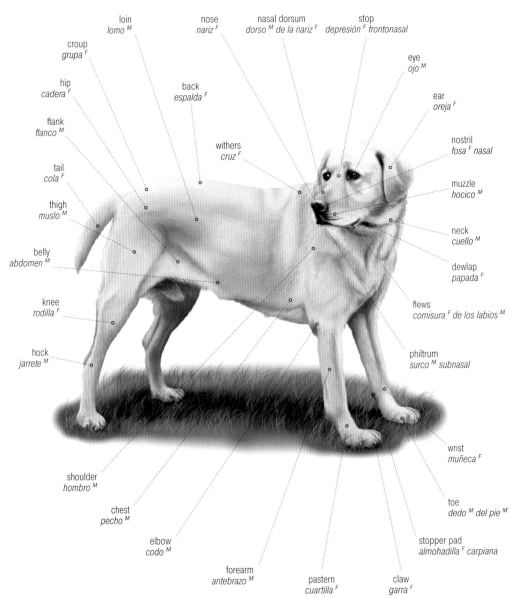

loin
lomo ^M

nose
nariz ^F

nasal dorsum
dorso ^M *de la nariz* ^F

stop
depresión ^F *frontonasal*

croup
grupa ^F

eye
ojo ^M

hip
cadera ^F

back
espalda ^F

ear
oreja ^F

flank
flanco ^M

withers
cruz ^F

nostril
fosa ^F *nasal*

tail
cola ^F

muzzle
hocico ^M

thigh
muslo ^M

neck
cuello ^M

belly
abdomen ^M

dewlap
papada ^F

knee
rodilla ^F

flews
comisura ^F *de los labios* ^M

hock
jarrete ^M

philtrum
surco ^M *subnasal*

wrist
muñeca ^F

shoulder
hombro ^M

toe
dedo ^M *del pie* ^M

chest
pecho ^M

stopper pad
almohadilla ^F *carpiana*

elbow
codo ^M

forearm
antebrazo ^M

pastern
cuartilla ^F

claw
garra ^F

British shorthair
británico ^M *de pelo* ^M *corto*

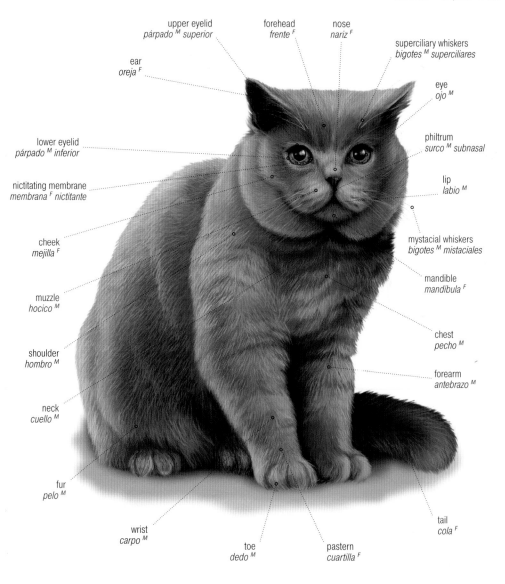

upper eyelid
párpado ^M *superior*

forehead
frente ^F

nose
nariz ^F

superciliary whiskers
bigotes ^M *superciliares*

ear
oreja ^F

eye
ojo ^M

lower eyelid
párpado ^M *inferior*

philtrum
surco ^M *subnasal*

nictitating membrane
membrana ^F *nictitante*

lip
labio ^M

cheek
mejilla ^F

mystacial whiskers
bigotes ^M *mistaciales*

mandible
mandíbula ^F

muzzle
hocico ^M

chest
pecho ^M

shoulder
hombro ^M

forearm
antebrazo ^M

neck
cuello ^M

fur
pelo ^M

tail
cola ^F

wrist
carpo ^M

toe
dedo ^M

pastern
cuartilla ^F

Norwegian forest cat
gato ^M *del bosque* ^M *de Noruega* ^F

Russian blue
azul ruso ^M

Maine coon
gato ^M *maine coon*

Persian cat
persa ^M

Siamese cat
siamés ^M

rabbit
conejo M

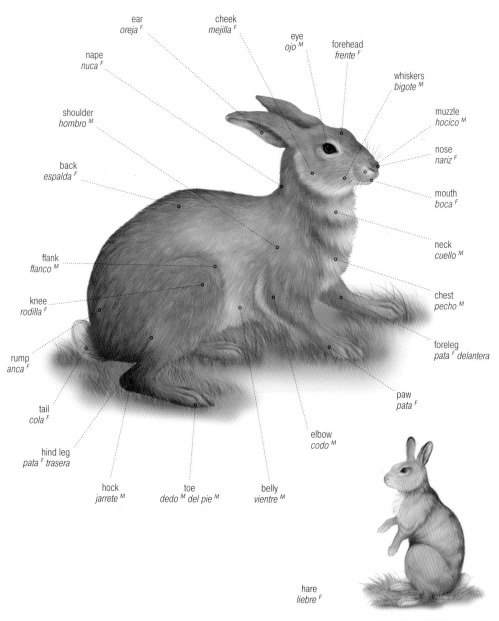

ear
oreja F

cheek
mejilla F

eye
ojo M

forehead
frente F

nape
nuca F

whiskers
bigote M

shoulder
hombro M

muzzle
hocico M

back
espalda F

nose
nariz F

mouth
boca F

neck
cuello M

flank
flanco M

knee
rodilla F

chest
pecho M

rump
anca F

foreleg
pata F *delantera*

tail
cola F

paw
pata F

hind leg
pata F *trasera*

elbow
codo M

hock
jarrete M

toe
dedo M *del pie* M

belly
vientre M

hare
liebre F

koala
koala ᴹ

head
cabeza ᶠ

ear
oreja ᶠ

cheek
mejilla ᶠ

eye
ojo ᴹ

mouth
boca ᶠ

nose
nariz ᶠ

forelimb
extremidad ᶠ *anterior*

hind limb
extremidad ᶠ *posterior*

chest
pecho ᴹ

opposable digit
dedo ᴹ *oponible*

digit
dedo ᴹ

hind paw
pata ᶠ *posterior*

forepaw
pata ᶠ *delantera*

claw
garra ᶠ

kangaroo
canguro ᴹ

opossum
zarigüeya ᶠ

house mouse
ratón ^M *común*

tail
cola ^F

hind limb
extremidad ^F *posterior*

fur
piel ^F

ear
oreja ^F

eye
ojo ^M

hind paw
garra ^F *posterior*

digit
dedo ^M

forelimb
extremidad ^F *anterior*

forepaw
zarpa ^F

claw
garra ^F

whiskers
bigotes ^M

nose
nariz ^F

field vole
topillo ^M *agreste*

brown rat
rata ^F *parda*

porcupine
puercoespín ^M

red-rumped agouti
aguti ^M brasileño

beaver
castor ^M

muskrat
rata ^F almizclera

chinchilla
chinchilla ^F

gray squirrel
ardilla ^F gris

marmot
marmota ^F

hamster
hámster ᴹ

guinea pig
conejillo ᴹ *de Indias* ᶠ / *cobayo* ᴹ

jerboa
jerbo ᴹ

chipmunk
ardilla ᶠ *rayada*

platypus
ornitorrinco ᴹ

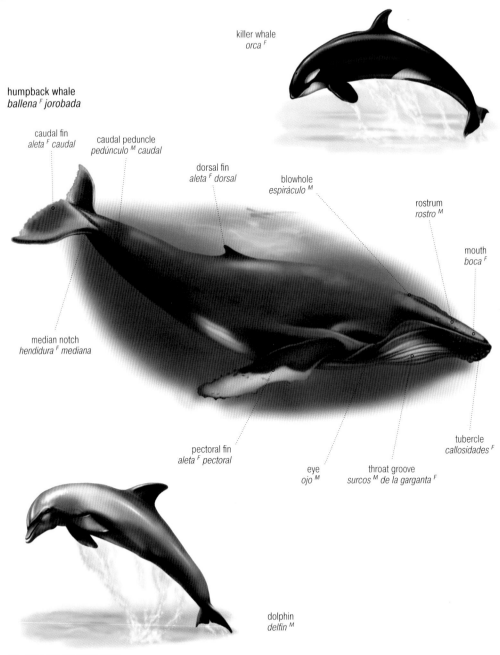

killer whale
orca ^F

humpback whale
ballena ^F *jorobada*

caudal fin
aleta ^F *caudal*

caudal peduncle
pedúnculo ^M *caudal*

dorsal fin
aleta ^F *dorsal*

blowhole
espiráculo ^M

rostrum
rostro ^M

mouth
boca ^F

median notch
hendidura ^F *mediana*

tubercle
callosidades ^F

pectoral fin
aleta ^F *pectoral*

eye
ojo ^M

throat groove
surcos ^M *de la garganta* ^F

dolphin
delfín ^M

blue whale
ballena ^F *azul*

fin whale
rorcual ^M *común*

beluga
beluga ^F

Galápagos tortoise
tortuga ^F de las galápagos

vertebral scute
escudo ^M vertebral

costal scute
escudo ^M costal

carapace
caparazón ^M

neck
cuello ^M

marginal scute
escudo ^M marginal

eye
ojo ^M

horny beak
pico ^M calloso

pygal plate
escudo ^M precentral

mouth
boca ^F

leg
pierna ^F

scale
escama ^F

plastron
plastrón ^M

claw
garra ^F

Blanding's turtle
tortuga ^F Blandingii

green sea turtle
tortuga ^F marina verde

chameleon
camaleón ^M

iguana
iguana ^F

monitor lizard
varano ^M

gecko
geco ^M

common wall lizard
lagartija ^F

Cuban crocodile
cocodrilo ^M *cubano*

caiman
caimán ^M

alligator
caimán ^M *americano*

Nile crocodile
cocodrilo ^M *del Nilo* ^M

Snakes
Serpientes ^F

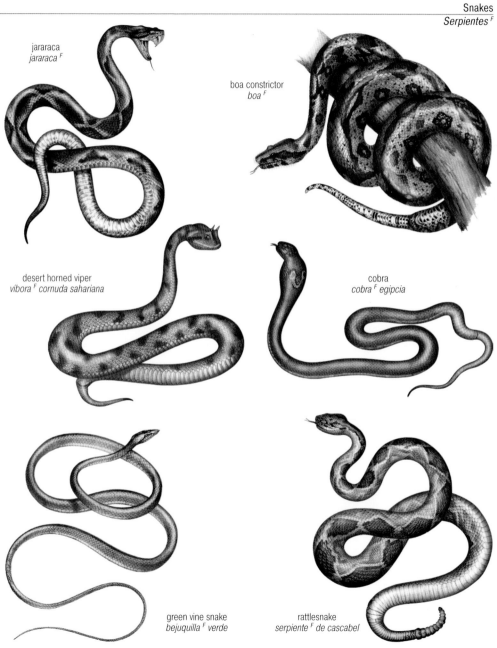

jararaca
jararaca ^F

boa constrictor
boa ^F

desert horned viper
víbora ^F *cornuda sahariana*

cobra
cobra ^F *egipcia*

green vine snake
bejuquilla ^F *verde*

rattlesnake
serpiente ^F *de cascabel*

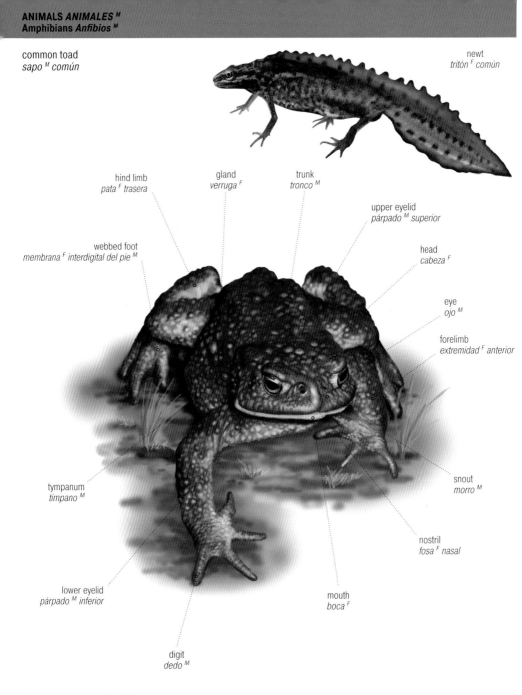

common toad
sapo ^M *común*

newt
tritón ^F *común*

hind limb
pata ^F *trasera*

gland
verruga ^F

trunk
tronco ^M

upper eyelid
párpado ^M *superior*

webbed foot
membrana ^F *interdigital del pie* ^M

head
cabeza ^F

eye
ojo ^M

forelimb
extremidad ^F *anterior*

snout
morro ^M

tympanum
tímpano ^M

nostril
fosa ^F *nasal*

lower eyelid
párpado ^M *inferior*

mouth
boca ^F

digit
dedo ^M

cane toad
sapo ᴹ *de caña* ᶠ

salamander
salamandra ᶠ

common frog
rana ᶠ *común*

tree frog
rana ᶠ *de cristal* ᴹ

edible frog
rana ᶠ *comestible*

bat
murciélago ^M

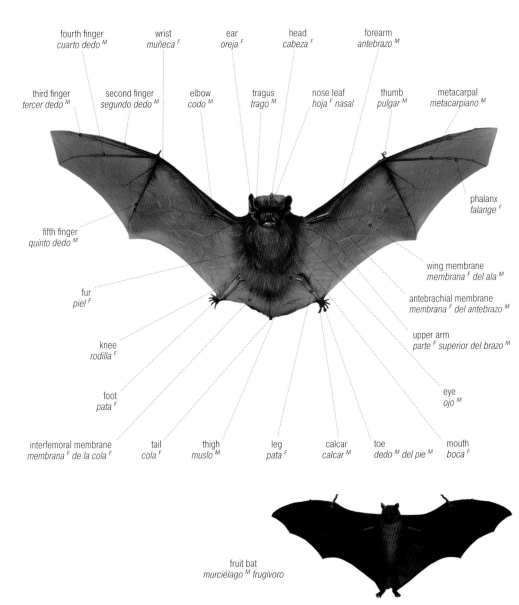

fourth finger
cuarto dedo ^M

wrist
muñeca ^F

ear
oreja ^F

head
cabeza ^F

forearm
antebrazo ^M

third finger
tercer dedo ^M

second finger
segundo dedo ^M

elbow
codo ^M

tragus
trago ^M

nose leaf
hoja ^F *nasal*

thumb
pulgar ^M

metacarpal
metacarpiano ^M

phalanx
falange ^F

fifth finger
quinto dedo ^M

fur
piel ^F

wing membrane
membrana ^F *del ala* ^M

antebrachial membrane
membrana ^F *del antebrazo* ^M

knee
rodilla ^F

upper arm
parte ^F *superior del brazo* ^M

foot
pata ^F

eye
ojo ^M

interfemoral membrane
membrana ^F *de la cola* ^F

tail
cola ^F

thigh
muslo ^M

leg
pata ^F

calcar
calcar ^M

toe
dedo ^M *del pie* ^M

mouth
boca ^F

fruit bat
murciélago ^M *frugívoro*

mole
topo ^M

head
cabeza ^F

eye
ojo ^M

body
cuerpo ^M

snout
morro ^M

fur
piel ^F

tail
cola ^F

finger
dedo ^F

claw
garra ^F

forelimb
extremidad ^F *anterior*

toe
dedo ^M *del pie* ^M

hind limb
extremidad ^F *posterior*

hedgehog
erizo ^M

pangolin
pangolín ^M

giant anteater
oso ^M *hormiguero*

armadillo
armadillo ^M

Japanese macaque
macaco ᴹ *japonés*

muzzle
hocico ᴹ

superciliary arch
arco ᴹ *superciliar*

fur
piel ᶠ

face
cara ᶠ

knee
rodilla ᶠ

nose
nariz ᶠ

arm
brazo ᴹ

mouth
boca ᶠ

hand
mano ᶠ

leg
pierna ᶠ

opposable digit
dedo ᴹ *oponible*

digit
dedo ᴹ

foot
pata ᶠ

nail
uña ᶠ

chimpanzee
chimpancé ᴹ

baboon
papión ᴹ *amarillo*

lemur
lémur ᴹ

lion tamarin
mono ^M tití

orangutan
orangután ^M

red howler monkey
mono ^M aullador rojo

slow loris
loris ^M perezosos

mandrill
mandril ^M

gorilla
gorila ^M

lobster
bogavante [M]

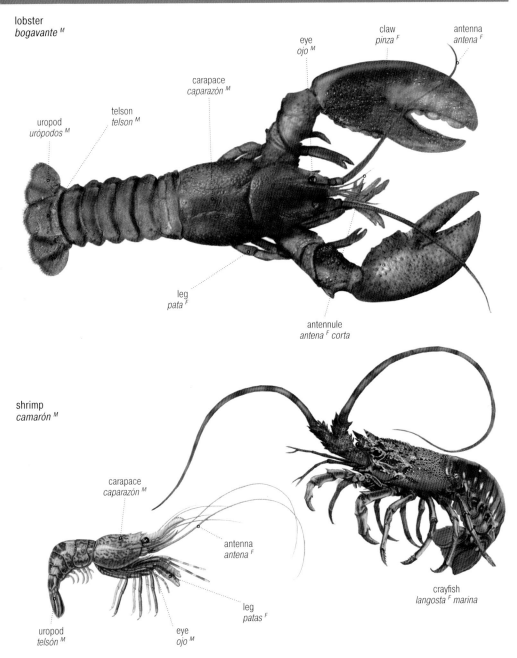

claw
pinza [F]

antenna
antena [F]

eye
ojo [M]

carapace
caparazón [M]

telson
telson [M]

uropod
urópodos [M]

leg
pata [F]

antennule
antena [F] *corta*

shrimp
camarón [M]

carapace
caparazón [M]

antenna
antena [F]

uropod
telsón [M]

eye
ojo [M]

leg
patas [F]

crayfish
langosta [F] *marina*

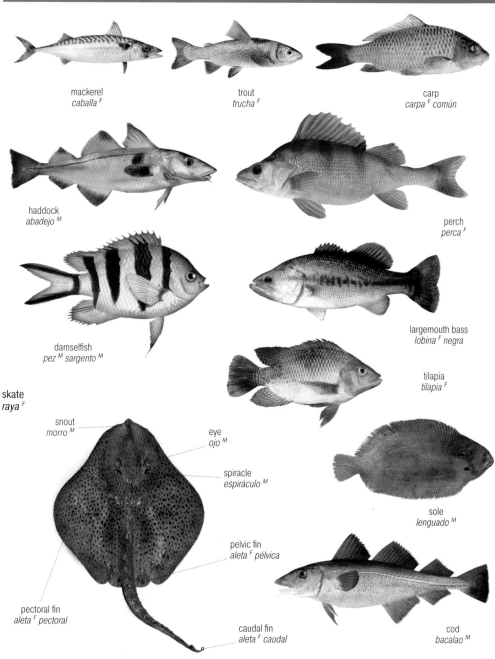

mackerel
caballa F

trout
trucha F

carp
carpa F *común*

haddock
abadejo M

perch
perca F

damselfish
pez M *sargento* M

largemouth bass
lobina F *negra*

tilapia
tilapia F

skate
raya F

snout
morro M

eye
ojo M

spiracle
espiráculo M

pelvic fin
aleta F *pélvica*

sole
lenguado M

pectoral fin
aleta F *pectoral*

caudal fin
aleta F *caudal*

cod
bacalao M

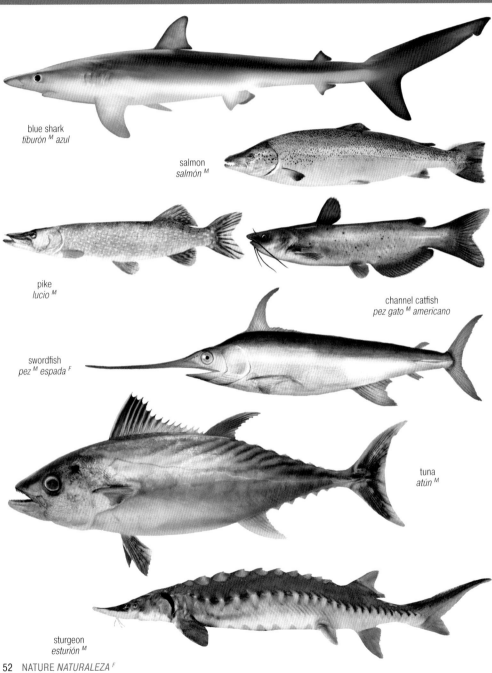

blue shark
tiburón ^M *azul*

salmon
salmón ^M

pike
lucio ^M

channel catfish
pez gato ^M *americano*

swordfish
pez ^M *espada* ^F

tuna
atún ^M

sturgeon
esturión ^M

octopus
pulpo ᴹ

mantle
manto ᴹ

siphon
sifón ᴹ

eye
ojo ᴹ

arm
tentáculo ᴹ

sucker
ventosa ᶠ

crab
cangrejo ᴹ

eyestalk
pedúnculo ᴹ *ocular*

antenna
antena ᶠ

leg
pata ᶠ

cheliped
pinza ᶠ

carapace
caparazón ᴹ

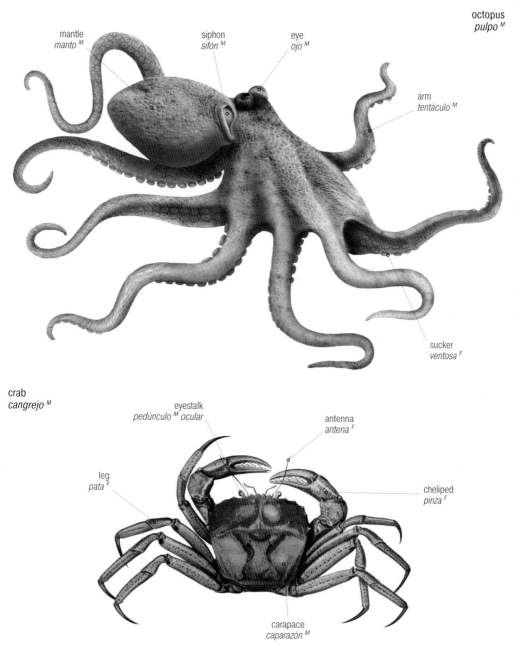

Eurasian jay
arrendajo ᴹ

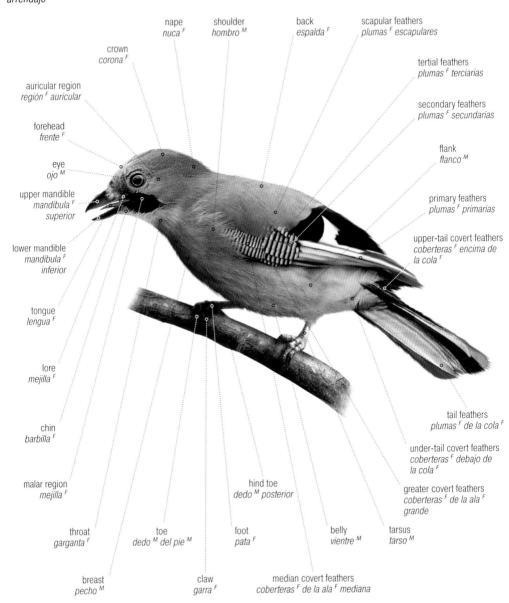

nape
nuca ᶠ

shoulder
hombro ᴹ

back
espalda ᶠ

scapular feathers
plumas ᶠ *escapulares*

crown
corona ᶠ

tertial feathers
plumas ᶠ *terciarias*

auricular region
región ᶠ *auricular*

secondary feathers
plumas ᶠ *secundarias*

forehead
frente ᶠ

flank
flanco ᴹ

eye
ojo ᴹ

upper mandible
mandíbula ᶠ
superior

primary feathers
plumas ᶠ *primarias*

lower mandible
mandíbula ᶠ
inferior

upper-tail covert feathers
coberteras ᶠ *encima de*
la cola ᶠ

tongue
lengua ᶠ

lore
mejilla ᶠ

tail feathers
plumas ᶠ *de la cola* ᶠ

chin
barbilla ᶠ

under-tail covert feathers
coberteras ᶠ *debajo de*
la cola ᶠ

malar region
mejilla ᶠ

hind toe
dedo ᴹ *posterior*

greater covert feathers
coberteras ᶠ *de la ala* ᶠ
grande

throat
garganta ᶠ

toe
dedo ᴹ *del pie* ᴹ

foot
pata ᶠ

belly
vientre ᴹ

tarsus
tarso ᴹ

breast
pecho ᴹ

claw
garra ᶠ

median covert feathers
coberteras ᶠ *de la ala* ᶠ *mediana*

Eurasian siskin
lúgano ^M

bullfinch
camachuelo ^M

common swift
vencejo ^M *común*

greater titmouse
herrerillo ^M *común*

pigeon
paloma ^F

red-backed shrike
alcaudón ^M *dorsirrojo*

blue jay
urraca ^F *azul*

hummingbird
colibrí ^M

black-capped chickadee
carbonero ^M *cabecinegro*

woodpecker
pájaro ^M *carpintero*

kingfisher
martín pescador ^M

cockatiel
cacatúa ^F *ninfa* ^F

barn swallow
golondrina ^F *común*

American goldfinch
jilguero ^M *americano*

cardinal
cardenal ^M

American robin
mirlo ^M *americano*

American crow
cuervo ^M *americano*

thrush
tordo ^M

nightingale
ruiseñor ^M

sparrow
gorrión ^M

starling
estornino ^M

owl
búho ^M

stork
cigüeña ^F

gyrfalcon
halcón ^M *gerifalte*

partridge
perdiz ^F

condor
cóndor ᴹ

bald eagle
águila ᶠ *calva*

ruffed grouse
perdiz ᶠ *martineta copetona*

rooster
gallo ᴹ

ostrich
avestruz ᶠ

sharp-tailed grouse
gallo ᴹ *de las praderas* ᶠ *rabudo*

peacock
pavo ᴹ *real*

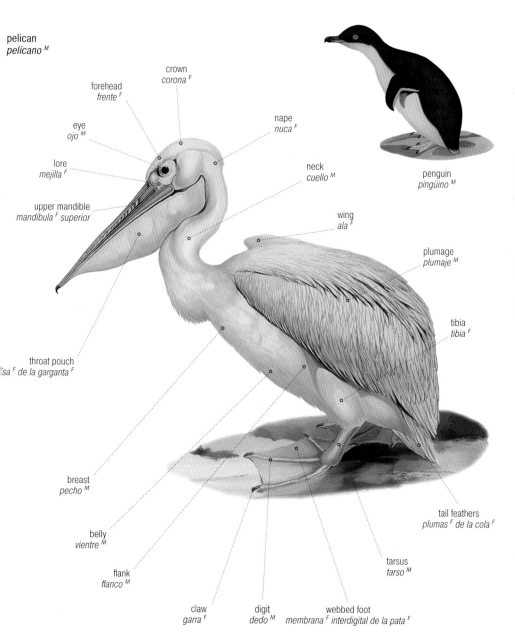

pelican
pelícano ^M

crown
corona ^F

forehead
frente ^F

eye
ojo ^M

nape
nuca ^F

lore
mejilla ^F

neck
cuello ^M

upper mandible
mandíbula ^F *superior*

wing
ala ^F

penguin
pingüino ^M

plumage
plumaje ^M

tibia
tibia ^F

throat pouch
sa ^F *de la garganta* ^F

breast
pecho ^M

belly
vientre ^M

flank
flanco ^M

claw
garra ^F

digit
dedo ^M

webbed foot
membrana ^F *interdigital de la pata* ^F

tarsus
tarso ^M

tail feathers
plumas ^F *de la cola* ^F

albatross
albatros M

mallard duck
pato M

tern
charrán M

gull
gaviota F

swan
cisne M

flamingo
flamenco M

goose
ganso M

heron
garza F

Arachnids
Arácnidos ^M

scorpion
escorpión ^M

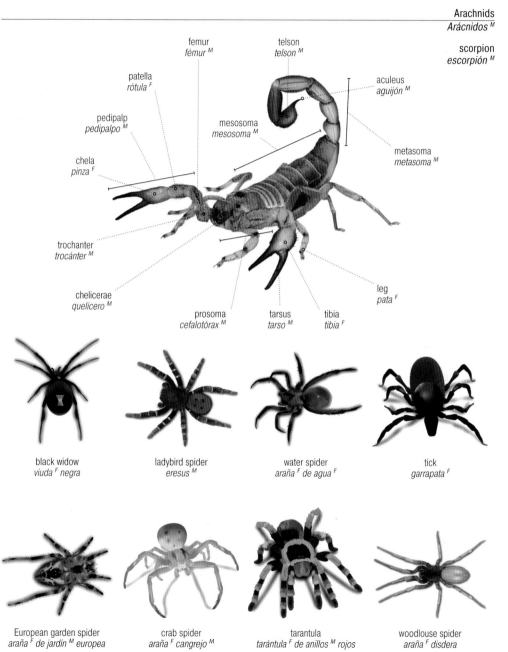

femur
fémur ^M

telson
telson ^M

patella
rótula ^F

aculeus
aguijón ^M

pedipalp
pedipalpo ^M

mesosoma
mesosoma ^M

metasoma
metasoma ^M

chela
pinza ^F

trochanter
trocánter ^M

leg
pata ^F

chelicerae
quelícero ^M

prosoma
cefalotórax ^M

tarsus
tarso ^M

tibia
tibia ^F

black widow
viuda ^F *negra*

ladybird spider
eresus ^M

water spider
araña ^F *de agua* ^F

tick
garrapata ^F

European garden spider
araña ^F *de jardín* ^M *europea*

crab spider
araña ^F *cangrejo* ^M

tarantula
tarántula ^F *de anillos* ^M *rojos*

woodlouse spider
araña ^F *disdera*

Beetles
Escarabajos ^M

Hercules beetle
escarbajo ^M *hércules*

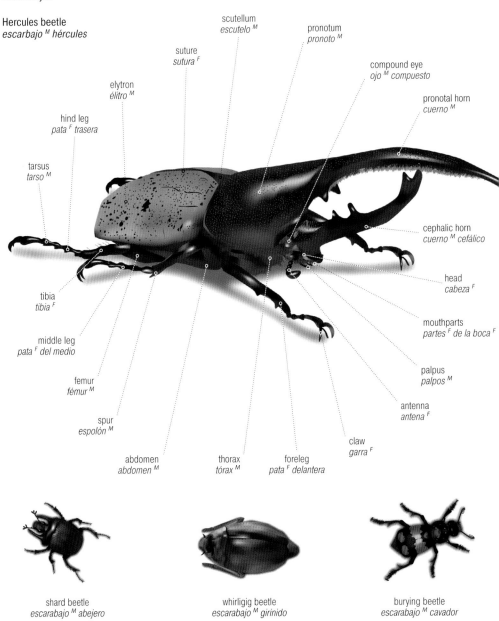

scutellum
escutelo ^M

pronotum
pronoto ^M

suture
sutura ^F

compound eye
ojo ^M *compuesto*

elytron
élitro ^M

pronotal horn
cuerno ^M

hind leg
pata ^F *trasera*

tarsus
tarso ^M

cephalic horn
cuerno ^M *cefálico*

head
cabeza ^F

tibia
tibia ^F

mouthparts
partes ^F *de la boca* ^F

middle leg
pata ^F *del medio*

palpus
palpos ^M

femur
fémur ^M

antenna
antena ^F

spur
espolón ^M

claw
garra ^F

abdomen
abdomen ^M

thorax
tórax ^M

foreleg
pata ^F *delantera*

shard beetle
escarabajo ^M *abejero*

whirligig beetle
escarabajo ^M *girínido*

burying beetle
escarabajo ^M *cavador*

Carabus problematicus (Lat.)
Carabus problematicus

furniture beetle
carcoma F

Sagra buqueti (Lat.)
Sagra buqueti

black vine weevil
gorgojo M *negro de la vid* F

cockchafer
escarabajo M *sanjuanero*

ladybug
mariquita F

thick-legged flower beetle
Oedemera nobilis

rhinoceros beetle
escarabajo M *rinoceronte* M *europeo*

stag beetle
ciervo M *volante*

Colorado potato beetle
escarabajo M *de la patata* F

rose chafer
Cetonia aurata

goliath beetle
escarabajo M *Goliat*

larch ladybug
Aphidecta obliterata

dung beetle
escarabajo M *pelotero*

flower beetle
escarabajo M *de las flores* F

golden scarab beetle
escarabajo M *dorado*

Butterflies and moths
Mariposas F *y polillas* F

swallowtail caterpillar
gusano M *de mariposa* F *macaón* M

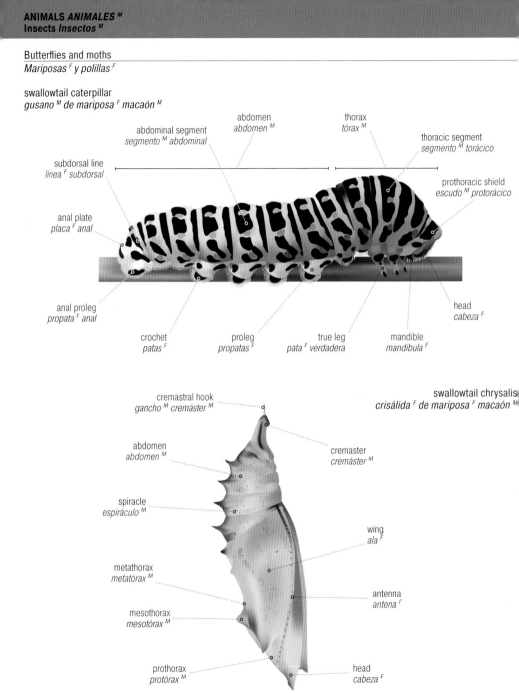

abdomen
abdomen M

thorax
tórax M

abdominal segment
segmento M *abdominal*

thoracic segment
segmento M *torácico*

subdorsal line
línea F *subdorsal*

prothoracic shield
escudo M *protorácico*

anal plate
placa F *anal*

anal proleg
propata F *anal*

head
cabeza F

crochet
patas F

proleg
propatas F

true leg
pata F *verdadera*

mandible
mandíbula F

cremastral hook
gancho M *cremáster* M

swallowtail chrysalis
crisálida F *de mariposa* F *macaón* M

abdomen
abdomen M

cremaster
cremáster M

spiracle
espiráculo M

wing
ala F

metathorax
metatórax M

antenna
antena F

mesothorax
mesotórax M

prothorax
protórax M

head
cabeza F

tiger swallowtail
papilo ^M *glaucus*

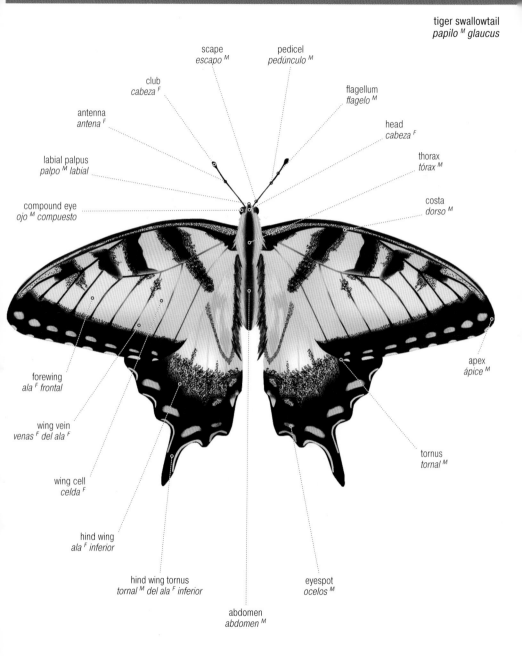

scape
escapo ^M

pedicel
pedúnculo ^M

club
cabeza ^F

flagellum
flagelo ^M

antenna
antena ^F

head
cabeza ^F

labial palpus
palpo ^M *labial*

thorax
tórax ^M

compound eye
ojo ^M *compuesto*

costa
dorso ^M

forewing
ala ^F *frontal*

apex
ápice ^M

wing vein
venas ^F *del ala* ^F

wing cell
celda ^F

tornus
tornal ^M

hind wing
ala ^F *inferior*

hind wing tornus
tornal ^M *del ala* ^F *inferior*

eyespot
ocelos ^M

abdomen
abdomen ^M

Adonis blue
mariposa ^F niña ^M celeste

clothes moth
polilla ^F

lappet moth
procesionaria ^F del pino ^M

cabbage white
blanquita de la col ^F

silkmoth
gusano ^M de seda ^F

monarch butterfly
mariposa ^F monarca

buff-tip
mariposa ^F pájaro ^M luna ^F

scarce swallowtail
podalirio ^M

brimstone
popilla ^F limonera

Apollo
apolo ^F

luna moth
Actias luna

black-veined white
blanca ^F *del majuelo* ^M

blue morpho
mariposa ^F *morpho azul*

Brahmin moth
Brahmaea wallichii

divana diva
divana ^F

purple emperor
Apatura iris ^F

Hercules moth
mariposa ^F *hércules*

spear-marked black moth
Rheumaptera hastata

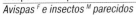

Wasps and wasp-like insects
Avispas ^F e insectos ^M parecidos

wasp
avispa ^F

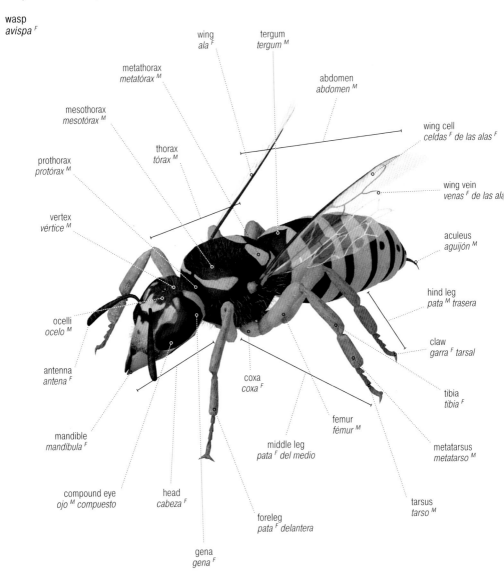

wing
ala ^F

tergum
tergum ^M

metathorax
metatórax ^M

abdomen
abdomen ^M

mesothorax
mesotórax ^M

wing cell
celdas ^F de las alas ^F

thorax
tórax ^M

prothorax
protórax ^M

wing vein
venas ^F de las ala

vertex
vértice ^M

aculeus
aguijón ^M

hind leg
pata ^M trasera

ocelli
ocelo ^M

claw
garra ^F tarsal

antenna
antena ^F

coxa
coxa ^F

tibia
tibia ^F

femur
fémur ^M

mandible
mandíbula ^F

middle leg
pata ^F del medio

metatarsus
metatarso ^M

compound eye
ojo ^M compuesto

head
cabeza ^F

tarsus
tarso ^M

foreleg
pata ^F delantera

gena
gena ^F

ant
hormiga ^F

buff-tailed bumblebee
abejorro ^M *común*

hornet
avispón ^M

red wood ant
hormiga ^F *roja de la madera* ^F

honey bee
abeja ^F *europea*

mud dauber
avispa ^F *alfarera*

True flies
Moscas ^M *verdaderas*

horsefly
tábano ^M

common housefly
mosca ^F

flesh fly
moscarda ^F *de la carne* ^F

little housefly
mosca ^F *doméstica*

blackfly
mosca ^F *negra*

blowfly
califórido ^M

mosquito
mosquito ^M

tsetse fly
mosca ^F *tse-tse*

Neoptera
Neópteros M

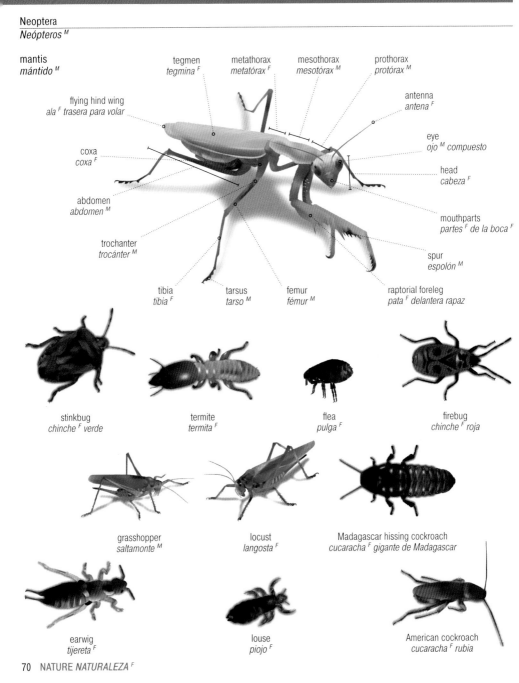

mantis
mántido M

tegmen
tegmina F

metathorax
metatórax F

mesothorax
mesotórax M

prothorax
protórax M

flying hind wing
ala F *trasera para volar*

antenna
antena F

eye
ojo M *compuesto*

coxa
coxa F

head
cabeza F

abdomen
abdomen M

mouthparts
partes F *de la boca* F

trochanter
trocánter M

spur
espolón M

tibia
tibia F

tarsus
tarso M

femur
fémur M

raptorial foreleg
pata F *delantera rapaz*

stinkbug
chinche F *verde*

termite
termita F

flea
pulga F

firebug
chinche F *roja*

grasshopper
saltamonte M

locust
langosta F

Madagascar hissing cockroach
cucaracha F *gigante de Madagascar*

earwig
tijereta F

louse
piojo F

American cockroach
cucaracha F *rubia*

Odonata
Odonatos ^M

dragonfly
libélula ^F

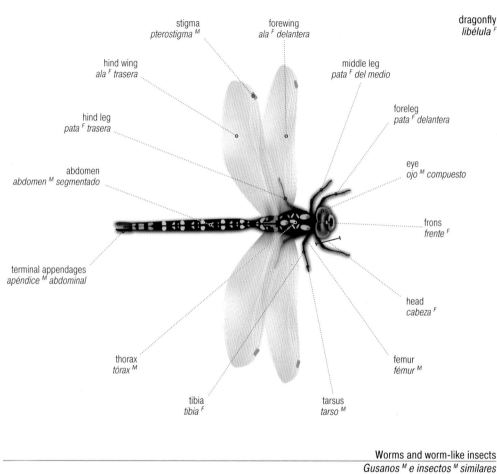

stigma
pterostigma ^M

forewing
ala ^F *delantera*

hind wing
ala ^F *trasera*

middle leg
pata ^F *del medio*

hind leg
pata ^F *trasera*

foreleg
pata ^F *delantera*

abdomen
abdomen ^M *segmentado*

eye
ojo ^M *compuesto*

frons
frente ^F

terminal appendages
apéndice ^M *abdominal*

head
cabeza ^F

thorax
tórax ^M

femur
fémur ^M

tibia
tibia ^F

tarsus
tarso ^M

Worms and worm-like insects
Gusanos ^M *e insectos* ^M *similares*

millipede
milpiés ^M

earthworm
lombriz ^F *de tierra* ^F

plant cell
célula ^F *vegetal*

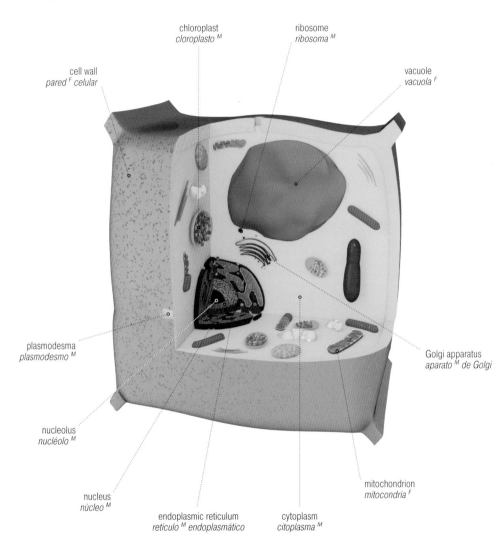

chloroplast
cloroplasto ^M

ribosome
ribosoma ^M

cell wall
pared ^F *celular*

vacuole
vacuola ^F

plasmodesma
plasmodesmo ^M

Golgi apparatus
aparato ^M *de Golgi*

nucleolus
nucléolo ^M

nucleus
núcleo ^M

mitochondrion
mitocondria ^F

endoplasmic reticulum
retículo ^M *endoplasmático*

cytoplasm
citoplasma ^M

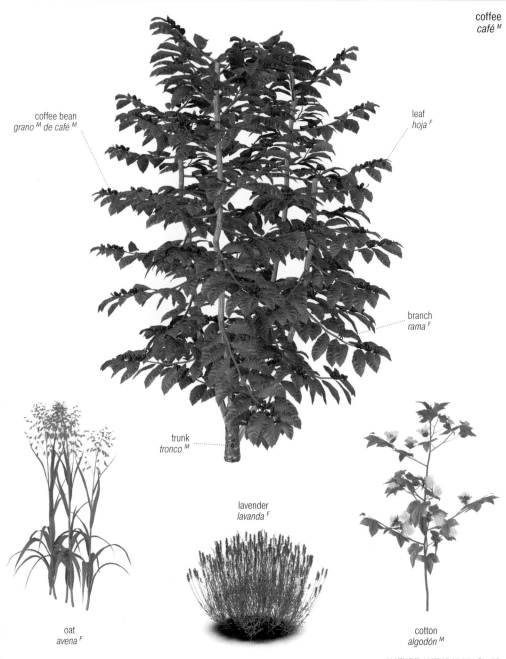

coffee
café ^M

coffee bean
grano ^M *de café* ^M

leaf
hoja ^F

branch
rama ^F

trunk
tronco ^M

lavender
lavanda ^F

oat
avena ^F

cotton
algodón ^M

grape
uva [F]

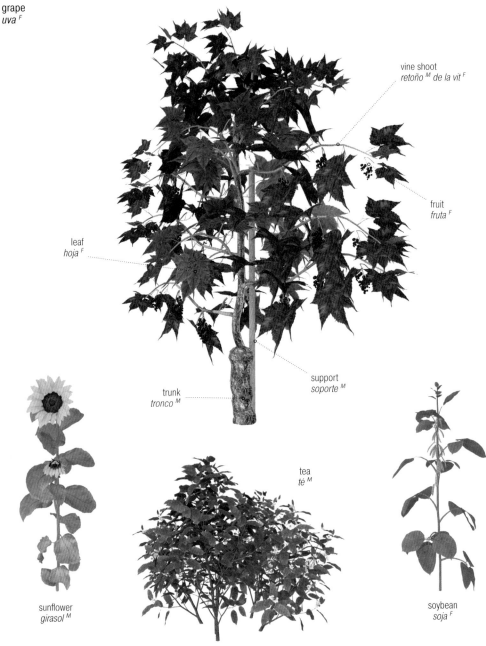

vine shoot
retoño [M] *de la vit* [F]

fruit
fruta [F]

leaf
hoja [F]

support
soporte [M]

trunk
tronco [M]

tea
té [M]

sunflower
girasol [M]

soybean
soja [F]

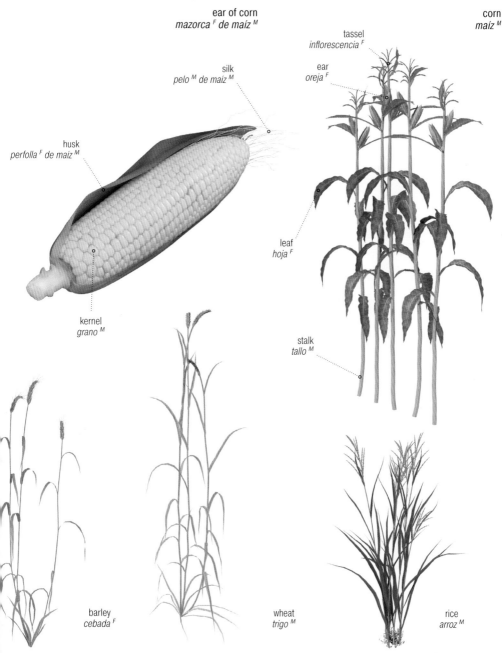

ear of corn
mazorca F *de maíz* M

corn
maíz M

tassel
inflorescencia F

silk
pelo M *de maíz* M

ear
oreja F

husk
perfolla F *de maíz* M

leaf
hoja F

kernel
grano M

stalk
tallo M

barley
cebada F

wheat
trigo M

rice
arroz M

geranium
geranio ^M

flower
flor ^M

petal
pétalo ^M

flower bud
capullo ^M *de flor* ^F

stalk
tallo ^M

leaf
hoja ^F

marigold
caléndula ^F

calla lily
cala ^F

hydrangea
hortensia ^F

Fruits and vegetables
Frutas ^F *y vegetales* ^M

strawberry
fresa ^F

flower
flor ^F

unripe berry
baya ^F *verde*

leaf
hoja ^F

stem
tallo ^M

berry
baya ^F

broccoli
brócoli ^M

cauliflower
coliflor ^F

lettuce
lechuga ^F

carrot
zanahoria ^F

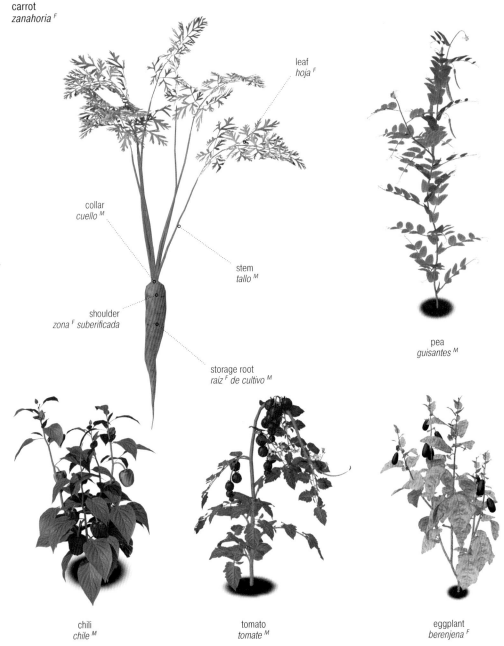

leaf
hoja ^F

collar
cuello ^M

stem
tallo ^M

shoulder
zona ^F *suberificada*

storage root
raíz ^F *de cultivo* ^M

pea
guisantes ^M

chili
chile ^M

tomato
tomate ^M

eggplant
berenjena ^F

zucchini
calabacín ^M

squash
calabacita ^M

watermelon
sandía ^F

cantaloupe
melón ^M

onion
cebolla ^F

cucumber
pepino ^M

pear
pera F

foliage
follaje M

branches
ramas F

fruit
fruto M

top
parte F *superior*

twig
ramita F

crown
copa F

branch
rama F

limb
rama F *madre*

trunk
tronco M

shallow root
raices F *superficiales*

rootlet
raicilla F

taproot
raiz F *primaria*

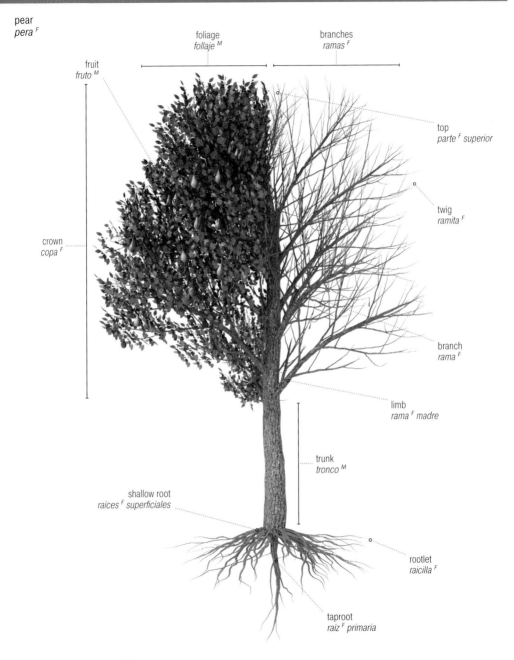

American sycamore
plátano ^M *occidental*

English oak
roble ^M *común*

apple
manzano ^M

holly
acebo ^M

palm tree
bjuvia ^M

European aspen
álamo ^M *temblón*

red oak
roble ^M *rojo*

ash
fresno ^M *norteño*

sugar maple
arce ^M *azucarero*

rubber tree
árbol ^M *de caucho* ^M

olive
olivo ᴹ

large-leaf linden
tilo ᴹ *de hoja* ᶠ *ancha*

black alder
aliso ᴹ *negro*

hawthorn
espino ᴹ *blanco*

ginkgo tree
gingko ᴹ

American beech
haya F *americana*

chestnut
castaño M

silver birch
abedul M *común*

hornbeam
carpe M

juniper
enebro M *común*

western red cedar
tuya F *gigante*

Caucasian fir
abeto M *del Cáucaso*

English yew
tejo M *común*

Colorado blue spruce
pícea ᶠ azul de Colorado

Italian cypress
ciprés ᴹ mediterráneo

red pine
pino ᴹ rojo

Norway spruce
pícea ᶠ común

white pine
pino ᴹ blanco

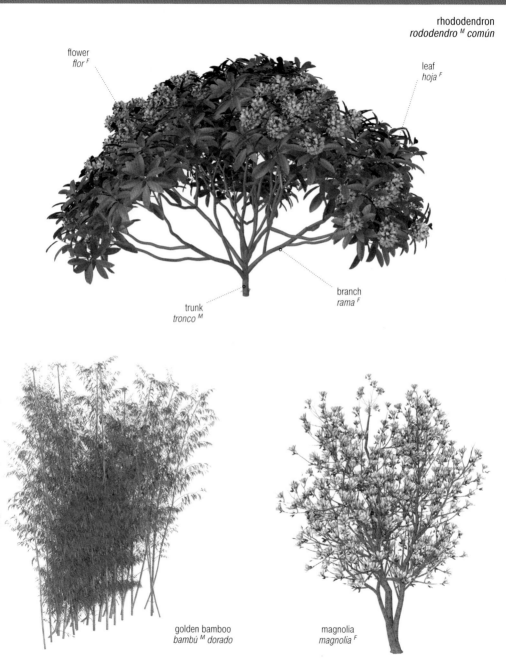

rhododendron
rododendro ^M *común*

flower
flor ^F

leaf
hoja ^F

branch
rama ^F

trunk
tronco ^M

golden bamboo
bambú ^M *dorado*

magnolia
magnolia ^F

structure of a flower
estructura ^F de una flor ^F

filament
filamento ^M

stigma
estigma ^M

style
estilo ^M

petal
pétalo ^M

anther
antera ^F

receptacle
receptáculo ^M

ovule
óvulo ^M

sepal
sépalo ^M

peduncle
pedúnculo ^M

ovary
ovario ^M

rose
rosa ^F

amaryllis
amarilis ^M

corolla
corola ^F

pistil
pistilo ^M

petal
pétalo ^M

thorn
espina ^F

leaf
hoja ^F

stamen
estambre ^M

stem
tallo ^M

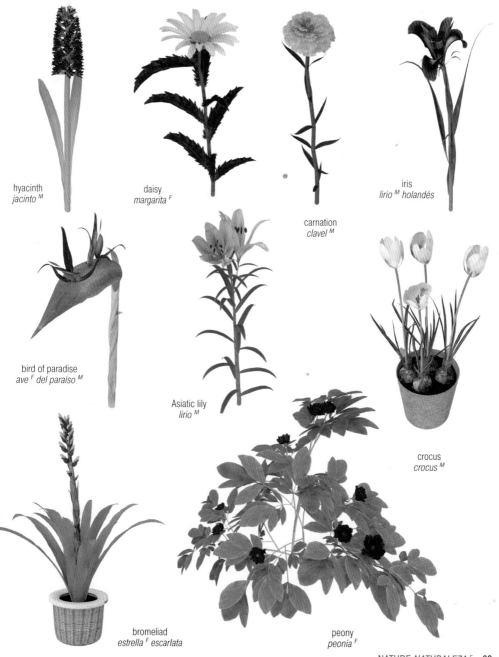

hyacinth
jacinto ^M

daisy
margarita ^F

carnation
clavel ^M

iris
lirio ^M *holandés*

bird of paradise
ave ^F *del paraíso* ^M

Asiatic lily
lirio ^M

crocus
crocus ^M

bromeliad
estrella ^F *escarlata*

peony
peonía ^F

orchid
orquídea ^F

gerbera daisy
margarita ^F *africana*

gladiolus
gladiolo ^M

tulip
tulipán ^M

Houseplants *Plantas* ^F *del hogar* ^M

dragon tree
dracaena ^F *de puntas* ^F *rojas*

leaf
hoja ^F

cactus
cactus ^M *de barril* ^M

trunk
tronco ^M

soil
tierra ^F

pot
tiesto ^M / *maceta* ^F

sago palm
palmera ^F *sagú*

weeping fig
Laurel ^M *de la India* ^F

ivy
hiedra ^F

croton
crotón ^M

fern
helecho ^M *común*

fan palm
palma ^F *de abanico* ^M

Aquatic plants *Plantas* ^f *acuáticas*

lotus
loto ^M

HUMAN BEING

SER HUMANO

anterior view of female body
vista F anterior del cuerpo M femenino

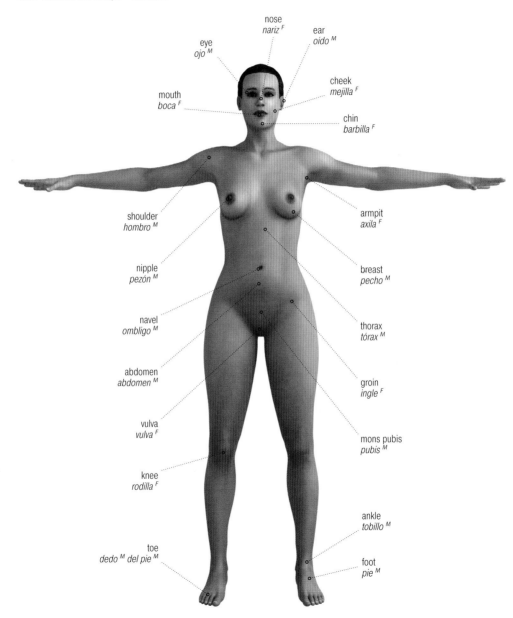

nose
nariz F

ear
oído M

eye
ojo M

cheek
mejilla F

mouth
boca F

chin
barbilla F

shoulder
hombro M

armpit
axila F

nipple
pezón M

breast
pecho M

navel
ombligo M

thorax
tórax M

abdomen
abdomen M

groin
ingle F

vulva
vulva F

mons pubis
pubis M

knee
rodilla F

ankle
tobillo M

toe
dedo M del pie M

foot
pie M

posterior view of female body
vista ^F *posterior del cuerpo* ^M *femenino*

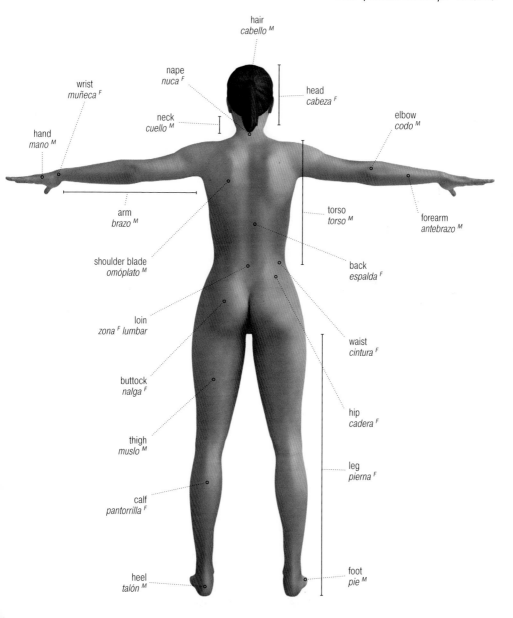

hair
cabello ^M

nape
nuca ^F

wrist
muñeca ^F

neck
cuello ^M

head
cabeza ^F

hand
mano ^M

elbow
codo ^M

arm
brazo ^M

torso
torso ^M

forearm
antebrazo ^M

shoulder blade
omóplato ^M

back
espalda ^F

loin
zona ^F *lumbar*

waist
cintura ^F

buttock
nalga ^F

hip
cadera ^F

thigh
muslo ^M

leg
pierna ^F

calf
pantorrilla ^F

heel
talón ^M

foot
pie ^M

anterior view of male body
vista F *anterior del cuerpo* M *masculino*

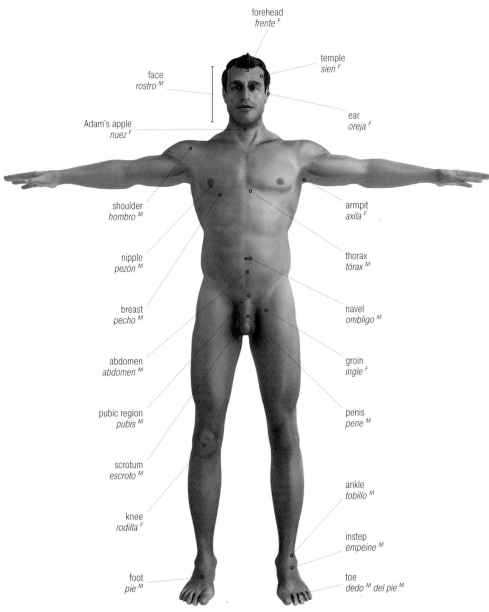

forehead
frente F

temple
sien F

face
rostro M

ear
oreja F

Adam's apple
nuez F

shoulder
hombro M

armpit
axila F

nipple
pezón M

thorax
tórax M

breast
pecho M

navel
ombligo M

abdomen
abdomen M

groin
ingle F

pubic region
pubis M

penis
pene M

scrotum
escroto M

ankle
tobillo M

knee
rodilla F

instep
empeine M

foot
pie M

toe
dedo M *del pie* M

posterior view of male body
vista F *posterior del cuerpo* M *masculino*

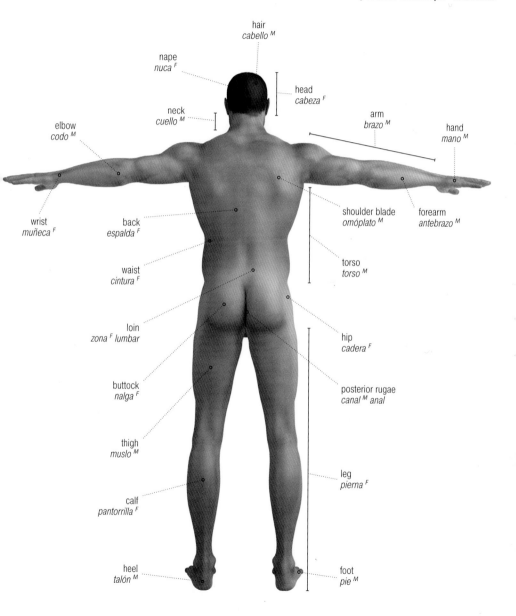

hair
cabello M

nape
nuca F

head
cabeza F

neck
cuello M

arm
brazo M

elbow
codo M

hand
mano M

wrist
muñeca F

back
espalda F

shoulder blade
omóplato M

forearm
antebrazo M

waist
cintura F

torso
torso M

loin
zona F *lumbar*

hip
cadera F

buttock
nalga F

posterior rugae
canal M *anal*

thigh
muslo M

leg
pierna F

calf
pantorrilla F

heel
talón M

foot
pie M

anterior view of main muscles
vista ^F *anterior de los músculos* ^M *principales*

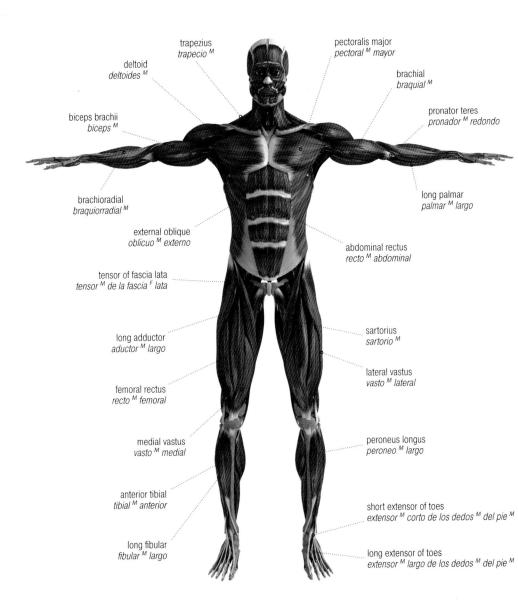

trapezius
trapecio ^M

deltoid
deltoides ^M

biceps brachii
bíceps ^M

brachioradial
braquiorradial ^M

external oblique
oblicuo ^M *externo*

tensor of fascia lata
tensor ^M *de la fascia* ^F *lata*

long adductor
aductor ^M *largo*

femoral rectus
recto ^M *femoral*

medial vastus
vasto ^M *medial*

anterior tibial
tibial ^M *anterior*

long fibular
fibular ^M *largo*

pectoralis major
pectoral ^M *mayor*

brachial
braquial ^M

pronator teres
pronador ^M *redondo*

long palmar
palmar ^M *largo*

abdominal rectus
recto ^M *abdominal*

sartorius
sartorio ^M

lateral vastus
vasto ^M *lateral*

peroneus longus
peroneo ^M *largo*

short extensor of toes
extensor ^M *corto de los dedos* ^M *del pie* ^M

long extensor of toes
extensor ^M *largo de los dedos* ^M *del pie* ^M

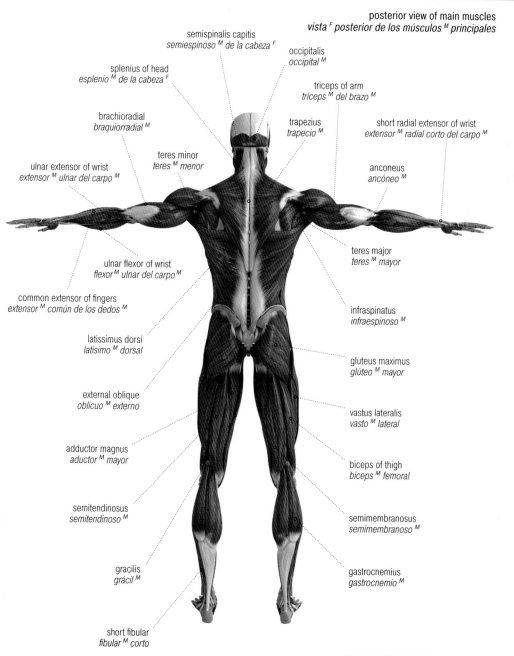

posterior view of main muscles
vista ᶠ *posterior de los músculos* ᴹ *principales*

semispinalis capitis
semiespinoso ᴹ *de la cabeza* ᶠ

occipitalis
occipital ᴹ

splenius of head
esplenio ᴹ *de la cabeza* ᶠ

triceps of arm
tríceps ᴹ *del brazo* ᴹ

brachioradial
braquiorradial ᴹ

trapezius
trapecio ᴹ

short radial extensor of wrist
extensor ᴹ *radial corto del carpo* ᴹ

ulnar extensor of wrist
extensor ᴹ *ulnar del carpo* ᴹ

teres minor
teres ᴹ *menor*

anconeus
ancóneo ᴹ

ulnar flexor of wrist
flexor ᴹ *ulnar del carpo* ᴹ

teres major
teres ᴹ *mayor*

common extensor of fingers
extensor ᴹ *común de los dedos* ᴹ

infraspinatus
infraespinoso ᴹ

latissimus dorsi
latísimo ᴹ *dorsal*

gluteus maximus
glúteo ᴹ *mayor*

external oblique
oblicuo ᴹ *externo*

vastus lateralis
vasto ᴹ *lateral*

adductor magnus
aductor ᴹ *mayor*

biceps of thigh
bíceps ᴹ *femoral*

semitendinosus
semitendinoso ᴹ

semimembranosus
semimembranoso ᴹ

gracilis
grácil ᴹ

gastrocnemius
gastrocnemio ᴹ

short fibular
fibular ᴹ *corto*

facial muscles
músculos ᴹ *faciales*

zygomaticus major muscle
músculo ᴹ *cigomático mayor*

frontalis
frontal ᴹ

temporal muscle
músculo ᴹ *temporal*

procerus muscle
músculo ᴹ *prócer*

occipitalis
occipital ᴹ

orbicularis oculi
orbicular ᴹ *de los ojos* ᴹ

masseter
masetero ᴹ

nasalis muscle
músculo ᴹ *nasal*

sternocleidomastoid
esternocleidomastoideo ᴹ

zygomaticus minor
músculo ᴹ *cigomático menor*

risorius
músculo ᴹ *risorio*

orbicularis oris
orbicular ᴹ *de la boca* ᴹ

trapezius muscle
músculo ᴹ *trapecio*

mentalis
músculo ᴹ *mentoniano*

sternothyroid muscle
esternotiroideo ᴹ

platysma muscle
músculo ᴹ *platisma*

depressor labii inferioris muscle
músculo ᴹ *depresor del labio* ᴹ *inferior*

depressor anguli oris muscle
músculo ᴹ *depresor del ángulo* ᴹ *de la boca* ᶠ

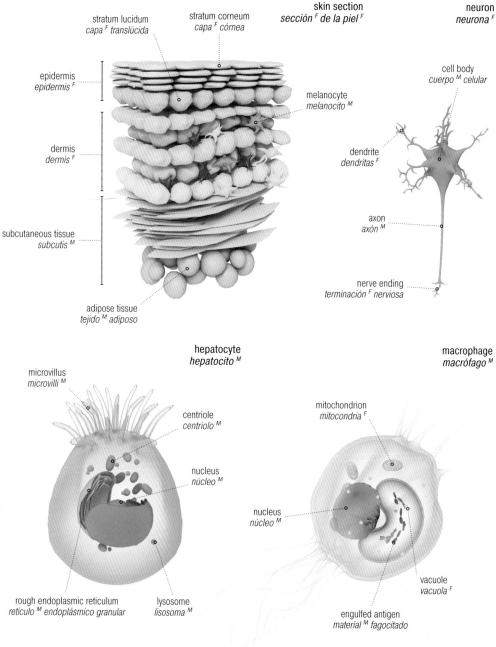

skin section
sección F *de la piel* F

neuron
neurona F

stratum lucidum
capa F *translúcida*

stratum corneum
capa F *córnea*

cell body
cuerpo M *celular*

epidermis
epidermis F

melanocyte
melanocito M

dendrite
dendritas F

dermis
dermis F

axon
axón M

subcutaneous tissue
subcutis M

nerve ending
terminación F *nerviosa*

adipose tissue
tejido M *adiposo*

hepatocyte
hepatocito M

macrophage
macrófago M

microvillus
microvilli M

mitochondrion
mitocondria F

centriole
centriolo M

nucleus
núcleo M

nucleus
núcleo M

rough endoplasmic reticulum
retículo M *endoplásmico granular*

lysosome
lisosoma M

vacuole
vacuola F

engulfed antigen
material M *fagocitado*

anterior view of skeleton
vista ^F *anterior del esqueleto* ^M

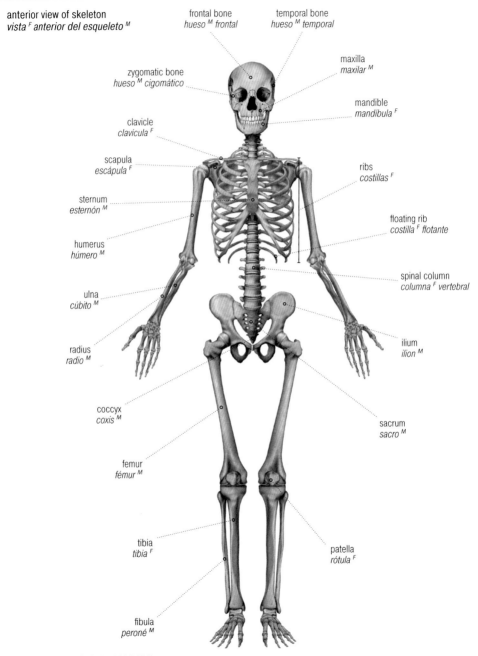

frontal bone
hueso ^M *frontal*

temporal bone
hueso ^M *temporal*

maxilla
maxilar ^M

mandible
mandíbula ^F

zygomatic bone
hueso ^M *cigomático*

clavicle
clavícula ^F

scapula
escápula ^F

ribs
costillas ^F

sternum
esternón ^M

floating rib
costilla ^F *flotante*

humerus
húmero ^M

spinal column
columna ^F *vertebral*

ulna
cúbito ^M

ilium
ilion ^M

radius
radio ^M

coccyx
coxis ^M

sacrum
sacro ^M

femur
fémur ^M

tibia
tibia ^F

patella
rótula ^F

fibula
peroné ^M

posterior view of skeleton
vista ᶠ *posterior del esqueleto* ᴹ

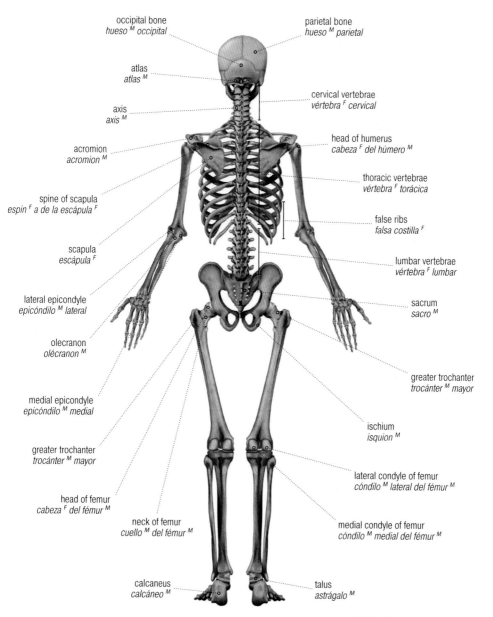

occipital bone
hueso ᴹ *occipital*

parietal bone
hueso ᴹ *parietal*

atlas
atlas ᴹ

cervical vertebrae
vértebra ᶠ *cervical*

axis
axis ᴹ

head of humerus
cabeza ᶠ *del húmero* ᴹ

acromion
acromion ᴹ

thoracic vertebrae
vértebra ᶠ *torácica*

spine of scapula
espin ᶠ *a de la escápula* ᶠ

false ribs
falsa costilla ᶠ

scapula
escápula ᶠ

lumbar vertebrae
vértebra ᶠ *lumbar*

lateral epicondyle
epicóndilo ᴹ *lateral*

sacrum
sacro ᴹ

olecranon
olécranon ᴹ

greater trochanter
trocánter ᴹ *mayor*

medial epicondyle
epicóndilo ᴹ *medial*

ischium
isquion ᴹ

greater trochanter
trocánter ᴹ *mayor*

lateral condyle of femur
cóndilo ᴹ *lateral del fémur* ᴹ

head of femur
cabeza ᶠ *del fémur* ᴹ

neck of femur
cuello ᴹ *del fémur* ᴹ

medial condyle of femur
cóndilo ᴹ *medial del fémur* ᴹ

calcaneus
calcáneo ᴹ

talus
astrágalo ᴹ

shoulder bones
huesos ^M *del hombro* ^M

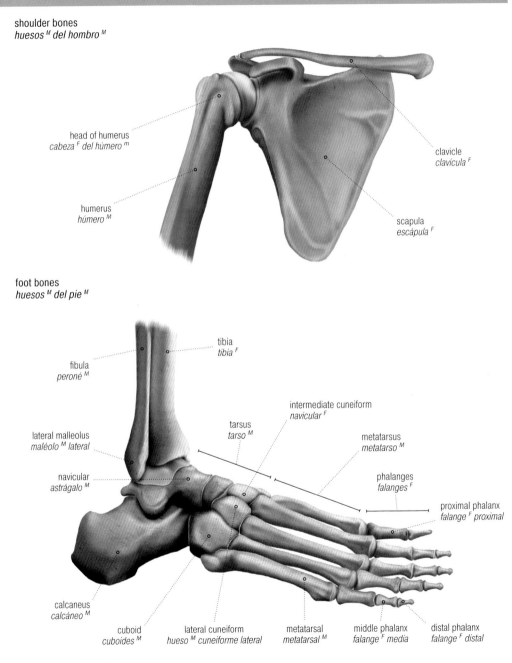

head of humerus
cabeza ^F *del húmero* ^m

clavicle
clavícula ^F

humerus
húmero ^M

scapula
escápula ^F

foot bones
huesos ^M *del pie* ^M

tibia
tibia ^F

fibula
peroné ^M

intermediate cuneiform
navicular ^F

tarsus
tarso ^M

metatarsus
metatarso ^M

lateral malleolus
maléolo ^M *lateral*

navicular
astrágalo ^M

phalanges
falanges ^F

proximal phalanx
falange ^F *proximal*

calcaneus
calcáneo ^M

cuboid
cuboides ^M

lateral cuneiform
hueso ^M *cuneiforme lateral*

metatarsal
metatarsal ^M

middle phalanx
falange ^F *media*

distal phalanx
falange ^F *distal*

hand bones
huesos ^M de la mano ^F

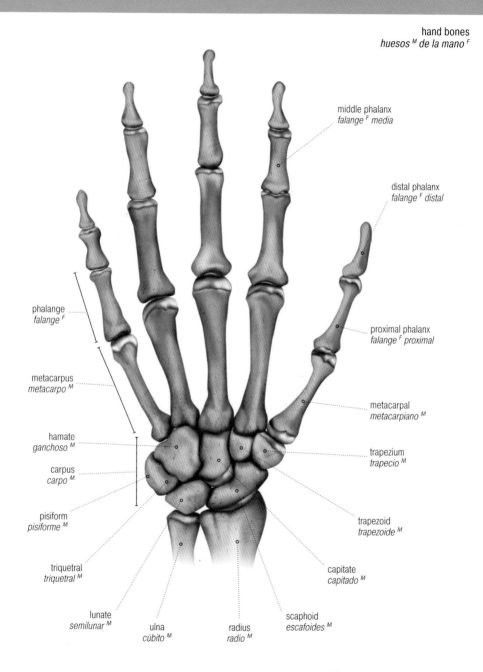

middle phalanx
falange ^F media

distal phalanx
falange ^F distal

phalange
falange ^F

proximal phalanx
falange ^F proximal

metacarpus
metacarpo ^M

metacarpal
metacarpiano ^M

hamate
ganchoso ^M

trapezium
trapecio ^M

carpus
carpo ^M

pisiform
pisiforme ^M

trapezoid
trapezoide ^M

triquetral
triquetral ^M

capitate
capitado ^M

lunate
semilunar ^M

ulna
cúbito ^M

radius
radio ^M

scaphoid
escafoides ^M

knee
rodilla F

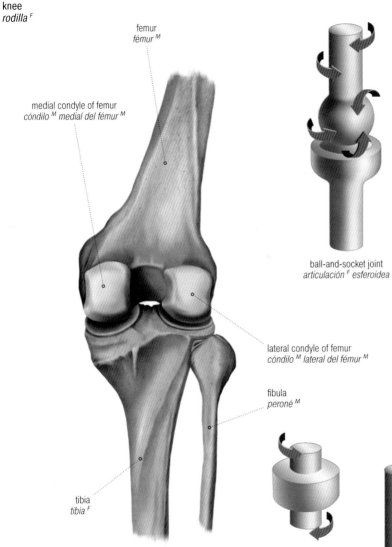

femur
fémur M

medial condyle of femur
cóndilo M *medial del fémur* M

lateral condyle of femur
cóndilo M *lateral del fémur* M

fibula
peroné M

tibia
tibia F

ball-and-socket joint
articulación F *esferoidea*

hinge joint
articulación F *en bisagra* F

pivot joint
articulación F *pivotante*

elbow
codo ᴹ

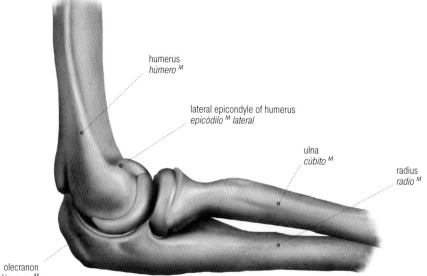

humerus
húmero ᴹ

lateral epicondyle of humerus
epicódilo ᴹ *lateral*

ulna
cúbito ᴹ

radius
radio ᴹ

olecranon
olécranon ᴹ

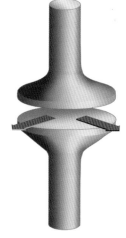

condyloid joint
articulación ꜰ *elipsoidea*

saddle joint
articulación ꜰ *en silla* ꜰ *de montar*

gliding joint
articulación ꜰ *deslizante*

spinal column
columna [F] *vertebral*

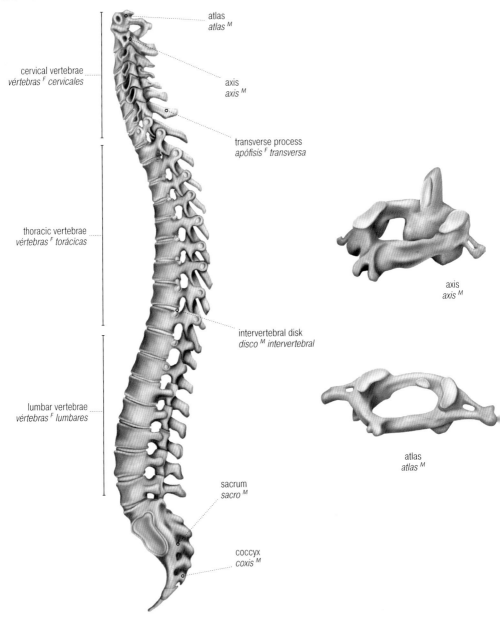

atlas
atlas [M]

axis
axis [M]

cervical vertebrae
vértebras [F] *cervicales*

transverse process
apófisis [F] *transversa*

thoracic vertebrae
vértebras [F] *torácicas*

axis
axís [M]

intervertebral disk
disco [M] *intervertebral*

lumbar vertebrae
vértebras [F] *lumbares*

atlas
atlas [M]

sacrum
sacro [M]

coccyx
coxis [M]

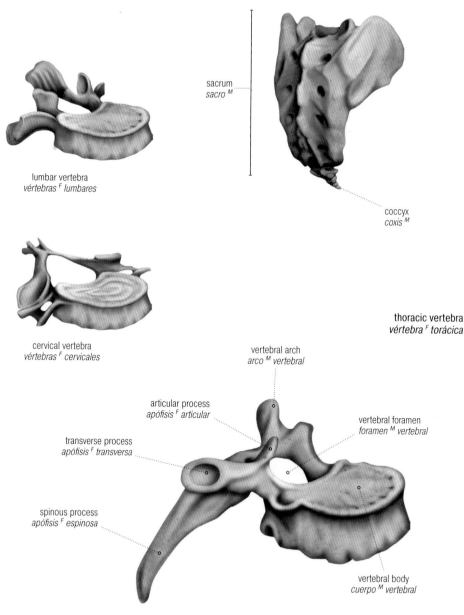

sacrum
sacro ᴹ

sacrum
sacro ᴹ

lumbar vertebra
vértebras ᶠ *lumbares*

coccyx
coxis ᴹ

thoracic vertebra
vértebra ᶠ *torácica*

cervical vertebra
vértebras ᶠ *cervicales*

vertebral arch
arco ᴹ *vertebral*

articular process
apófisis ᶠ *articular*

vertebral foramen
foramen ᴹ *vertebral*

transverse process
apófisis ᶠ *transversa*

spinous process
apófisis ᶠ *espinosa*

vertebral body
cuerpo ᴹ *vertebral*

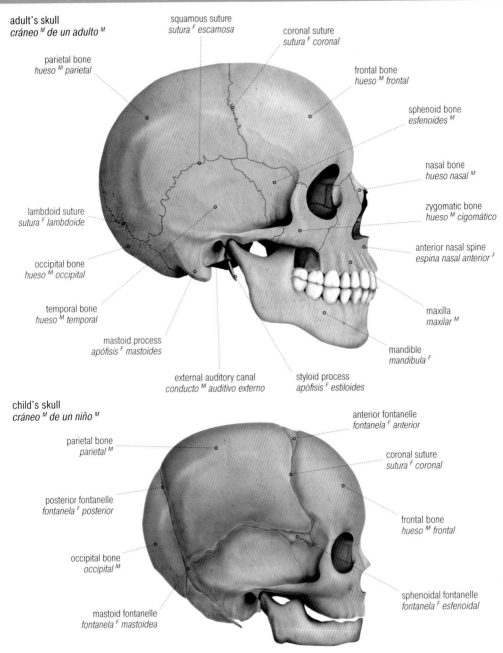

adult's skull
cráneo M *de un adulto* M

squamous suture
sutura F *escamosa*

coronal suture
sutura F *coronal*

parietal bone
hueso M *parietal*

frontal bone
hueso M *frontal*

sphenoid bone
esfenoides M

nasal bone
hueso nasal M

zygomatic bone
hueso M *cigomático*

lambdoid suture
sutura F *lambdoide*

anterior nasal spine
espina nasal anterior F

occipital bone
hueso M *occipital*

temporal bone
hueso M *temporal*

maxilla
maxilar M

mastoid process
apófisis F *mastoides*

mandible
mandíbula F

external auditory canal
conducto M *auditivo externo*

styloid process
apófisis F *estiloides*

child's skull
cráneo M *de un niño* M

anterior fontanelle
fontanela F *anterior*

parietal bone
parietal M

coronal suture
sutura F *coronal*

posterior fontanelle
fontanela F *posterior*

frontal bone
hueso M *frontal*

occipital bone
occipital M

sphenoidal fontanelle
fontanela F *esfenoidal*

mastoid fontanelle
fontanela F *mastoidea*

teeth and skull
dentadura y cráneo ᶠ

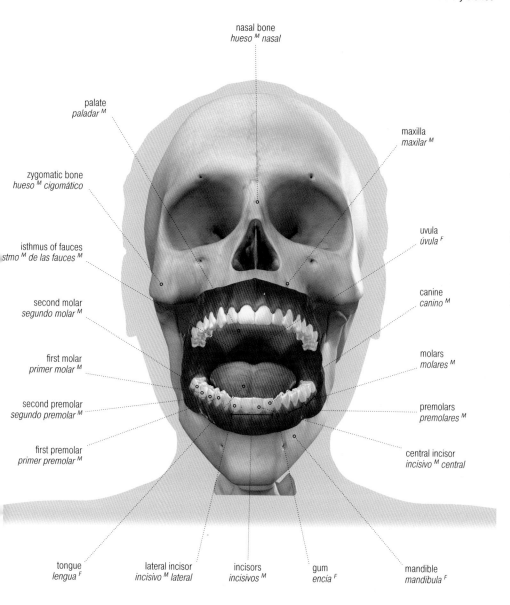

nasal bone
hueso ᴹ *nasal*

palate
paladar ᴹ

maxilla
maxilar ᴹ

zygomatic bone
hueso ᴹ *cigomático*

uvula
úvula ᶠ

isthmus of fauces
stmo ᴹ *de las fauces* ᴹ

canine
canino ᴹ

second molar
segundo molar ᴹ

first molar
primer molar ᴹ

molars
molares ᴹ

second premolar
segundo premolar ᴹ

premolars
premolares ᴹ

first premolar
primer premolar ᴹ

central incisor
incisivo ᴹ *central*

tongue
lengua ᶠ

lateral incisor
incisivo ᴹ *lateral*

incisors
incisivos ᴹ

gum
encía ᶠ

mandible
mandíbula ᶠ

cross section of molar
sección F *transversal de un molar* F

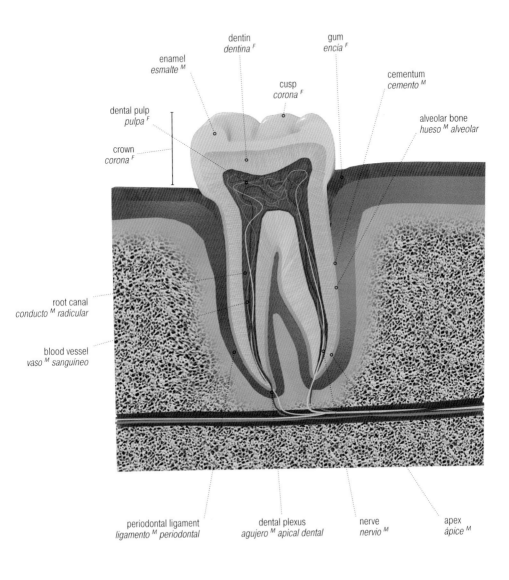

dentin
dentina F

gum
encía F

enamel
esmalte M

cusp
corona F

cementum
cemento M

dental pulp
pulpa F

alveolar bone
hueso M *alveolar*

crown
corona F

root canal
conducto M *radicular*

blood vessel
vaso M *sanguíneo*

periodontal ligament
ligamento M *periodontal*

dental plexus
agujero M *apical dental*

nerve
nervio M

apex
ápice M

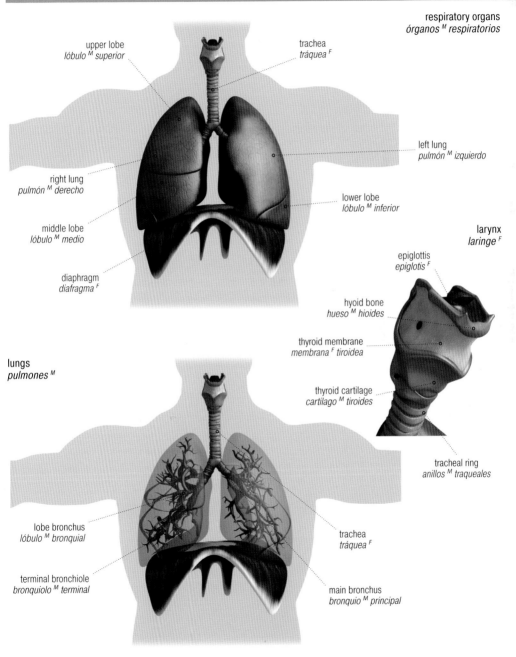

respiratory organs
órganos ᴹ respiratorios

upper lobe
lóbulo ᴹ superior

trachea
tráquea ᶠ

left lung
pulmón ᴹ izquierdo

right lung
pulmón ᴹ derecho

lower lobe
lóbulo ᴹ inferior

middle lobe
lóbulo ᴹ medio

larynx
laringe ᶠ

diaphragm
diafragma ᶠ

epiglottis
epiglotis ᶠ

hyoid bone
hueso ᴹ hioides

thyroid membrane
membrana ᶠ tiroidea

lungs
pulmones ᴹ

thyroid cartilage
cartílago ᴹ tiroides

tracheal ring
anillos ᴹ traqueales

lobe bronchus
lóbulo ᴹ bronquial

trachea
tráquea ᶠ

terminal bronchiole
bronquiolo ᴹ terminal

main bronchus
bronquio ᴹ principal

principal arteries
arterias ᶠ principales

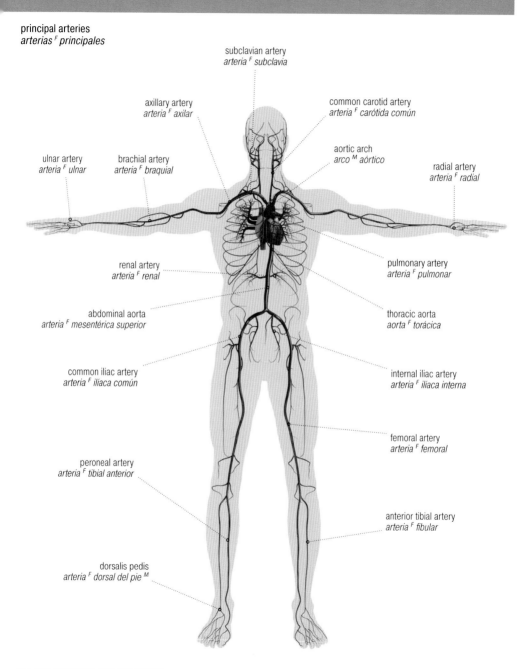

subclavian artery
arteria ᶠ subclavia

axillary artery
arteria ᶠ axilar

common carotid artery
arteria ᶠ carótida común

ulnar artery
arteria ᶠ ulnar

brachial artery
arteria ᶠ braquial

aortic arch
arco ᴹ aórtico

radial artery
arteria ᶠ radial

renal artery
arteria ᶠ renal

pulmonary artery
arteria ᶠ pulmonar

abdominal aorta
arteria ᶠ mesentérica superior

thoracic aorta
aorta ᶠ torácica

common iliac artery
arteria ᶠ ilíaca común

internal iliac artery
arteria ᶠ ilíaca interna

femoral artery
arteria ᶠ femoral

peroneal artery
arteria ᶠ tibial anterior

anterior tibial artery
arteria ᶠ fibular

dorsalis pedis
arteria ᶠ dorsal del pie ᴹ

principal veins
venas ᶠ principales

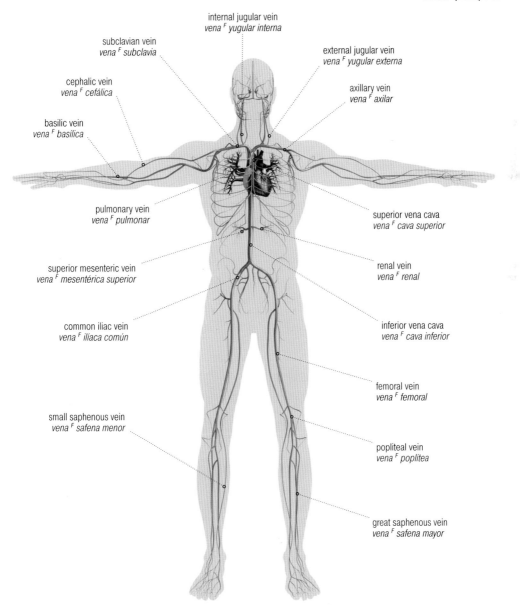

internal jugular vein
vena ᶠ yugular interna

subclavian vein
vena ᶠ subclavia

external jugular vein
vena ᶠ yugular externa

cephalic vein
vena ᶠ cefálica

axillary vein
vena ᶠ axilar

basilic vein
vena ᶠ basílica

pulmonary vein
vena ᶠ pulmonar

superior vena cava
vena ᶠ cava superior

superior mesenteric vein
vena ᶠ mesentérica superior

renal vein
vena ᶠ renal

common iliac vein
vena ᶠ ilíaca común

inferior vena cava
vena ᶠ cava inferior

femoral vein
vena ᶠ femoral

small saphenous vein
vena ᶠ safena menor

popliteal vein
vena ᶠ poplítea

great saphenous vein
vena ᶠ safena mayor

heart
corazón ^M

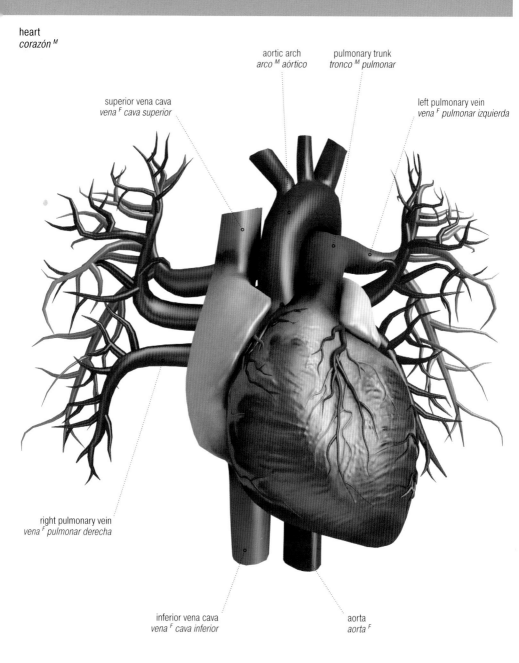

aortic arch
arco ^M *aórtico*

pulmonary trunk
tronco ^M *pulmonar*

superior vena cava
vena ^F *cava superior*

left pulmonary vein
vena ^F *pulmonar izquierda*

right pulmonary vein
vena ^F *pulmonar derecha*

inferior vena cava
vena ^F *cava inferior*

aorta
aorta ^F

cross section of heart
sección ^F transversal de corazón ^M

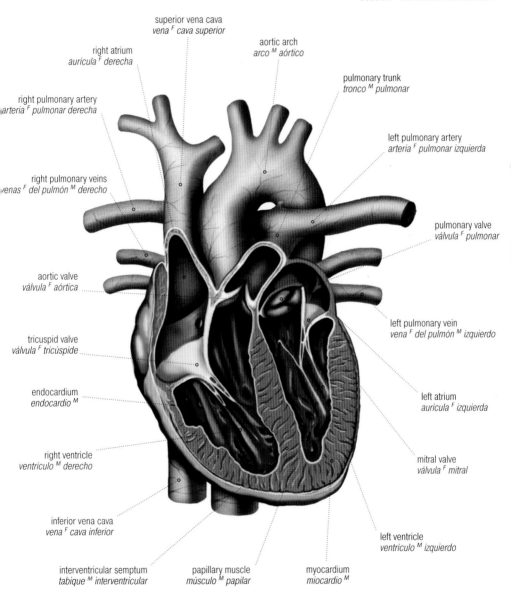

superior vena cava
vena ^F cava superior

aortic arch
arco ^M aórtico

right atrium
aurícula ^F derecha

pulmonary trunk
tronco ^M pulmonar

right pulmonary artery
arteria ^F pulmonar derecha

left pulmonary artery
arteria ^F pulmonar izquierda

right pulmonary veins
venas ^F del pulmón ^M derecho

pulmonary valve
válvula ^F pulmonar

aortic valve
válvula ^F aórtica

left pulmonary vein
vena ^F del pulmón ^M izquierdo

tricuspid valve
válvula ^F tricúspide

endocardium
endocardio ^M

left atrium
aurícula ^F izquierda

right ventricle
ventrículo ^M derecho

mitral valve
válvula ^F mitral

inferior vena cava
vena ^F cava inferior

left ventricle
ventrículo ^M izquierdo

interventricular semptum
tabique ^M interventricular

papillary muscle
músculo ^M papilar

myocardium
miocardio ^M

anterior view of brain
vista F *anterior del cerebro* M

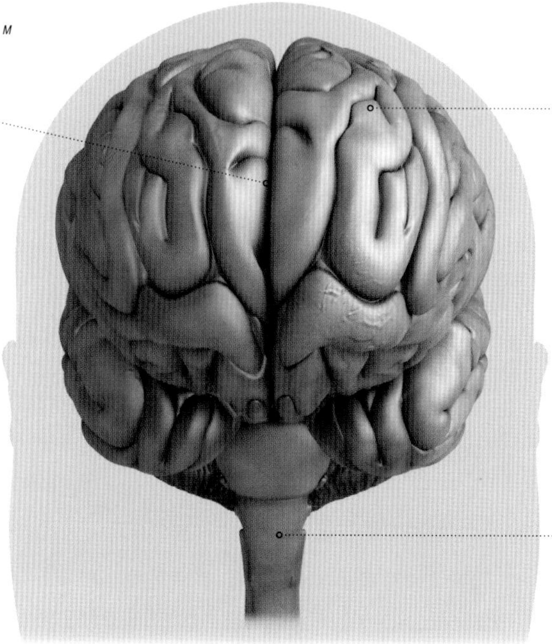

longitudinal fissure
fisura F *longitudinal*

cerebral cortex
corteza F *cerebral*

medulla oblongata
médula oblongada F

posterior view of brain
vista F *posterior del cerebro* M

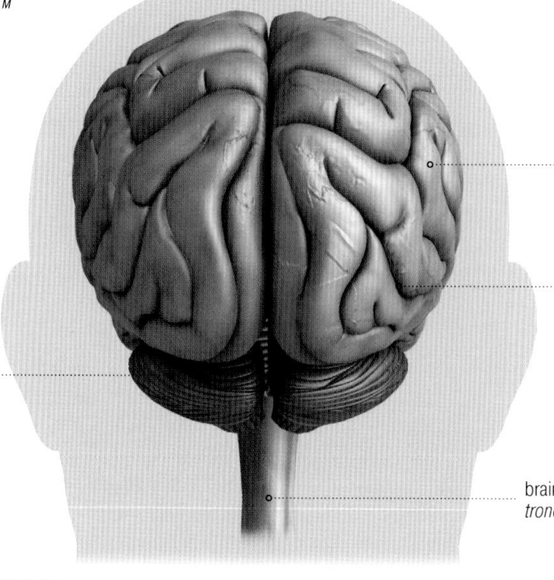

gyrus
giro M

sulcus
surco M

cerebellum
cerebelo M

brain stem
tronco M *del encéfalo* M

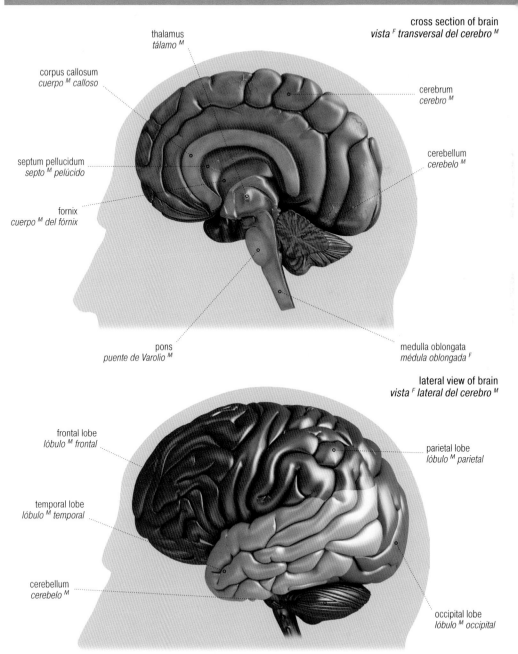

cross section of brain
vista F *transversal del cerebro* M

thalamus
tálamo M

corpus callosum
cuerpo M *calloso*

cerebrum
cerebro M

septum pellucidum
septo M *pelúcido*

cerebellum
cerebelo M

fornix
cuerpo M *del fórnix*

pons
puente de Varolio M

medulla oblongata
médula oblongada F

lateral view of brain
vista F *lateral del cerebro* M

frontal lobe
lóbulo M *frontal*

parietal lobe
lóbulo M *parietal*

temporal lobe
lóbulo M *temporal*

cerebellum
cerebelo M

occipital lobe
lóbulo M *occipital*

main structure of nervous system
estructura ꟳ principal del sistema ᴹ nervioso

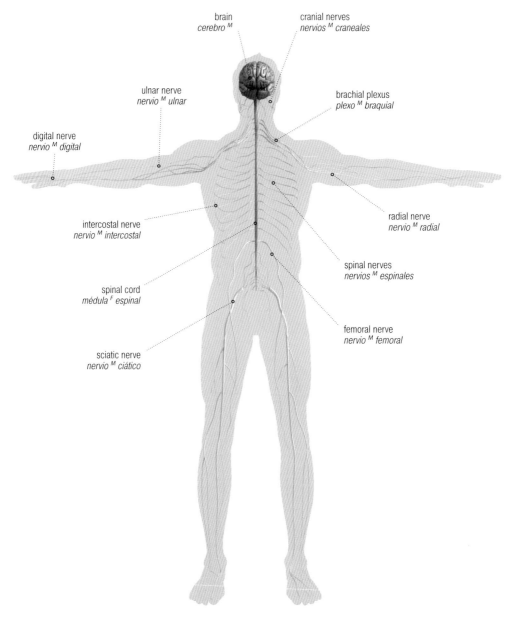

brain
cerebro ᴹ

cranial nerves
nervios ᴹ craneales

ulnar nerve
nervio ᴹ ulnar

brachial plexus
plexo ᴹ braquial

digital nerve
nervio ᴹ digital

intercostal nerve
nervio ᴹ intercostal

radial nerve
nervio ᴹ radial

spinal nerves
nervios ᴹ espinales

spinal cord
médula ꟳ espinal

femoral nerve
nervio ᴹ femoral

sciatic nerve
nervio ᴹ ciático

lymphatic organs
órganos **M** *linfáticos*

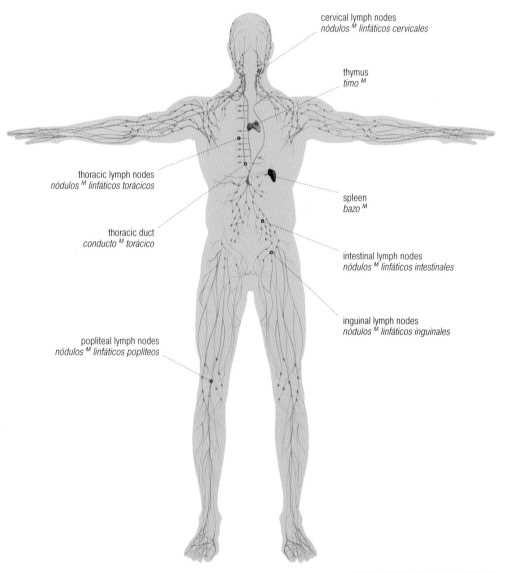

cervical lymph nodes
nódulos **M** *linfáticos cervicales*

thymus
timo **M**

thoracic lymph nodes
nódulos **M** *linfáticos torácicos*

spleen
bazo **M**

thoracic duct
conducto **M** *torácico*

intestinal lymph nodes
nódulos **M** *linfáticos intestinales*

inguinal lymph nodes
nódulos **M** *linfáticos inguinales*

popliteal lymph nodes
nódulos **M** *linfáticos poplíteos*

breast
pecho ᴹ

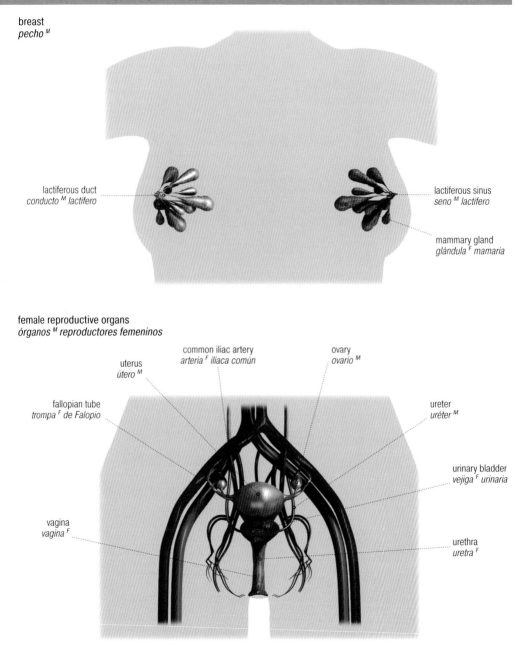

lactiferous duct
conducto ᴹ *lactifero*

lactiferous sinus
seno ᴹ *lactifero*

mammary gland
glándula ᶠ *mamaria*

female reproductive organs
órganos ᴹ *reproductores femeninos*

uterus
útero ᴹ

common iliac artery
arteria ᶠ *iliaca común*

ovary
ovario ᴹ

fallopian tube
trompa ᶠ *de Falopio*

ureter
uréter ᴹ

urinary bladder
vejiga ᶠ *urinaria*

vagina
vagina ᶠ

urethra
uretra ᶠ

male reproductive organs
órganos ^M *reproductores masculinos*

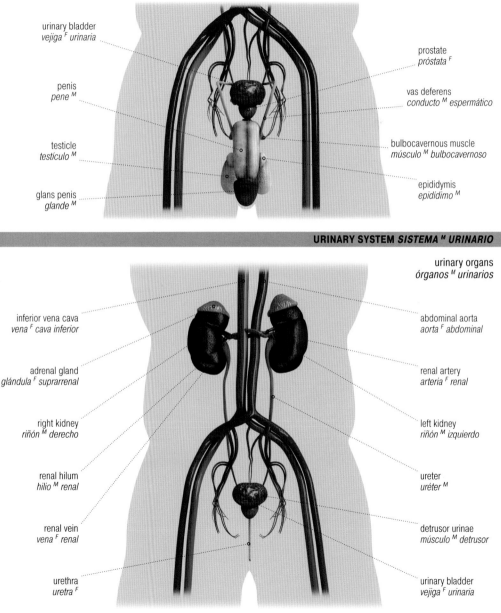

urinary bladder
vejiga ^F *urinaria*

penis
pene ^M

testicle
testículo ^M

glans penis
glande ^M

prostate
próstata ^F

vas deferens
conducto ^M *espermático*

bulbocavernous muscle
músculo ^M *bulbocavernoso*

epididymis
epidídimo ^M

URINARY SYSTEM *SISTEMA* ^M *URINARIO*

urinary organs
órganos ^M *urinarios*

inferior vena cava
vena ^F *cava inferior*

adrenal gland
glándula ^F *suprarrenal*

right kidney
riñón ^M *derecho*

renal hilum
hilio ^M *renal*

renal vein
vena ^F *renal*

urethra
uretra ^F

abdominal aorta
aorta ^F *abdominal*

renal artery
arteria ^F *renal*

left kidney
riñón ^M *izquierdo*

ureter
uréter ^M

detrusor urinae
músculo ^M *detrusor*

urinary bladder
vejiga ^F *urinaria*

anterior view of digestive system
vista ^F anterior del sistema ^M digestivo

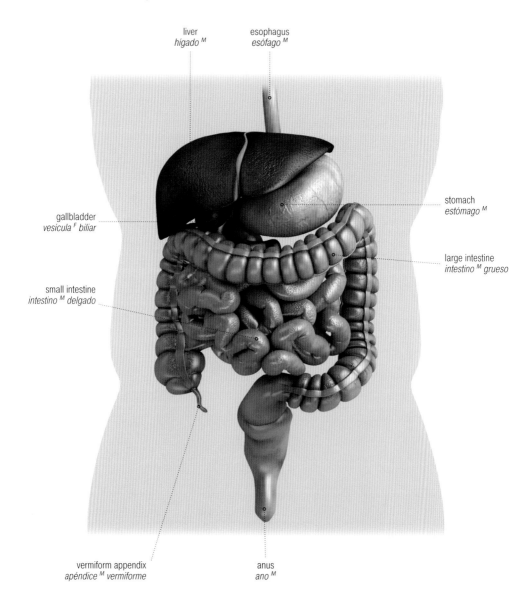

liver
hígado ^M

esophagus
esófago ^M

stomach
estómago ^M

gallbladder
vesícula ^F *biliar*

large intestine
intestino ^M *grueso*

small intestine
intestino ^M *delgado*

vermiform appendix
apéndice ^M *vermiforme*

anus
ano ^M

posterior view of digestive system
vista ᶠ posterior del sistema ᴹ digestivo

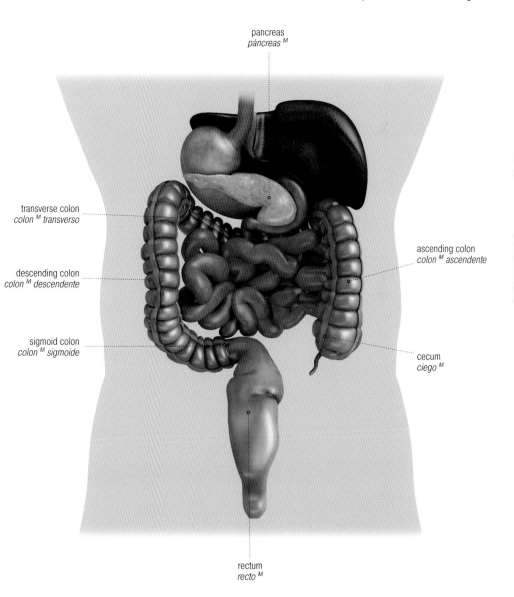

pancreas
páncreas ᴹ

transverse colon
colon ᴹ *transverso*

ascending colon
colon ᴹ *ascendente*

descending colon
colon ᴹ *descendente*

sigmoid colon
colon ᴹ *sigmoide*

cecum
ciego ᴹ

rectum
recto ᴹ

female endocrine system
sistema ^M *endocrino femenino*

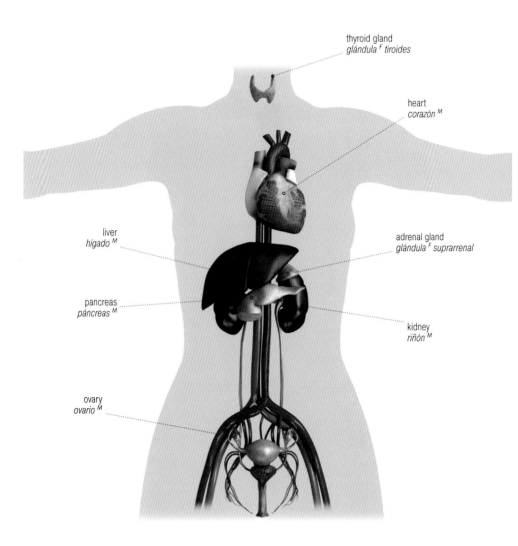

thyroid gland
glándula ^F *tiroides*

heart
corazón ^M

liver
hígado ^M

adrenal gland
glándula ^F *suprarrenal*

pancreas
páncreas ^M

kidney
riñón ^M

ovary
ovario ^M

hand
mano ᶠ

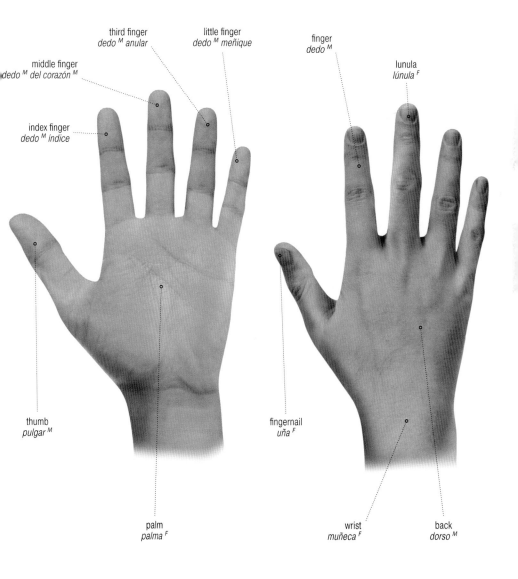

third finger
dedo ᴹ *anular*

little finger
dedo ᴹ *meñique*

middle finger
dedo ᴹ *del corazón* ᴹ

finger
dedo ᴹ

lunula
lúnula ᶠ

index finger
dedo ᴹ *índice*

thumb
pulgar ᴹ

fingernail
uña ᶠ

palm
palma ᶠ

wrist
muñeca ᶠ

back
dorso ᴹ

ear
oído ^M

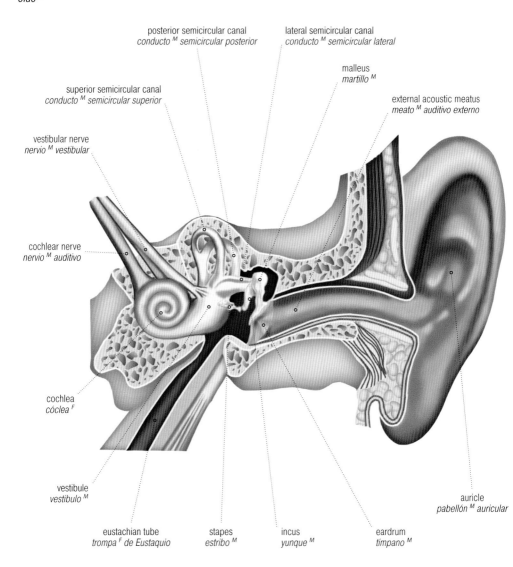

posterior semicircular canal
conducto ^M *semicircular posterior*

lateral semicircular canal
conducto ^M *semicircular lateral*

malleus
martillo ^M

superior semicircular canal
conducto ^M *semicircular superior*

external acoustic meatus
meato ^M *auditivo externo*

vestibular nerve
nervio ^M *vestibular*

cochlear nerve
nervio ^M *auditivo*

cochlea
cóclea ^F

vestibule
vestíbulo ^M

auricle
pabellón ^M *auricular*

eustachian tube
trompa ^F *de Eustaquio*

stapes
estribo ^M

incus
yunque ^M

eardrum
tímpano ^M

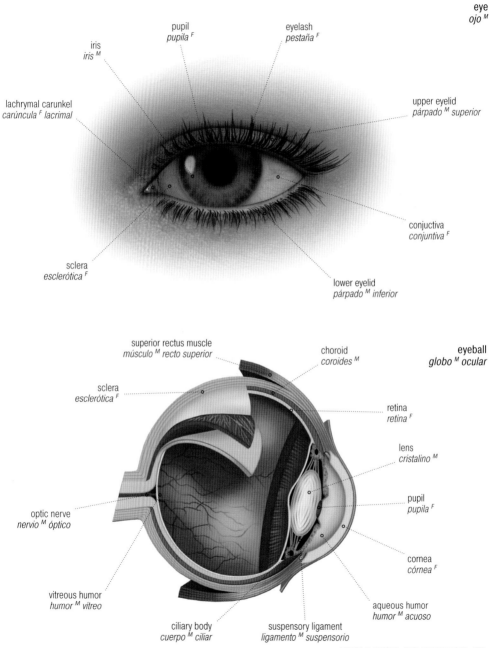

eye
ojo ᴹ

pupil
pupila ᶠ

eyelash
pestaña ᶠ

iris
iris ᴹ

upper eyelid
párpado ᴹ *superior*

lachrymal carunkel
carúncula ᶠ *lacrimal*

conjuctiva
conjuntiva ᶠ

sclera
esclerótica ᶠ

lower eyelid
párpado ᴹ *inferior*

superior rectus muscle
músculo ᴹ *recto superior*

choroid
coroides ᴹ

eyeball
globo ᴹ *ocular*

sclera
esclerótica ᶠ

retina
retina ᶠ

lens
cristalino ᴹ

optic nerve
nervio ᴹ *óptico*

pupil
pupila ᶠ

cornea
córnea ᶠ

vitreous humor
humor ᴹ *vítreo*

aqueous humor
humor ᴹ *acuoso*

ciliary body
cuerpo ᴹ *ciliar*

suspensory ligament
ligamento ᴹ *suspensorio*

HEALTH AND MEDICINE

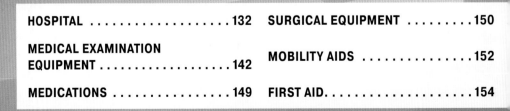

SALUD Y MEDICINA

angiography room
sala ᶠ *de angiografía* ᶠ

video monitor
monitor ᴹ *de vídeo* ᴹ

camera housing
recinto ᴹ *de la cámara* ᶠ

C-arm crawler carriage
carro ᴹ *móvil de brazo* ᴹ *en C*

mattress
colchón ᴹ

radiologist
radiólogo ᴹ

image intensifier
intensificador de imagen ᴹ

angiography machine
angiógrafo ᴹ

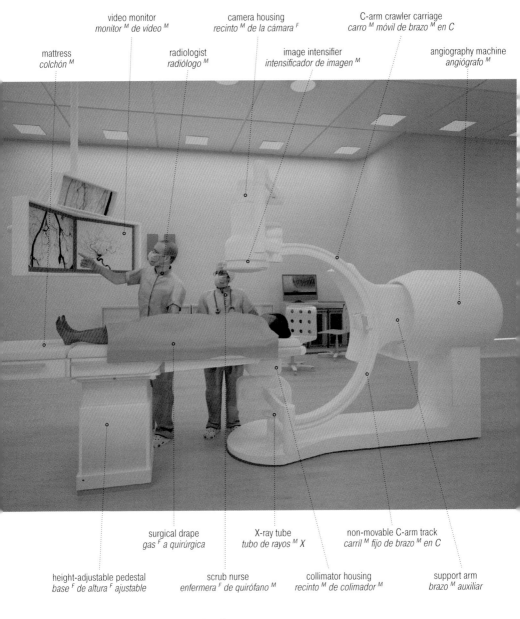

surgical drape
gas ᶠ *a quirúrgica*

X-ray tube
tubo de rayos ᴹ *X*

non-movable C-arm track
carril ᴹ *fijo de brazo* ᴹ *en C*

height-adjustable pedestal
base ᶠ *de altura* ᶠ *ajustable*

scrub nurse
enfermera ᶠ *de quirófano* ᴹ

collimator housing
recinto ᴹ *de colimador* ᴹ

support arm
brazo ᴹ *auxiliar*

MRI (magnetic resonance imaging) room
sala ᶠ de resonancia ᶠ magnética

file cabinet
archivo ᴹ

technician's room
sala ᶠ de operadores

screened glass
pantalla ᶠ de cristal ᴹ

display device
pantalla ᶠ

MRI scanner
escáner ᴹ de IRM

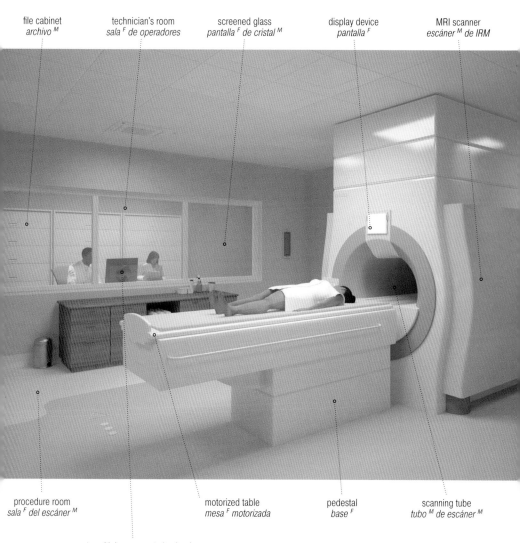

procedure room
sala ᶠ del escáner ᴹ

motorized table
mesa ᶠ motorizada

pedestal
base ᶠ

scanning tube
tubo ᴹ de escáner ᴹ

computer with image-capturing hardware
PC ᴹ con sistema ᶠ de captura ᶠ de imágenes ᶠ

operating room
sala ^F *de operaciones* ^F

video monitor
monitor ^M *de vídeo* ^M

surgical mask
mascarilla ^F *de operaciones* ^F

multi-movement pendant
brazo ^M *multimovimiento*

ceiling light
luces ^F

scrub nurse
enfermera ^F *de quirófano* ^M

anesthesiologist
anestesista ^M

operating light
luz ^F *principal*

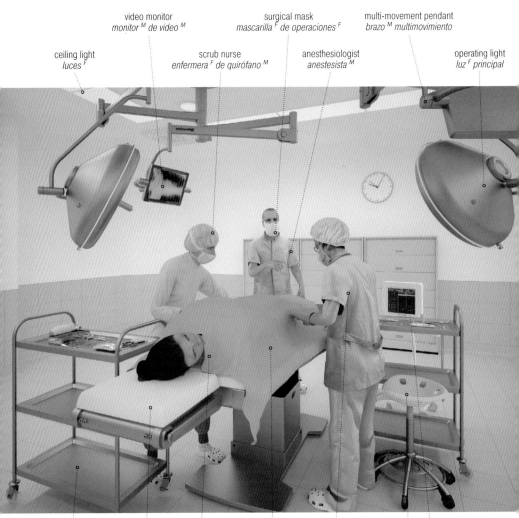

instrument cart
carrito ^M *de instrumental* ^M

patient
paciente ^M

surgeon
cirujano ^M

patient monitor
monitor ^M *del paciente*

operating table
mesa ^F *de operaciones* ^F

surgical drape
sábana ^F *quirúrgica* ^F

adjustable stool
taburete ^M *ajustable*

hospital room
habitación ᶠ de hospital ᴹ

privacy screen
biombo ᴹ

IV (intravenous) stand
soporte ᴹ para bolsa ᶠ intravenosa

nurse call button
botón ᴹ para llamar a la enfermera ᶠ

over-bed light
lámpara ᶠ

medical utility table
mesa ᶠ para instrumental ᴹ médico

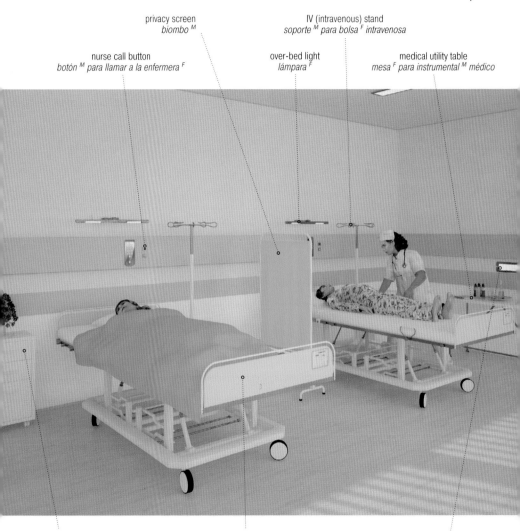

bedside table
mesa ᶠ auxiliar

adjustable hospital bed
cama ᶠ regulable de hospital ᴹ

wall light
luz ᶠ de pared ᶠ

intensive care unit
unidad ^F *de cuidados* ^M *intensivos*

patient monitor
monitor ^M *del paciente* ^M

patient connection panel
panel ^M *de conexión* ^F *con el paciente* ^M

waveform fields
campos ^M *de onda* ^F

numeric fields
campos ^M *de parámetro* ^M

cart
carrito ^M

bedside table
mesa ^F *auxiliar*

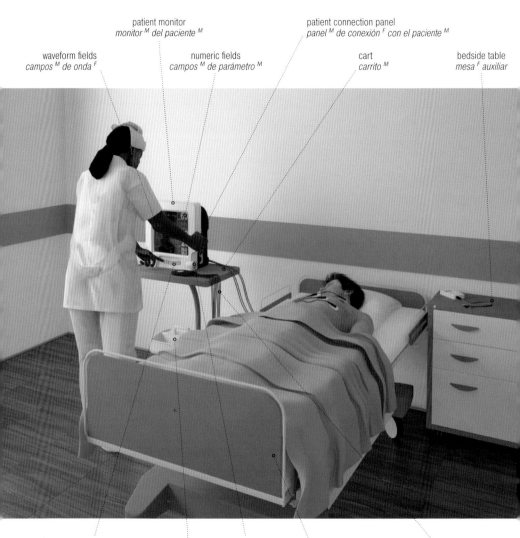

function buttons
botones ^M *de funciones* ^F

trim knob
perilla ^F *de ajuste* ^M

adjustable hospital bed
cama ^F *regulable de hospital* ^M

cables
cables ^M

utility basket
cesta ^F *de instrumental* ^M

physical therapy room
unidad [F] *de medicina* [F] *deportiva y rehabilitación* [F]

physical therapist
fisioterapeuta [M]

treatment table
camilla [F] *de tratamiento* [M]

fitness ball
pelota [F] *de ejercicio* [M]

bolster
almohada [F]

adjustable stool
taburete [M] *ajustable*

treadmill
cinta [F] *para caminar*

gynecological examination room
sala ^F *de examen* ^M *ginecológico*

doctor's writing pad
bloc ^M *del médico* ^M

ceiling-mounted monitor
monitor ^M *anclado al techo* ^M

examination chair
silla ^F *de exploración* ^F

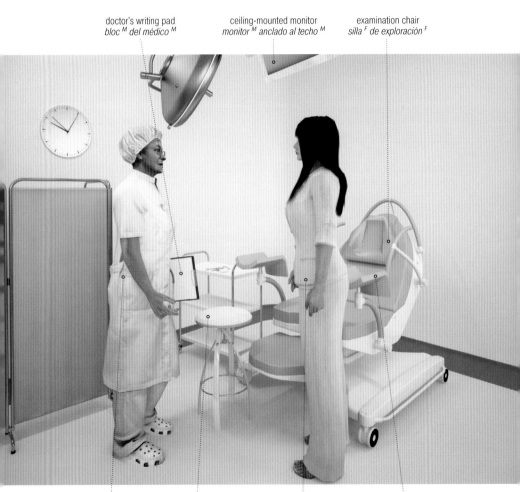

gynecologist
ginecóloga ^F

instrument cart
carrito ^M *de instrumental* ^M

patient
paciente ^M

leg support
soporte ^M *para piernas* ^F

neonatal intensive care unit
unidad *F* *de cuidados* *M* *intensivos para neonatos*

anesthesia monitor
monitor *M* *de anestesia* *F*

mattress tray
base *F* *del colchón* *M*

incubator
incubadora *F*

mattress
colchón *M*

canopy
cubierta *F*

newborn
niño *M* *recién nacido*

porthole
acceso *M* *para las manos* *M*

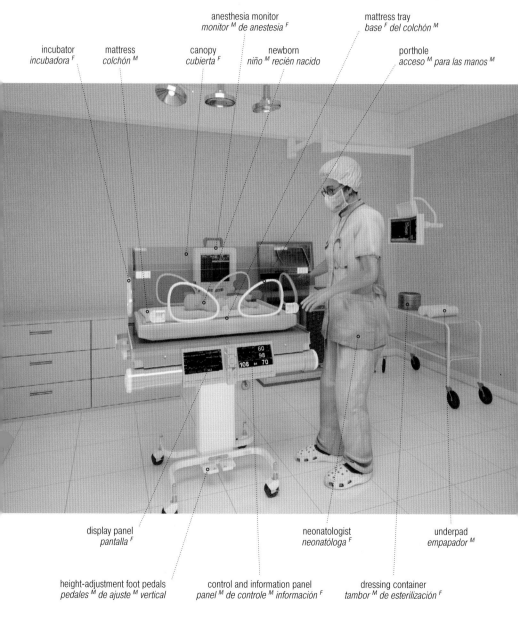

display panel
pantalla *F*

neonatologist
neonatóloga *F*

underpad
empapador *M*

height-adjustment foot pedals
pedales *M* *de ajuste* *M* *vertical*

control and information panel
panel *M* *de controle* *M* *información* *F*

dressing container
tambor *M* *de esterilización* *F*

dental room
sala ᶠ dental

emesis basin
batea ᶠ

dental chair
sillón ᴹ de dentista ᴹ

operating light
lámpara ᶠ operatoria

delivery system
bandeja ᶠ de utensilios ᴹ

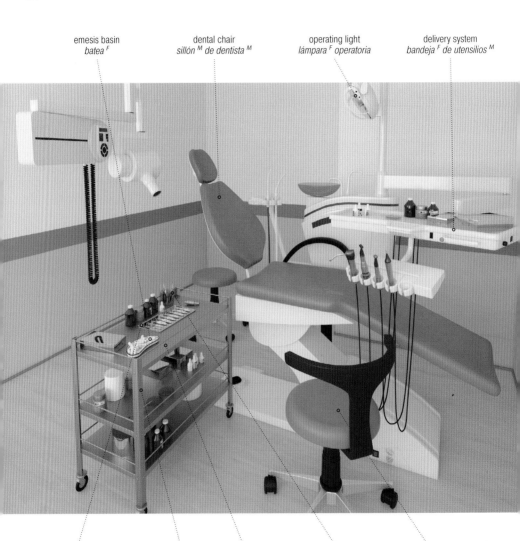

dental mirror
espejo ᴹ bucal

Mayo instrument stand
mesa ᶠ instrumental de Mayo

work tray
bandeja ᶠ de trabajo ᴹ

dental tweezers
pinzas ᶠ dentales

adjustable stool
taburete ᴹ ajustable

psychotherapy room
sala F *de psicoterapia* F

therapy couch
sillón M *de terapia* F

therapist's chair
silla F *para el terapeuta* F

therapist's notes
apuntes M *del terapeuta* F

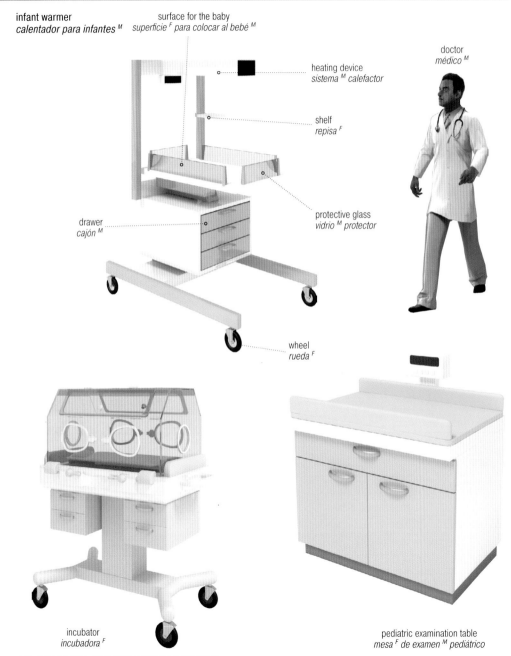

infant warmer
calentador para infantes ᴹ

surface for the baby
superficie ᶠ *para colocar al bebé* ᴹ

heating device
sistema ᴹ *calefactor*

shelf
repisa ᶠ

doctor
médico ᴹ

drawer
cajón ᴹ

protective glass
vidrio ᴹ *protector*

wheel
rueda ᶠ

incubator
incubadora ᶠ

pediatric examination table
mesa ᶠ *de examen* ᴹ *pediátrico*

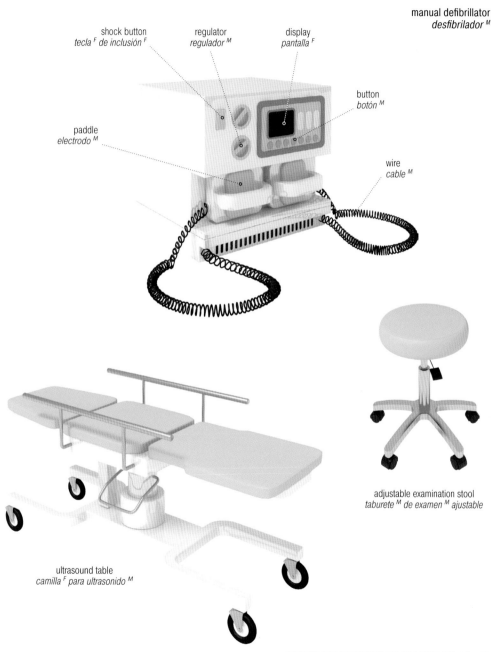

manual defibrillator
desfibrilador ᴹ

shock button
tecla ᶠ de inclusión ᶠ

regulator
regulador ᴹ

display
pantalla ᶠ

button
botón ᴹ

paddle
electrodo ᴹ

wire
cable ᴹ

adjustable examination stool
taburete ᴹ de examen ᴹ ajustable

ultrasound table
camilla ᶠ para ultrasonido ᴹ

electric hospital bed
cama ᶠ eléctrica

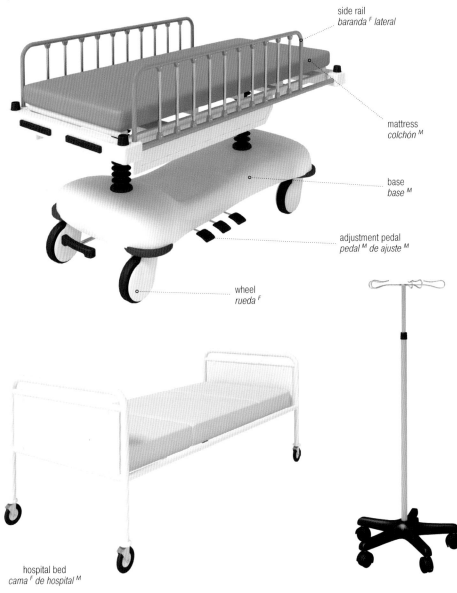

side rail
baranda ᶠ lateral

mattress
colchón ᴹ

base
base ᴹ

adjustment pedal
pedal ᴹ de ajuste ᴹ

wheel
rueda ᶠ

hospital bed
cama ᶠ de hospital ᴹ

IV (intravenous) stand
soporte ᴹ para bolsa ᶠ intravenosa

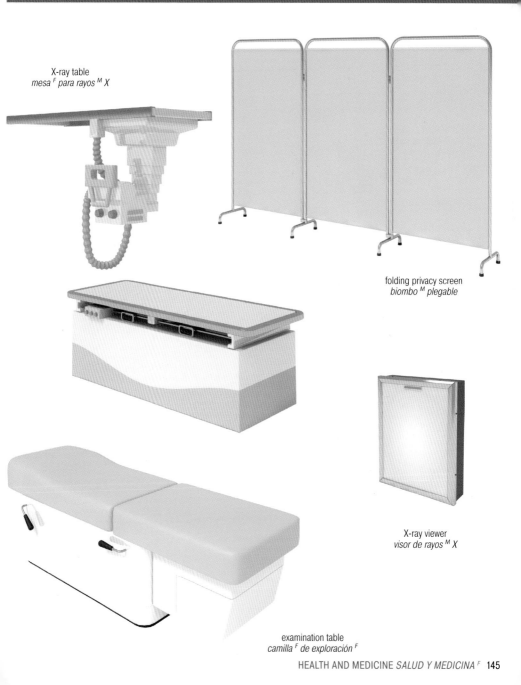

X-ray table
mesa ᶠ para rayos ᴹ X

folding privacy screen
biombo ᴹ plegable

X-ray viewer
visor de rayos ᴹ X

examination table
camilla ᶠ de exploración ᶠ

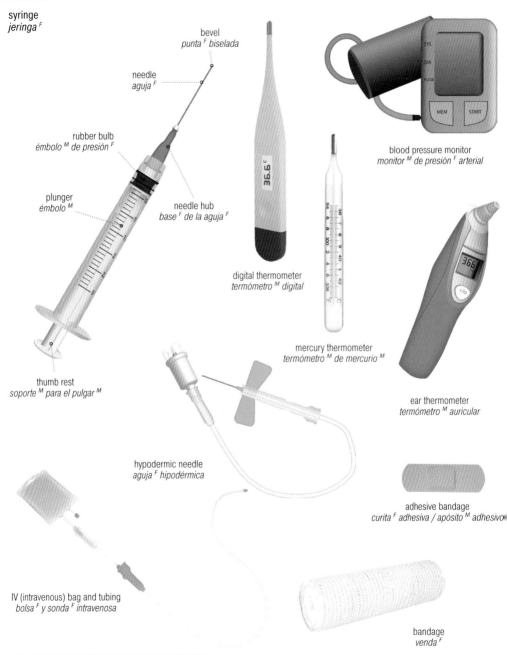

syringe
jeringa ᶠ

bevel
punta ᶠ biselada

needle
aguja ᶠ

rubber bulb
émbolo ᴹ de presión ᶠ

plunger
émbolo ᴹ

needle hub
base ᶠ de la aguja ᶠ

thumb rest
soporte ᴹ para el pulgar ᴹ

digital thermometer
termómetro ᴹ digital

mercury thermometer
termómetro ᴹ de mercurio ᴹ

blood pressure monitor
monitor ᴹ de presión ᶠ arterial

ear thermometer
termómetro ᴹ auricular

hypodermic needle
aguja ᶠ hipodérmica

adhesive bandage
curita ᶠ adhesiva / apósito ᴹ adhesivo

IV (intravenous) bag and tubing
bolsa ᶠ y sonda ᶠ intravenosa

bandage
venda ᶠ

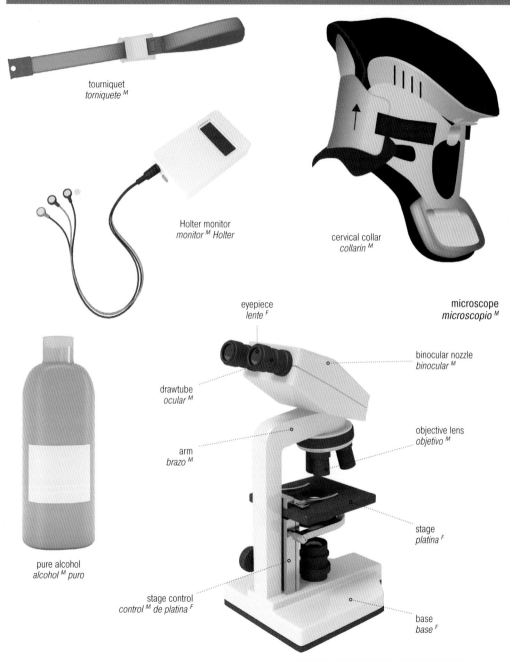

tourniquet
torniquete ^M

Holter monitor
monitor ^M *Holter*

cervical collar
collarín ^M

eyepiece
lente ^F

microscope
microscopio ^M

binocular nozzle
binocular ^M

drawtube
ocular ^M

objective lens
objetivo ^M

arm
brazo ^M

stage
platina ^F

pure alcohol
alcohol ^M *puro*

stage control
control ^M *de platina* ^F

base
base ^F

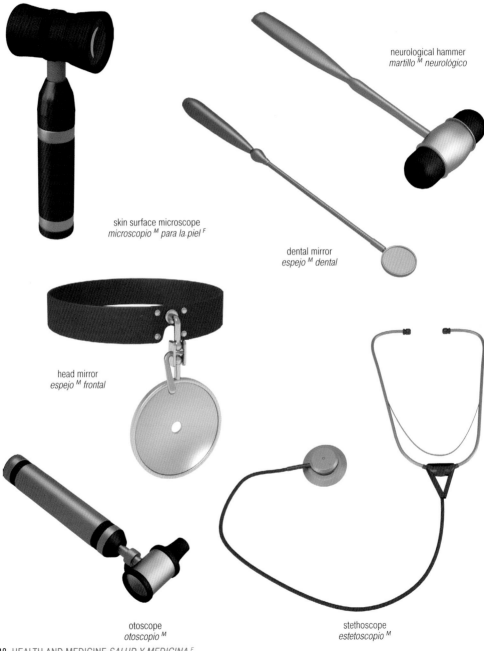

neurological hammer
martillo ᴹ neurológico

skin surface microscope
microscopio ᴹ para la piel ᶠ

dental mirror
espejo ᴹ dental

head mirror
espejo ᴹ frontal

otoscope
otoscopio ᴹ

stethoscope
estetoscopio ᴹ

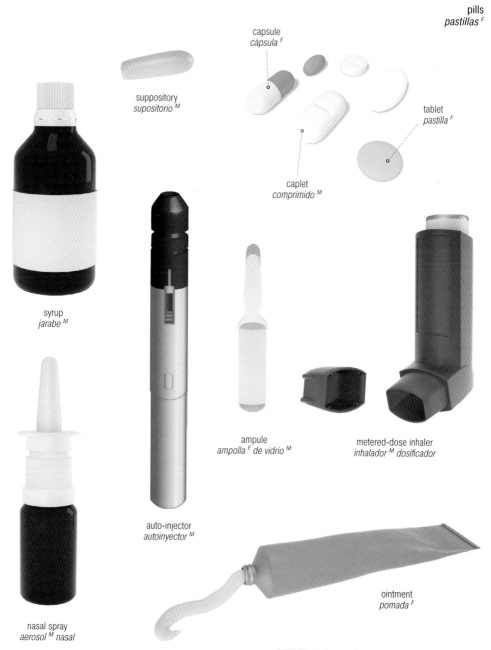

pills
pastillas F

capsule
cápsula F

suppository
supositorio M

tablet
pastilla F

caplet
comprimido M

syrup
jarabe M

ampule
ampolla F *de vidrio* M

metered-dose inhaler
inhalador M *dosificador*

auto-injector
autoinyector M

nasal spray
aerosol M *nasal*

ointment
pomada F

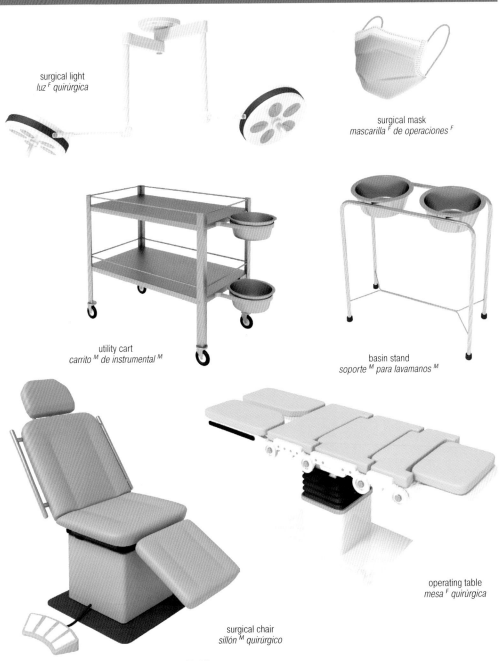

surgical light
luz [F] *quirúrgica*

surgical mask
mascarilla [F] *de operaciones* [F]

utility cart
carrito [M] *de instrumental* [M]

basin stand
soporte [M] *para lavamanos* [M]

surgical chair
sillón [M] *quirúrgico*

operating table
mesa [F] *quirúrgica*

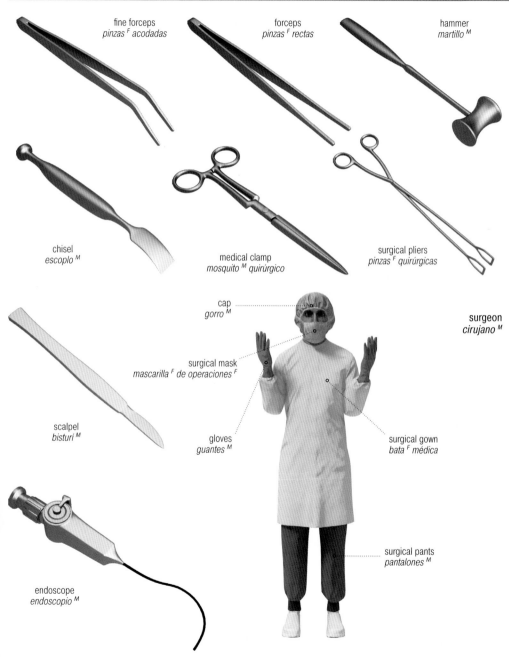

fine forceps
pinzas F *acodadas*

forceps
pinzas F *rectas*

hammer
martillo M

chisel
escoplo M

medical clamp
mosquito M *quirúrgico*

surgical pliers
pinzas F *quirúrgicas*

cap
gorro M

surgeon
cirujano M

surgical mask
mascarilla F *de operaciones* F

scalpel
bisturí M

gloves
guantes M

surgical gown
bata F *médica*

surgical pants
pantalones M

endoscope
endoscopio M

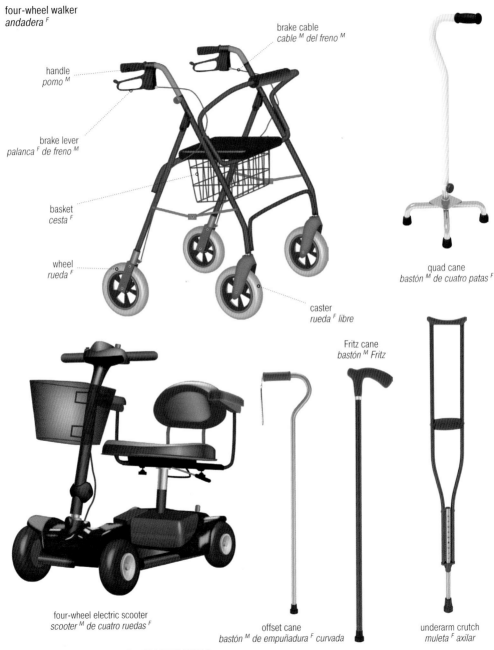

four-wheel walker
andadera ᶠ

brake cable
cable ᴹ del freno ᴹ

handle
pomo ᴹ

brake lever
palanca ᶠ de freno ᴹ

basket
cesta ᶠ

wheel
rueda ᶠ

caster
rueda ᶠ libre

quad cane
bastón ᴹ de cuatro patas ᶠ

Fritz cane
bastón ᴹ Fritz

four-wheel electric scooter
scooter ᴹ de cuatro ruedas ᶠ

offset cane
bastón ᴹ de empuñadura ᶠ curvada

underarm crutch
muleta ᶠ axilar

electric wheelchair
silla ꟳ de ruedas ꟳ eléctrica

back
respaldo ᴹ

control stick
palanca ꟳ de control ꟳ

handle
pomo ᴹ

armrest
reposabrazos ᴹ

seat
asiento ᴹ

electric drive
motor ᴹ eléctrico

wheel
rueda ꟳ

footboard
reposapies ᴹ

caster
rueda ꟳ libre

back
respaldo ᴹ

forearm crutch
muleta ꟳ de antebrazo ᴹ

clothing guard
protector ᴹ

wheelchair
silla ꟳ de ruedas ꟳ

handle
mango ᴹ

arm
brazo ᴹ

armrest
reposabrazos ᴹ

seat
asiento ᴹ

push rim
aros ᴹ de empuje ᴹ

caster
rueda ꟳ libre

hub
buje ᴹ

large wheel
rueda ꟳ grande

footrest
reposapies ᴹ

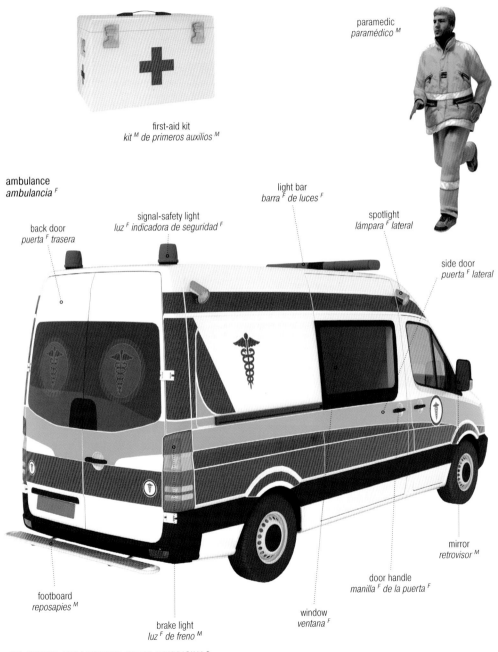

paramedic
paramédico ^M

first-aid kit
kit ^M *de primeros auxilios* ^M

ambulance
ambulancia ^F

light bar
barra ^F *de luces* ^F

signal-safety light
luz ^F *indicadora de seguridad* ^F

spotlight
lámpara ^F *lateral*

back door
puerta ^F *trasera*

side door
puerta ^F *lateral*

mirror
retrovisor ^M

door handle
manilla ^F *de la puerta* ^F

footboard
reposapies ^M

window
ventana ^F

brake light
luz ^F *de freno* ^M

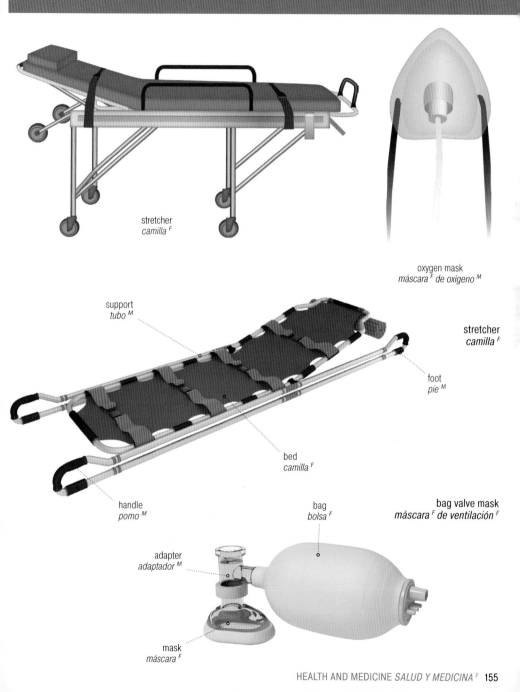

stretcher
camilla ^F

oxygen mask
máscara ^F *de oxígeno* ^M

support
tubo ^M

stretcher
camilla ^F

foot
pie ^M

bed
camilla ^F

handle
pomo ^M

bag
bolsa ^F

bag valve mask
máscara ^F *de ventilación* ^F

adapter
adaptador ^M

mask
máscara ^F

HOUSING

HOGAR

ground floor of house
planta ᶠ *baja de una casa* ᶠ

kitchen
cocina ᶠ

cabinets
estantes ᴹ

powder room
baño ᴹ *de invitados* ᴹ

stairs
escaleras ᶠ

refrigerator
nevera ᶠ

breakfast bar
mesa ᶠ *de desayuno* ᴹ

bar stool
taburetes ᴹ

dining room
comedor ᴹ

mailbox
buzón ᴹ

dining table
mesa ᶠ *de comedor* ᴹ

picture
cuadro ᴹ

dining chair
sillas ᶠ *de comedor* ᴹ

front door
puerta ᶠ *principal*

front steps
escalones ᴹ *de la entrada* ᶠ

doorbell
timbre ᴹ

patio
terraza ᶠ

patio umbrella
sombrilla para terraza ᶠ

fence
valla ᶠ

flower bed
parterres ᴹ

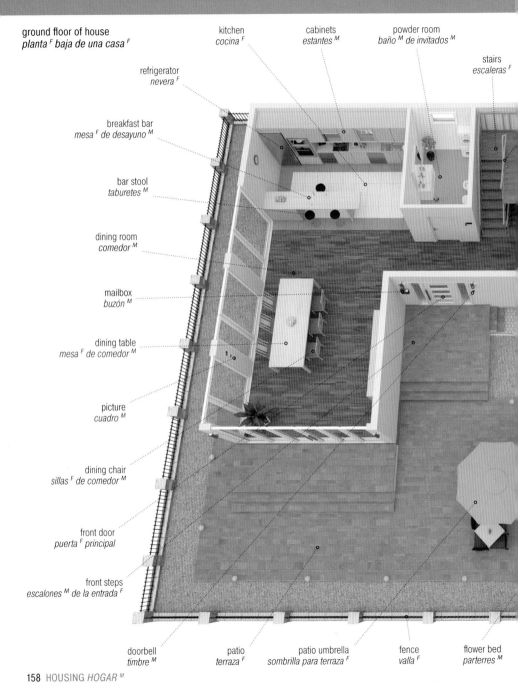

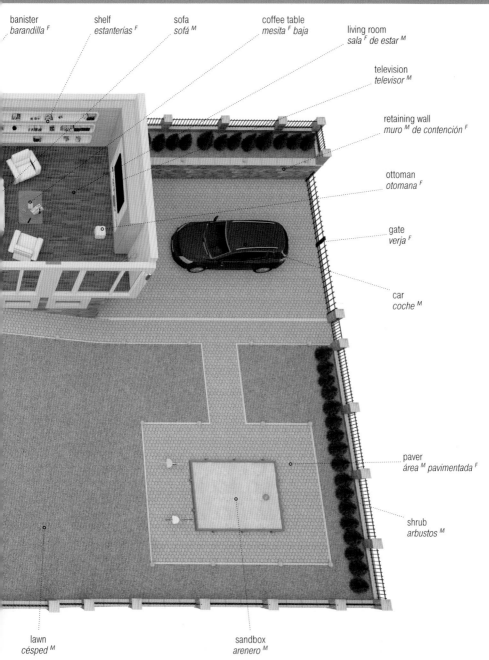

banister
barandilla *F*

shelf
estanterias *F*

sofa
sofá *M*

coffee table
mesita *F* *baja*

living room
sala *F* *de estar* *M*

television
televisor *M*

retaining wall
muro *M* *de contención* *F*

ottoman
otomana *F*

gate
verja *F*

car
coche *M*

paver
área *M* *pavimentada* *F*

shrub
arbustos *M*

lawn
césped *M*

sandbox
arenero *M*

second floor of house
primer piso ᴹ *de una casa* ᶠ

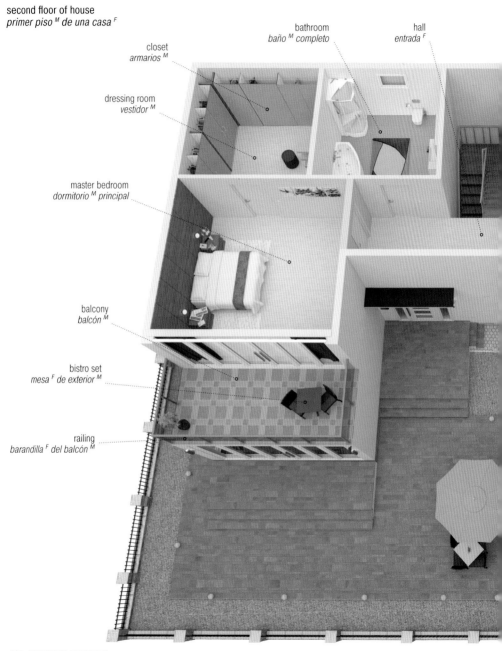

closet
armarios ᴹ

dressing room
vestidor ᴹ

bathroom
baño ᴹ *completo*

hall
entrada ᶠ

master bedroom
dormitorio ᴹ *principal*

balcony
balcón ᴹ

bistro set
mesa ᶠ *de exterior* ᴹ

railing
barandilla ᶠ *del balcón* ᴹ

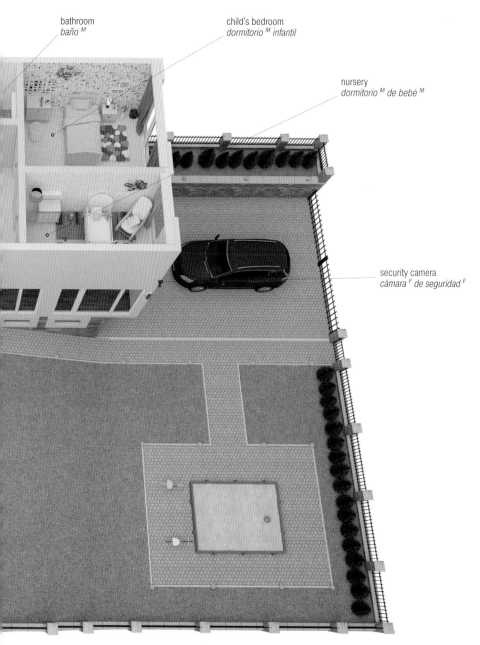

bathroom
baño M

child's bedroom
dormitorio M *infantil*

nursery
dormitorio M *de bebé* M

security camera
cámara F *de seguridad* F

exterior of house
exterior ᴹ del hogar ᴹ

balcony
balcón ᴹ

roof
tejado ᴹ

roof hatch
compuerta ᶠ del techo ᴹ

front door
puerta ᶠ principal

porch
porche ᴹ

patio umbrella
sombrilla ᶠ para terraza ᶠ

patio
terraza ᶠ

bistro set
mesa ᶠ de exterior ᴹ

flower bed
parterres ᴹ

lawn
césped ᴹ

sandbox
arenero ᴹ

fence
valla ᶠ

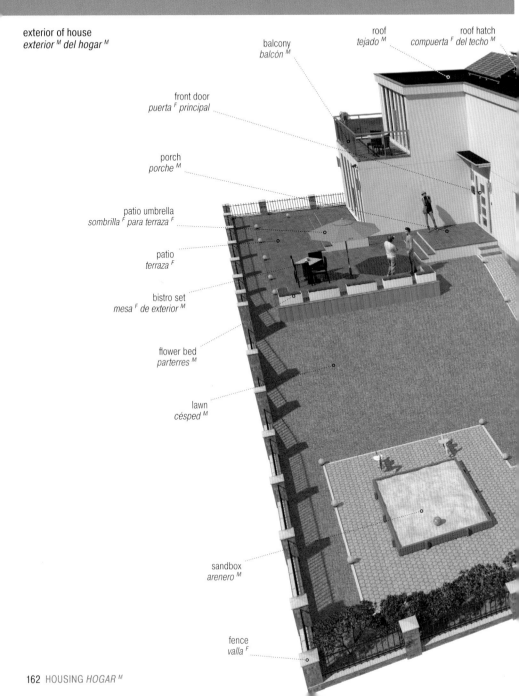

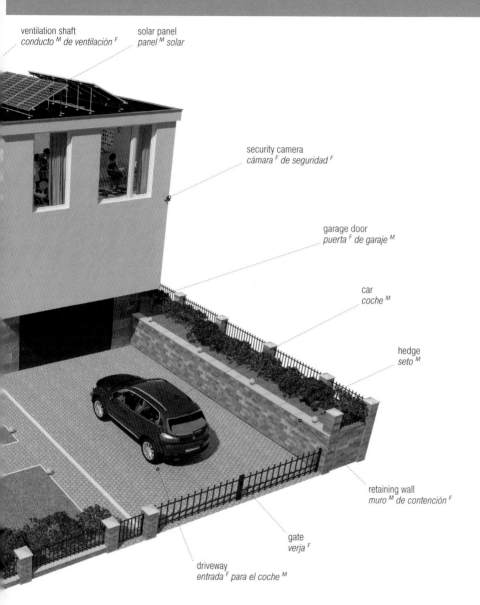

ventilation shaft
conducto ^M *de ventilación* ^F

solar panel
panel ^M *solar*

security camera
cámara ^F *de seguridad* ^F

garage door
puerta ^F *de garaje* ^M

car
coche ^M

hedge
seto ^M

retaining wall
muro ^M *de contención* ^F

gate
verja ^F

driveway
entrada ^F *para el coche* ^M

apartment building
bloque ᴹ *de apartamentos* ᴹ

facade
fachada ᶠ

penthouse
penthouse ᴹ

balcony door
puerta ᶠ *del balcón* ᴹ

balcony
balcón ᴹ

balcony railing
barandilla ᶠ *del balcón* ᴹ

resident
residente ᴹ

window
ventana ᶠ

intercom
intercomunicador ᴹ

main entrance
entrada ᶠ *principal*

satellite dish
antena ᶠ *parabólica*

antenna
antena ᶠ

patio umbrella
sombrilla para terraza ᶠ

patio
terraza ᶠ

living room
sala ᶠ de estar

book
libro ᴹ

fruit bowl
frutero ᴹ

bookshelf
librero ᴹ

sofa
sofá ᴹ

magazine
revista ᶠ

coffee table
mesita ᶠ baja

remote control
control ᴹ remoto

DVD
DVD ᴹ

DVD player
reproductor ᴹ *de DVD* ᴹ

television
televisor ᴹ

shelf
estante ᴹ

cushion
cojín ᴹ

armchair
sillón ᴹ

ottoman
otomana ᶠ

potted plant
planta ᶠ *de interior* ᴹ

master bedroom
dormitorio ^M *principal*

curtain
cortina ^F

light fixture
lámpara ^F

photograph
foto ^F

nightstand
mesa ^F *de noche* ^F

rug
alfombra ^F

book
libro ^M

bed
cama ^F

pillow
almohada ^F

light switch
interruptor ^M *de luz* ^F

closet door
puerta ^F *de armario* ^M

telephone
teléfono ^M

electrical outlet
enchufe ^M

hardwood floor
suelo ^M *de madera* ^F

bathroom
sala ^F *de baño* ^M

recessed light
luz ^F *empotrada*

shower cubicle
cuarto ^M *de la ducha* ^F

tile
azulejo ^M

bath towel
toalla ^F *de baño* ^M

faucet
grifo ^M

shampoo
champú ^M

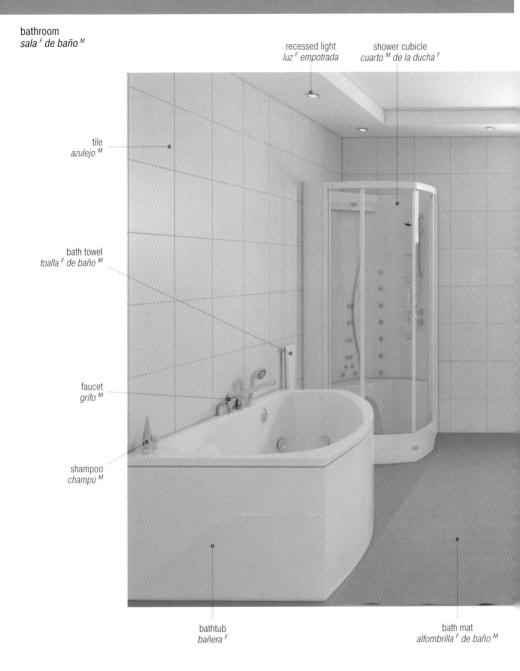

bathtub
bañera ^F

bath mat
alfombrilla ^F *de baño* ^M

window
ventana ᶠ

toilet
inodoro ᴹ

mirror
espejo ᴹ

fan
extractor ᴹ

medicine cabinet
botiquin ᴹ

soap dish
jabonera ᶠ

faucet
grifo ᴹ

toothbrush
cepillo ᴹ *de dientes* ᴹ

toothbrush holder
vaso ᴹ *para cepillo* ᴹ
de dientes ᴹ

lotion
crema ᶠ

sink
lavabo ᴹ

hand towel
toalla ᶠ *de mano* ᴹ

floor
suelo ᴹ

toilet paper
papel ᴹ *higiénico*

toilet brush
cepillo ᴹ *para limpiar*
el inodoro ᴹ

wastebasket
papelera ᶠ

vanity
mueble ᴹ *de baño* ᴹ

girl's room
dormitorio [M] *de niña* [F]

wall decal
vinilo [M] *decorativo*

clock
reloj [M]

photograph
fotografía [F]

chest of drawers
cajonera [F]

pillow
almohada [F]

sheets
sábanas [F]

bed
cama [F]

wallpaper
papel ^M *tapiz* ^M

picture
cuadro ^M

lamp
lámpara ^F

toy
juguete ^M

nightstand
mesita ^F *de noche* ^F

hardwood floor
suelo ^M *de madera* ^F

throw rug
alfombra ^F

nursery
dormitorio ^M *del bebé* ^M

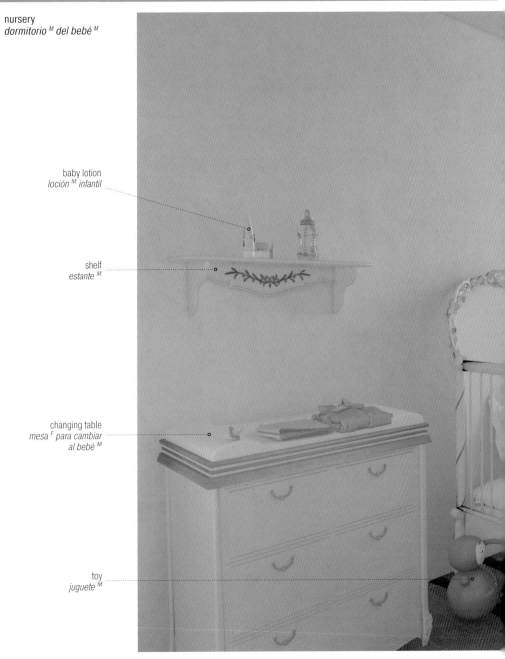

baby lotion
loción ^M *infantil*

shelf
estante ^M

changing table
mesa ^F *para cambiar*
al bebé ^M

toy
juguete ^M

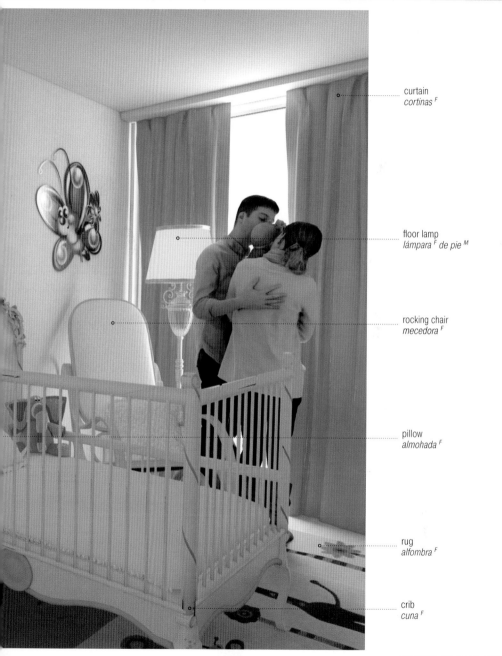

curtain
cortinas ^F

floor lamp
lámpara ^F *de pie* ^M

rocking chair
mecedora ^F

pillow
almohada ^F

rug
alfombra ^F

crib
cuna ^F

Children's furniture
Muebles M *infantiles*

changing table
mesa F *para cambiar al bebé* M

knob
tirador M

drawer
cajón M

leg
pata F

shelf
estante M

armoire
armario M

high chair
sillita F *alta*

back
respaldo M

desk and chair
mesa F *y silla* F

desk
escritorio M

tray
bandeja F

seat
asiento M

leg
pata F

footrest
reposapiés M

chair
silla F

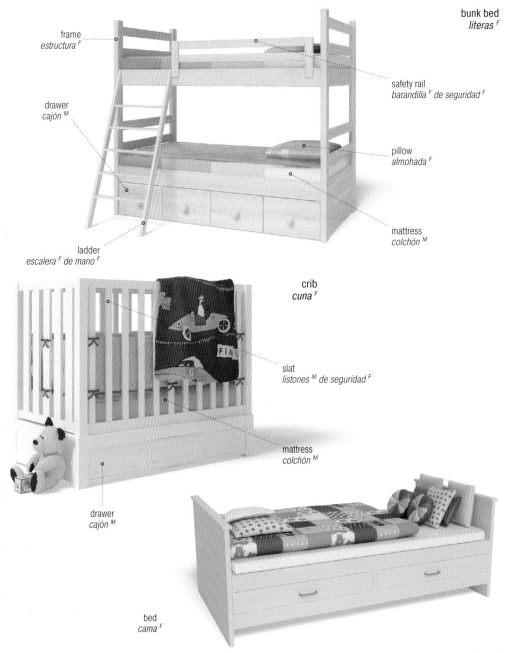

bunk bed
literas ^F

frame
estructura ^F

safety rail
barandilla ^F *de seguridad* ^F

drawer
cajón ^M

pillow
almohada ^F

mattress
colchón ^M

ladder
escalera ^F *de mano* ^F

crib
cuna ^F

slat
listones ^M *de seguridad* ^F

mattress
colchón ^M

drawer
cajón ^M

bed
cama ^F

kitchen
cocina ᶠ

picture
foto ᶠ

clock
reloj ᴹ

refrigerator
nevera ᶠ

microwave
microondas ᴹ

breakfast bar
barra americana ᶠ

bar stool
taburete ᴹ

oven
horno ᴹ

coffee machine
cafetera ᶠ

wine fridge
frigorífico ᴹ *para vino* ᴹ

range hood
campana F

wine glass
copa F *de vino* M

canister
bote M

cup
taza F

faucet
grifo M

cabinet
alacenas F

cooktop
tapa F *de cocina* F

countertop
encimera F

dishwasher
lavavajillas M

sink
fregadero M

tiled floor
suelo M *de baldosas* M

Large appliances
Electrodomésticos ^M *de cocina* ^F

refrigerator
nevera ^F

shelf
estante ^M

egg tray
bandeja ^F *de huevos* ^M

refrigerator compartment door
puerta ^F *de la nevera* ^F

side-by-side refrigerator and freezer
nevera ^F *de doble puerta* ^F

handle
asa ^F

freezer compartment
congelador ^M

microwave
microondas ^M

crisper
cajón ^M *de las verduras* ^F
de la nevera ^F

drawer
cajón ^M

handle
asa ^F

clock timer
temporizador ^M

freezer compartment door
puerta ^F *del congelador* ^M

window
ventana ^F

cooktop
fogones ^M

turntable
bandeja ^F *giratoria*

door
puerta ^F

control panel
panel ^M *de control* ^M

range hood
extractor M

dishwasher
lavavajillas M

ventilation duct
conducto M de ventilación F

handle
asa F

power button
interruptor M

control knob
dial M selector de función F

indicator light
indicador M

door
puerta F

filter
filtro M

screen
pantalla F protectora

display
monitor M

gas range
cocina F de gas M

cooktop control knob
mando M de control M de cocina F

burner
fogón M

handle
asa F

oven control knob
mando M de control M del horno M

electric range
cocina F eléctrica

oven
horno M

Small appliances
Electrodomésticos M *pequeños*

espresso machine
cafetera F *espresso* F

pressure gauge
medidor M *de presión* F

cup-warming tray
bandeja F *calienta tazas* F

group head
cabezal M

water tank
depósito M *de agua* F

filter holder
cesto M *del filtro* M

spout
pico M

handle
mango M

coffee grinder
molinillo M *de café* M

steam nozzle
boquilla F *de vapor* M

drip tray
bandeja F *de goteo* M

automatic drip coffeemaker
cafetera F *de goteo* M

lid
tapa F *del filtro* M

water-level indicator
indicador M *del nivel* M *de agua* F

basket
cesto M *del filtro* M

lid-release button
botón M *para abrir la*
tapa F

pot lid
tapa F *de la cafetera* F

handle
mango M

pot
cafetera F

warming plate
placa F *calentadora*

water reservoir
depósito M *de agua* F

blender
batidora F

juicer
extractor ᴹ *de jugos* ᴹ

pusher
empujador ᴹ

feed tube
tubo ᴹ *de alimentación* ᶠ

filter
filtro ᴹ

lid
tapa ᶠ

pulp container
depósito ᴹ *de pulpa* ᶠ

safety latch
gancho ᴹ *de seguridad* ᶠ

spout
pico ᴹ

power button
interruptor ᴹ

motor housing
compartimento ᴹ *del motor* ᴹ

immersion blender
batidora ᶠ *de mano* ᴹ

electric kettle
tetera ᶠ *eléctrica*

electric citrus juicer
exprimidor ᴹ *de cítricos* ᴹ

reamer
exprimidor ᴹ

spout
pico ᴹ

strainer
colador ᴹ

spout
pico ᴹ

lid
tapa ᶠ

lid-release button
botón ᴹ *para abrir la tapa* ᶠ

power switch
interruptor ᴹ

bowl
jarra ᶠ

juice-level indicator
indicador ᴹ *de nivel* ᴹ *de zumo*

motor housing
compartimento ᴹ *del motor* ᴹ

base
soporte ᴹ

indicator light
luz ᶠ *indicadora*

jug
jarra ᶠ

toaster oven
horno ^M tostador

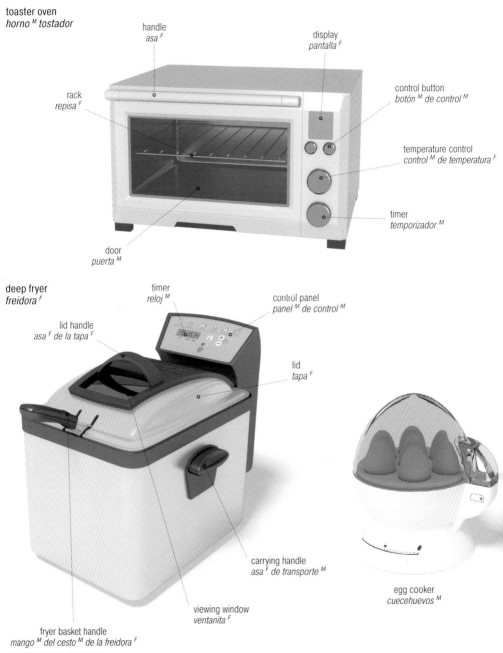

handle
asa ^F

display
pantalla ^F

control button
botón ^M de control ^M

rack
repisa ^F

temperature control
control ^M de temperatura ^F

timer
temporizador ^M

door
puerta ^M

deep fryer
freidora ^F

timer
reloj ^M

control panel
panel ^M de control ^M

lid handle
asa ^F de la tapa ^F

lid
tapa ^F

carrying handle
asa ^F de transporte ^M

egg cooker
cuecehuevos ^M

viewing window
ventanita ^F

fryer basket handle
mango ^M del cesto ^M de la freidora ^F

slot
ranura ^F

toaster
tostadora ^F

control buttons
botones ^M *de control* ^M

lever
palanca ^F

crumb tray
bandeja ^F *recogemigas*

browning control
control ^M *de potencia* ^F

table grill
parrilla ^F *de mesa* ^F

waffle iron
gofrera ^F

bread maker
máquina ^F *de pan* ^M

window
ventana ^F

liquid-crystal display (LCD)
pantalla ^F *de cristal* ^M *líquido*

lid
tapa ^F

control buttons
botones ^M *de control* ^M

food processor
robot M *de cocina* F

feed tube
tubo M *de entrada* F

handle
mango M

blade
cuchilla F

bowl
tazón M

motor housing
compartimento M *del motor* M

control pad
panel M *de control* M

control buttons
botones M *de control* M

stand mixer
batidora F *de pedestal* M

tilt-back head
cabeza F *móvil*

dehydrator
deshidratadora F

mixing bowl
tazón M *de mezclar*

beater
varilla F *de batir*

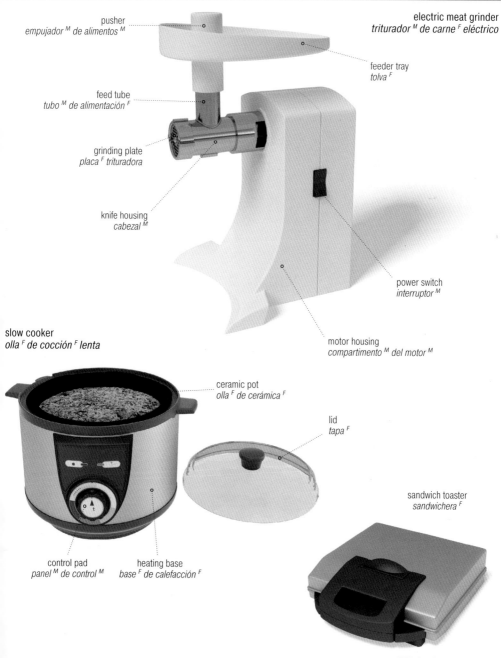

pusher
empujador M *de alimentos* M

electric meat grinder
triturador M *de carne* F *eléctrico*

feeder tray
tolva F

feed tube
tubo M *de alimentación* F

grinding plate
placa F *trituradora*

knife housing
cabezal M

power switch
interruptor M

motor housing
compartimento M *del motor* M

slow cooker
olla F *de cocción* F *lenta*

ceramic pot
olla F *de cerámica* F

lid
tapa F

sandwich toaster
sandwichera F

control pad
panel M *de control* M

heating base
base F *de calefacción* F

table setting
disposición [F] *de la mesa* [F]

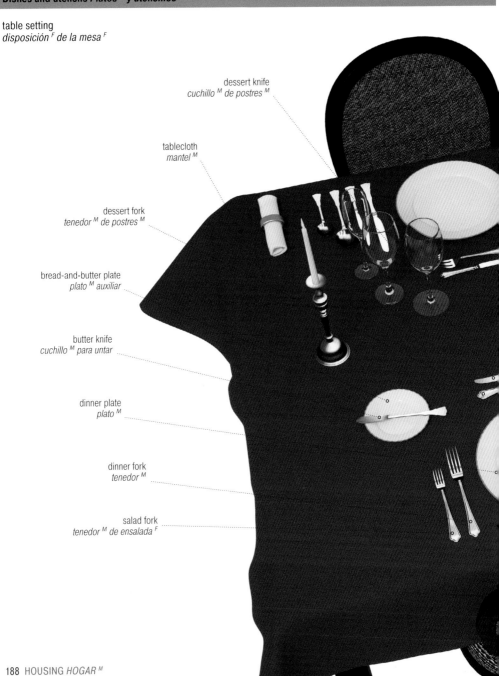

dessert knife
cuchillo [M] *de postres* [M]

tablecloth
mantel [M]

dessert fork
tenedor [M] *de postres* [M]

bread-and-butter plate
plato [M] *auxiliar*

butter knife
cuchillo [M] *para untar*

dinner plate
plato [M]

dinner fork
tenedor [M]

salad fork
tenedor [M] *de ensalada* [F]

candle
vela F

red wine glass
copa F *de vino* M *tinto*

candlestick
candelero M

white wine glass
copa F *de vino* M *blanco*

ice bucket
cubitera F

champagne flute
copa F *alta de champán* M

napkin
servilleta F

teaspoon
cucharilla F

soupspoon
cuchara F

fish knife
cuchillo M *de aperitivo* M

dinner knife
cuchillo M

Cutlery
Cubertería F

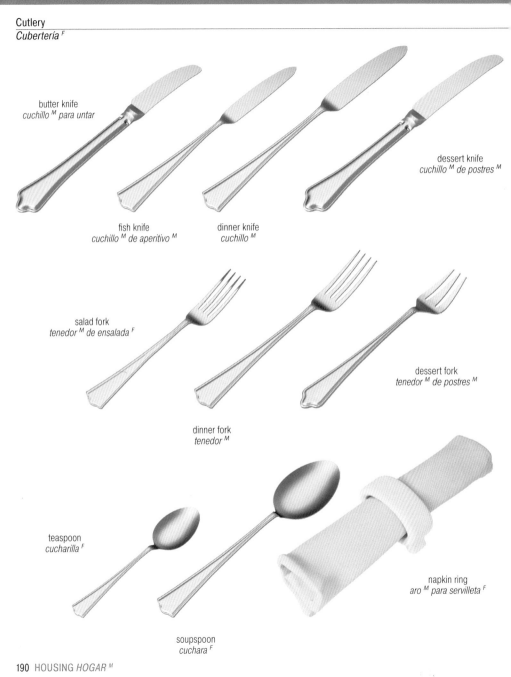

butter knife
cuchillo M *para untar*

dessert knife
cuchillo M *de postres* M

fish knife
cuchillo M *de aperitivo* M

dinner knife
cuchillo M

salad fork
tenedor M *de ensalada* F

dessert fork
tenedor M *de postres* M

dinner fork
tenedor M

teaspoon
cucharilla F

napkin ring
aro M *para servilleta* F

soupspoon
cuchara F

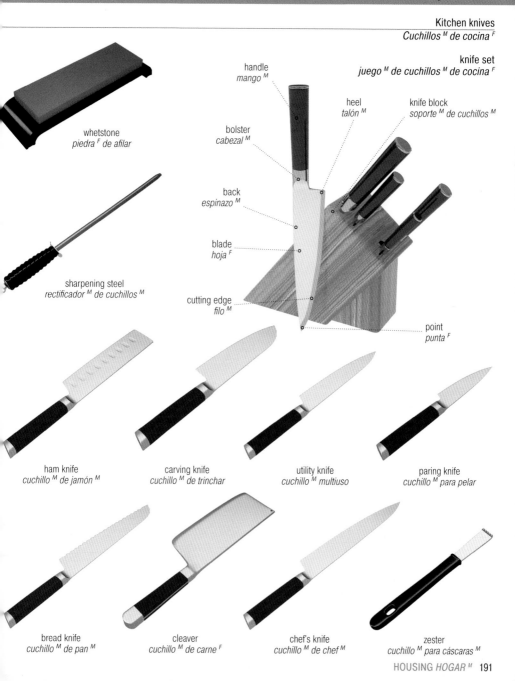

Kitchen knives
Cuchillos ᴹ de cocina ᶠ

knife set
juego ᴹ de cuchillos ᴹ de cocina ᶠ

handle
mango ᴹ

heel
talón ᴹ

knife block
soporte ᴹ de cuchillos ᴹ

whetstone
piedra ᶠ de afilar

bolster
cabezal ᴹ

back
espinazo ᴹ

blade
hoja ᶠ

sharpening steel
rectificador ᴹ de cuchillos ᴹ

cutting edge
filo ᴹ

point
punta ᶠ

ham knife
cuchillo ᴹ de jamón ᴹ

carving knife
cuchillo ᴹ de trinchar

utility knife
cuchillo ᴹ multiuso

paring knife
cuchillo ᴹ para pelar

bread knife
cuchillo ᴹ de pan ᴹ

cleaver
cuchillo ᴹ de carne ᶠ

chef's knife
cuchillo ᴹ de chef ᴹ

zester
cuchillo ᴹ para cáscaras ᴹ

Tableware
Vajilla F

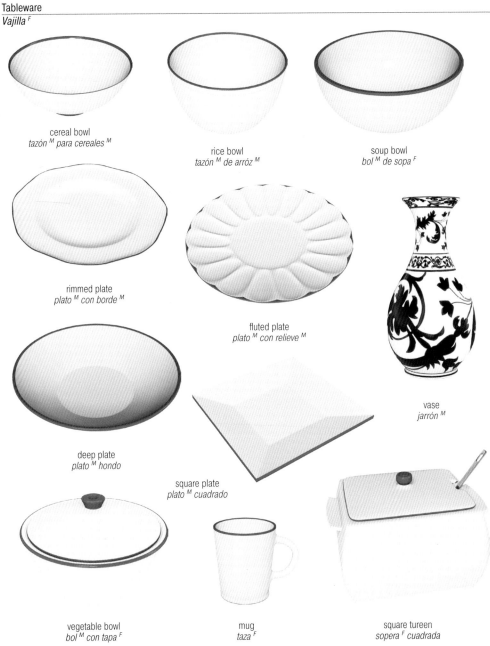

cereal bowl
tazón M *para cereales* M

rice bowl
tazón M *de arróz* M

soup bowl
bol M *de sopa* F

rimmed plate
plato M *con borde* M

fluted plate
plato M *con relieve* M

vase
jarrón M

deep plate
plato M *hondo*

square plate
plato M *cuadrado*

vegetable bowl
bol M *con tapa* F

mug
taza F

square tureen
sopera F *cuadrada*

platter
plato [M] *de servir*

dinner plate
plato [M] *llano*

dessert plate
plato [M] *de postres* [M]

spoon rest
portacucharas [M]

dessert bowl
tazón [M] *de postres* [M]

cup and saucer
taza [F] *y plato* [M]

soup tureen
fuente [F]

teapot
tetera [F]

creamer
jarra [F] *de leche* [F]

sugar bowl
azucarero [M]

Kitchen utensils
Utensilios [M] *de cocina* [F]

electronic kitchen scale
balanza [F] *digital de cocina* [F]

bowl
bandeja [F]

fondue set
fondue [F]

cube slicer
cortador [M] *en cubitos* [M]

fondue pot
recipiente [M] *para fondue* [F]

burner
quemador [M]

platform
plataforma [F]

stand
soporte [M]

fondue fork
tenedor [M] *para fondue* [F]

display
pantalla [F]

bowl
tazón [M]

corkscrew
sacacorchos [M]

tray
bandeja [F]

bread box
panera [F]

manual coffee grinder
molinillo [M] *de café* [M]

roll-top lid
tapadera [F] *corredera*

pastry blender
amasadora F

citrus juicer
exprimidor M de cítricos M

pot grabber
agarrador M

meat thermometer
termómetro M de cocina F

mezzaluna
medialuna F

peeler
pelador M

apple corer and slicer
cortador M de manzanas F

grater
rallador M

pastry brush
brocha F de repostería F

milk frother
batidor M de leche F

sieve
colador M

cutting board
tabla de cortar ᶠ

baking sheet
bandeja ᶠ *de cocina* ᶠ

bottle carrier
portabotellas ᴹ

baking rack
rejilla ᶠ *de horno* ᴹ

measuring spoon
cuchara ᶠ *de medir*

measuring cup
taza ᶠ *de medir*

funnel
embudo ᴹ

sifter
cedazo ᴹ

bottle opener
destapador ᴹ *de botellas* ᶠ

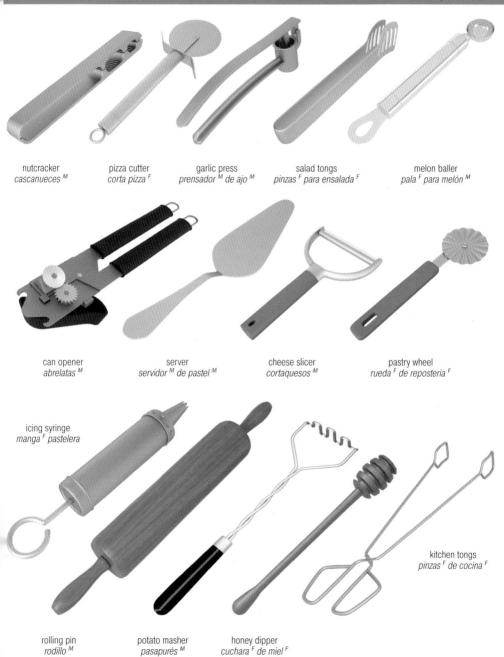

nutcracker
cascanueces M

pizza cutter
corta pizza F

garlic press
prensador M de ajo M

salad tongs
pinzas F para ensalada F

melon baller
pala F para melón M

can opener
abrelatas M

server
servidor M de pastel M

cheese slicer
cortaquesos M

pastry wheel
rueda F de repostería F

icing syringe
manga F pastelera

kitchen tongs
pinzas F de cocina F

rolling pin
rodillo M

potato masher
pasapurés M

honey dipper
cuchara F de miel F

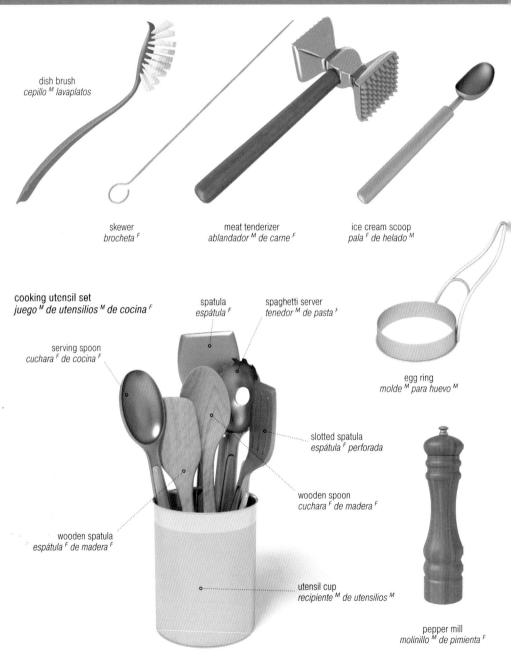

dish brush
cepillo M *lavaplatos*

skewer
brocheta F

meat tenderizer
ablandador M *de carne* F

ice cream scoop
pala F *de helado* M

cooking utensil set
juego M *de utensilios* M *de cocina* F

spatula
espátula F

spaghetti server
tenedor M *de pasta* F

serving spoon
cuchara F *de cocina* F

egg ring
molde M *para huevo* M

slotted spatula
espátula F *perforada*

wooden spoon
cuchara F *de madera* F

wooden spatula
espátula F *de madera* F

utensil cup
recipiente M *de utensilios* M

pepper mill
molinillo M *de pimienta* F

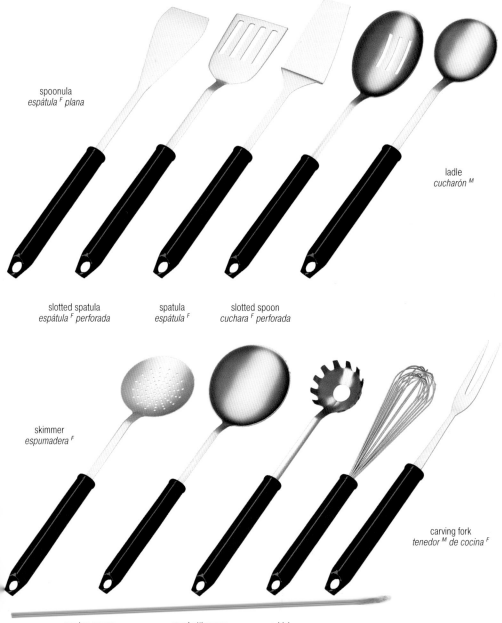

spoonula
espátula F *plana*

ladle
cucharón M

slotted spatula
espátula F *perforada*

spatula
espátula F

slotted spoon
cuchara F *perforada*

skimmer
espumadera F

carving fork
tenedor M *de cocina* F

serving spoon
cuchara F *de servir*

spaghetti server
tenedor M *de pasta* F

whisk
batidor M

coffee carafe
jarra F de café M

measuring cup
taza F de medir

ice bucket
cubitera F

mold
molde M para pasteles M

mortar and pestle
mortero M y pilón M

plastic storage container
recipiente M de plástico M

mixing bowl
bol M mezclador

saucepan
cacerola F

kettle
pava F

pie dish
molde M para tartas F

double boiler
cacerola F para baño M Maria F

wok
wok M

skillet
sartén F

frying pan
sartén F

casserole dish
cacerola F ovalada

stock pot
olla F sopera F

colander
colador M

salad spinner
centrifugador M de ensalada F

loaf pan
molde M de pan M

roasting pan
bandeja F para asados M

Glassware
Cristalería F

water glass
vaso M *de agua* F

champagne flute
copa F *alta de champán* M

white wine glass
copa F *de vino* M *blanco*

Alsace glass
copa F *de vino* M *del Alsacia* F

decanter
decantador M

cocktail glass
copa F *de cóctel* M

champagne glass
copa F *baja de champán* M

sherry glass
copa F *de jerez* M

brandy snifter
copa F *de coñac* M

burgundy glass
copa F *de Borgoña* F

port glass
copa F *de oporto* M

red wine glass
copa F *de vino* M *tinto*

liqueur glass
copa F *de licor* M

beer mug
jarra F *de cerveza* F

beer glass
vaso M *de cerveza* F

old-fashioned glass
vaso M *de whisky* M

Tables
Mesas ᶠ

console table
consola ᶠ

nightstand
mesilla ᶠ *de noche* ᶠ

dining table
mesa ᶠ *de comedor* ᴹ

writing desk
escritorio ᴹ

end table
mesa ^{F} *auxiliar*

top
parte ^{F} *superior*

telephone table
mesita ^{F} *de teléfono* ^{M}

leg
pata ^{F}

tempered glass
vidrio ^{M} *templado*

patio table
mesa ^{F} *de terraza* ^{F}

base
base ^{F}

vanity
tocador ^{M}

coffee table
mesita ^{F} *baja*

Chairs
Sillas ^F

bergère
poltrona ^F

leather armchair
sillón ^M *de cuero* ^M

back
respaldo ^M

arm
brazo ^M

seat
asiento ^M

leg
pata ^F

armchair
sillón ^M

stool
taburete ^M

Voltaire chair
silla ^F *francesa*

easy chair
butaca ^F

cushioned armchair
sillón ^M *acolchado*

kitchen chair
silla F de cocina F

folding chair
silla F plegable

stacking chair
silla F apilable

dining chair
mesa F de comedor M

rocking chair
mecedora F

bar stool
taburete M de bar M

back
respaldo M

seat
asiento M

upholstery
tapizado M

director's chair
silla F de director M

front leg
pata F delantera

back leg
pata F trasera

Sofas
Sofás ᴹ

sectional sofa
sofá ᴹ *seccional*

backrest
respaldo ᴹ

seat cushion
asiento ᴹ *acolchado*

leg
pata ᶠ

arm
brazo ᴹ

ottoman
otomana ᶠ

loveseat
sofá ᴹ *estrecho*

bench
banco ᴹ *acolchado*

chaise longe
chaiselongue ᶠ

Storage furniture
Muebles ^M *para almacenaje* ^M

liquor cabinet
mueble ^M *bar*

drawer
cajón ^M

door
puerta ^F

shelf
estante ^M

pull
tirador ^M

leg
pata ^F

chest of drawers
cajonera ^F

sofa table
mesa ^F *de sofá* ^M

display cabinet
vitrina ^F

glass door
puerta ^F *de cristal* ^M

pull
tirador ^M

sideboard
aparador ^M

drawer
cajón ^M

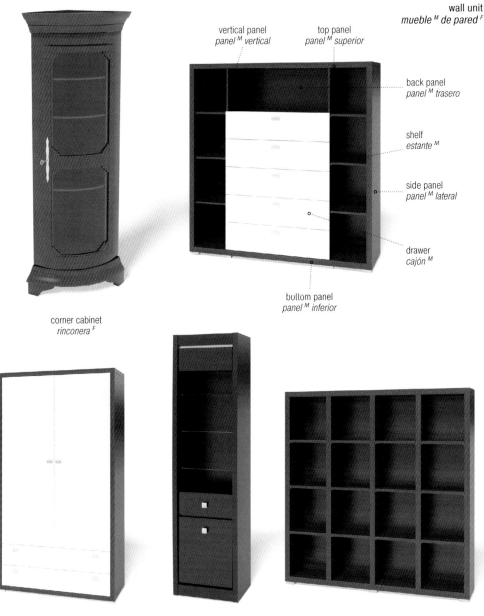

wall unit
mueble ᴹ *de pared* ᶠ

vertical panel
panel ᴹ *vertical*

top panel
panel ᴹ *superior*

back panel
panel ᴹ *trasero*

shelf
estante ᴹ

side panel
panel ᴹ *lateral*

drawer
cajón ᴹ

bottom panel
panel ᴹ *inferior*

corner cabinet
rinconera ᶠ

armoire
armario ᴹ *ropero*

chiffonier
chifonier ᴹ

bookcase
librero ᴹ

Domestic appliances
Electrodomésticos ᴹ

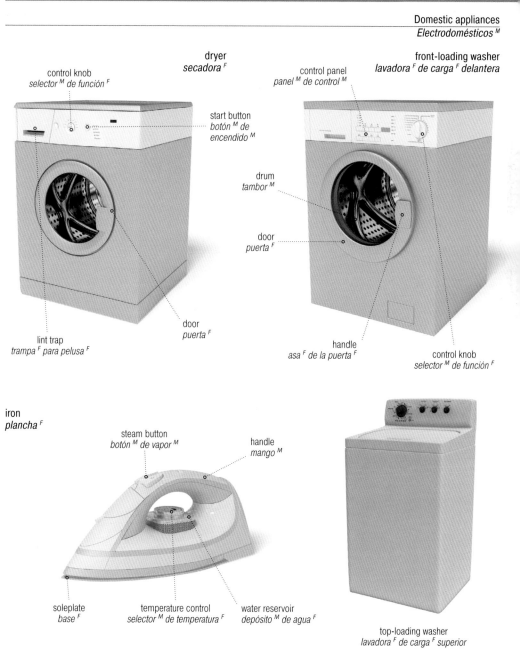

dryer
secadora ᶠ

control knob
selector ᴹ *de función* ᶠ

start button
botón ᴹ *de*
encendido ᴹ

door
puerta ᶠ

lint trap
trampa ᶠ *para pelusa* ᶠ

front-loading washer
lavadora ᶠ *de carga* ᶠ *delantera*

control panel
panel ᴹ *de control* ᴹ

drum
tambor ᴹ

door
puerta ᶠ

handle
asa ᶠ *de la puerta* ᶠ

control knob
selector ᴹ *de función* ᶠ

iron
plancha ᶠ

steam button
botón ᴹ *de vapor* ᴹ

handle
mango ᴹ

soleplate
base ᶠ

temperature control
selector ᴹ *de temperatura* ᶠ

water reservoir
depósito ᴹ *de agua* ᶠ

top-loading washer
lavadora ᶠ *de carga* ᶠ *superior*

ceiling fan
ventilador *M* *de techo* *M*

pedestal fan
ventilador *M* *de pie* *M*

oscillation control
mecanismo *M* *de oscilación*

blade
aspa *F*

ceiling mount
soporte *M* *de montaje* *M*

safety guard
protector *M* *de seguridad* *F*

rod
barra *F* *vertical*

motor housing
compartimento *M* *del motor* *M*

motor housing
compartimento *M* *del motor*

speed control
control *M* *de velocidad* *F*

height adjustment
ajuste *M* *de altura* *F*

blade
aspa *M*

stand
soporte *M*

ductless air conditioner
aparato *M* *de aire* *M* *acondicionado interior*

base
base *F*

canister vacuum cleaner
aspiradora *F*

power switch
interruptor *M*

pipe
tubo *M* *de succión* *F*

handheld vacuum cleaner
aspiradora *F* *de mano* *F*

hose
manguera *F*

storage compartment release button
botón *M* *de apertura* *F* *del depósito* *M*

wheel
rueda *F*

ventillation grille
rejilla *F* *de ventilación* *F*

rug and floor brush
cepillo *M* *para pisos* *M*
y alfombras *F*

robotic vacuum cleaner
aspiradora *F* *automática*

upright vacuum cleaner
aspiradora *F* *vertical*

Audiovisual equipment
Equipo ᴹ audiovisual

television
televisor ᴹ

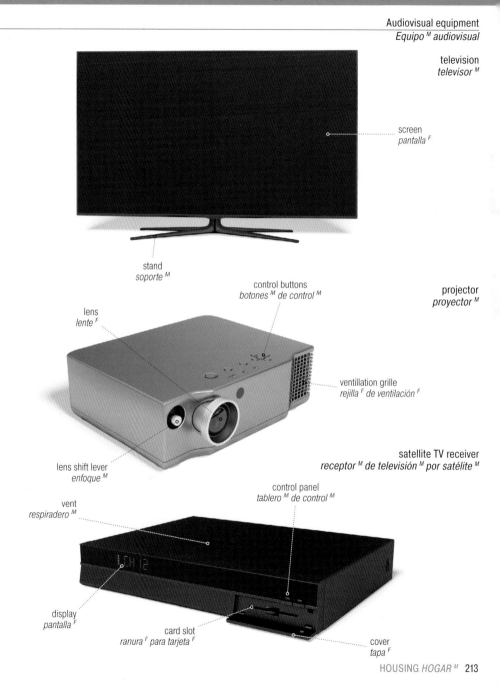

screen
pantalla ᶠ

stand
soporte ᴹ

control buttons
botones ᴹ *de control* ᴹ

projector
proyector ᴹ

lens
lente ᶠ

ventillation grille
rejilla ᶠ *de ventilación* ᶠ

lens shift lever
enfoque ᴹ

satellite TV receiver
receptor ᴹ *de televisión* ᴹ *por satélite* ᴹ

control panel
tablero ᴹ *de control* ᴹ

vent
respiradero ᴹ

display
pantalla ᶠ

card slot
ranura ᶠ *para tarjeta* ᶠ

cover
tapa ᶠ

sound system
sistema ^M *de sonido* ^M

main speaker
altavoz ^M *principal*

subwoofer
subwoofer ^M

surround speaker
altavoz ^M *central*

stand
soporte ^M

base
base ^F

headphones
auriculares ^M

headband
montura ^F

ear cushion
almohadilla ^F *acústica*

earphone
auricular ^M

casing
revestimiento ^M

input button
botón ^M *de entrada* ^F

standby button
botón ^M *de standby* ^M

volume control
control ^M *de volumen* ^M

remote control
control ^M *remoto*

image format button
botón ^M *de formato* ^M
de imagen ^F

play button
botón ^M *de reproducción* ^M

control pad
rueda ^F *de control* ^M

DVD player and amplifier
reproductor ^M *de DVD* ^M

DVD slot
ranura ^F *para DVD* ^M

DVD player
reproductor ^M *de DVD* ^M

control pad
teclado ^M *de control* ^M

volume control
control ^M *de volumen* ^M

channel scan button
botón ^M *de búsqueda* ^F
de canales ^M

channel selector buttons
botones ^M *selectores* ^M
de canales ^M

amplifier
amplificador ^M

control panel
tablero ^M *de control* ^M

display
pantalla ^F

function button
botón ^M *de selección* ^F
de modo ^M

Lightbulbs
Bombillas ꜰ

incandescent lightbulb
bombilla ꜰ incandescente

compact fluorescent lightbulb (CFL)
bombilla ꜰ de bajo consumo ᴹ

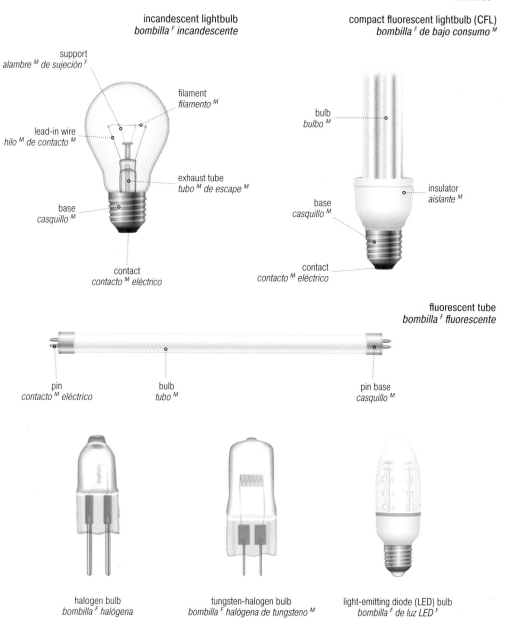

support
alambre ᴹ de sujeción ꜰ

filament
filamento ᴹ

lead-in wire
hilo ᴹ de contacto ᴹ

exhaust tube
tubo ᴹ de escape ᴹ

base
casquillo ᴹ

contact
contacto ᴹ eléctrico

bulb
bulbo ᴹ

insulator
aislante ᴹ

base
casquillo ᴹ

contact
contacto ᴹ eléctrico

fluorescent tube
bombilla ꜰ fluorescente

pin
contacto ᴹ eléctrico

bulb
tubo ᴹ

pin base
casquillo ᴹ

halogen bulb
bombilla ꜰ halógena

tungsten-halogen bulb
bombilla ꜰ halógena de tungsteno ᴹ

light-emitting diode (LED) bulb
bombilla ꜰ de luz LED ꜰ

Light fixtures and lamps
Lámparas ^F *e iluminación* ^F

chandelier
araña ^F

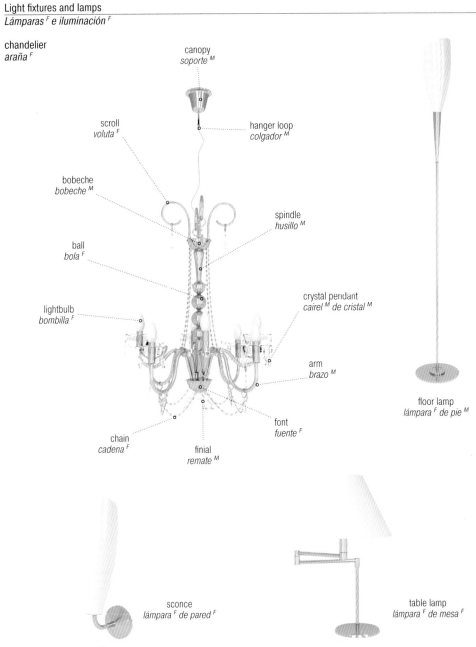

canopy
soporte ^M

scroll
voluta ^F

hanger loop
colgador ^M

bobeche
bobeche ^M

spindle
husillo ^M

ball
bola ^F

crystal pendant
cairel ^M *de cristal* ^M

lightbulb
bombilla ^F

arm
brazo ^M

font
fuente ^F

chain
cadena ^F

finial
remate ^M

floor lamp
lámpara ^F *de pie* ^M

sconce
lámpara ^F *de pared* ^F

table lamp
lámpara ^F *de mesa* ^F

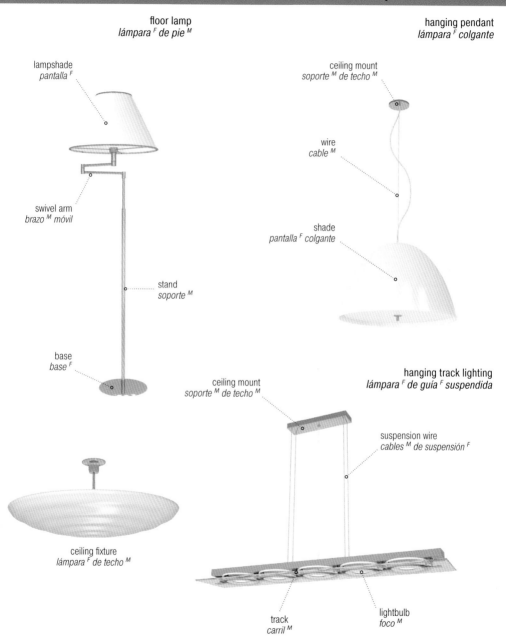

floor lamp
lámpara ᶠ de pie ᴹ

hanging pendant
lámpara ᶠ colgante

lampshade
pantalla ᶠ

ceiling mount
soporte ᴹ de techo ᴹ

wire
cable ᴹ

swivel arm
brazo ᴹ móvil

shade
pantalla ᶠ colgante

stand
soporte ᴹ

base
base ᶠ

hanging track lighting
lámpara ᶠ de guía ᶠ suspendida

ceiling mount
soporte ᴹ de techo ᴹ

suspension wire
cables ᴹ de suspensión ᶠ

ceiling fixture
lámpara ᶠ de techo ᴹ

track
carril ᴹ

lightbulb
foco ᴹ

Electrical fittings
Accesorios ᴹ *eléctricos*

light socket
portalámparas ᴹ

cross section of a plug
sección ꜰ *transversal de un enchufe* ᴹ

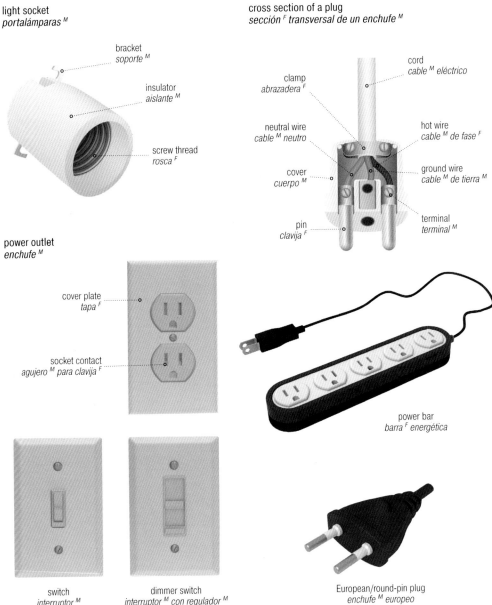

bracket
soporte ᴹ

insulator
aislante ᴹ

screw thread
rosca ꜰ

cord
cable ᴹ *eléctrico*

clamp
abrazadera ꜰ

neutral wire
cable ᴹ *neutro*

hot wire
cable ᴹ *de fase* ꜰ

cover
cuerpo ᴹ

ground wire
cable ᴹ *de tierra* ᴹ

pin
clavija ꜰ

terminal
terminal ᴹ

power outlet
enchufe ᴹ

cover plate
tapa ꜰ

socket contact
agujero ᴹ *para clavija* ꜰ

power bar
barra ꜰ *energética*

switch
interruptor ᴹ

dimmer switch
interruptor ᴹ *con regulador* ᴹ

European/round-pin plug
enchufe ᴹ *europeo*

flat mop
mopa ^F

mop
mopa ^F

handle
palo ^M

broom
escoba ^F

mop head
cabeza ^F *de la mopa* ^F

bucket
cubo ^M

dustpan
recogedor ^M

scrub brush
cepillo ^M *de cerdas* ^F

wastebasket
cesto ^M *de basura* ^F

aquarium
acuario ᴹ

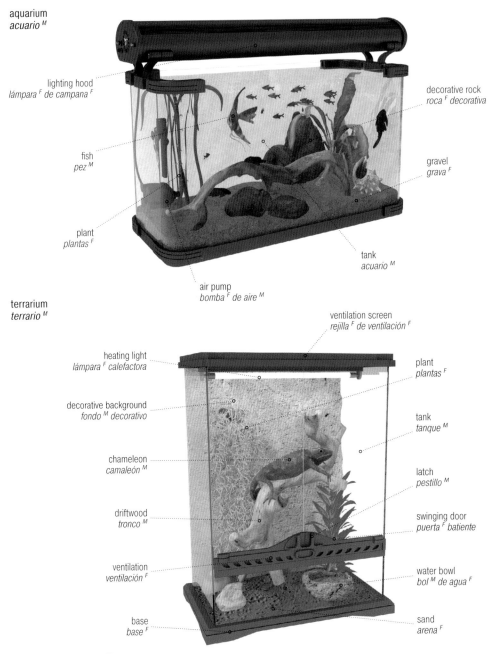

lighting hood
lámpara ᶠ *de campana* ᶠ

decorative rock
roca ᶠ *decorativa*

fish
pez ᴹ

gravel
grava ᶠ

plant
plantas ᶠ

tank
acuario ᴹ

air pump
bomba ᶠ *de aire* ᴹ

terrarium
terrario ᴹ

ventilation screen
rejilla ᶠ *de ventilación* ᶠ

heating light
lámpara ᶠ *calefactora*

plant
plantas ᶠ

decorative background
fondo ᴹ *decorativo*

tank
tanque ᴹ

chameleon
camaleón ᴹ

latch
pestillo ᴹ

driftwood
tronco ᴹ

swinging door
puerta ᶠ *batiente*

ventilation
ventilación ᶠ

water bowl
bol ᴹ *de agua* ᶠ

base
base ᶠ

sand
arena ᶠ

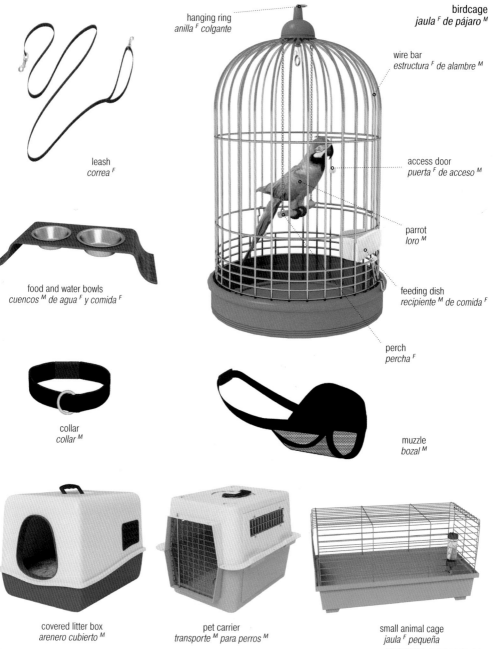

hanging ring
anilla *F* *colgante*

birdcage
jaula *F* *de pájaro* *M*

wire bar
estructura *F* *de alambre* *M*

leash
correa *F*

access door
puerta *F* *de acceso* *M*

parrot
loro *M*

food and water bowls
cuencos *M* *de agua* *F* *y comida* *F*

feeding dish
recipiente *M* *de comida* *F*

perch
percha *F*

collar
collar *M*

muzzle
bozal *M*

covered litter box
arenero cubierto *M*

pet carrier
transporte *M* *para perros* *M*

small animal cage
jaula *F* *pequeña*

Curtain rods
Barras ^F *de cortina* ^F

wooden curtain rod
barra ^F *de cortina* ^F *de madera* ^F

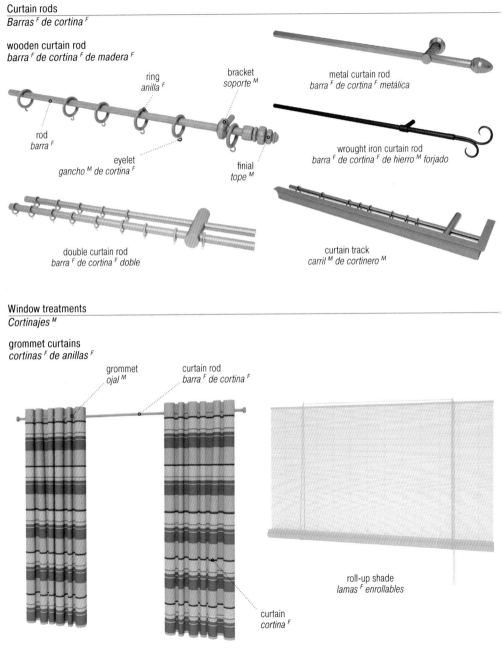

ring
anilla ^F

bracket
soporte ^M

metal curtain rod
barra ^F *de cortina* ^F *metálica*

rod
barra ^F

eyelet
gancho ^M *de cortina* ^F

finial
tope ^M

wrought iron curtain rod
barra ^F *de cortina* ^F *de hierro* ^M *forjado*

double curtain rod
barra ^F *de cortina* ^F *doble*

curtain track
carril ^M *de cortinero* ^M

Window treatments
Cortinajes ^M

grommet curtains
cortinas ^F *de anillas* ^F

grommet
ojal ^M

curtain rod
barra ^F *de cortina* ^F

roll-up shade
lamas ^F *enrollables*

curtain
cortina ^F

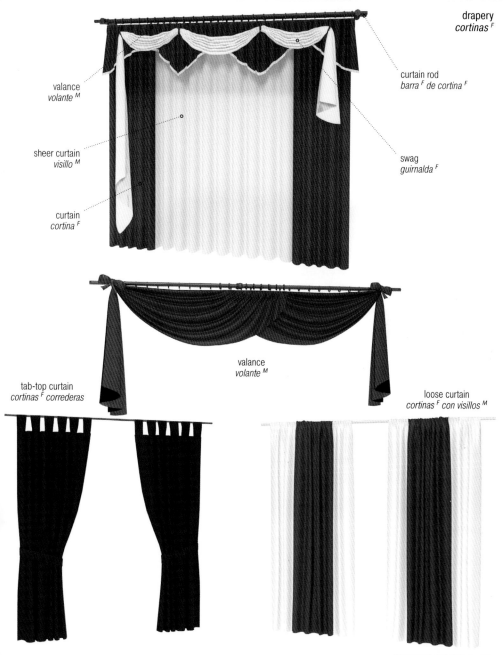

drapery
cortinas^F

valance
volante^M

curtain rod
barra^F de cortina^F

sheer curtain
visillo^M

swag
guirnalda^F

curtain
cortina^F

valance
volante^M

tab-top curtain
cortinas^F correderas

loose curtain
cortinas^F con visillos^M

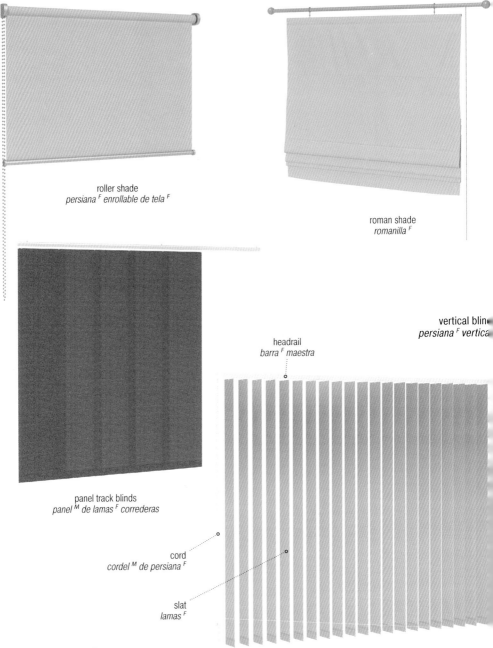

roller shade
persiana F enrollable de tela F

roman shade
romanilla F

vertical blin•
persiana F vertica

headrail
barra F maestra

panel track blinds
panel M de lamas F correderas

cord
cordel M de persiana F

slat
lamas F

kitchen curtains
cortinillas F de cocina F

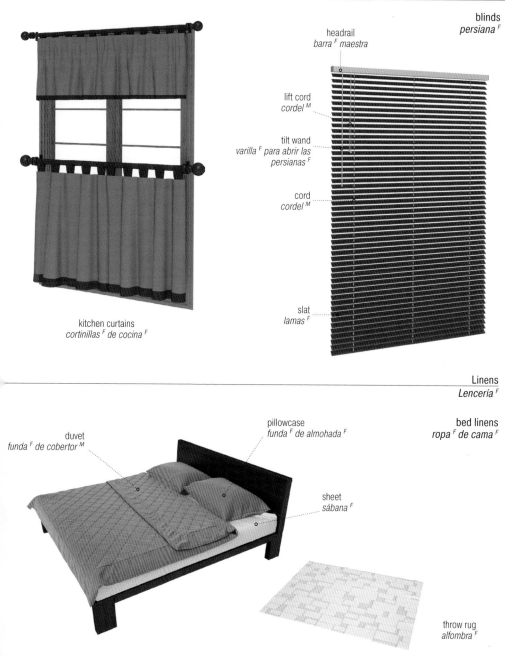

blinds
persiana F

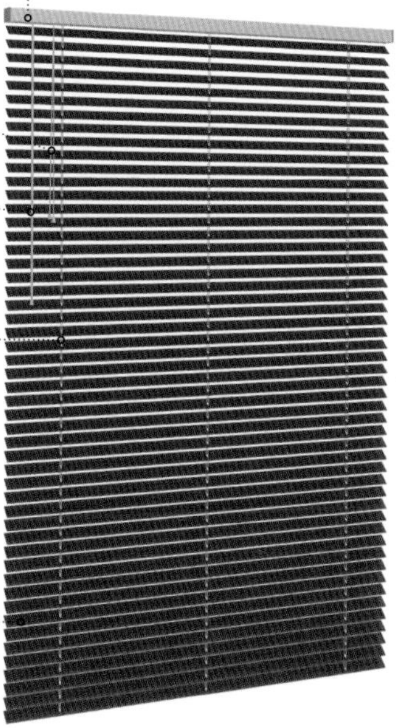
headrail
barra F maestra
lift cord
cordel M
tilt wand
varilla F para abrir las persianas F
cord
cordel M
slat
lamas F

Linens
Lencería F

bed linens
ropa F de cama F

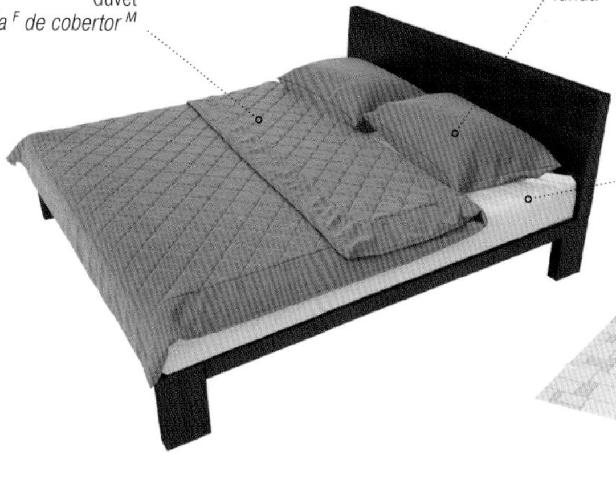
duvet
funda F de cobertor M
pillowcase
funda F de almohada F
sheet
sábana F

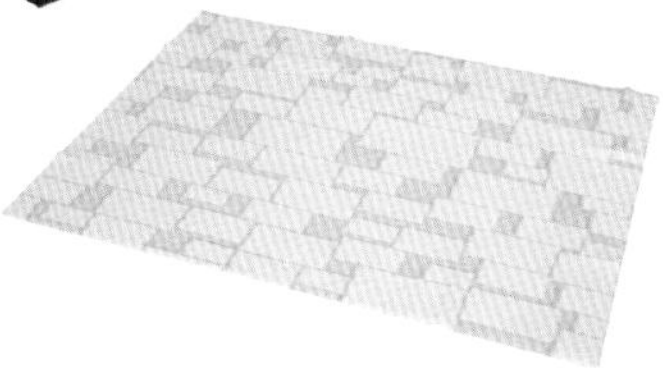

throw rug
alfombra F

brick house
casa F de ladrillo M

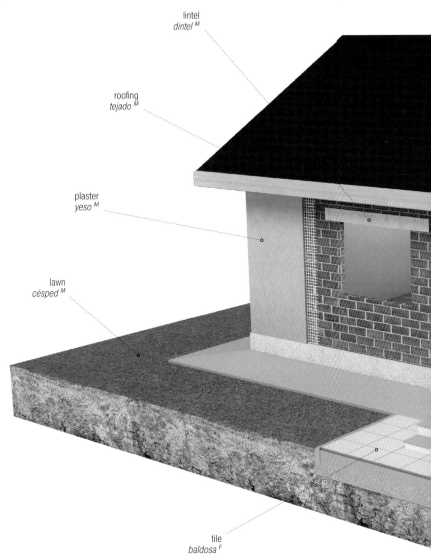

lintel
dintel M

roofing
tejado M

plaster
yeso M

lawn
césped M

tile
baldosa F

roof underlayment
techo M *intermedio*

roof batten
listones M *del techo* M

ridge beam
viga F *cumbrera*

rafter
alfarda F

attic floor
suelo M *del desván* M

ceiling joist
viguetas F *del techo* M

hardwood floor
suelo M *de madera* F

underlay
suelo M *intermedio*

subfloor
suelo M *subyacente*

floor joist
viguetas F *del suelo* M

foundation
base F

footing
cimientos M

front porch
porche M

front step
escalón M

reinforced concrete house
casa F *de hormigón* M *armado*

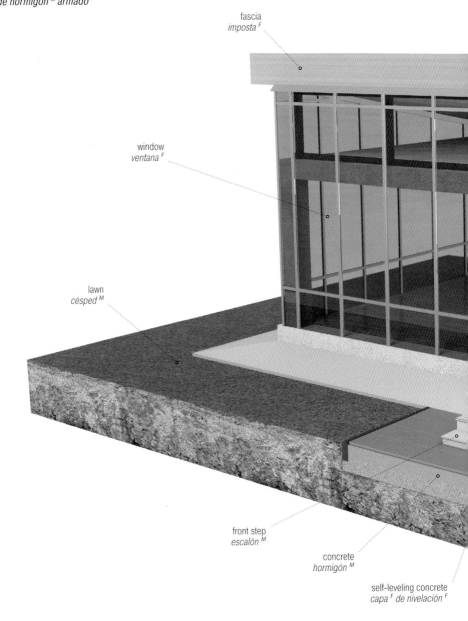

fascia
imposta F

window
ventana F

lawn
césped M

front step
escalón M

concrete
hormigón M

self-leveling concrete
capa F *de nivelación* F

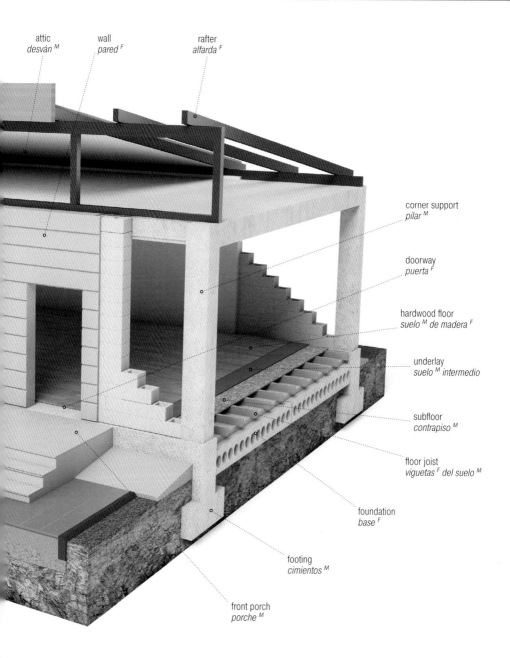

attic
desván M

wall
pared F

rafter
alfarda F

corner support
pilar M

doorway
puerta F

hardwood floor
suelo M *de madera* F

underlay
suelo M *intermedio*

subfloor
contrapiso M

floor joist
viguetas F *del suelo* M

foundation
base F

footing
cimientos M

front porch
porche M

wooden-frame house
casa F de madera F

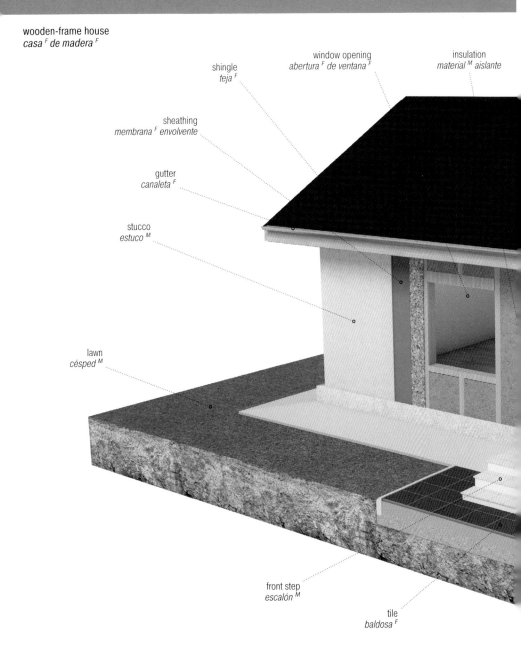

shingle
teja F

window opening
abertura F de ventana F

insulation
material M aislante

sheathing
membrana F envolvente

gutter
canaleta F

stucco
estuco M

lawn
césped M

front step
escalón M

tile
baldosa F

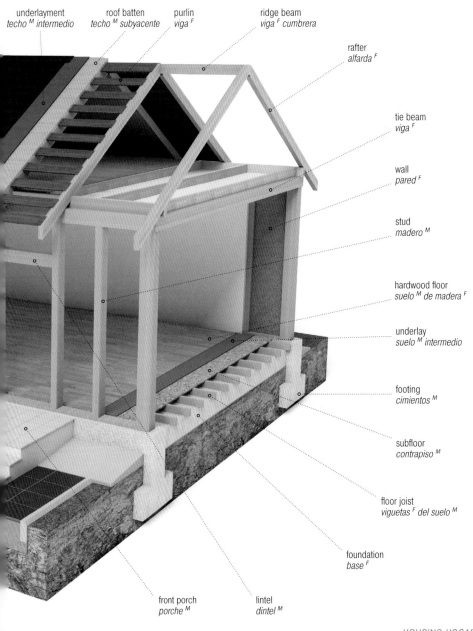

underlayment
techo M *intermedio*

roof batten
techo M *subyacente*

purlin
viga F

ridge beam
viga F *cumbrera*

rafter
alfarda F

tie beam
viga F

wall
pared F

stud
madero M

hardwood floor
suelo M *de madera* F

underlay
suelo M *intermedio*

footing
cimientos M

subfloor
contrapiso M

floor joist
viguetas F *del suelo* M

foundation
base F

front porch
porche M

lintel
dintel M

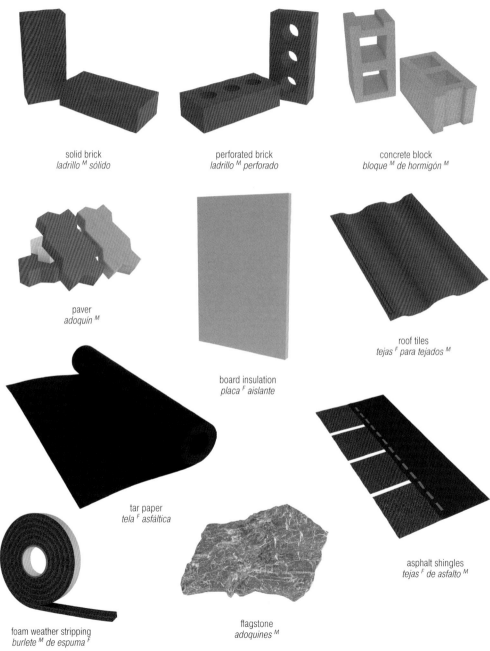

solid brick
ladrillo [M] *sólido*

perforated brick
ladrillo [M] *perforado*

concrete block
bloque [M] *de hormigón* [M]

paver
adoquin [M]

board insulation
placa [F] *aislante*

roof tiles
tejas [F] *para tejados* [M]

tar paper
tela [F] *asfáltica*

asphalt shingles
tejas [F] *de asfalto* [M]

foam weather stripping
burlete [M] *de espuma* [F]

flagstone
adoquines [M]

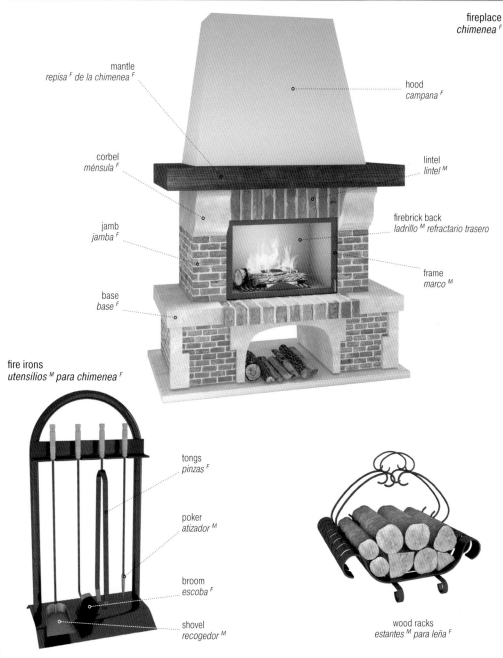

fireplace
chimenea ^F

mantle
repisa ^F *de la chimenea* ^F

hood
campana ^F

corbel
ménsula ^F

lintel
lintel ^M

jamb
jamba ^F

firebrick back
ladrillo ^M *refractario trasero*

frame
marco ^M

base
base ^F

fire irons
utensilios ^M *para chimenea* ^F

tongs
pinzas ^F

poker
atizador ^M

broom
escoba ^F

shovel
recogedor ^M

wood racks
estantes ^M *para leña* ^F

forced-air heating and air-conditioning system
sistema [M] *forzado de calefacción* [F] *y aire* [M] *acondicionado*

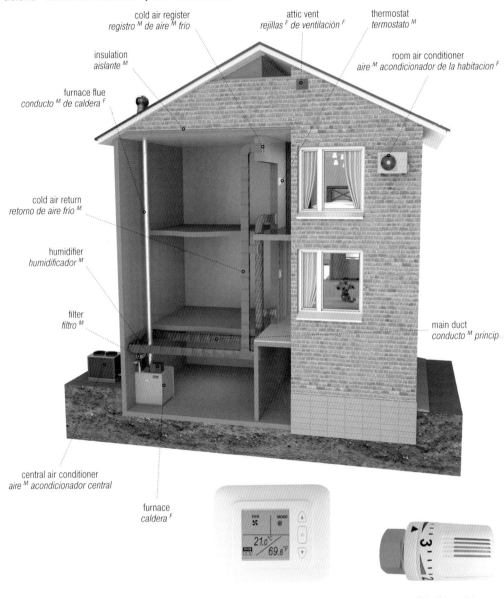

cold air register
registro [M] *de aire* [M] *frío*

attic vent
rejillas [F] *de ventilación* [F]

thermostat
termostato [M]

insulation
aislante [M]

room air conditioner
aire [M] *acondicionador de la habitacion* [F]

furnace flue
conducto [M] *de caldera* [F]

cold air return
retorno de aire frío [M]

humidifier
humidificador [M]

filter
filtro [M]

main duct
conducto [M] *princip*

central air conditioner
aire [M] *acondicionador central*

furnace
caldera [F]

room thermostat
termostato [M] *de habitación* [F]

radiator thermostat
termostato [M] *de radiador* [M]

column radiator
radiador ^M *de columna* ^F

cover grille
rejilla ^F *de cubierta* ^F

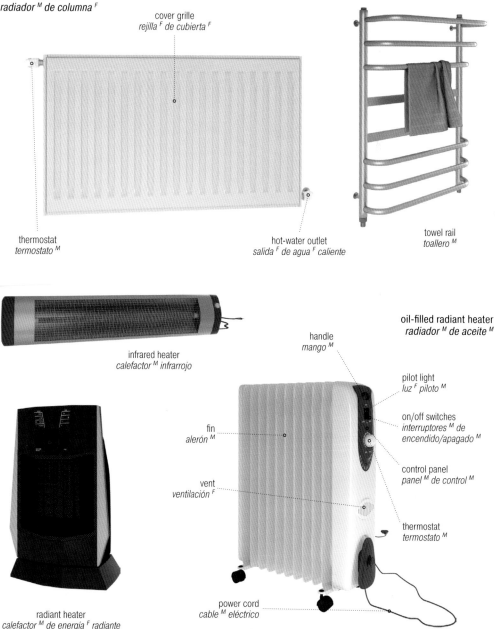

thermostat
termostato ^M

hot-water outlet
salida ^F *de agua* ^F *caliente*

towel rail
toallero ^M

infrared heater
calefactor ^M *infrarrojo*

oil-filled radiant heater
radiador ^M *de aceite* ^M

handle
mango ^M

pilot light
luz ^F *piloto* ^M

on/off switches
interruptores ^M *de encendido/apagado* ^M

fin
alerón ^M

control panel
panel ^M *de control* ^M

vent
ventilación ^F

thermostat
termostato ^M

radiant heater
calefactor ^M *de energía* ^F *radiante*

power cord
cable ^M *eléctrico*

plumbing system
sistema M de fontanería F

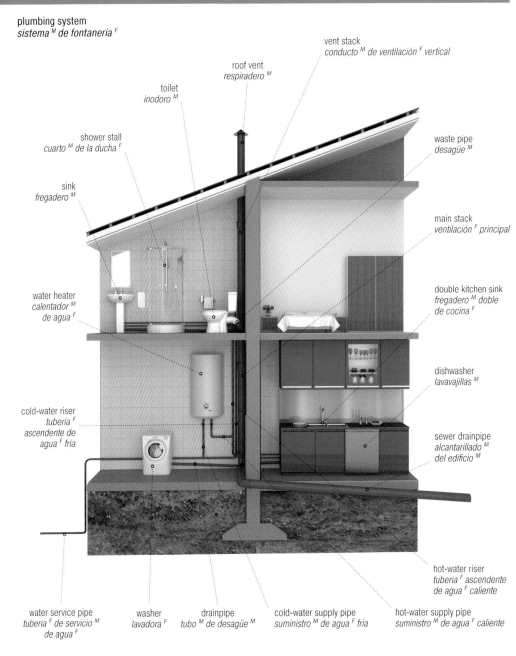

vent stack
conducto M de ventilación F vertical

roof vent
respiradero M

toilet
inodoro M

waste pipe
desagüe M

shower stall
cuarto M de la ducha F

sink
fregadero M

main stack
ventilación F principal

water heater
calentador M
de agua F

double kitchen sink
fregadero M doble
de cocina F

dishwasher
lavavajillas M

cold-water riser
tubería F
ascendente de
agua F fría

sewer drainpipe
alcantarillado M
del edificio M

hot-water riser
tubería F ascendente
de agua F caliente

water service pipe
tubería F de servicio M
de agua F

washer
lavadora F

drainpipe
tubo M de desagüe M

cold-water supply pipe
suministro M de agua F fría

hot-water supply pipe
suministro M de agua F caliente

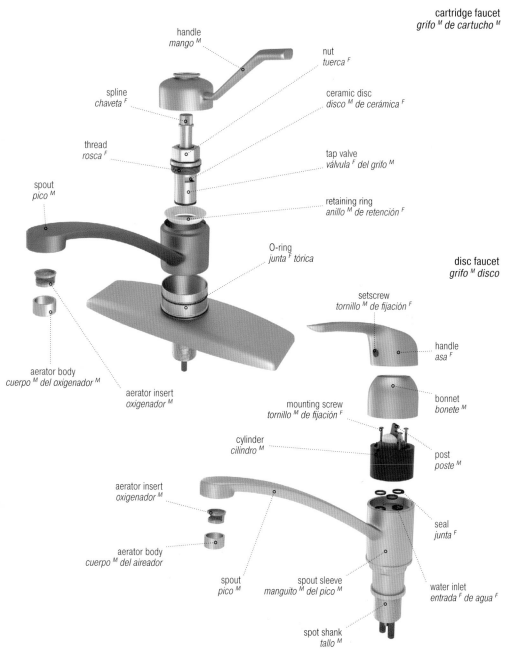

cartridge faucet
grifo M *de cartucho* M

handle
mango M

nut
tuerca F

spline
chaveta F

ceramic disc
disco M *de cerámica* F

thread
rosca F

tap valve
válvula F *del grifo* M

spout
pico M

retaining ring
anillo M *de retención* F

O-ring
junta F *tórica*

disc faucet
grifo M *disco*

setscrew
tornillo M *de fijación* F

handle
asa F

aerator body
cuerpo M *del oxigenador* M

aerator insert
oxigenador M

bonnet
bonete M

mounting screw
tornillo M *de fijación* F

cylinder
cilindro M

post
poste M

aerator insert
oxigenador M

seal
junta F

aerator body
cuerpo M *del aireador* M

spout
pico M

spout sleeve
manguito M *del pico* M

water inlet
entrada F *de agua* F

spot shank
tallo M

toilet
inodoro [M]

seat cover
tapa [F] *del inodoro* [M]

seat
asiento [M]

toilet bowl
taza [F]

tank lid
tapa [F] *de la cisterna* [F]

flush handle
palanca [F] *de la cisterna* [F]

tank
cisterna [F]

waste pipe
bajante [M]

stem faucet
tallo [M] *del grifo* [M]

handle
mango [M]

gland nut
tuerca [F] *del prensaestopas* [F]

packing
prensaestopas [M]

thread
rosca [F]

spindle
husillo [M]

stem washer
arandela [F] *de vástago* [M]

ball valve
válvula [F] *esférica*

handle
palanca [F]

retaining ring
anillo [M] *de retención* [F]

thread
rosca [F]

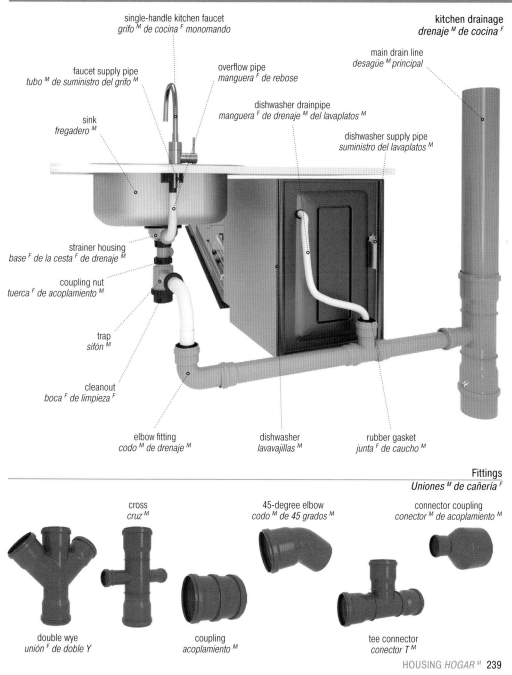

single-handle kitchen faucet
grifo M de cocina F monomando

kitchen drainage
drenaje M de cocina F

faucet supply pipe
tubo M de suministro del grifo M

overflow pipe
manguera F de rebose

main drain line
desagüe M principal

dishwasher drainpipe
manguera F de drenaje M del lavaplatos M

sink
fregadero M

dishwasher supply pipe
suministro del lavaplatos M

strainer housing
base F de la cesta F de drenaje M

coupling nut
tuerca F de acoplamiento M

trap
sifón M

cleanout
boca F de limpieza F

elbow fitting
codo M de drenaje M

dishwasher
lavavajillas M

rubber gasket
junta F de caucho M

Fittings
Uniones M de cañería F

cross
cruz M

45-degree elbow
codo M de 45 grados M

connector coupling
conector M de acoplamiento M

double wye
unión F de doble Y

coupling
acoplamiento M

tee connector
conector T M

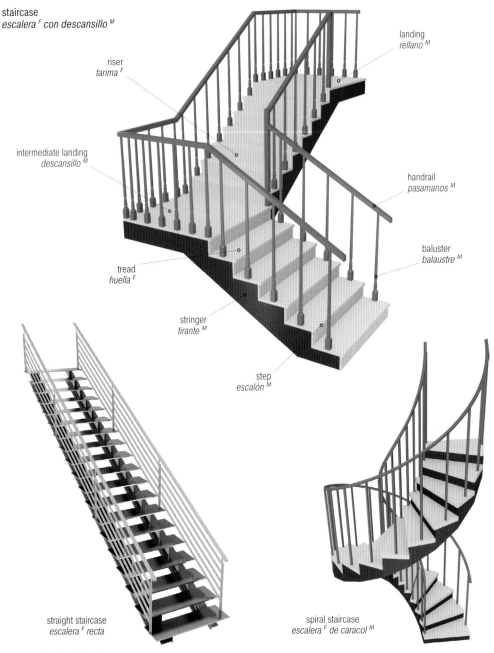

staircase
escalera F *con descansillo* M

landing
rellano M

riser
tarima F

intermediate landing
descansillo M

handrail
pasamanos M

tread
huella F

baluster
balaustre M

stringer
tirante M

step
escalón M

straight staircase
escalera F *recta*

spiral staircase
escalera F *de caracol* M

gabled roof
tejado ᴹ de pendiente ᶠ inclinada

shingles
tejas ᶠ

sheathing
forro ᴹ envolvente

ridge beam
viga ᶠ cumbrera

collar tie
falso tirante ᴹ

rafter
alfarda ᶠ

side post
puntal ᴹ

beam
viga ᶠ

fascia
imposta ᶠ

rafter plate
travesaño ᴹ

low-pitch roof
tejado ᴹ de pendiente ᶠ suave

gambrel roof
mansarda ᶠ

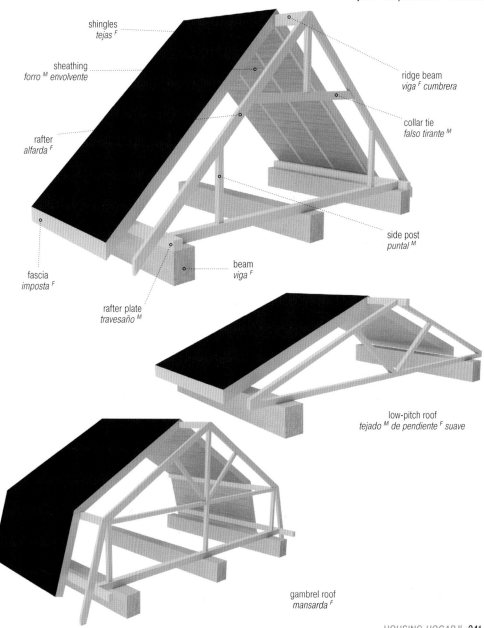

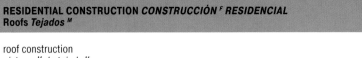

roof construction
sistema M de tejado M

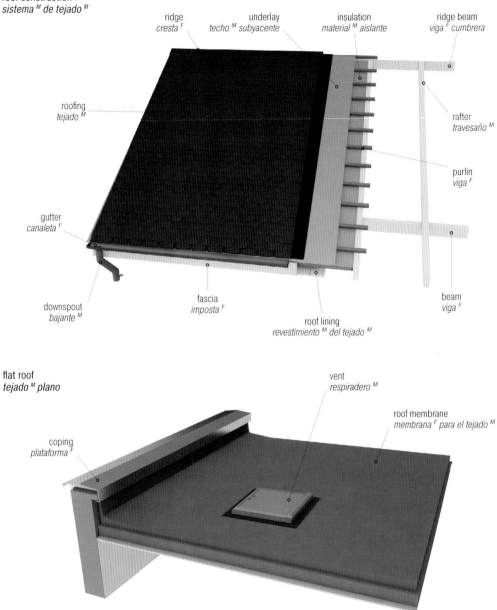

ridge
cresta F

underlay
techo M subyacente

insulation
material M aislante

ridge beam
viga F cumbrera

roofing
tejado M

rafter
travesaño M

purlin
viga F

gutter
canaleta F

downspout
bajante M

fascia
imposta F

beam
viga F

roof lining
revestimiento M del tejado M

flat roof
tejado M plano

vent
respiradero M

roof membrane
membrana F para el tejado M

coping
plataforma F

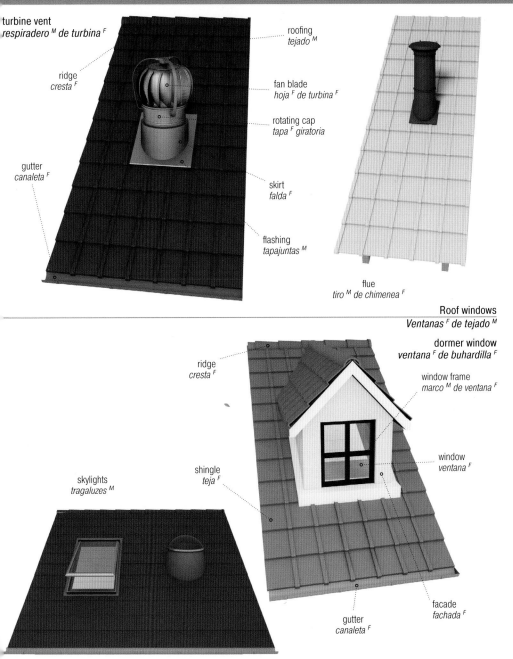

turbine vent
respiradero [M] *de turbina* [F]

ridge
cresta [F]

gutter
canaleta [F]

roofing
tejado [M]

fan blade
hoja [F] *de turbina* [F]

rotating cap
tapa [F] *giratoria*

skirt
falda [F]

flashing
tapajuntas [M]

flue
tiro [M] *de chimenea* [F]

Roof windows
Ventanas [F] *de tejado* [M]

dormer window
ventana [F] *de buhardilla* [F]

ridge
cresta [F]

window frame
marco [M] *de ventana* [F]

skylights
tragaluces [M]

shingle
teja [F]

window
ventana [F]

facade
fachada [F]

gutter
canaleta [F]

swimming pool
pileta ^F / *piscina* ^F

ladder
escalera ^F

deck
cubierta ^F

overflow drain
drenaje ^M

gutter
canaleta ^F

wall
muro ^M

diving board
trampolín ^M

drain
desagüe ^M

pump
bomba ^F

filter
filtro ^M

hatch
trampilla ^F

inflatable toy
juguete ^M *inflable*

swim ring
flotador ^M

sauna
sauna ᶠ

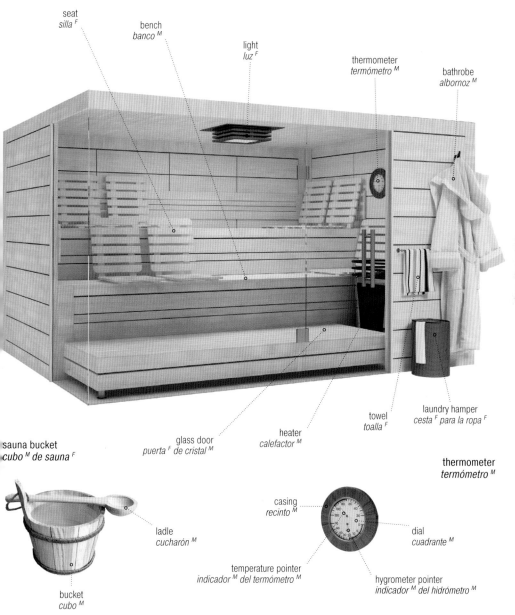

seat
silla ᶠ

bench
banco ᴹ

light
luz ᶠ

thermometer
termómetro ᴹ

bathrobe
albornoz ᴹ

sauna bucket
cubo ᴹ *de sauna* ᶠ

glass door
puerta ᶠ *de cristal* ᴹ

heater
calefactor ᴹ

towel
toalla ᶠ

laundry hamper
cesta ᶠ *para la ropa* ᶠ

thermometer
termómetro ᴹ

ladle
cucharón ᴹ

casing
recinto ᴹ

dial
cuadrante ᴹ

temperature pointer
indicador ᴹ *del termómetro* ᴹ

hygrometer pointer
indicador ᴹ *del hidrómetro* ᴹ

bucket
cubo ᴹ

roof
techo ^M

gazebo
glorieta ^F

table
mesa ^F

deck chair
silla ^F *de terraza* ^F

bench
banco ^M

bistro set
muebles ^M *de exterior* ^M

support beam
puntal ^M

table
mesa ^F *de exterior* ^M

floor
suelo ^M

chair
silla ^F *de exterior* ^M

bench
banco ^M

lounger
tumbona ᶠ

sofa
sofá ᴹ

folding table
mesa ᶠ *plegable*

folding bench
banco ᴹ *plegable*

porch swing
balancín ᴹ

bridge
puente ᴹ

patio umbrella
sombrilla F para terraza F

fountain
fuente F

fence
valla F

patio heater
calefactor M de terraza F

reflector
reflector M

shade
pantalla F

burner
quemador M

sconce
farola F

ventilation hole
abertura F de ventilación F

propane tank housing
*compartimiento M del
tanque M de gas M*

base
base F

decorative light
lámpara F decorativa

lamppost
poste M de luz F

stake light
lámpara F de suelo M

barbecue
barbacoa ^F */ parrilla* ^F

lid
tapa ^F

control pad
panel ^M *de control* ^M

grill rack
rejilla ^F *de parrilla* ^F

meat
carne ^F

gas cylinder
tanque ^M *de gas* ^M

wheel
rueda ^F

storage rack
estante ^M *de almacenamiento* ^M

hibachi
barbacoa ^F *de picnic* ^M

outdoor fireplace
parrilla ^F *para exteriores* ^M

grill
parrilla ^F

lid
tapa ^F

electric grill
parrilla ^F *eléctrica*

bowl
depósito ^M *de carbón* ^M

barbecue utensils
utensilios ᴹ de barbacoa ꟳ

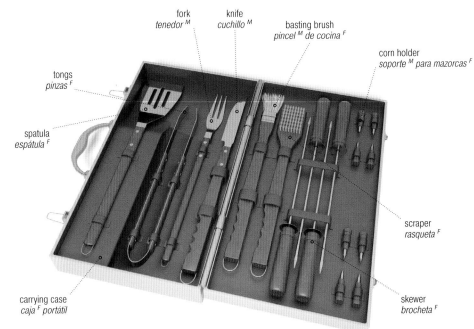

fork
tenedor ᴹ

knife
cuchillo ᴹ

basting brush
pincel ᴹ de cocina ꟳ

corn holder
soporte ᴹ para mazorcas ꟳ

tongs
pinzas ꟳ

spatula
espátula ꟳ

scraper
rasqueta ꟳ

carrying case
caja ꟳ portátil

skewer
brocheta ꟳ

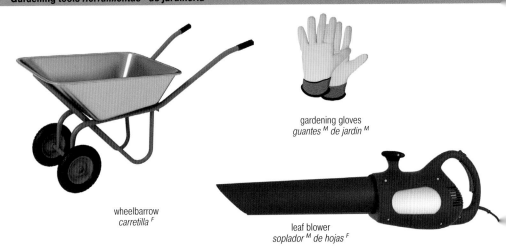

gardening gloves
guantes ᴹ de jardín ᴹ

wheelbarrow
carretilla ꟳ

leaf blower
soplador ᴹ de hojas ꟳ

snow scoop
quitanieves [M]

plastic snow shovel
pala [F] *de nieve* [F] *de plástico* [M]

metal snow shovel
pala [F] *de nieve* [F] *metálica*

leaf rake
rastrillo [M] *de jardín* [M]

level rake
rastrillo [M]

garden fork
horca [F] *de jardín* [M]

hoe
azada [F]

weeder
palita [F] *de jardín* [M]

hand rake
cultivador [M] *de mano* [F]

hand cultivator
cultivador [M] *de mano* [F]

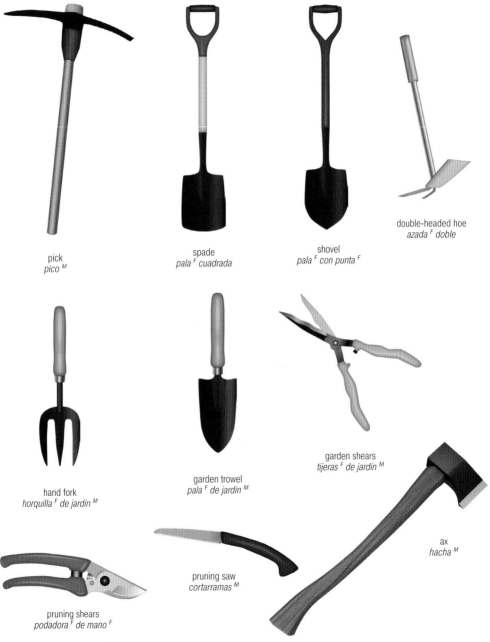

pick
pico M

spade
pala F *cuadrada*

shovel
pala F *con punta* F

double-headed hoe
azada F *doble*

hand fork
horquilla F *de jardín* M

garden trowel
pala F *de jardín* M

garden shears
tijeras F *de jardín* M

pruning shears
podadora F *de mano* F

pruning saw
cortarramas M

ax
hacha M

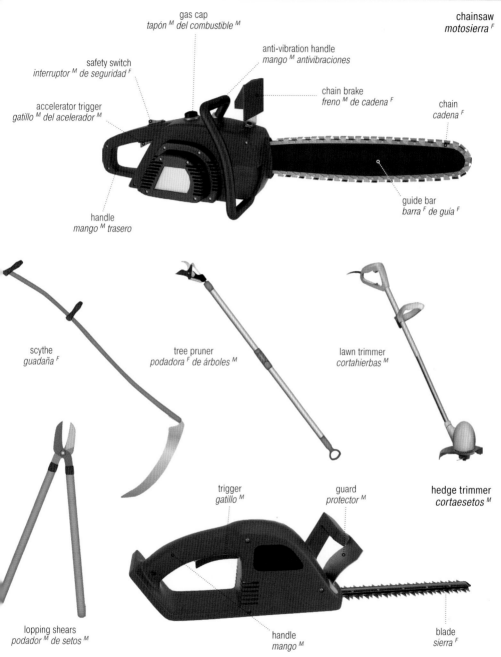

gas cap
tapón ^M *del combustible* ^M

chainsaw
motosierra ^F

anti-vibration handle
mango ^M *antivibraciones*

safety switch
interruptor ^M *de seguridad* ^F

chain brake
freno ^M *de cadena* ^F

chain
cadena ^F

accelerator trigger
gatillo ^M *del acelerador* ^M

guide bar
barra ^F *de guía* ^F

handle
mango ^M *trasero*

scythe
guadaña ^F

tree pruner
podadora ^F *de árboles* ^M

lawn trimmer
cortahierbas ^M

trigger
gatillo ^M

guard
protector ^M

hedge trimmer
cortaesetos ^M

lopping shears
podador ^M *de setos* ^M

handle
mango ^M

blade
sierra ^F

lawn mower
cortacésped [M]

handle
mango [M]

control lever
palanca [F] *de control* [M] *del acelerador* [M]

safety handle
barra [F] *de control* [M]

gas tank
depósito [M] *de combustible* [M]

string trimmer
cortabordes [M]

grass catcher
depósito [M] *de césped* [M]

air filter
filtro [M] *de aire* [M]

wheel
rueda [F]

impulse sprinkler
aspersor [M] *de impacto* [M]

oscillating sprinkler
aspersor [M] *oscilante*

watering wand
aspersor [M]

pistol nozzle
boquilla [F] *de pistola* [F]

watering can
regadera [F]

garden hose
manguera [F] *de jardín* [M]

hose reel
carrete portamangueras [M]

flaring tool
expansor [M] *de tubos* [M]

wing nut
tuerca [F] *de mariposa* [F]

clamp
abrazadera [F]

tube slot
ranura [F] *circular*

mount
montura [F]

pipe wrench
llave [F] *inglesa*

pipe cutter
tijera [F] *cortatubos*

plumber's snake
sistema [M] *de limpieza* [F] *de alcantarillas* [F]

plunger
desatascador [M]

tongue-and-groove pliers
alicate [M] *de unión* [F] *deslizante*

pipe threader
machuelo [M]

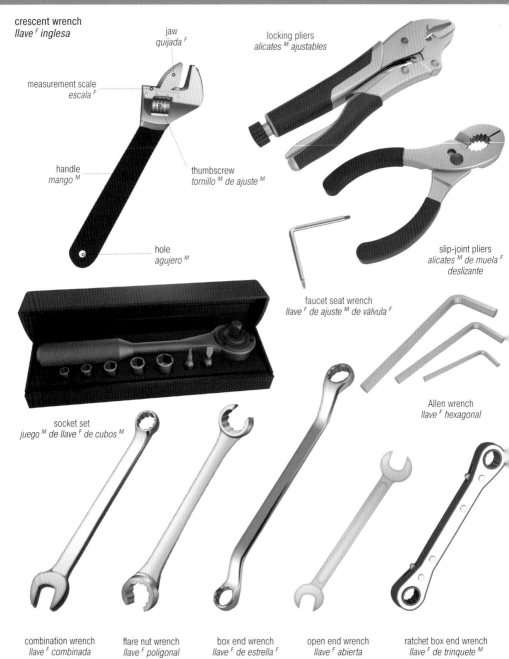

crescent wrench
llave ^F *inglesa*

jaw
quijada ^F

locking pliers
alicates ^M *ajustables*

measurement scale
escala ^F

handle
mango ^M

thumbscrew
tornillo ^M *de ajuste* ^M

hole
agujero ^M

slip-joint pliers
alicates ^M *de muela* ^F
deslizante

faucet seat wrench
llave ^F *de ajuste* ^M *de válvula* ^F

Allen wrench
llave ^F *hexagonal*

socket set
juego ^M *de llave* ^F *de cubos* ^M

combination wrench
llave ^F *combinada*

flare nut wrench
llave ^F *poligonal*

box end wrench
llave ^F *de estrella* ^F

open end wrench
llave ^F *abierta*

ratchet box end wrench
llave ^F *de trinquete* ^M

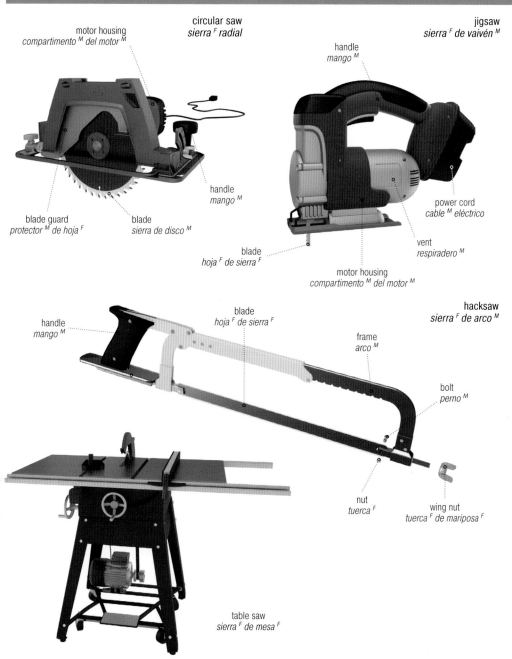

circular saw
sierra F *radial*

motor housing
compartimento M *del motor* M

jigsaw
sierra F *de vaivén* M

handle
mango M

handle
mango M

blade guard
protector M *de hoja* F

blade
sierra de disco M

power cord
cable M *eléctrico*

blade
hoja F *de sierra* F

vent
respiradero M

motor housing
compartimento M *del motor* M

blade
hoja F *de sierra* F

hacksaw
sierra F *de arco* M

handle
mango M

frame
arco M

bolt
perno M

nut
tuerca F

wing nut
tuerca F *de mariposa* F

table saw
sierra F *de mesa* F

hand saw
sierra F *de mano* F

backsaw
serrucho M *de costilla* F

compass saw
sierra F *de calar*

Sanding and polishing tools *Herramientas* F *para lijar y pulir*

orbital sander
lijadora F *orbital*

power cord
cable M *eléctrico*

motor housing
compartimento M *del motor* M

electric grinder
esmerilador M *eléctrico*

dust collection bag
bolsa F *colectora de polvo* M

belt sander
lijadora F *de correa* F

motor housing
compartimento M *del motor* M

fastening
cierre M

sanding pad
almohadilla F *lijadora*

power cord
cable M *eléctrico*

sanding belt
cinta F *lijadora*

dust collection bag
bolsa F *colectora de polvo* M

pulley
polea F

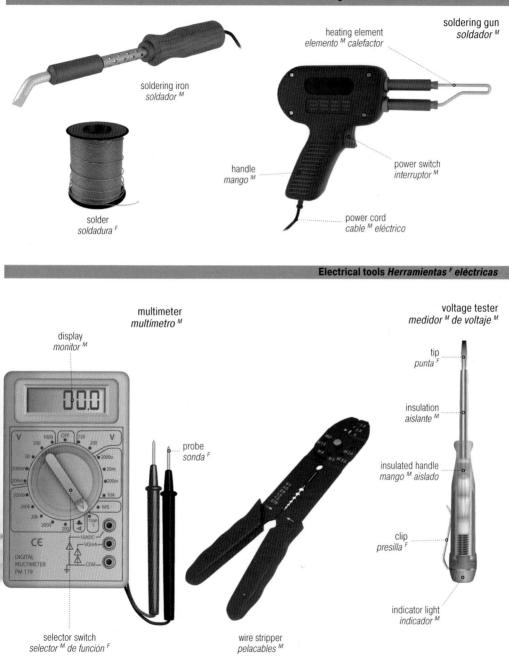

heating element
elemento M *calefactor*

soldering gun
soldador M

soldering iron
soldador M

handle
mango M

power switch
interruptor M

solder
soldadura F

power cord
cable M *eléctrico*

Electrical tools *Herramientas* F *eléctricas*

multimeter
multímetro M

voltage tester
medidor M *de voltaje* M

display
monitor M

tip
punta F

insulation
aislante M

probe
sonda F

insulated handle
mango M *aislado*

clip
presilla F

DIGITAL
MULTIMETER
PM 119

CE

indicator light
indicador M

selector switch
selector M *de función* F

wire stripper
pelacables M

electric drill
taladro ^M *eléctrico*

speed selector switch
selector ^M *de velocidad* ^F *de giro* ^M

chuck
portabrocas ^M

bit
broca ^F

motor housing
compartimento ^M
del motor ^M

trigger switch
interruptor ^M

reversing switch
selector ^M *de dirección* ^F *de giro* ^M

handle
mango ^M

battery
batería ^F

auger bit
barrena ^F

spade bit
broca ^F *fresadora*

battery
batería ^F

drill press
mandrinadora ^F

hammer drill
taladro ^M *de impacto* ^M

feed lever
palanca ^F *de descenso*

twist drill bit
broca ^F

tip
filo ^M

protective screen
pantalla ^F *protectora*

motor housing
compartimento ^M *del motor* ^M

drill bit
broca ^F

land
rosca ^F

column
soporte ^M

table
mesa ^F

flute
muesca ^F

masonry drill bit
broca ^F *de mampostería* ^F

base
base ^F

claw hammer
martillo ᴹ *sacaclavos*

claw
oreja ᶠ *de martillo* ᴹ

face
cabeza ᶠ

shaft
vara ᶠ

handle
mango ᴹ

crowbar
pata ᶠ *de cabra* ᶠ

masonry hammer
martillo ᴹ *de albañilería* ᶠ

mallet
mazo ᴹ

nail gun
pistola ᶠ *de clavos* ᴹ

nail set
punzón ᴹ

electric stapler
grapadora ᶠ *eléctrica*

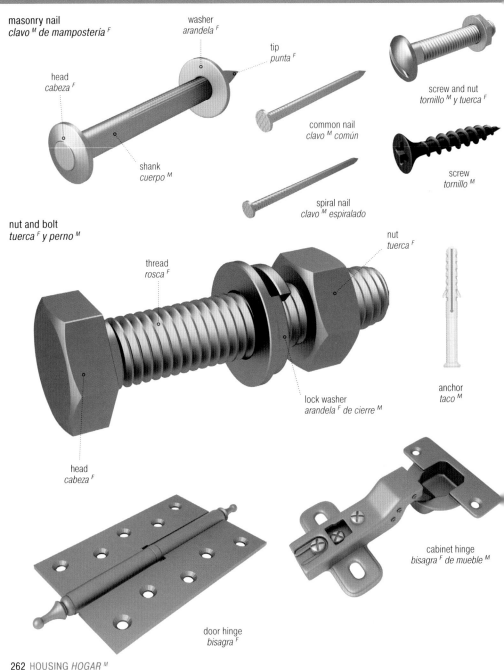

masonry nail
clavo ᴹ *de mampostería* ᶠ

washer
arandela ᶠ

tip
punta ᶠ

head
cabeza ᶠ

shank
cuerpo ᴹ

common nail
clavo ᴹ *común*

spiral nail
clavo ᴹ *espiralado*

screw and nut
tornillo ᴹ *y tuerca* ᶠ

screw
tornillo ᴹ

nut and bolt
tuerca ᶠ *y perno* ᴹ

thread
rosca ᶠ

nut
tuerca ᶠ

head
cabeza ᶠ

lock washer
arandela ᶠ *de cierre* ᴹ

anchor
taco ᴹ

cabinet hinge
bisagra ᶠ *de mueble* ᴹ

door hinge
bisagra ᶠ

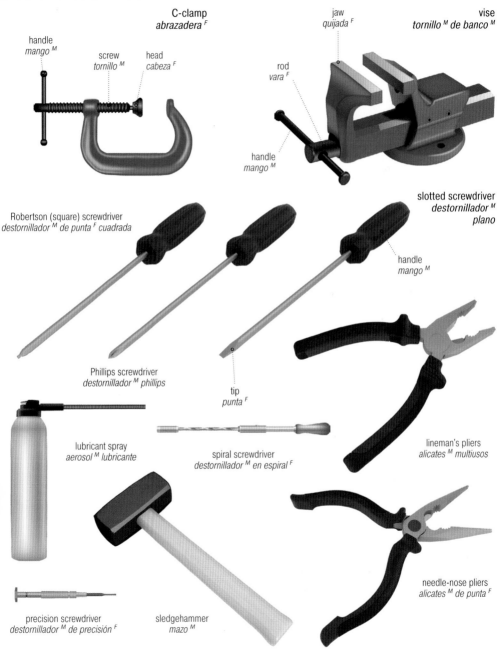

C-clamp
abrazadera [F]

handle
mango [M]

screw
tornillo [M]

head
cabeza [F]

jaw
quijada [F]

vise
tornillo [M] *de banco* [M]

rod
vara [F]

handle
mango [M]

slotted screwdriver
destornillador [M]
plano

Robertson (square) screwdriver
destornillador [M] *de punta* [F] *cuadrada*

handle
mango [M]

Phillips screwdriver
destornillador [M] *phillips*

tip
punta [F]

lubricant spray
aerosol [M] *lubricante*

spiral screwdriver
destornillador [M] *en espiral* [F]

lineman's pliers
alicates [M] *multiusos*

precision screwdriver
destornillador [M] *de precisión* [F]

sledgehammer
mazo [M]

needle-nose pliers
alicates [M] *de punta* [F]

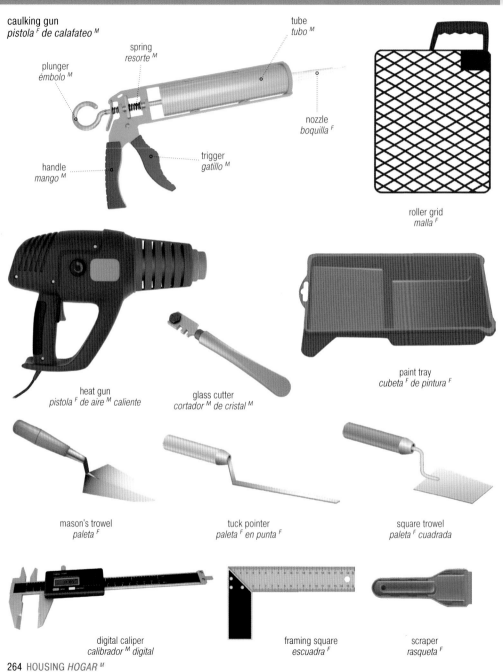

caulking gun
pistola F *de calafateo* M

spring
resorte M

plunger
émbolo M

tube
tubo M

nozzle
boquilla F

handle
mango M

trigger
gatillo M

roller grid
malla F

heat gun
pistola F *de aire* M *caliente*

glass cutter
cortador M *de cristal* M

paint tray
cubeta F *de pintura* F

mason's trowel
paleta F

tuck pointer
paleta F *en punta* F

square trowel
paleta F *cuadrada*

digital caliper
calibrador M *digital*

framing square
escuadra F

scraper
rasqueta F

cement mixer
hormigonera [F]

platform stepladder
escalera [F] *de plataforma* [F]

shelf
soporte [M]

leg
pata [F]

leg tip
almohadilla [F]

extension ladder
escalera [F] *extensible*

step
escalón [M]

tape measure
cinta [F] *métrica*

spirit level
nivel [M]

paint sprayer
pistola [F] *de pintura* [F]

paint reservoir
depósito [M] *de pintura* [F]

bricklayer's hammer
martillo [M] *de mampostería* [F]

paintbrush
brocha [F]

handle
mango [M]

paint roller
rodillo [M] *de pintor* [M]

trigger
gatillo [M]

fluid adjustment screw
tornillo [M] *de ajuste* [M]

roller
rodillo [M]

nozzle
boquilla [F]

handle
mango [M]

FOOD

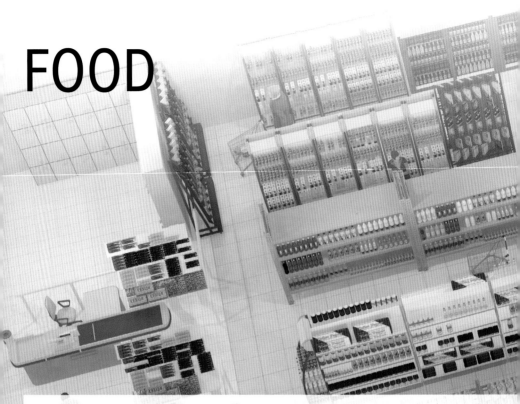

ALIMENTOS

bacon
tocino ^M

bologna
salchicha ^F *boloñesa*

cooked sausage
salchicha ^F *ahumada cocida*

foie gras
foie gras ^M

breakfast sausage
salchicha ^F *fresca*

sausage meat
salchicha ^F *ahumada fresca*

kielbasa sausage
salchicha ^F *polaca*

prosciutto
jamón ^M *prosciutto* ^M

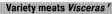

bratwurst sausage
embutido ^M *crudo*

salami
embutido ^M *seco*

pâté
paté ^M

weiner
salchicha ^F *vienesa*

Variety meats *Vísceras* ^F

beef liver
hígado ^M *de res* ^F

chicken liver
hígado ^M *de pollo* ^M

heart
corazón ^M

kidney
riñón ^M

tongue
lengua ^F

chicken
pollo ᴹ

duck
pato ᴹ

goose
ganso ᴹ

chicken wing
alitas ꟳ de pollo ᴹ

chicken breast
pechuga ꟳ de pollo ᴹ

chicken egg
huevos ᴹ de gallina ꟳ

chicken leg
muslos ᴹ de pollo ᴹ

Game *Animales ᴹ de caza ꟳ*

quail
codorniz ꟳ

quail egg
huevo ᴹ de codorniz ꟳ

pheasant
faisán ᴹ

guinea fowl
pintada ꟳ

rabbit
conejo ᴹ

partridge
perdiz ꟳ

Lamb
Cordero ᴹ

cuts of lamb
cortes ᴹ *de cordero* ᴹ

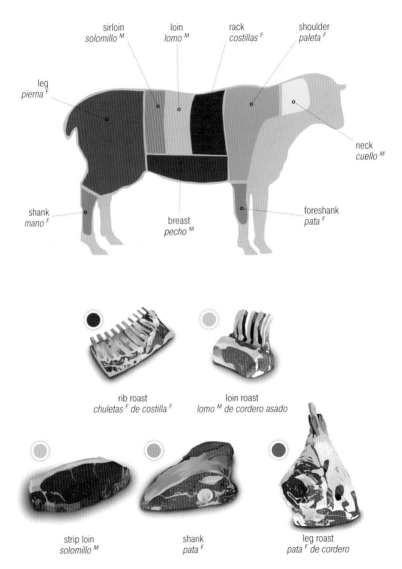

sirloin
solomillo ᴹ

loin
lomo ᴹ

rack
costillas ᶠ

shoulder
paleta ᶠ

leg
pierna ᶠ

neck
cuello ᴹ

shank
mano ᶠ

breast
pecho ᴹ

foreshank
pata ᶠ

rib roast
chuletas ᶠ *de costilla* ᶠ

loin roast
lomo ᴹ *de cordero asado*

strip loin
solomillo ᴹ

shank
pata ᶠ

leg roast
pata ᶠ *de cordero*

Pork
Cerdo ^M

cuts of pork
cortes ^M *de cerdo* ^M

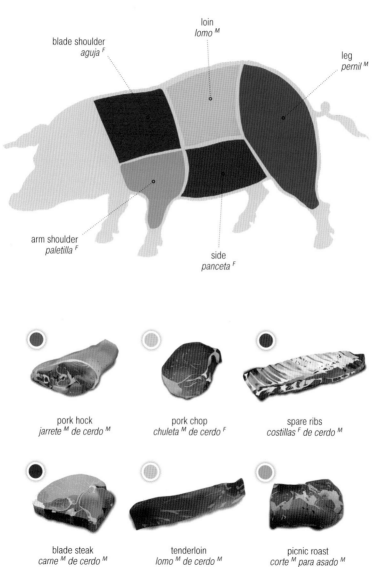

loin
lomo ^M

blade shoulder
aguja ^F

leg
pernil ^M

arm shoulder
paletilla ^F

side
panceta ^F

pork hock
jarrete ^M *de cerdo* ^M

pork chop
chuleta ^M *de cerdo* ^F

spare ribs
costillas ^F *de cerdo* ^M

blade steak
carne ^M *de cerdo* ^M

tenderloin
lomo ^M *de cerdo* ^M

picnic roast
corte ^M *para asado* ^M

Beef
Carne F *de res* F

cuts of beef
cortes M *de carne* F *de res* F

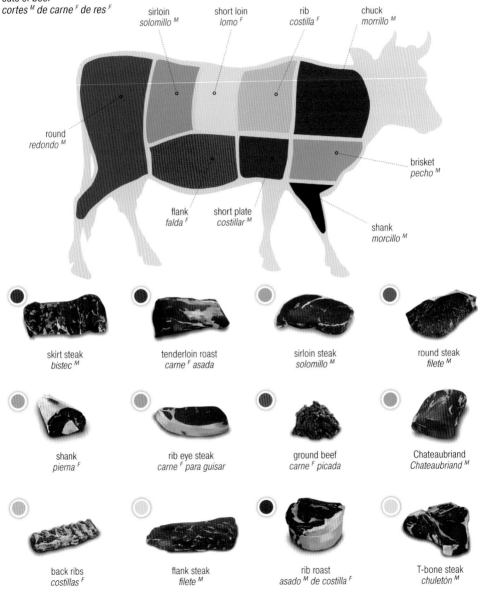

sirloin
solomillo M

short loin
lomo F

rib
costilla F

chuck
morrillo M

round
redondo M

brisket
pecho M

flank
falda F

short plate
costillar M

shank
morcillo M

skirt steak
bistec M

tenderloin roast
carne F *asada*

sirloin steak
solomillo M

round steak
filete M

shank
pierna F

rib eye steak
carne F *para guisar*

ground beef
carne F *picada*

Chateaubriand
Chateaubriand M

back ribs
costillas F

flank steak
filete M

rib roast
asado M *de costilla* F

T-bone steak
chuletón M

Veal
Ternera ^F

cuts of veal
cortes ^M *de ternera* ^F

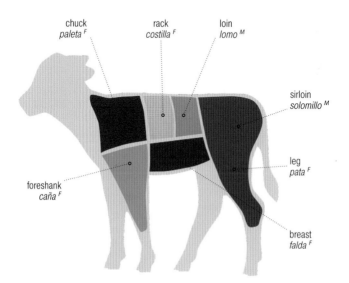

chuck
paleta ^F

rack
costilla ^F

loin
lomo ^M

sirloin
solomillo ^M

leg
pata ^F

breast
falda ^F

foreshank
caña ^F

blade roast
asado ^M *de paleta* ^F

breast
falda ^F *de ternera* ^F

rib chop
chuleta ^F *de ternera* ^F

shank
jarrete ^M *de ternera* ^F

cutlet
filete ^M *de ternera* ^F

Milk and cream
Leche ^F *y nata* ^F

kefir
kéfir ^M

cow's milk
leche ^F *de vaca* ^F

goat's milk
leche ^F *de cabra* ^F

lactose-free milk
leche ^F *sin lactosa* ^F

evaporated milk
leche ^F *evaporada*

sour cream
crema ^F *agria*

whipped cream
crema ^F *batida*

yogurt
yogur ^M

cream cheese
queso ^M *crema* ^F

butter
mantequilla ^F

buttermilk
suero ^M *de leche* ^F

Cheeses
Quesos ^M

mozzarella
mozzarella ^F

cottage cheese
requesón ^M

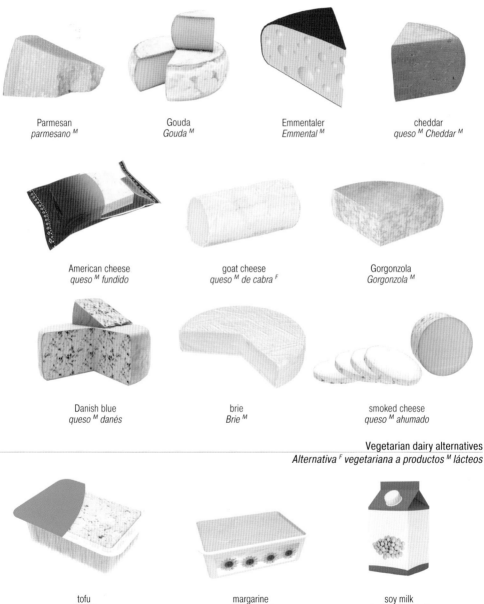

Parmesan
parmesano ᴹ

Gouda
Gouda ᴹ

Emmentaler
Emmental ᴹ

cheddar
queso ᴹ *Cheddar* ᴹ

American cheese
queso ᴹ *fundido*

goat cheese
queso ᴹ *de cabra* ᶠ

Gorgonzola
Gorgonzola ᴹ

Danish blue
queso ᴹ *danés*

brie
Brie ᴹ

smoked cheese
queso ᴹ *ahumado*

Vegetarian dairy alternatives
Alternativa ᶠ *vegetariana a productos* ᴹ *lácteos*

tofu
tofu ᴹ

margarine
margarina ᶠ

soy milk
leche ᶠ *de soja* ᶠ

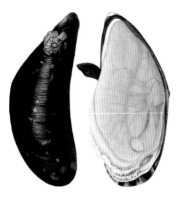

mussel
mejillón ^M

salmon roe
huevas ^F *de salmón* ^M

caviar
caviar ^M

clam
almeja ^F

scallop
vieira ^F

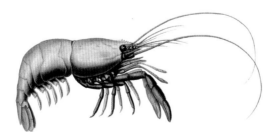

shrimp
camarón ^M

snail
caracol ^M

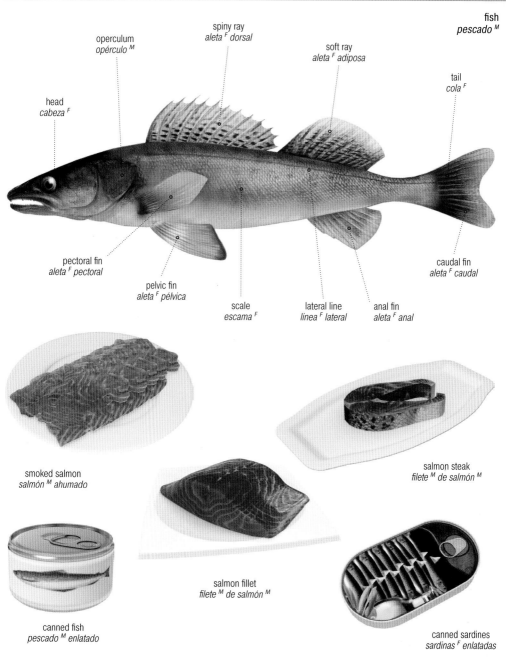

fish
pescado ᴹ

spiny ray
aleta ᶠ *dorsal*

operculum
opérculo ᴹ

soft ray
aleta ᶠ *adiposa*

tail
cola ᶠ

head
cabeza ᶠ

pectoral fin
aleta ᶠ *pectoral*

pelvic fin
aleta ᶠ *pélvica*

scale
escama ᶠ

lateral line
línea ᶠ *lateral*

anal fin
aleta ᶠ *anal*

caudal fin
aleta ᶠ *caudal*

smoked salmon
salmón ᴹ *ahumado*

salmon steak
filete ᴹ *de salmón* ᴹ

salmon fillet
filete ᴹ *de salmón* ᴹ

canned fish
pescado ᴹ *enlatado*

canned sardines
sardinas ᶠ *enlatadas*

Leaf vegetables
Verduras ᶠ *de hoja* ᶠ

red cabbage
col ᶠ *lombarda*

Brussels sprout
coles ᶠ *de Bruselas*

white cabbage
repollo ᴹ

Belgian endive
escarola ᶠ

corn salad
canónigo ᴹ

curly kale
col ᶠ *rizada*

garden sorrel
acedera ᶠ

Boston lettuce
lechuga ᶠ *francesa*

iceberg lettuce
lechuga ᶠ *iceberg*

Chinese cabbage
col ᶠ *china*

radicchio
achicoria ᶠ *roja*

arugula
rúcula ᶠ

romaine lettuce
lechuga ᶠ *romana*

green cabbage
col ᶠ *Savoy*

spinach
espinaca ᶠ

bok choy
bok choy ᴹ

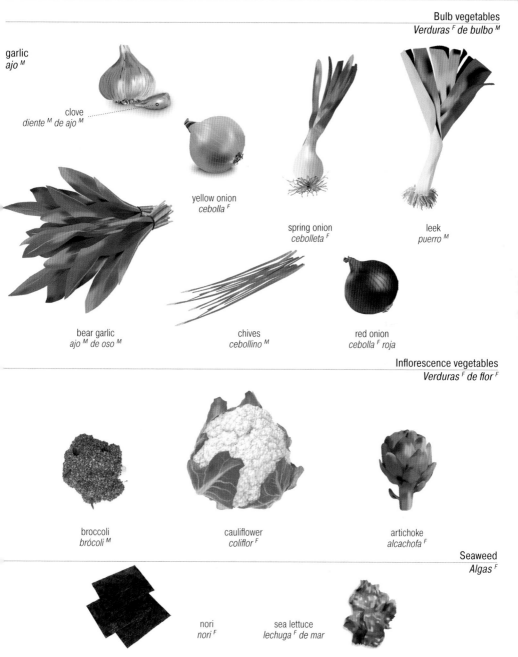

Bulb vegetables
Verduras **ᶠ** *de bulbo* **ᴹ**

garlic
ajo **ᴹ**

clove
diente **ᴹ** *de ajo* **ᴹ**

yellow onion
cebolla **ᶠ**

spring onion
cebolleta **ᶠ**

leek
puerro **ᴹ**

bear garlic
ajo **ᴹ** *de oso* **ᴹ**

chives
cebollino **ᴹ**

red onion
cebolla **ᶠ** *roja*

Inflorescence vegetables
Verduras **ᶠ** *de flor* **ᶠ**

broccoli
brócoli **ᴹ**

cauliflower
coliflor **ᶠ**

artichoke
alcachofa **ᶠ**

Seaweed
Algas **ᶠ**

nori
nori **ᶠ**

sea lettuce
lechuga **ᶠ** *de mar*

Fruit vegetables
Hortalizas ^F *de fruto* ^M

olives
aceitunas ^F

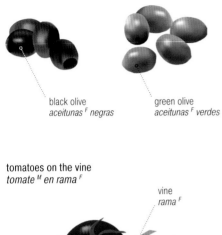

black olive
aceitunas ^F *negras*

green olive
aceitunas ^F *verdes*

avocado
aguacate ^M / *palta* ^F

tomatoes on the vine
tomate ^M *en rama* ^F

vine
rama ^F

zucchini
calabacín ^M

pattypan squash
calabaza ^F *pattypan*

okra
quimbombó ^M

green chili pepper
chile ^M *verde largo*

tomato
tomate ^M

red chili pepper
chiles ^M

buttercup squash
calabaza ^F *buttercup*

pumpkin
calabaza ^F

yellow pepper
pimiento ^M *amarillo*

sweet pepper
pimiento ^M

acorn squash
calabacín ^M

red pepper
pimiento ^M *rojo*

green pepper
pimiento ^M *verde*

eggplant
berenjena ^F

cucumber
pepino ^M

Root vegetables
Verduras ᶠ *de raíz* ᶠ

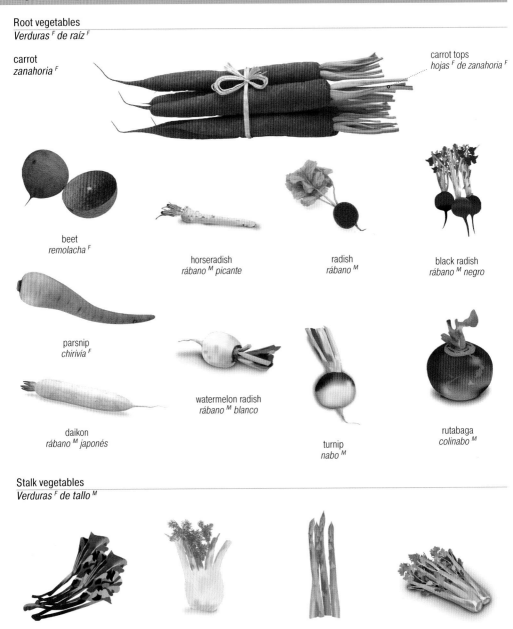

carrot
zanahoria ᶠ

carrot tops
hojas ᶠ *de zanahoria* ᶠ

beet
remolacha ᶠ

horseradish
rábano ᴹ *picante*

radish
rábano ᴹ

black radish
rábano ᴹ *negro*

parsnip
chirivía ᶠ

daikon
rábano ᴹ *japonés*

watermelon radish
rábano ᴹ *blanco*

turnip
nabo ᴹ

rutabaga
colinabo ᴹ

Stalk vegetables
Verduras ᶠ *de tallo* ᴹ

rhubarb
ruibarbo ᴹ

fennel
hinojo ᴹ

asparagus
espárrago ᴹ

celery
apio ᴹ

Tuber vegetables
Tubérculos ^M

Jerusalem artichoke
alcachofa ^F *de Jerusalén*

kohlrabi
colirrábano ^M

potato
patata ^F

sweet potato
boniato ^M

Legumes
Leguminosas ^F

white kidney bean
judía ^F

black-eyed pea
frijol ^M *de ojo* ^M *negro*

chickpea
garbanzos ^M

lentil
lentejas ^F

adzuki bean
frijol ^M *rojo*

red kidney bean
alubias ^F *rojas*

pinto bean
frijol ^M *pintado*

peanut
cacahuete ^M/*maní* ^M

mung bean
frijol ^M *chino*

green bean
judías ^F *verdes*

pea
guisantes ^M

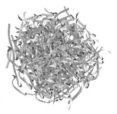

bean sprouts
brotes ^M/*germinados* ^M

porcini mushroom
hongo ᴹ porcini

stem
tallo ᴹ

cap
sombrero ᴹ

oyster mushroom
champiñón ᴹ ostra

enoki mushroom
Enokitake ᴹ

cremini
champiñón ᴹ marrón

button mushroom
champiñón ᴹ común

chanterelle
rebozuelo ᴹ

honey mushroom
hongo ᴹ de miel

morel
colmenilla ᶠ

wood ear
oreja ᶠ de Judas

truffle
trufa ᶠ

russula
rúsula ᶠ

saffron milk cap
níscalo ᴹ

shiitake
shiitake ᴹ

slippery jack
boleto ᴹ anillado

bay bolete
boleto ^M *bayo*

red aspen bolete
boleto ^M *anaranjado*

birch bolete
boleto ^M *birch*

suede bolete
boleto ^M *gamuza*

Nuts Nueces ^F

walnut
nuez ^F

shell
cáscara ^F *de nuez* ^F

coconut
coco ^M

almond
almendra ^F

hazelnut
avellana ^F

pine nut
piñón ^M

Brazil nut
nuez ^F *de Brasil*

cashew
merey ^M */ nuez* ^F *de cajú*

macadamia nut
nuez ^F *de macadamia*

chestnut
castaña ^F

pistachio
pistacho ^M

pecan
nuez ^F *pacana*

black mustard
grano M *de mostaza* F *negra*

black pepper
pimienta F *negra*

caraway
comino M

cardamom
cardamomo M

white pepper
pimienta F *blanca*

cinnamon
canela F

bird's eye chili pepper
pimiento M *rojo*

dried chili
pimiento M *seco*

ginger
jengibre M

ground pepper
pimienta F *molida*

jalapeño
jalapeño M

juniper berry
bayas F *de enebro* M

nutmeg
nuez F *moscada*

paprika
pimentón M

pink peppercorn
pimienta F *rosa*

poppy seed
semillas F *de amapola* F

clove
clavo M *de olor*

saffron
azafrán M

white mustard
grano M *de mostaza* F *blan*

cayenne pepper
pimienta F *de Cayena*

table salt
sal F *de mesa* F

turmeric
cúrcuma F

sea salt
sal F *de mar*

curry powder
polvo M *de curry*

anise
anís ^M

basil
albahaca ^F

bay leaf
hojas ^F *de laurel* ^M

caper
alcaparra ^F

cilantro
cilantro ^M

dill
eneldo ^M

rosemary
romero ^M

fennel
hinojo ^M

garden cress
mastuerzo ^M

parsley
perejil ^M

lemongrass
citronela ^F

mint
menta ^F

mugwort
artemisa ^F

sage
salvia ^F

thyme
tomillo ^M

tarragon
estragón ^M

oregano
orégano ^M

purple basil
albahaca ^F *morada*

lemon balm
melisa ^F

Tea and coffee *Té* ^M *y café* ^M

black tea
té ^M *negro*

herbal tea
té ^M *de hierbas* ^F

green coffee bean
granos ^M *de café* ^M *verde*

ground coffee
café ^M *molido*

instant coffee
café ^M *instantáneo*

oolong tea
té ^M *oolong*

white tea

green tea
té ^M *verde*

white tea
té ^M *blanco*

roasted coffee bean
granos ^M *de café* ^M *tostado*

wheat
trigo ᴹ

rye
centeno ᴹ

corn
maíz ᴹ

rice
arroz ᴹ

buckwheat
alforfón ᴹ

quinoa
quinua ᶠ

millet
mijo ᴹ

oats
avena ᶠ

spelt
escanda ᶠ

barley
cebada ᶠ

wild rice
arroz ᴹ *salvaje*

Flour
Harina ᶠ

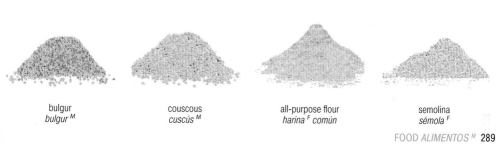

bulgur
bulgur ᴹ

couscous
cuscús ᴹ

all-purpose flour
harina ᶠ *común*

semolina
sémola ᶠ

Tropical fruits
Frutas ᶠ *tropicales*

banana
banana ᶠ

flesh
pulpa ᶠ

papaya
papaya ᶠ

flesh
pulpa ᶠ

skin
piel ᶠ

seeds
semillas ᶠ

lychee
lichi ᴹ

carambola
fruta ᶠ *de estrella*

cherimoya
chirimoya ᶠ

durian
durián ᴹ

fig
higo ᴹ

guava
guayaba ᶠ

Asian pear
pera ᶠ *oriental*

horned melon
melón ᴹ *africano*

pomegranate
granada ^F

membrane
mesocarpio ^M

skin
piel ^F

aril
semilla ^F

pineapple
piña ^F

feijoa
feijoa ^F

kiwifruit
kiwi ^M

mango
mango ^M

mangosteen
mangostán ^M

dragon fruit
fruta ^F *del dragón* ^M

persimmon
caqui ^M

passion fruit
maracuyá ^M */ parchita* ^F

rambutan
rambután ^M

tamarillo
tamarillo ^M

Citrus fruits
Cítricos ^M

clementine
clementina ^F

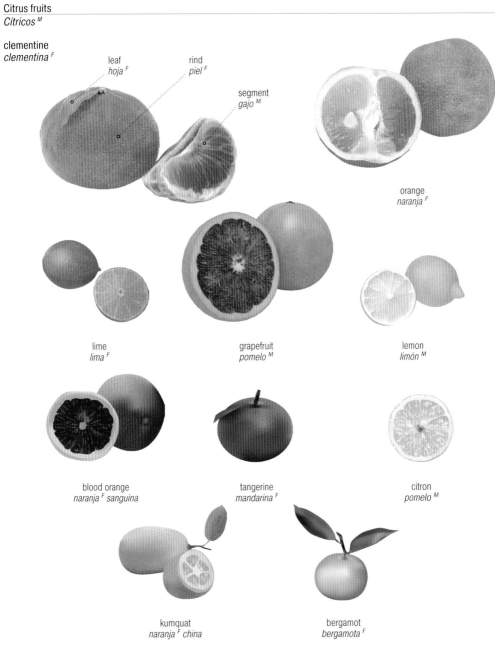

leaf
hoja ^F

rind
piel ^F

segment
gajo ^M

orange
naranja ^F

lime
lima ^F

grapefruit
pomelo ^M

lemon
limón ^M

blood orange
naranja ^F *sanguina*

tangerine
mandarina ^F

citron
pomelo ^M

kumquat
naranja ^F *china*

bergamot
bergamota ^F

Berries
Bayas ^F

cranberry
arándano ^M *agrio*

red grape
uva ^F *negra*

white grape
uva ^F *blanca*

red currant
grosella ^F *roja*

cloudberry
mora ^F *de los pantanos* ^M

raspberry
frambuesa ^F

strawberry
fresa ^F

blackberry
mora ^F

gooseberry
grosella ^F

black currant
grosella ^F *negra*

blueberry
arándano ^M *azul*

cape gooseberry
uchuva ^F

elderberry
saúco ^M

lingonberry
arándano ^M *rojo*

Melons
Melones ᴹ

cantaloupe
melón ᴹ

watermelon
sandía ᶠ

yellow watermelon
sandía ᶠ *amarilla*

honeydew melon
melón ᴹ *de almizcle* ᴹ

canary melon
melón ᴹ *dulce*

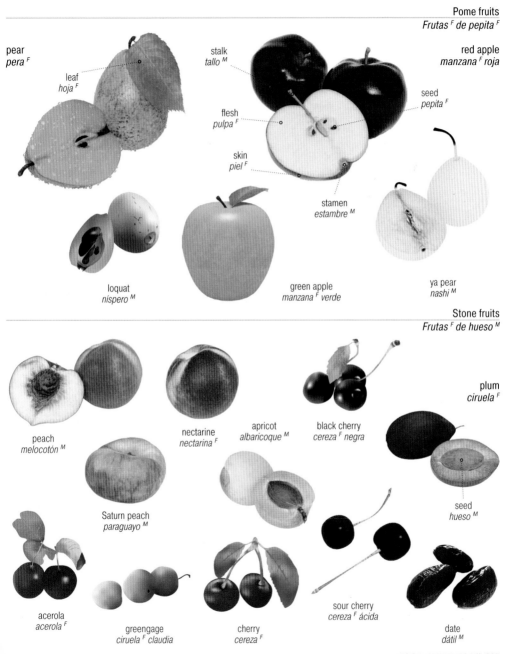

Pome fruits
Frutas F *de pepita* F

pear
pera F

leaf
hoja F

stalk
tallo M

flesh
pulpa F

skin
piel F

stamen
estambre M

red apple
manzana F *roja*

seed
pepita F

loquat
níspero M

green apple
manzana F *verde*

ya pear
nashi M

Stone fruits
Frutas F *de hueso* M

peach
melocotón M

nectarine
nectarina F

apricot
albaricoque M

black cherry
cereza F *negra*

plum
ciruela F

Saturn peach
paraguayo M

seed
hueso M

acerola
acerola F

greengage
ciruela F *claudia*

cherry
cereza F

sour cherry
cereza F *ácida*

date
dátil M

aioli
alioli ᴹ

barbecue sauce
salsa ᶠ *barbacoa*

salsa
salsa ᶠ

mustard
mostaza ᶠ

Italian dressing
aderezo ᴹ *italiano*

ketchup
salsa ᶠ *de tomate* ᴹ */ cátsup* ᴹ

mayonnaise
mayonesa ᶠ

French dressing
aderezo ᴹ *francés*

harissa
harissa ᶠ

pesto
pesto ᴹ

rémoulade
remoulade ᶠ

sambal oelek
sambal ᴹ

tomato paste
concentrado ᴹ *de tomate* ᴹ

tamarind paste
pasta ᶠ *de tamarindo* ᴹ

wasabi
wasabi ᴹ

tomato puree
puré ᴹ *de tomate* ᴹ

balsamic vinegar
vinagre ᴹ *balsámico*

cider vinegar
vinagre ᴹ *de manzana* ᶠ

chili oil
salsa ᶠ *picante*

white wine vinegar
vinagre ᴹ *de vino blanco* ᴹ

soy sauce
salsa ᶠ *de soja* ᶠ

white vinegar
vinagre ᴹ *destilado*

Oils *Aceites* ᴹ

sunflower oil
aceite ᴹ *de girasol* ᴹ

walnut oil
aceite ᴹ *de nuez* ᶠ

soybean oil
aceite ᴹ *de soja* ᶠ

sesame oil
aceite ᴹ *de ajonjoli* ᴹ

corn oil
aceite ᴹ *de maíz* ᴹ

olive oil
aceite ᴹ *de oliva* ᶠ

peanut oil
aceite ᴹ *de cacahuete* ᴹ

pumpkin seed oil
aceite ᴹ *de semillas* ᶠ *de calabaza* ᶠ

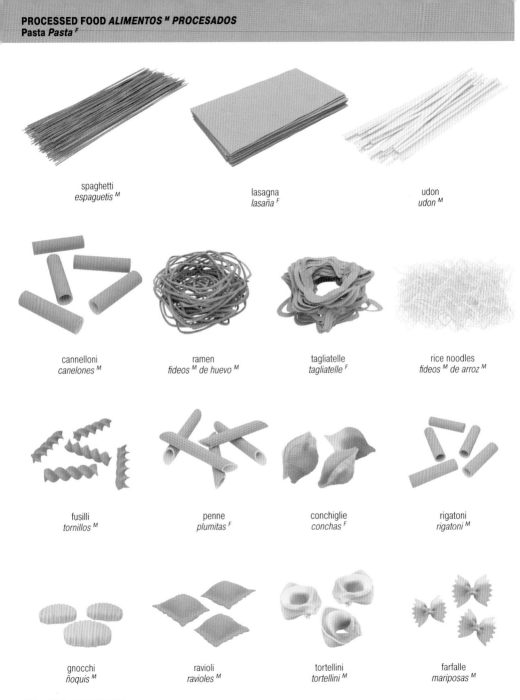

spaghetti
espaguetis *M*

lasagna
lasaña *F*

udon
udon *M*

cannelloni
canelones *M*

ramen
fideos *M* *de huevo* *M*

tagliatelle
tagliatelle *F*

rice noodles
fideos *M* *de arroz* *M*

fusilli
tornillos *M*

penne
plumitas *F*

conchiglie
conchas *F*

rigatoni
rigatoni *M*

gnocchi
ñoquis *M*

ravioli
ravioles *M*

tortellini
tortellini *M*

farfalle
mariposas *M*

baguette
baguette ᶠ

crust
corteza ᶠ

multi-grain bread
pan ᴹ *multi grano* ᴹ

slice
rebanada ᶠ

sunflower seed
semillas ᶠ *de girasol* ᴹ

crumb
miga ᶠ

white bread
pan ᴹ *blanco*

toast
tostada ᶠ

challah
jalá ᴹ

bagel
bagel ᴹ

pretzel
pretzel ᴹ

stuffed pastry
pastelito ᴹ *relleno*

whole wheat roll
panecillo ᴹ *integral*

coarse rye bread
pan ᴹ *de centeno* ᴹ

sourdough bread
pan ᴹ *de centeno* ᴹ *grueso*

jelly doughnut
dónut ^M *de mermelada* ^F

powdered sugar
azúcar ^M *glas*

doughnut
dónut ^M

sugar cookie
galleta ^F

chocolate cookie
galleta ^F *de chocolate* ^M

kifli
kifli ^M

Spritzkuchen
Spritzkuchen ^M

butter cookie
galleta ^F *de mantequilla* ^F

layer cake
pastel ^M *de varias capas* ^F

jelly roll
brazo ^M *de gitano*

bread roll
panecillo ^M

oatmeal cookie
galleta ^F *de avena* ^F

vatrushka
vatrushka ^F

croissant
cruasán ^M

waffle
gofre ^M

rusk
bizcocho ^M

cheesecake
tarta ᶠ de queso ᴹ

fruit sauce
cobertura ᶠ de mermelada ᶠ

Bundt cake
pastel ᴹ para café ᴹ

cupcake
magdalena ᶠ

fruit tartlet
tartaleta ᶠ de frutas ᶠ

cherry tart
tartaleta ᶠ de cerezas ᶠ

blueberry pie
tarta ᶠ de arándanos ᴹ

banana bread
pan ᴹ de plátano ᴹ

cake
pastel ᴹ

chocolate torte
pastel ᴹ de chocolate ᴹ

ice cream cone
barquilla ^F *de helado* ^M

sundae
copa ^M *de helado* ^M

wafer
barquillo ^M

chocolate sauce
chocolate ^M *fundido*

ice cream
helado ^M

crushed nut
trocito ^M *de nueces* ^F

cone
barquilla ^F

scoop of ice cream
bola ^F *de helado* ^M

dessert
postre ^M

fruit coulis
coulis ^M *de frutas* ^F

panna cotta
panna ^F *cotta*

sundae glass
copa ^F *de helado* ^M

jam
mermelada ^F

jar
bote ^M

lid
tapa ^F

whipped cream
crema ^F *batida*

honey
miel ^F

jar
tarro ^M

rubber seal
sello ^M *de goma* ^M

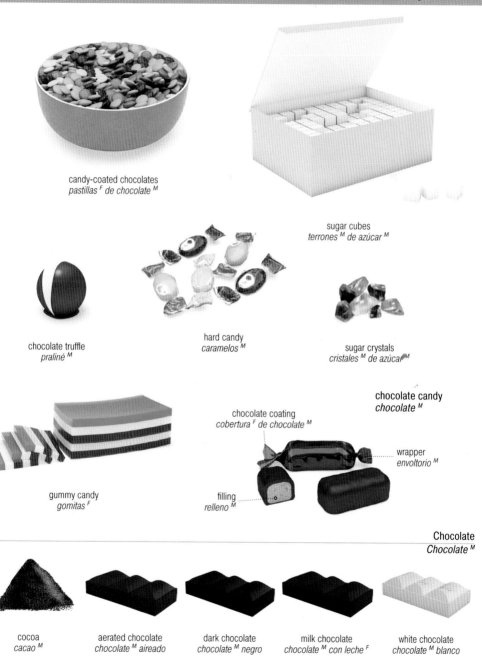

candy-coated chocolates
pastillas ᶠ *de chocolate* ᴹ

sugar cubes
terrones ᴹ *de azúcar* ᴹ

chocolate truffle
praliné ᴹ

hard candy
caramelos ᴹ

sugar crystals
cristales ᴹ *de azúcar* ᴹ

chocolate candy
chocolate ᴹ

chocolate coating
cobertura ᶠ *de chocolate* ᴹ

wrapper
envoltorio ᴹ

gummy candy
gomitas ᶠ

filling
relleno ᴹ

Chocolate
Chocolate ᴹ

cocoa
cacao ᴹ

aerated chocolate
chocolate ᴹ *aireado*

dark chocolate
chocolate ᴹ *negro*

milk chocolate
chocolate ᴹ *con leche* ᶠ

white chocolate
chocolate ᴹ *blanco*

hot dog
perro M caliente

mustard
mostaza F

hot dog bun
bollito M

weiner
salchicha F

Greek salad
ensalada F griega

chips
patatas F chips

french fries
papas F fritas

pizza
pizza F

toppings
ingredientes M extra

crust
borde M

pizza peel
paleta F para pizza F

cola
refresco M

slice of pizza
porción M de pizza M

chips and dip
nachos ^M

salsa
salsa ^F

sandwich
bocadillo ^M / *sándwich* ^M

wrap
burrito ^M

coffee
café ^M

hamburger
hamburguesa ^F

popcorn
palomitas ^F *de maíz* ^M

doner kebab / shawarma / gyro
shawarma ^M

breakfast cereal
cereal M *de desayuno* M

milk
leche F

rolled oats
copos M *de avena* F

blueberry
arándanos M

soft-boiled egg
huevo M *pasado por agua* F

cream of vegetable soup
crema F *de verduras* F

fried egg
huevo M *frito*

appetizer
aperitivo M

olive oil
aceite M *de oliva* F

bread
pan M

dipping bowl
tazón M *de salsa* F

green olive
aceitunas F *verdes*

black olive
aceitunas F *negras*

serving board
tabla F *para cortar*

roast turkey
pavo^M *asado*

breast
pechuga^F

leg
muslo^M

stuffing
relleno^M

tomato soup
sopa^F *de tomate*^M

wing
alita^F

spaghetti and sauce
pasta^F *con salsa*^F

hors d'oeuvre
canapé^M

spaghetti
espaguetis^M

skewer
pincho^M

bocconcini
mozzarella^F

grated cheese
queso^M *rallado*

tomato sauce
salsa^F *de tomate*^M

whipped cream
crema^F *batida*

pancakes
panquecas^F

basil
albahaca^F

crouton
pan^M *tostado*

cherry tomato
tomate^M *cherry*

pancake
panqueca^F

green tea
té F *verde*

teapot
tetera F

tea
té M

tea bowl
taza F *de té* M

sushi
sushi M

avocado
aguacate M */ palta* F

rice
arroz M

nori
alga F *nori*

tobiko (flying fish roe)
huevas F *de pez* M *volador*

chopsticks
palillos M

chopstick
palillo M *chino*

chopstick rest
soporte M *para palillos* M

gari (pickled ginger)
gari (gengibre M *encurtido)*

soy sauce
salsa F *de soja* F

chow mein
fideos M *chinos*

chopstick
palillos M

miso soup
sopa F *miso* M

fortune cookie
galleta F *de la suerte* F

cappuccino
capuchino M

espresso
espresso M

black tea
té M *negro*

hot chocolate
chocolate M *caliente*

creamer
jarrita F *de leche* F

coffee
taza F *de café* M

milkshake
batido M

straw
pajita F / *pitillo* M

fruit
fruta F

beverage with ice and lime
bebida F *con lima* F *y hielo* M

lemonade
limonada F

pineapple juice
zumo M de piña F

orange juice
zumo M de naranja F

peach juice
zumo M de melocotón M

pomegranate juice
zumo M de granada F

apple juice
zumo M de manzana F

grape juice
zumo M de uva F

tomato juice
zumo M de tomate M

bottled water
agua F de mesa F

cap
tapón M

label
etiqueta F

barcode
código M de barras F

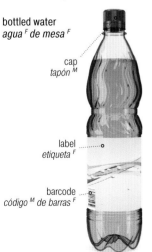

sparkling water
*agua F mineral
con gas M*

still mineral water
agua F mineral

canned pop
refresco M enlatado

wine stopper
tapón ^M *para vino* ^M

red wine
vino ^M *tinto*

white wine
vino ^M *blanco*

champagne
champán ^M

cognac
coñac ^M

vodka
vodka ^M

whiskey
whisky ^M

garnish
guarnición ^F

cocktail
cóctel ^F

beer
cerveza ^F

cocktail glass
copa ^F *de cóctel* ^M

CLOTHING AND ACCESSORIES

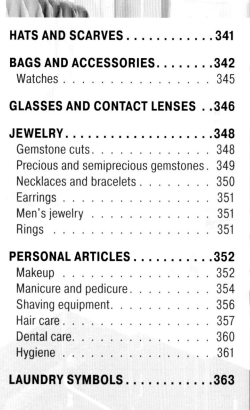

ROPA Y ACCESORIOS

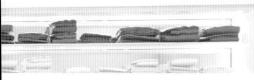

fashion show
desfile ^M *de moda* ^F

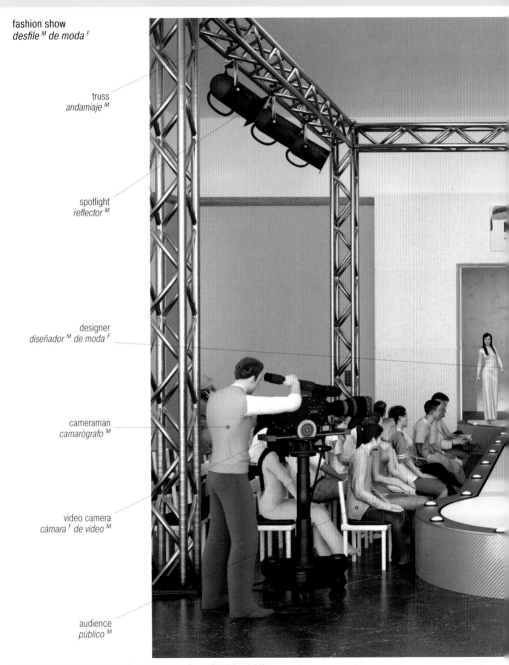

truss
andamiaje ^M

spotlight
reflector ^M

designer
diseñador ^M *de moda* ^F

cameraman
camarógrafo ^M

video camera
cámara ^F *de vídeo* ^M

audience
público ^M

sign
panel ᴹ *publicitario*

model
modelo ᴹ

photographer
fotógrafo ᴹ

uplight
luces ᶠ *de suelo* ᴹ

runway
pasarela ᶠ

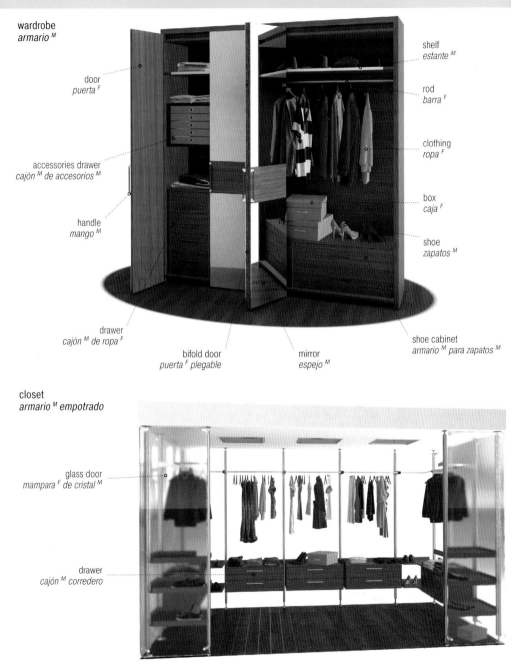

wardrobe
armario ᴹ

door
puerta ᶠ

accessories drawer
cajón ᴹ *de accesorios* ᴹ

handle
mango ᴹ

drawer
cajón ᴹ *de ropa* ᶠ

bifold door
puerta ᶠ *plegable*

mirror
espejo ᴹ

shelf
estante ᴹ

rod
barra ᶠ

clothing
ropa ᶠ

box
caja ᶠ

shoe
zapatos ᴹ

shoe cabinet
armario ᴹ *para zapatos* ᴹ

closet
armario ᴹ *empotrado*

glass door
mampara ᶠ *de cristal* ᴹ

drawer
cajón ᴹ *corredero*

coat
brigo ^M

collar
cuello ^M

sleeve
manga ^F

pocket
bolsillo ^M

button
botón ^M

jacket
chaqueta ^F

trench coat
impermeable ^M

fleece jacket
chaqueta ^F *acolchada*

sweat suit
chándal ^M

MEN'S CLOTHES *ROPA* ᴹ *DE CABALLEROS* ᴹ
Suits and formal accessories *Trajes* ᴹ *y accesorios* ᴹ

vest
chaleco ᴹ

bow tie
pajarita ᶠ

double-breasted jacket
abrigo ᴹ *de doble botonadura* ᶠ

suit
traje ᴹ

necktie
corbata ᶠ

Pants *Pantalones* ᴹ

jeans
vaqueros ᴹ

waistband
pretina ᶠ

belt
cinturón ᴹ

punch hole
agujero ᴹ

belt loop
trabilla ᶠ

belt loop
trabilla ᶠ *para el cinturón* ᴹ

pocket
bolsillo ᴹ

zipper
bragueta ᶠ

buckle
hebilla ᶠ

pant leg
pernera ᶠ *del pantalón* ᴹ

Bermuda shorts
bermudas ᶠ

suspenders
tirantes ᴹ

pants
pantalones ᴹ

hoodie
sudadera ^F

sweatshirt
jersey ^M *de punto*

three-button sweater
jersey ^M

zip-front cardigan
chaqueta ^F

sweater
suéter ^M

zip hoodie
sudadera ^F *con capucha* ^F

cardigan
cárdigan ^M *de caballero* ^M

dress shirt
camisa ^F *con puños* ^M

collar
cuello ^M

button
botón ^M

sleeve
manga ^F

cuff
puño ^M

plaid shirt
camisa ^F *de cuadritos* ^M

polo shirt
camisa ^F *estilo* ^M *polo*

V-neck
cuello ^M *en V*

T-shirt
camiseta ^F

short sleeve
manga ^F *corta*

double-pocket shirt
camisa ^F *con bolsillos* ^M

short-sleeved shirt
camisa ^F *de manga* ^F *corta*

swim briefs
bañador M *de slip*

square-cut trunks
bañador M *largo*

trunks
short de baño M

boxer shorts
calzoncillos M *bóxer*

briefs
calzoncillos M *de slip*

ocks
alcetines M

ribbed top
tobillo M *de canalé* M

leg
pierna F

heel
talón M

foot
pie M

toe
punta F

sole
planta F

long underwear
calzoncillos M *largos*

undershirt
camiseta F *interior*

trench coat
trenca [F] *larga*

collar
cuello [M]

button
botón [M]

belt
cinturón [M]

sleeve
manga [F]

parka
chaqueta [F] *acolchada*

biker jacket
chaqueta [F] *de motorista* [M/F]

peacoat
abrigo [M] *de marinero* [M]

poncho
poncho [M]

fur coat
abrigo [M] *de piel* [F]

denim jacket
chaqueta ^F *vaquera*

wool coat
abrigo ^M *de lana* ^F

double-breasted overcoat
abrigo ^M *de doble botonadura*

sheepskin jacket
abrigo ^M *de piel* ^F *de borrego* ^M

overcoat
trenca ^F

down coat
abrigo ^M *de plumón* ^M

maternity pants
pantalones ^M *de maternidad* ^F

belt loop
trabilla ^F *para el cinturón* ^M

waistband
pretina ^F

pocket
bolsillo ^M

seam
costura ^F

slim-fit pants
pantalones ^M *ajustados*

jeggings
jeggings ^M

wide-leg pants
pantalones ^M *de pierna* ^F *ancha*

pant leg
pernera ^F *del pantalón* ^M

bell-bottomed jeans
vaqueros ^M *de campana* ^F

straight-leg jeans
vaqueros ^M *rectos*

slim-fit jeans
vaqueros ^M *ajustados*

shorts
pantalones ^M *cortos*

spaghetti strap dress
vestido M *con correa* F *de espagueti*

sheath dress
vestido M *de una pieza* F

strap
tirante M

draped neckline
escote M *drapeado*

belt
cinturón M

skirt
falda F

halter dress
vestido M *atado al cuello* M

drop-waist dress
vestido M *de cintura* F *suelta* F

shirtdress
vestido M *camisero* M

A-line dress
vestido ^M con línea ^F en A

sleeve
manga ^F

jersey dress
vestido ^M de tela ^F de jersey

strapless gown
vestido ^M sin tirantes

maxi skirt
falda ^F larga

jumpsuit
mono ^M

sundress
vestido ^M veraniego

cap-sleeve dress
vestido^M *de mangas*^F *cortas*

V-neck
cuello^M *en V*

bodice
corpiño^M

skirt
falda^F

wedding dress
vestido^M *de novia*^F

pencil skirt
falda^F *tubo*^M

maxi dress
vestido^M *largo*

minidress
minivestido^M

short-sleeved shirt
blusa F *de manga* F *corta*

sleeve
manga F

button
botón M

bolero
bolero M

tunic sweater
suéter M

tank top
top M

ruffled top
blusa F *drapeada*

spencer
blazer M *corto*

peasant blouse
blusa F *campesina*

blouse
blusa F

blazer
blazer ^M clásico

batwing-sleeve top
jersey ^M de mangas ^F de murciélago ^M

pocket
bolsillo ^M

long cardigan
cárdigan ^M largo

T-shirt
camiseta ^F

polo shirt
camisa ^F polo ^M de señora ^F

three-quarter sleeve top
top ^M de manga ^F larga

short cardigan
cárdigan ^M corto

sweater vest
chaleco ^M tejido ^M

elastic-waist top
top ^M con cintura ^F elástica

cover-up
túnica ^F de playa ^F

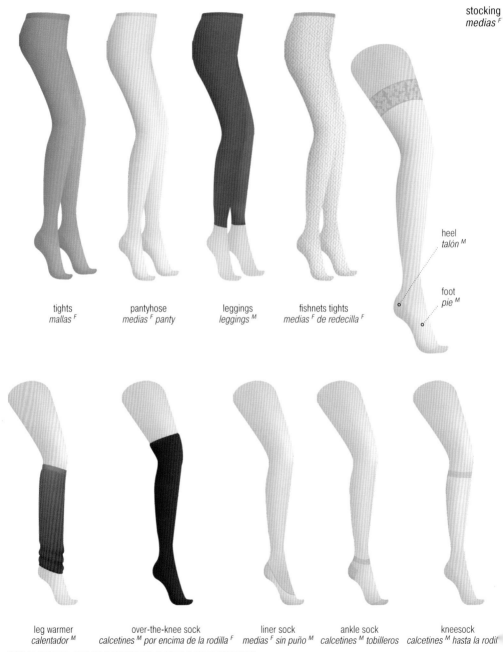

stocking
medias ^F

heel
talón ^M

foot
pie ^M

tights
mallas ^F

pantyhose
medias ^F *panty*

leggings
leggings ^M

fishnets tights
medias ^F *de redecilla* ^F

leg warmer
calentador ^M

over-the-knee sock
calcetines ^M *por encima de la rodilla* ^F

liner sock
medias ^F *sin puño* ^M

ankle sock
calcetines ^M *tobilleros*

kneesock
calcetines ^M *hasta la rodil*

corselet
corsé ^M

shoulder strap
tira ^F *para el hombro* ^M

cup
copa ^F

zipper
cremallera ^F

dressing gown
negligé ^M

camisole and briefs
camiseta ^F *de tirantes* ^M *y bragas* ^F

baby-doll
picardías ^M

corset
corpiño ^M

body shaper
corsé ^M *todo en uno*

slip
combinación ^F

push-up bra and panties
sujetador M *y bragas* M *push-up*

shoulder strap
tira F *para el hombro* M

bra
sujetador M

cup
copa F

waistband
cintura F

panties
bragas F

sweat suit
chándal M

sports bra
sujetador M *deportivo*

nightgown
camisón M

teddy
body M

pajamas
pijama M

garter belt
liguero M

garter
liga F

camisole
camiseta F *de tirantes* M

bra and thong set
sujetador M *y tanga* M

nursing bra
sujetador M *de lactancia* F

bathrobe
albornoz M

Swimwear *Trajes* M *de baño* M

tankini
tankini M

one-piece swimsuit
traje M *de baño* M *de una pieza* F

sarong
pareo M

bikini
bikini M

diaper bag
bolsa ᶠ portapañales ᴹ

baby sling
fular ᴹ portabebés ᴹ

cloth baby carrier
portabebés ᴹ de tela ᶠ

bib
babero ᴹ

nursing pillow
cojín ᴹ de lactancia ᶠ

hooded towel
toalla ᶠ con capucha ᶠ

pacifier
chupón ᴹ

pacifier clip
cinta ᶠ para chupón ᴹ

teething ring
mordedor ᴹ

baby monitor
monitor ᴹ de bebés ᴹ

baby bouncer
mecedora ᶠ para bebé ᴹ

harness
arnés ᴹ de seguridad ᶠ

backpack baby carrier
mochila ᶠ portabebés ᴹ

stroller
cochecito ᴹ de paseo ᴹ

hood
capota ᶠ

handle
manillar ᴹ

wheel
rueda ᶠ

lightweight stroller
cochecito ᴹ de paseo ᴹ

basket
cesta ᶠ

brake
freno ᴹ

play mat
manta ᶠ de actividades ᶠ

baby bathtub
bañera ᶠ para bebé ᴹ

toy
juguete ᴹ

tub
bañera ᶠ

mat
colchoneta ᶠ

disposable diaper
pañal ᴹ desechable

potty chair
orinal ᴹ

onesie
enterizo ᴹ / mameluco ᴹ

toilet seat reducer
asiento ᴹ adaptador ᴹ para inodoro ᴹ

fastener
cierre ᴹ

backstay
contrafuerte ᴹ

dress shoes
zapato ᴹ *de vestir*

tongue
lengüeta ᶠ

quarter
cuarto ᴹ

sole
suela ᶠ

lace
cordón ᴹ

heel
tacón ᴹ

toe cap
puntera ᶠ

sneaker
zapatilla ᶠ *deportiva*

cross-trainer
zapatillas ᶠ *de deporte* ᴹ

basketball shoe
zapatos ᴹ *de baloncesto* ᴹ

high-top sneaker
zapatillas ᶠ *deportivas altas*

oxford
Oxfords ᴹ

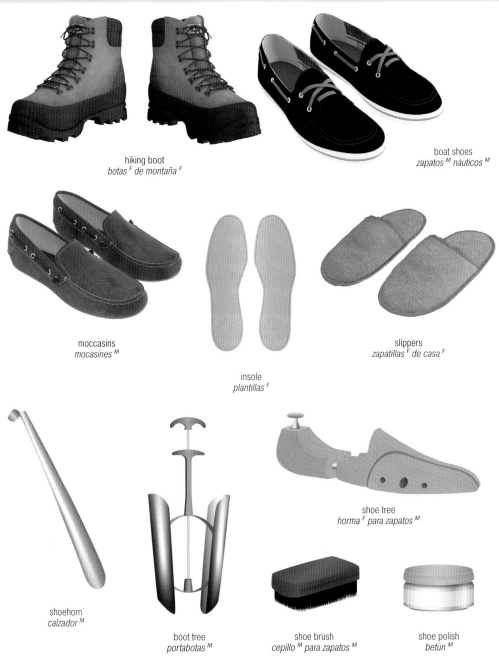

hiking boot
botas ^F de montaña ^F

boat shoes
zapatos ^M náuticos ^M

moccasins
mocasines ^M

insole
plantillas ^F

slippers
zapatillas ^F de casa ^F

shoe tree
horma ^F para zapatos ^M

shoehorn
calzador ^M

boot tree
portabotas ^M

shoe brush
cepillo ^M para zapatos ^M

shoe polish
betún ^M

ankle-strap sandals
sandalias [F] *con tira* [F] *en el tobillo* [M]

platform pumps
zapatos [M] *de tacón* [M]

heel
tacón [M]

platform
plataforma [F]

strap
tira [F]

toe
puntera [F]

sole
suela [F]

ballet flats
zapatillas [F] *de bailarina* [F]

high-heeled boot
bota [F] *de tacón* [M] *alto*

high-heeled sandal
sandalia [F] *de tacón* [M] *alto*

sandal
sandalia [F]

slippers
zapatillas ^F

peep-toe ankle boot
botas ^F *de tacón* ^M *alto con punta* ^F *abierta*

peep-toe flat
bailarina ^F *con punta* ^F *abierta*

biker boots
bota ^F *de motorista* ^M

ankle boots
botín ^M

wedge boot
bota ^F *con suela* ^F *de cuña* ^F

peep-toe pump
zapato ^M *con punta abierta* ^F

pump
zapato ^M *de salón* ^M

wedge sandal
sandalia ^F *de cuña*

stocking cap
gorro ^M con pompón ^M

sun hat
pamela ^F

pom-pom
pompón ^M

hatband
banda ^F del sombrero ^M

crown
corona ^F

brim
ala ^F

straw hat
sombrero ^M de paja ^F

fedora
sombrero ^M fedora ^M

cloche
sombrero ^M de señora ^F

cap
gorra ^F

flatcap
gorra ^F irlandesa

earflap cap
gorro ^M tapaorejas ^F

baseball cap
gorra ^F de béisbol ^M

scarf
pañuelo ^M de señora ^F

gloves
guantes ^M

fingerless gloves
guantes ^M cortos

umbrella
paraguas M

ring
contera F

canopy
tejido M

shank
bastón M

spreader
extensor M

rib
varilla F

handle
asa F

garment bag
portatrajes M

backpack
mochila F *deportiva*

telescopic umbrella
paraguas M *plegable*

briefcase
portafolio M

retractable handle
asa F *extensible*

suitcase
maleta F

carry-on bag
equipaje M *de mano* F

zipper
cremallera F

handle
asa F

pocket
bolsillo M

strap
correa F

pocket
bolsillo M

document case
portadocumentos M

cell-phone case
funda F *para teléfono* M *móvil*

checkbook holder
libreta F *de cheques* M

card case
tarjetero M

key case
cartera F *con llavero* M

coin purse
monedero M

underarm portfolio
cartera F *sin asa* F

wallet
billetera F

clutch
clutch M

writing case
cartera F *portadocumentos* M

evening bag
bolso M *de noche* F

passport holder
funda M *para pasaporte* M

backpack purse
mochila F

shoulder bag
bandolera F

men's bag
bolso M *para hombre* M

carrier bag
bolsa F *de compras* F

schoolbag
mochila F *escolar*

sea bag
petate M

handbag
bolso M *de mano* F

vanity bag
neceser M

drawstring bag
bolsito M *con cierre* M *de cordón* F

laptop bag
bolso M *para computadora* F *portátil*

tote purse
bolso M *capazo*

attaché case
maletín M

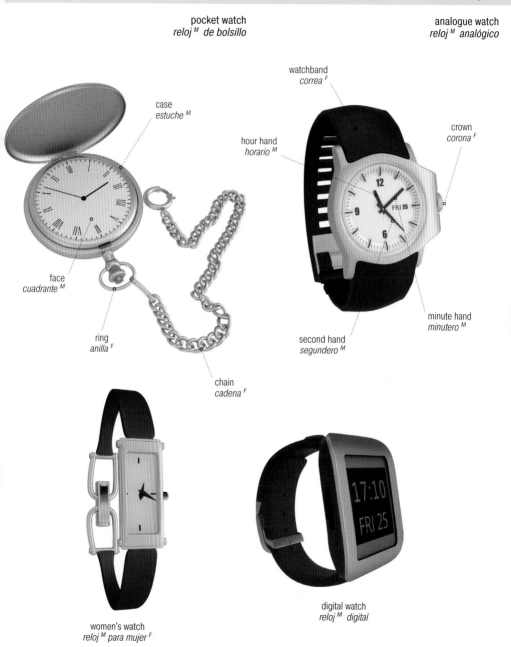

pocket watch
reloj M *de bolsillo*

analogue watch
reloj M *analógico*

watchband
correa F

case
estuche M

hour hand
horario M

crown
corona F

face
cuadrante M

ring
anilla F

chain
cadena F

second hand
segundero M

minute hand
minutero M

women's watch
reloj M *para mujer* F

digital watch
reloj M *digital*

sunglasses
gafas ᶠ *de sol* ᴹ

nose pad
plaqueta ᶠ

bridge
puente ᴹ

temple
patilla ᶠ

frame
montura ᶠ

lens
lente ᶠ

eyeglasses
gafas ᶠ

half-rimmed glasses
gafas ᶠ *de media montura* ᶠ

clip-on sunglasses
lentes ᶠ *de sol* ᴹ *enganchables*

bifocal lens
lentes ᶠ *bifocales*

opera glasses
binoculares ᴹ *para ópera* ᶠ

monocle
monóculo ᴹ

soft contact lenses
lentes M de contacto blandos M

hard contact lenses
lentes M de contacto duros

disposable contact lenses
lentes M de contacto desechables

lens case
estuche M para lentes M de contacto

antique lens case
estuche M antiguo M para lentes M de contacto

multipurpose solution
solución F multiusos

lubricant eye drops
gotas F oculares lubricantes

cleaning cloth
paño M para limpiar las gafas F

glasses case
estuche M para gafas F

glasses cord
tira F para las gafas F

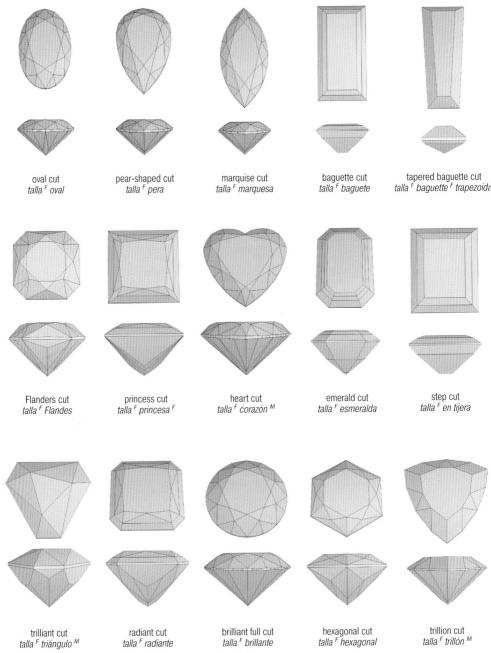

oval cut
talla F *oval*

pear-shaped cut
talla F *pera*

marquise cut
talla F *marquesa*

baguette cut
talla F *baguete*

tapered baguette cut
talla F *baguette* F *trapezoida*

Flanders cut
talla F *Flandes*

princess cut
talla F *princesa* F

heart cut
talla F *corazón* M

emerald cut
talla F *esmeralda*

step cut
talla F *en tijera*

trilliant cut
talla F *triángulo* M

radiant cut
talla F *radiante*

brilliant full cut
talla F *brillante*

hexagonal cut
talla F *hexagonal*

trillion cut
talla F *trillón* M

diamond
diamante M

amethyst
amatista F

aquamarine
aguamarina F

tourmaline
turmalina F

blue topaz
topacio M *azul*

ruby
rubí M

emerald
esmeralda F

garnet
granate M

sapphire
zafiro M

quartz crystal
cristal M *de cuarzo* M

malachite
malaquita F

moonstone
piedra F *de luna* F

jade
jade M

onyx
ónix M

opal
ópalo M

ivory
marfil M

lapis lazuli
lapislázuli M

turquoise
turquesa F

tigereye
ojo M *de tigre* M

agate
ágata F

tiara
tiara ^F

charm bracelet
pulsera ^F *de dijes* ^M

cuff
brazalete ^M

leather bangle
brazalete ^M *de cuero* ^M

locket
medallón ^M

rhinestone
estrás ^M

pearl necklace
collar ^M *de perlas* ^F

cameo
camafeo ^M

choker
gargantilla ^F

brooch
broche ^M

filigree pendant
pendiente ^M *de filigrana* ^F

pendant
pendiente ^M

navel ring stud
adorno ^M *para piercing* ^M
del ombligo ^M

silver pendant
pendiente ^M *de plata* ^F

jewelry box
joyero ^M

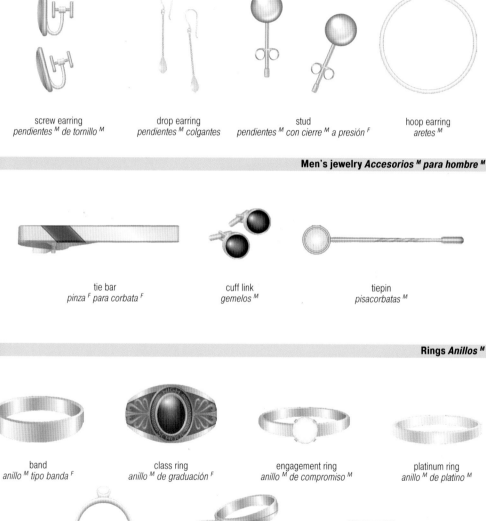

screw earring
pendientes ^M de tornillo ^M

drop earring
pendientes ^M colgantes

stud
pendientes ^M con cierre ^M a presión ^F

hoop earring
aretes ^M

Men's jewelry Accesorios ^M **para hombre** ^M

tie bar
pinza ^F para corbata ^F

cuff link
gemelos ^M

tiepin
pisacorbatas ^M

Rings Anillos ^M

band
anillo ^M tipo banda ^F

class ring
anillo ^M de graduación ^F

engagement ring
anillo ^M de compromiso ^M

platinum ring
anillo ^M de platino ^M

solitaire ring
anillo ^M solitario

wedding ring
alianza ^F de boda ^F

signet ring
anillo ^M de sello ^M

powder blush
colorete ^M en polvo ^M

mirror
espejo ^M

blush
colorete ^M

makeup brush
brocha ^F de maquillaje ^M

compact
compacto ^M

eye shadow
sombra ^F de ojos ^M

powder puff
almohadilla ^F para aplicar maquillaje

washcloth
toallita ^F facial

loose eye shadow
sombra ^F de ojos ^M suelta

makeup remover pad
discos ^M de algodón ^M

pressed face powder
polvo ^M compacto

face cream
crema ^F facial

loose face powder
polvo ^M suelto

makeup remover
removedor ^M de maquillaje ^M

cotton swab
hisopo M de algodón M

eyelash curler
rizador M de pestañas F

brow brush and lash comb
cepillo M para cejas F y peine M para pestañas F

tweezers
pinzas F de depilar

lip gloss
brillo M de labios M

eye cream
crema F para los ojos M

concealer
corrector M

lipstick
pintura F de labios M

lip balm
crema F de labios M

loose powder brush
brocha F para polvo M suelto

liquid eye shadow
sombra F de ojos M líquida

liquid eyeliner
delineador M de ojos M líquido

mascara
rímel M

PERSONAL ARTICLES *ARTÍCULOS ᴹ DE HIGIENE ᶠ PERSONAL*
Makeup *Maquillaje ᴹ*

lip brush
pincel ᴹ para labios ᴹ

eyebrow pencil
lápiz ᴹ de cejas ᴹ

fan brush
pincel ᴹ facial

lip liner
perfilador ᴹ de labios ᴹ

liquid foundation
base ᶠ líquida

Manicure and pedicure *Manicura ᶠ y pedicura ᶠ*

nail polish
esmalte ᴹ de uñas ᶠ

nail polish remover
quitaesmalte ᴹ

cuticle nippers
alicates ᴹ corta cutículas ᶠ

nail clippers
cortauñas ᴹ

safety scissors
tijeras ᶠ de seguridad ᶠ

toenail scissors
tijeras ᶠ para pedicura ᶠ

nail scissors
tijeras ᶠ para uñas ᶠ

cuticle scissors
tijeras ᶠ para cutículas ᶠ

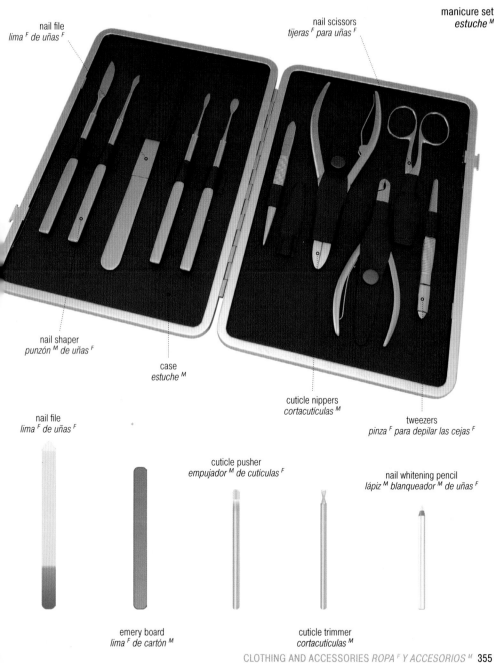

nail file
lima F *de uñas* F

nail scissors
tijeras F *para uñas* F

manicure set
estuche M

nail shaper
punzón M *de uñas* F

case
estuche M

cuticle nippers
cortacutículas M

tweezers
pinza F *para depilar las cejas* F

nail file
lima F *de uñas* F

cuticle pusher
empujador M *de cutículas* F

nail whitening pencil
lápiz M *blanqueador* M *de uñas* F

emery board
lima F *de cartón* M

cuticle trimmer
cortacutículas M

electric shaver
máquina F de afeitar eléctrica

head
cabezal M

housing
cuerpo M

power button
botón M de encendido M

flexible power cord
cable M flexible

shaving cream
espuma F de afeitar

disposable razor blade
hojilla F de afeitar desechable

aftershave
loción M para después del afeita

cleaning brush
cepillo M de limpieza F

disposable razor
hojilla F de afeitar desechable

men's razo
afeitadora M para hombre

head
cabezal M

hair clippers
rasuradora F eléctrica

blade
cuchilla F

lubricating strip
banda F lubricante

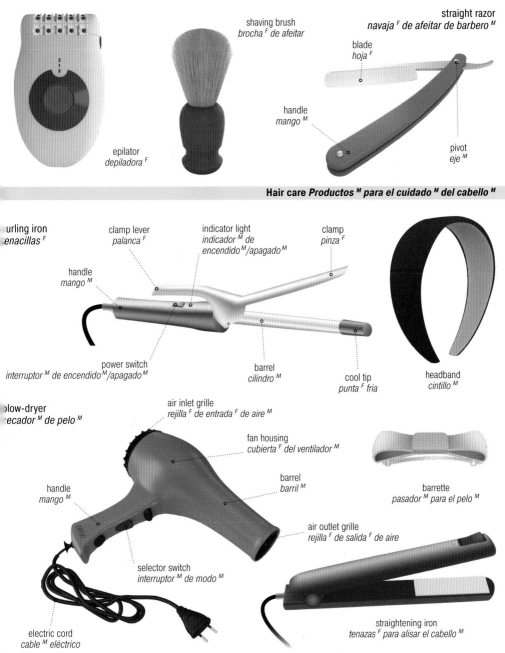

shaving brush
brocha ᶠ de afeitar

straight razor
navaja ᶠ de afeitar de barbero ᴹ

blade
hoja ᶠ

handle
mango ᴹ

pivot
eje ᴹ

epilator
depiladora ᶠ

Hair care *Productos ᴹ para el cuidado ᴹ del cabello ᴹ*

urling iron
enacillas ᶠ

clamp lever
palanca ᶠ

indicator light
*indicador ᴹ de
encendido ᴹ/apagado ᴹ*

clamp
pinza ᶠ

handle
mango ᴹ

power switch
interruptor ᴹ de encendido ᴹ/apagado ᴹ

barrel
cilindro ᴹ

cool tip
punta ᶠ fría

headband
cintillo ᴹ

low-dryer
ecador ᴹ de pelo ᴹ

air inlet grille
rejilla ᶠ de entrada ᶠ de aire ᴹ

fan housing
cubierta ᶠ del ventilador ᴹ

barrel
barril ᴹ

barrette
pasador ᴹ para el pelo ᴹ

handle
mango ᴹ

air outlet grille
rejilla ᶠ de salida ᶠ de aire ᴹ

selector switch
interruptor ᴹ de modo ᴹ

straightening iron
tenazas ᶠ para alisar el cabello ᴹ

electric cord
cable ᴹ eléctrico

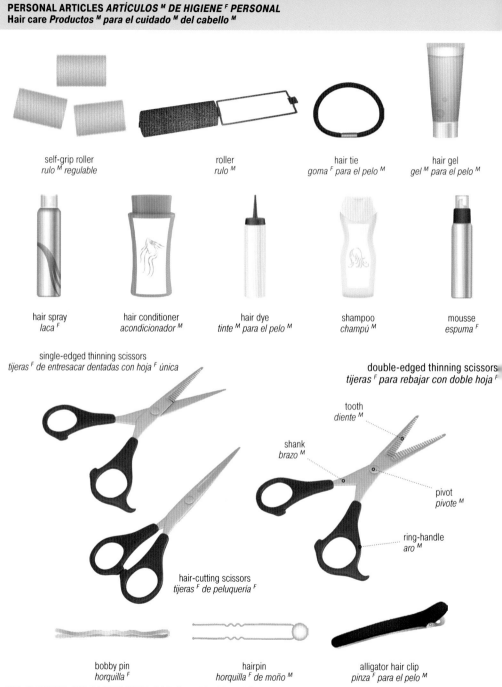

self-grip roller
rulo ᴹ *regulable*

roller
rulo ᴹ

hair tie
goma ᶠ *para el pelo* ᴹ

hair gel
gel ᴹ *para el pelo* ᴹ

hair spray
laca ᶠ

hair conditioner
acondicionador ᴹ

hair dye
tinte ᴹ *para el pelo* ᴹ

shampoo
champú ᴹ

mousse
espuma ᶠ

single-edged thinning scissors
tijeras ᶠ *de entresacar dentadas con hoja* ᶠ *única*

double-edged thinning scissors
tijeras ᶠ *para rebajar con doble hoja* ᶠ

tooth
diente ᴹ

shank
brazo ᴹ

pivot
pivote ᴹ

ring-handle
aro ᴹ

hair-cutting scissors
tijeras ᶠ *de peluquería* ᶠ

bobby pin
horquilla ᶠ

hairpin
horquilla ᶠ *de moño* ᴹ

alligator hair clip
pinza ᶠ *para el pelo* ᴹ

rake comb
peine ^M rastrillo

quill brush
cepillo ^M redondo

vent brush
cepillo ^M esqueleto ^M

round brush
cepillo ^M redondo

tint brush
brocha ^F para teñir

wave clip
pinza ^F para el pelo ^M

hair pick
peine ^M Afro

paddle brush
cepillo ^M plano

tail comb
peine ^M púa ^F

pitchfork comb
peine ^M ahuecador

barber comb
peine ^M de peluquero ^M

teaser comb
peine ^M para cardado ^M

battery-operated toothbrush
cepillo ᴹ *de dientes* ᴹ *eléctrico*

bristles
cerdas ᶠ

on/off button
botón ᴹ *de encendido* ᴹ

charger base
soporte ᴹ *de carga* ᶠ

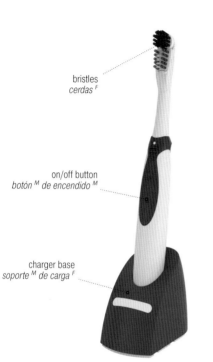

toothbrush
cepillo ᴹ *de dientes* ᴹ

gum stimulator
estimulador ᴹ *de encías* ᶠ

dental floss
hilo ᴹ *dental*

toothpaste
pasta ᶠ *dentífrica*

mouthwash
enjuague ᴹ *bucal*

sanitary pad
toallas ^F sanitarias

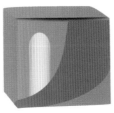

tampon
tampones ^M

pantyliner
salva slips ^M

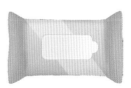

wipe
toallitas ^F

natural sponge
esponja ^F natural

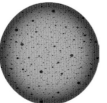

synthetic sponge
esponja ^F sintética

toilet paper
papel ^M higiénico

wax strip
bandas ^F de cera ^F

soap dish
jabonera ^F

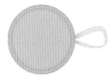

soap
jabón ^M

loofah
esponja ^F vegetal

condom
preservativo ^M

depilatory cream
crema ^F depilatoria

sunscreen
protector ^M solar

bronzer
bronceador ^M corporal

liquid soap
jabón ^M líquido

eau de parfum
eau de parfum ^F

bubble bath
baño ^M *de espuma* ^F

shower gel
gel ^M *de ducha* ^F

spray-on deodorant
desodorante ^M *en espray* ^M

eau de toilette
eau de toilette ^F

nail brush
cepillo ^M *de baño* ^M

moisturizer
humectante ^M

solid deodorant
desodorante ^M *sólido*

bath bomb
bomba ^F *de baño* ^M

toiletry bag
bolsa ^F *de aseo* ^M

bath sheet
toalla ^F *de baño* ^M *grande*

exfoliating glove
guante ^M *de masaje* ^M

bath towel
toalla ^F *de baño* ^M

washing symbols
símbolos ^M *de lavandería* ^F

do not wash
no lavar

wash in warm water
lavar en agua ^F *tibia*

hand wash
lavar a mano ^M

drying symbols
símbolos ^M *de secado* ^M

tumble dry at any heat
secadora ^F *a cualquier temperatura* ^F

tumble dry at low heat
secar en secadora ^F *a baja temperatura* ^F

tumble dry at medium heat
secar en secadora ^F *a temperatura media* ^F

do not tumble dry
no secar en la secadora ^F

ironing symbols
símbolos ^M *de planchado* ^M

   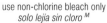

iron at low setting
planchar a baja temperatura ^F

iron at medium setting
planchar a temperatura ^F *media*

iron at high setting
planchar a alta temperatura ^F

do not iron
no planchar

bleaching symbols
símbolos ^M *de uso* ^M *de lejía* ^F

use any bleach
se puede usar lejía ^F

use non-chlorine bleach only
solo lejía sin cloro ^M

do not bleach
no usar lejía ^F

dry cleaning
limpieza ^F *al seco* ^M

dry clean
lavar en seco ^M

do not dry clean
no lavar en seco

SOCIETY

SOCIEDAD

parents and children
padres M *e hijos* M

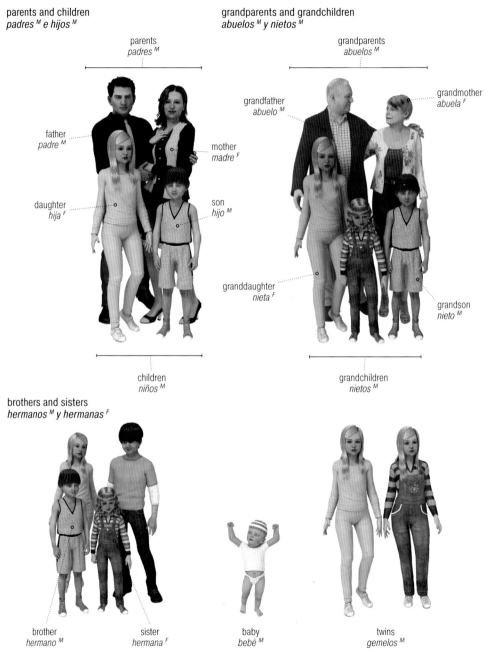

parents
padres M

father
padre M

mother
madre F

daughter
hija F

son
hijo M

children
niños M

grandparents and grandchildren
abuelos M *y nietos* M

grandparents
abuelos M

grandfather
abuelo M

grandmother
abuela F

granddaughter
nieta F

grandson
nieto M

grandchildren
nietos M

brothers and sisters
hermanos M *y hermanas* F

brother
hermano M

sister
hermana F

baby
bebé M

twins
gemelos M

stages of life: female
etapas F *de la vida* F *: mujeres* F

stages of life: male
etapas F *de la vida* F *: hombres* M

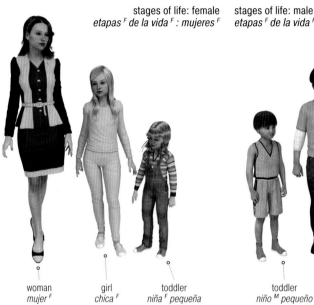
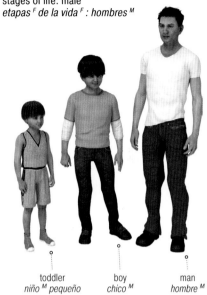

woman
mujer F

girl
chica F

toddler
niña F *pequeña*

toddler
niño M *pequeño*

boy
chico M

man
hombre M

Body types
Tipos M *de cuerpos* M

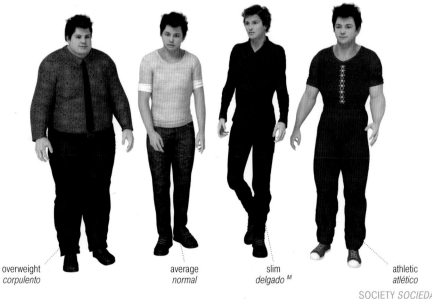

overweight
corpulento

average
normal

slim
delgado M

athletic
atlético

classroom
salón M de clase F

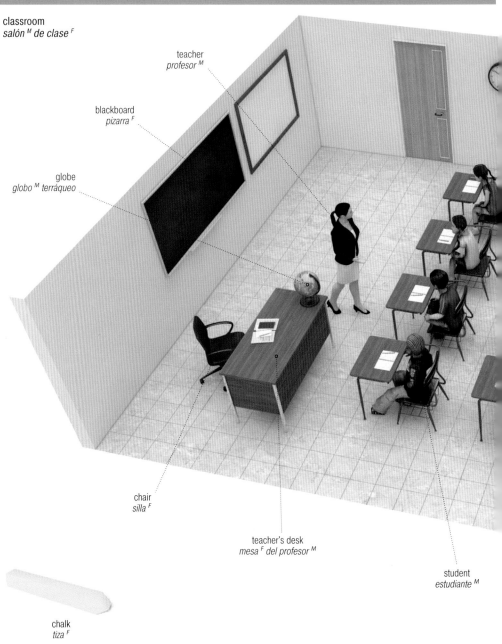

teacher
profesor M

blackboard
pizarra F

globe
globo M terráqueo

chair
silla F

teacher's desk
mesa F del profesor M

student
estudiante M

chalk
tiza F

bulletin board
tablón ^M de anuncios ^M

bookcase
librero ^M

desk
escritorio ^M

lecture hall
salón ^M *de conferencias* ^F

professor
profesor ^M

blackboard
pizarra ^F

desk
mesa ^F *del profesor* ^M

seat
asiento ^M

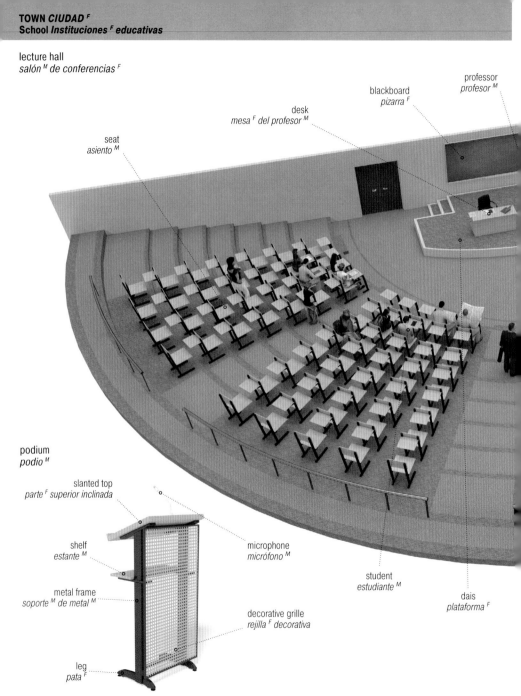

podium
podio ^M

slanted top
parte ^F *superior inclinada*

shelf
estante ^M

metal frame
soporte ^M *de metal* ^M

microphone
micrófono ^M

student
estudiante ^M

dais
plataforma ^F

decorative grille
rejilla ^F *decorativa*

leg
pata ^F

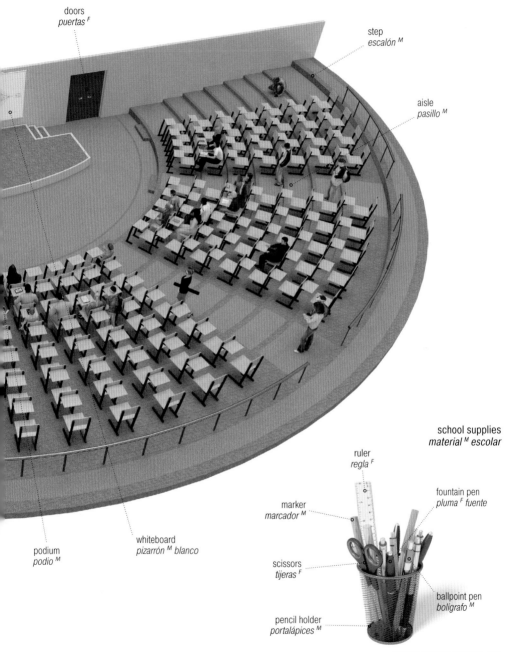

doors
puertas F

step
escalón M

aisle
pasillo M

school supplies
material M *escolar*

ruler
regla F

marker
marcador M

fountain pen
pluma F *fuente*

scissors
tijeras F

ballpoint pen
bolígrafo M

podium
podio M

whiteboard
pizarrón M *blanco*

pencil holder
portalápices M

residential neighborhood
área ^F *residencial*

high-rise apartment building
bloque ^M *de apartamentos* ^M

intersection
intersección ^F

parking lot
playa ^F *de estacionamiento* ^M

townhouse
casa ^F *adosada*

front yard
jardín ^M *delantero*

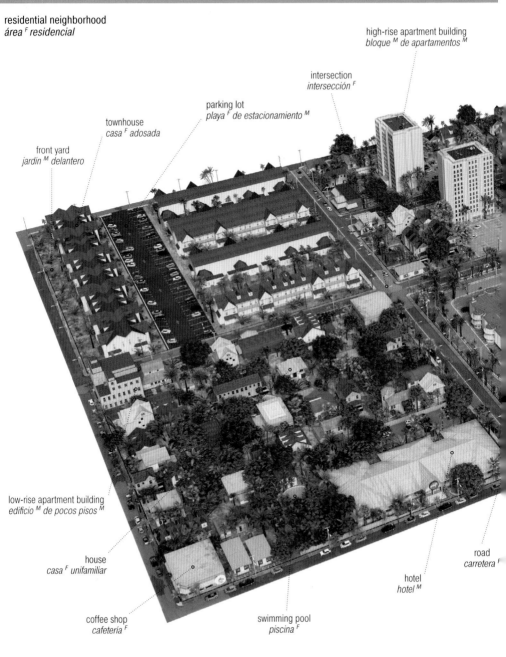

low-rise apartment building
edificio ^M *de pocos pisos* ^M

house
casa ^F *unifamiliar*

road
carretera ^F

hotel
hotel ^M

coffee shop
cafetería ^F

swimming pool
piscina ^F

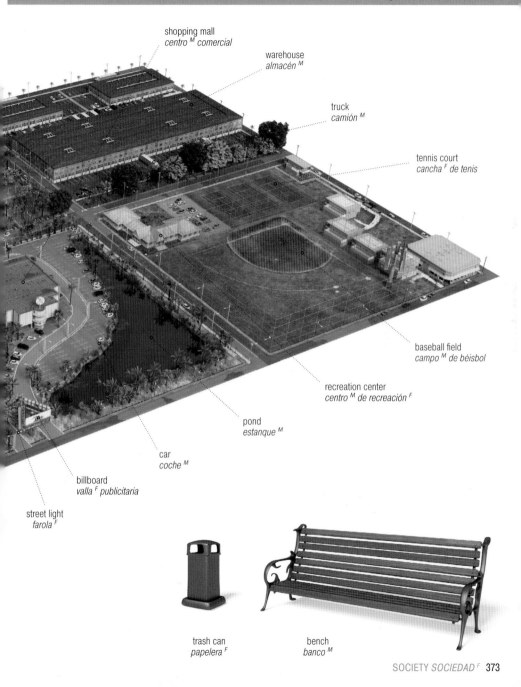

shopping mall
centro ^M *comercial*

warehouse
almacén ^M

truck
camión ^M

tennis court
cancha ^F *de tenis*

baseball field
campo ^M *de béisbol*

recreation center
centro ^M *de recreación* ^F

pond
estanque ^M

car
coche ^M

billboard
valla ^F *publicitaria*

street light
farola ^F

trash can
papelera ^F

bench
banco ^M

downtown
centro M *urbano*

helipad
helipuerto M

helicopter
helicóptero M

crane
grúa F

skyscraper
rascacielo M

construction site
lugar M *en obras* F

restaurant
restaurante M

museum
museo M

building
edificio M

container
contenedor M

truck
camión M

cement truck
camión M *hormigonero*

satellite dish
antena F *parabólica*

solar panel
panel M *solar*

car
coche M

road
carretera F

hospital
hospital M

supermarket
supermercado M

antenna
mástil M *de la ante*

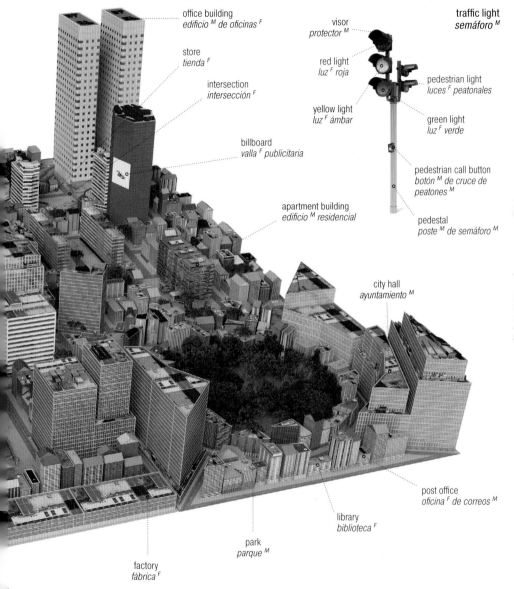

office building
edificio ^M *de oficinas* ^F

store
tienda ^F

intersection
intersección ^F

billboard
valla ^F *publicitaria*

apartment building
edificio ^M *residencial*

traffic light
semáforo ^M

visor
protector ^M

red light
luz ^F *roja*

yellow light
luz ^F *ámbar*

pedestrian light
luces ^F *peatonales*

green light
luz ^F *verde*

pedestrian call button
botón ^M *de cruce de*
peatones ^M

pedestal
poste ^M *de semáforo* ^M

city hall
ayuntamiento ^M

post office
oficina ^F *de correos* ^M

library
biblioteca ^F

park
parque ^M

factory
fábrica ^F

penthouse
penthouse ^M

shopping mall
centro M comercial

sporting goods store
tienda F de artículos M deportivos

travel agency
agencia F de viajes M

cosmetics store
tienda F de cosméticos M

maintenance worker
empleado M de mantenimiento M

jewelry store
joyería F

skylight
tragaluz M

railing
barandilla F

potted plant
planta F decorativa

bridge
puente M

clothing store
tienda F de ropa F

housewares store
*tienda F de artículos M
para el hogar M*

vending machine
máquina F expendedora

security guard
vigilante M

bench
banco M

menswear store
*tienda F de ropa F
de hombre M*

department store
*tienda F por
departamentos M*

trash can
cesto M de basura F

customer
cliente M

information stand
puesto M de información F

electronics store
tienda ^F de electrónica ^F

information display
panel ^M de información ^F

newsstand
puesto ^M de venta ^F de periódicos ^M

toy store
juguetería ^F

lighting store
tienda ^F de lámparas ^F

coffee shop
cafetería ^F

automated teller machine (ATM)
cajero ^M automático

bakery
panadería ^F

table and chairs
mesa ^F y sillas ^F

baby-changing room
cuarto ^M para cambiar al bebé ^M

restroom
baño ^M

janitor
empleado ^M de limpieza ^M

supermarket
supermercado [M]

prepared foods
mostrador [M] *de comida* [F] *preparada*

baked goods
productos [M] *de panadería* [F] *y confitería* [F]

drinks fridge
nevera [F] *de bebidas* [F]

display freezer
exhibidor [M] *de comida* [F] *congelada*

frozen foods
productos [M] *congelados*

locker
casillero [M]

drinks
bebidas [F]

security guard
vigilante [M] *de seguridad* [F]

conveyor belt
banda [F] *transportadora*

cashier
cajero [M]

chair
silla [F]

counter
mostrador [M]

basket
cesta [F]

customer
cliente [M]

railing
barandilla [F]

store entrance/exit
entrada [F] */salida* [F]
de la tienda [F]

anti-theft sensor
sensor [M] *antirrobo*

fruits and vegetables
frutas [F] *y vegetales* [M]

shopping cart
carrito [M] *de la compra* [F]

magazine stand
estante [M] *para revistas* [F]

newspaper and magazine rack
estante [M] *de periódicos* [M] *y revistas*

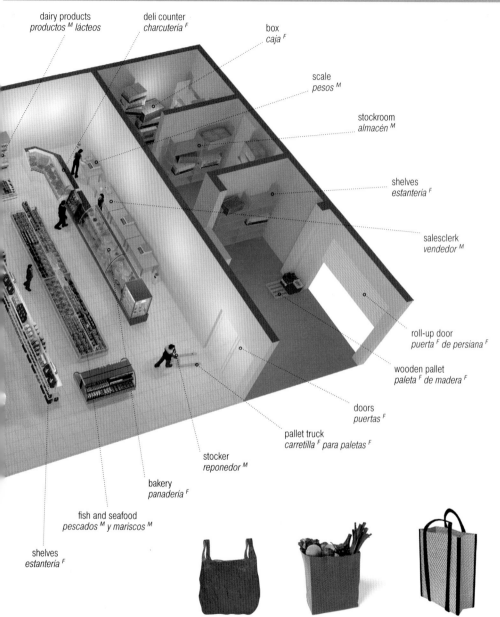

dairy products
productos M *lácteos*

deli counter
charcutería F

box
caja F

scale
pesos M

stockroom
almacén M

shelves
estantería F

salesclerk
vendedor M

roll-up door
puerta F *de persiana* F

wooden pallet
paleta F *de madera* F

doors
puertas F

pallet truck
carretilla F *para paletas* F

stocker
reponedor M

bakery
panadería F

fish and seafood
pescados M *y mariscos* M

shelves
estantería F

plastic bag
bolsa F *de plástico*

paper grocery bag
bolsa F *de papel* M
para víveres M

reusable grocery bag
bolsa F *de compras* F *reusable*

coffee house
cafetería F

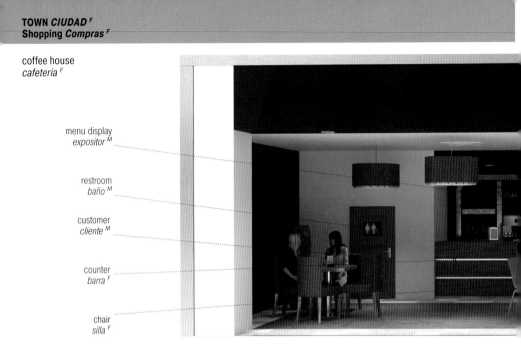

menu display
expositor M

restroom
baño M

customer
cliente M

counter
barra F

chair
silla F

bakery
panadería F

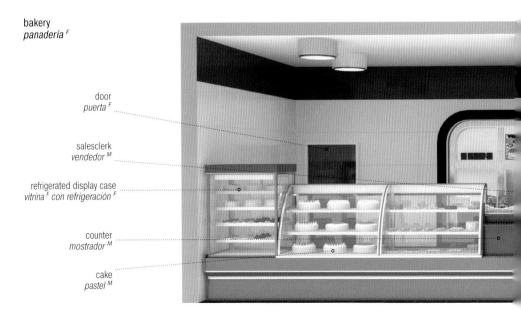

door
puerta F

salesclerk
vendedor M

refrigerated display case
vitrina F *con refrigeración* F

counter
mostrador M

cake
pastel M

storefront sign
letrero ^M

exhaust fan
extractor ^M

pendant light
lámpara ^F *colgante*

barista
encargado ^M
de la cafetería ^F

waitress
camarera ^F

table
mesa ^F

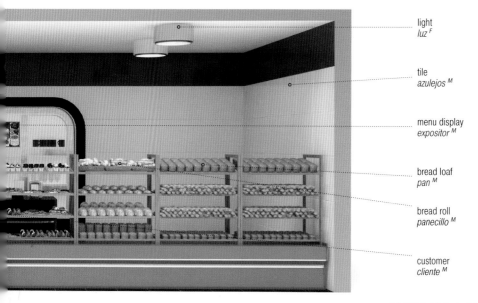

light
luz ^F

tile
azulejos ^M

menu display
expositor ^M

bread loaf
pan ^M

bread roll
panecillo ^M

customer
cliente ^M

cosmetics store
tienda ^F de cosméticos ^M

mirror
espejo ^M

display
expositor ^M

store manager
gerente ^M de la tienda ^F

computer
computadora ^F portátil

counter
mostrador ^M

electronics store
tienda ^F de electrónica ^F

tablet
tableta ^F

monitor
monitor ^M

cellular phone
teléfono ^M móvil

counter
mostrador ^M

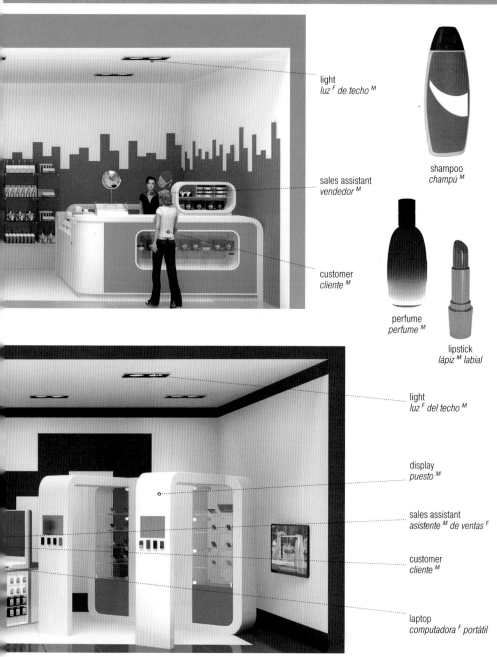

light
luz ^F *de techo* ^M

sales assistant
vendedor ^M

customer
cliente ^M

shampoo
champú ^M

perfume
perfume ^M

lipstick
lápiz ^M *labial*

light
luz ^F *del techo* ^M

display
puesto ^M

sales assistant
asistente ^M *de ventas* ^F

customer
cliente ^M

laptop
computadora ^F *portátil*

clothing store
tienda ^F de ropa ^F

hooks
perchero ^M

curtain
cortina ^F

hangers
ganchos ^M de ropa ^F

fitting room
probador ^M

bench
banco ^M

full-length mirror
espejo ^M de cuerpo ^M entero

display table
mesa ^F de exhibición ^M

clothes rod
barra F *para colgar ropa* F

mannequin
maniquí M

shelves
estantería F

checkout computer
terminal M *de caja* F

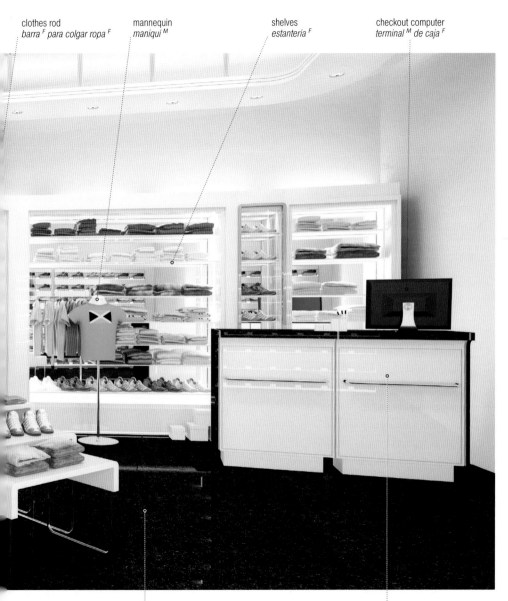

sales and merchandise area
área F *de ventas* F *y mercancías* F

counter
caja F

bar
bar [M]

draft beer taps
tiradores [M] *de cerveza* [F]

patron
cliente [M] *habitual*

waitress
camarera [F]

bar counter
barra [F]

bar stool
taburete [M]

liquor bottle
botella ^F de licor ^M

coffee machine
máquina ^f de café ^M

point-of-sale computer
computadora ^F de punto ^M de venta ^F

wine rack
botellero ^M

bartender
barman ^M

rack of glasses
estante ^M de copas ^F de cristal ^M

napkin dispenser
servilletero ^M

refrigerator
nevera ^F

restaurant
restaurante M

prep table
encimera F

chef
chef M

kitchen
cocina F

bus cart
carrito M

storage room
almacén M

walk-in cooler
cámara F *frigorífica*

grand piano
piano M *de cola* F

bartender
barman M

bar counter
barra F

piano bar
salón M *del piano* M

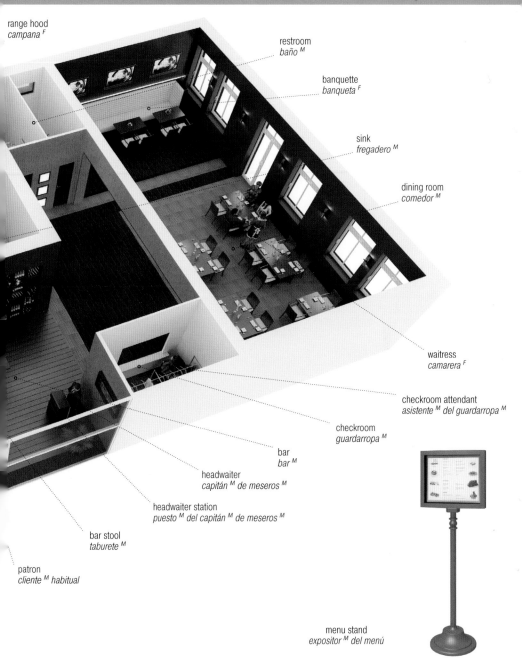

range hood
campana F

restroom
baño M

banquette
banqueta F

sink
fregadero M

dining room
comedor M

waitress
camarera F

checkroom attendant
asistente M *del guardarropa* M

checkroom
guardarropa M

bar
bar M

headwaiter
capitán M *de meseros* M

headwaiter station
puesto M *del capitán* M *de meseros* M

bar stool
taburete M

patron
cliente M *habitual*

menu stand
expositor M *del menú*

fast-food restaurant
restaurante ^M de comida ^F rápida

cash register
caja ^F registradora

beverage dispenser
dispensador ^M de bebidas

menu board
pantalla ^F de menú ^M

salt and pepper shakers
salero ^M y pimentero ^M

counter
mostrador ^M

napkin dispenser
servilletero ^M

waitress
camarera ^F

glasses
cristalería ^F

light
lámpara F

table
mesa F

patron
cliente M *habitual*

window
ventana F

chair
silla F

squeeze bottle
bote M *de salsa* F

napkin holder
servilletero M

banquette
banqueta F

reception
recepción M

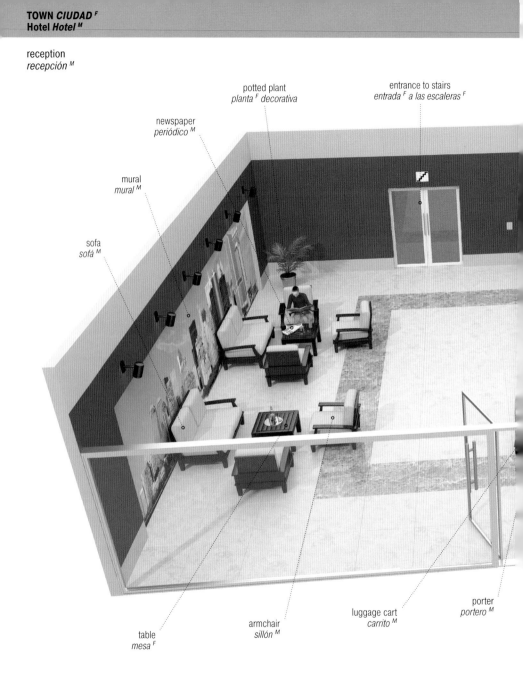

newspaper
periódico M

potted plant
planta F *decorativa*

entrance to stairs
entrada F *a las escaleras* F

mural
mural M

sofa
sofá M

table
mesa F

armchair
sillón M

luggage cart
carrito M

porter
portero M

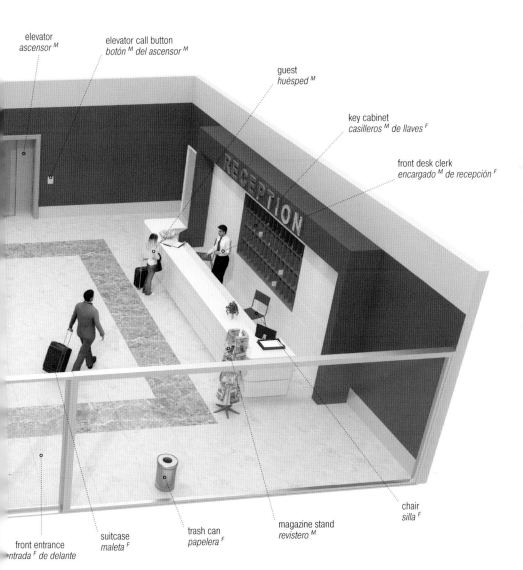

elevator
ascensor [M]

elevator call button
botón [M] *del ascensor* [M]

guest
huésped [M]

key cabinet
casilleros [M] *de llaves* [F]

front desk clerk
encargado [M] *de recepción* [F]

RECEPTION

chair
silla [F]

front entrance
ntrada [F] *de delante*

suitcase
maleta [F]

trash can
papelera [F]

magazine stand
revistero [M]

hotel room
habitación ^F *de hotel* ^M

ventilation fan
ventilador ^M *extractor*

toilet paper
papel ^M *higiénico*

toilet
inodoro ^M

flush buttons
botones ^M *para
descargar el inodoro* ^M

toilet brush
escobilla ^F

bathtub
tina ^F *de baño* ^M

trash can
papelera ^F

towel
toalla ^F

mirror
espejo ^M

sink
lavabo ^M

bath mat
alfombrilla ^F

front door
puerta ^F *delantera*

tiled floor
suelo ^M *de baldosas* ^F

coat hook
percha ^F

shelf
estante ^M

shower enclosure
ducha ^F

closet
armario ^M

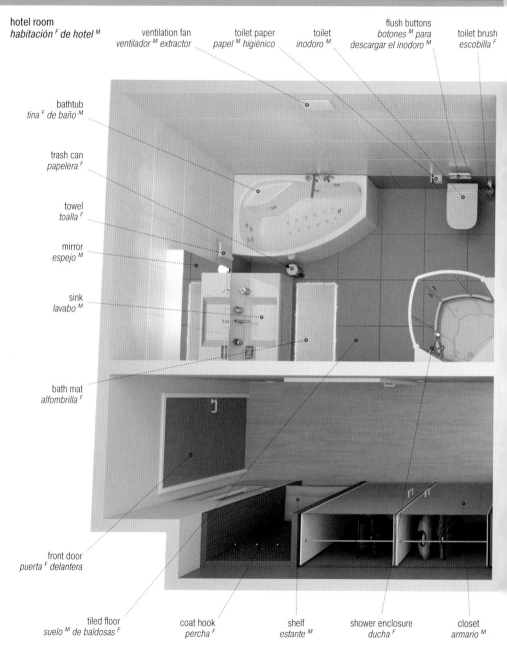

night table
mesita ^F *de noche* ^F

book
libro ^M

newspaper
periódico ^M

bed
cama ^F

telephone
teléfono ^M

wall sconce
luz ^F *de pared* ^F

remote control
control ^M *remoto*

vase with flowers
jarrón ^M *con flores* ^F

curtain
cortina ^F

rug
alfombra ^F

blanket
manta ^F

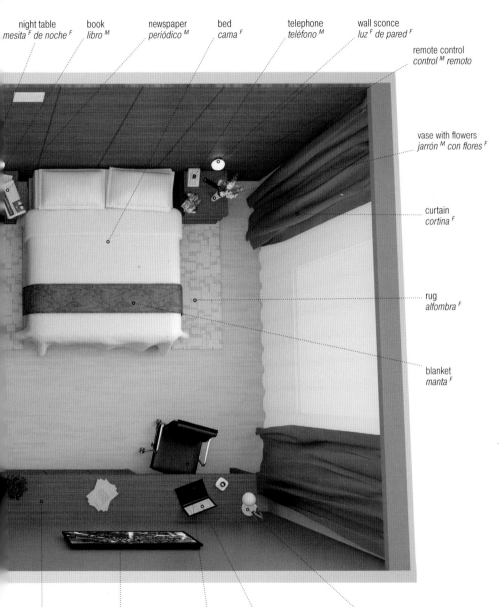

desk
escritorio ^M

television
televisor ^M

desk chair
silla ^F *de escritorio* ^M

laptop
computadora ^F *portátil*

desk lamp
lámpara de escritorio ^M

auditorium
auditorio ^M

projector screen
pantalla ^F *del proyector* ^M

head table
mesa ^F *principal*

podium
podio ^M

microphone
micrófono ^M

gooseneck
cuello ^M *flexible*

grille
rejilla ^F

dais
plataforma ^F

indicator light
luz ^F *indicadora*

power switch
interruptor ^M *de encendido* ^M/*apagado* ^M

control button
botón ^M *de control* ^M

base
base ^F

microphone
micrófono ^M

video camera
video cámara ^F

simultaneous interpretation booth
cabina ^F *de interpretación* ^F *simultánea*

soundproof window
ventana ^F *a prueba de sonidos* ^M

conference table
mesa ^F *de conferencia* ^F

desk chair
silla ^F *de escritorio* ^M

door
puerta ^F

floor
suelo ^M

Police department
Policía ^F

police officer
oficial ^M *de policía* ^F

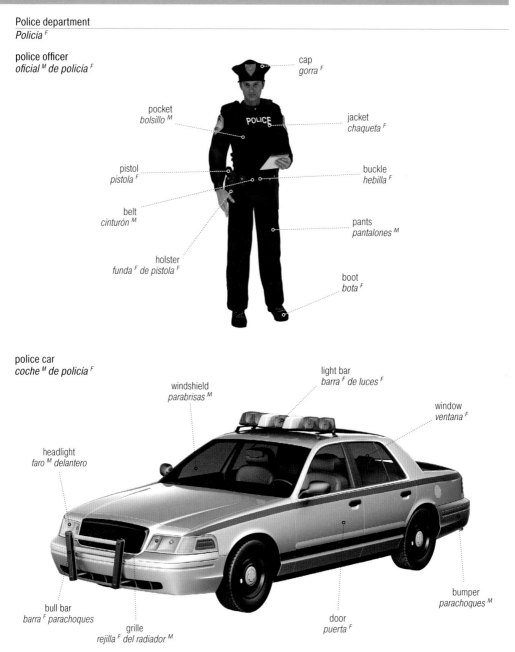

cap
gorra ^F

pocket
bolsillo ^M

jacket
chaqueta ^F

pistol
pistola ^F

buckle
hebilla ^F

belt
cinturón ^M

pants
pantalones ^M

holster
funda ^F *de pistola* ^F

boot
bota ^F

police car
coche ^M *de policía* ^F

light bar
barra ^F *de luces* ^F

windshield
parabrisas ^M

window
ventana ^F

headlight
faro ^M *delantero*

bull bar
barra ^F *parachoques*

grille
rejilla ^F *del radiador* ^M

door
puerta ^F

bumper
parachoques ^M

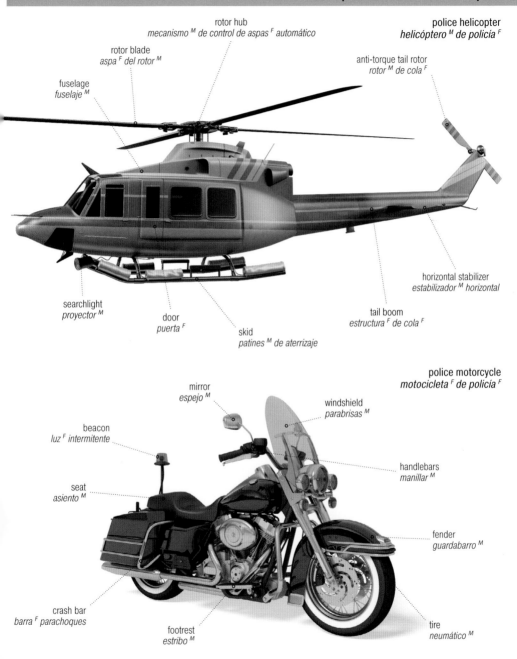

rotor hub
mecanismo [M] *de control de aspas* [F] *automático*

police helicopter
helicóptero [M] *de policía* [F]

rotor blade
aspa [F] *del rotor* [M]

anti-torque tail rotor
rotor [M] *de cola* [F]

fuselage
fuselaje [M]

searchlight
proyector [M]

door
puerta [F]

skid
patines [M] *de aterrizaje*

tail boom
estructura [F] *de cola* [F]

horizontal stabilizer
estabilizador [M] *horizontal*

police motorcycle
motocicleta [F] *de policía* [F]

mirror
espejo [M]

windshield
parabrisas [M]

beacon
luz [F] *intermitente*

handlebars
manillar [M]

seat
asiento [M]

fender
guardabarro [M]

crash bar
barra [F] *parachoques*

footrest
estribo [M]

tire
neumático [M]

Fire department
Bomberos ^M

firefighter
bombero ^M

helmet
casco ^M

face mask
protector ^M *de seguridad* ^F

reflective band
banda ^F *reflectante*

turnouts
chaqueta ^F

rubber boot
botas ^M *de goma* ^F

storage compartment
compartimento ^M

fire truck: front view
camión ^M *de bomberos* ^M *: vista delantera*

light bar
barra ^F *de luces* ^F

rearview mirror
espejo ^M *retrovisor* ^M *lateral*

blind-spot mirror
espejo ^M *para punto* ^M *ciego*

650

grille
rejilla ^F *del radiador* ^M

spotlight
foco ^M *reflector* ^M

front step
parachoque ^M

front outrigger
soporte ^M *frontal*

grab handle
mango ^M

fire truck: back view
camión ^M *de bomberos* ^M *: vista trasera*

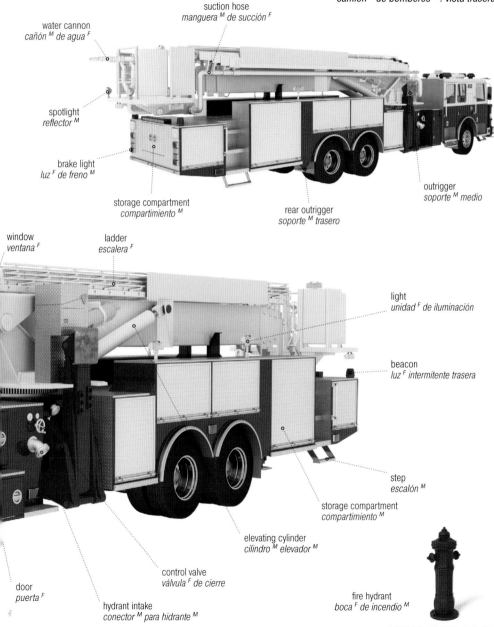

water cannon
cañón ^M *de agua* ^F

suction hose
manguera ^M *de succión* ^F

spotlight
reflector ^M

brake light
luz ^F *de freno* ^M

storage compartment
compartimiento ^M

rear outrigger
soporte ^M *trasero*

outrigger
soporte ^M *medio*

window
ventana ^F

ladder
escalera ^F

light
unidad ^F *de iluminación*

beacon
luz ^F *intermitente trasera*

step
escalón ^M

storage compartment
compartimiento ^M

elevating cylinder
cilindro ^M *elevador* ^M

control valve
válvula ^F *de cierre*

door
puerta ^F

hydrant intake
conector ^M *para hidrante* ^M

fire hydrant
boca ^F *de incendio* ^M

Information signs
Señales F informativas

telephone
teléfono M

post office
correo M

currency exchange
cambio de divisas F

first aid
primeros auxilios M

lost and found
objetos M perdidos

checkroom
guardarropa M

baggage lockers
guarda equipajes M

down escalator
escalera F mecánica, hacia abajo

up escalator
escalera F mecánica, hacia arriba

stairs
escaleras F

elevator
ascensor M

men's restroom
baño M de caballeros M

women's restroom
baño M de damas F

restroom
baño M

baby changing area
área F para cambiar pañales M

waiting room
sala F de espera F

information
información F

lodging
hotel M

airport
aeropuerto M

litter barrel
cesto M *de basura* F

taxi stand
parada F *de taxi* M

bus stop
parada F *de autobús* M

ground transportation
transporte M *terrestre*

train station
estación F *de trenes* M

ferry terminal
terminal F *de ferry* M

car rental
alquiler de coches M

restaurant
restaurante M

coffee shop
cafetería F

bar
bar M

baggage claim
patio M *de equipaje* M

parking
estacionamiento M

smoking area
área M *de fumadores* M

wheelchair access
acceso ^M *para personas* ^F
en sillas ^F *de ruedas* ^F

tent camping
área ^F *de campamento* ^M

trailer camping
campamento ^M *en caravana* ^F

hospital
hospital ^M

picnic area
área ^F *de picnic* ^M

fire extinguisher
extintor ^M

service station
estación ^F *de servicios* ^M

Wi-Fi zone
zona ^F *Wi-Fi*

campfire area
área ^F *para fogatas* ^F

automatic teller machine (ATM)
cajero ^M *automático*

dog-walking area
área ^F *para perros* ^M

swimming area
área ^F *de natación* ^F

drinking water
agua ^F *potable*

video surveillance
vídeo ^M *de vigilancia*

hiking trail
sendero ^M

auto mechanic
taller ^M *de reparación* ^F

Hazard signs
Símbolos ᴹ de peligro ᴹ

corrosive to skin and metals
*corrosivo ᴹ para la piel ᶠ y los
metales ᴹ*

gases under pressure
gases ᴹ comprimidos

flammable materials, self-reactives,
organic peroxides
*materiales ᴹ inflamables, materiales ᴹ
reactivos, peróxidos ᴹ orgánicos*

explosives, self-reactives
explosivos ᴹ

aquatic toxicity
tóxico ᴹ para el medio acuático ᴹ

oxidizers
agentes ᴹ oxidantes

health hazard
peligro ᴹ para la salud ᶠ

acute toxicity
altamente tóxico

Workplace safety signs
Señales ᶠ de precaución ᶠ

eye protection
*obligatorio el uso de gafas ᶠ
protectoras*

respiratory system protection
*obligatorio el uso de
protección ᶠ respiratoria*

foot protection
*obligatorio el uso de
calzado ᴹ protector*

hand protection
*obligatorio el uso de guantes ᴹ
protectores*

head protection
obligatorio el uso de casco ᴹ

protective clothing
*obligatorio el uso de ropa ᶠ
de seguridad ᶠ*

face shield
*obligatorio el uso de
pantalla ᶠ facial*

ear protection
*obligatorio el uso de
protectores ᴹ auditivos*

Warning signs
Señales F de advertencia F

poison
veneno M

radioactive
sustancia F radioactiva

irritant
irritante M

flammable
inflamable M

magnetic field
campo M magnético

high voltage
alto voltaje M

slippery
superficie F resbaladiza

corrosive to skin and metals
*corrosivo M para la piel F
y los metales M*

Prohibition signs
Símbolos M de prohibición

not drinking water
no es agua F potable

cell phone use prohibited
*prohibido usar teléfonos M
móviles*

no open flame
*prohibido fumar y encender
fuego M*

photography prohibited
prohibido tomar fotos F

no smoking
prohibido fumar

pets prohibited
no se permiten las mascotas F

no access
acceso M cerrado

stop
alto M

Emergency signs
Señales F *de emergencia* F

first aid
primeros auxilios M

emergency telephone
teléfono M *de emergencias* F

assembly point
punto M *de encuentro* M

automated external defibrillator
(AED)
desfibrilador M *externo automático*
(DEA)

eye wash station
estación F *para lavar los ojos* M

doctor
médico M

in case of emergency break glass
en caso M *de emergencia* F *rompa el cristal* M

emergency exit
salida F *de emergencia* F

Fire safety signs
Señales F *de prevención* F *de incendios* M

fire hose
manguera F *de incendios* M

ladder
escalera F

fire extinguisher
extintor M

fire alarm
alarma F *contra incendio* M

fire-fighting equipment
equipo M *contra incendio* M

emergency phone
teléfono M *de emergencia* F

directional arrow
indicador M *de dirección* F

Asia
Asia [F]

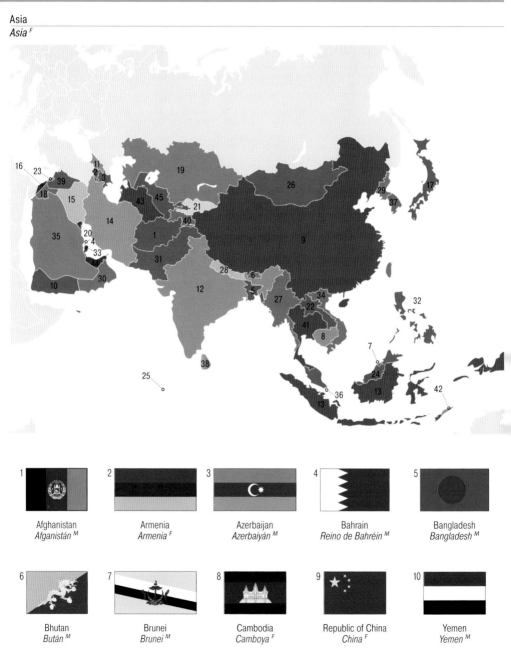

1
Afghanistan
Afganistán [M]

2
Armenia
Armenia [F]

3
Azerbaijan
Azerbaiyán [M]

4
Bahrain
Reino de Bahréin [M]

5
Bangladesh
Bangladesh [M]

6
Bhutan
Bután [M]

7
Brunei
Brunei [M]

8
Cambodia
Camboya [F]

9
Republic of China
China [F]

10
Yemen
Yemen [M]

11	12	13	14	15
Georgia *Georgia* F	India *India* F	Indonesia *Indonesia* F	Iran *Irán* M	Iraq *Iraq* M

16	17	18	19	20
Israel *Israel* M	Japan *Japón* M	Jordan *Jordania* M	Kazakhstan *Kazajstán* M	Kuwait *Kuwait* M

21	22	23	24	25
Kyrgyzstan *Kirguistán* M	Laos *Laos* M	Lebanon *Líbano* M	Federation of Malaysia *Malasia* F	Maldives *Maldivas* F

26	27	28	29	30
Mongolia *Mongolia* F	Myanmar *Myanmar* M	Nepal *Nepal* M	North Korea *Corea del Norte* F	Oman *Omán* M

31	32	33	34	35
Pakistan *Pakistán* M	Philippines *Filipinas* F	Qatar *Qatar* M	Vietnam *Vietnam* M	Saudi Arabia *Arabia Saudí* M

36	37	38	39	40
Singapore *Singapur* M	South Korea *Corea del Sur* F	Sri Lanka *Sri Lanka* F	Syria *Siria* F	Tajikistan *Tayikistán* M

41

Thailand
Tailandia *F*

42

East Timor
Timor Oriental *M*

43

Turkmenistan
Turkmenistán *M*

44

United Arab Emirates
Emiratos Árabes Unidos *M*

45

Uzbekistan
Uzbekistán *M*

Europe
Europa *F*

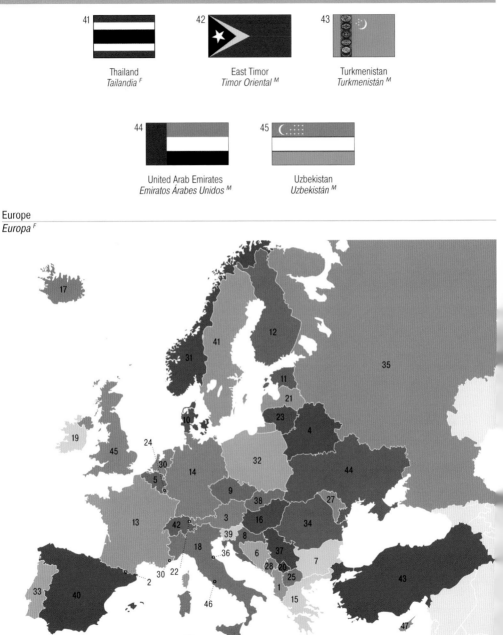

1 Albania
Albania F

2 Andorra
Andorra F

3 Austria
Austria F

4 Belarus
Bielorrusia F

5 Belgium
Bélgica F

6 Bosnia and Herzegovina
Bosnia y Herzegovina F

7 Bulgaria
Bulgaria F

8 Croatia
Croacia F

9 Czech Republic
Republica Checa F

10 Denmark
Dinamarca F

11 Estonia
Estonia F

12 Finland
Finlandia F

13 France
Francia F

14 Germany
Alemania F

15 Greece
Grecia F

16 Hungary
Hungria F

17 Iceland
Islandia F

18 Italy
Italia F

19 Ireland
Irlanda F

20 Kosovo
Kosovo M

21 Latvia
Letonia F

22 Liechtenstein
Liechtenstein M

23 Lithuania
Lituania F

24 Luxembourg
Luxemburgo M

25 Macedonia
Macedonia F

26 Malta
Malta F

27 Moldova
Moldavia F

28 Monaco
Mónaco M

29 Montenegro
Montenegro M

30 Netherlands
Países Bajos M

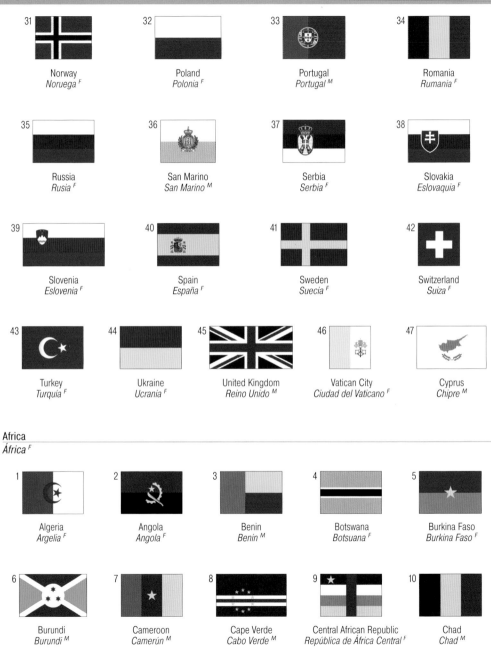

31 Norway
Noruega ^F

32 Poland
Polonia ^F

33 Portugal
Portugal ^M

34 Romania
Rumania ^F

35 Russia
Rusia ^F

36 San Marino
San Marino ^M

37 Serbia
Serbia ^F

38 Slovakia
Eslovaquia ^F

39 Slovenia
Eslovenia ^F

40 Spain
España ^F

41 Sweden
Suecia ^F

42 Switzerland
Suiza ^F

43 Turkey
Turquía ^F

44 Ukraine
Ucrania ^F

45 United Kingdom
Reino Unido ^M

46 Vatican City
Ciudad del Vaticano ^F

47 Cyprus
Chipre ^M

Africa
África ^F

1 Algeria
Argelia ^F

2 Angola
Angola ^F

3 Benin
Benín ^M

4 Botswana
Botsuana ^F

5 Burkina Faso
Burkina Faso ^F

6 Burundi
Burundi ^M

7 Cameroon
Camerún ^M

8 Cape Verde
Cabo Verde ^M

9 Central African Republic
República de África Central ^F

10 Chad
Chad ^M

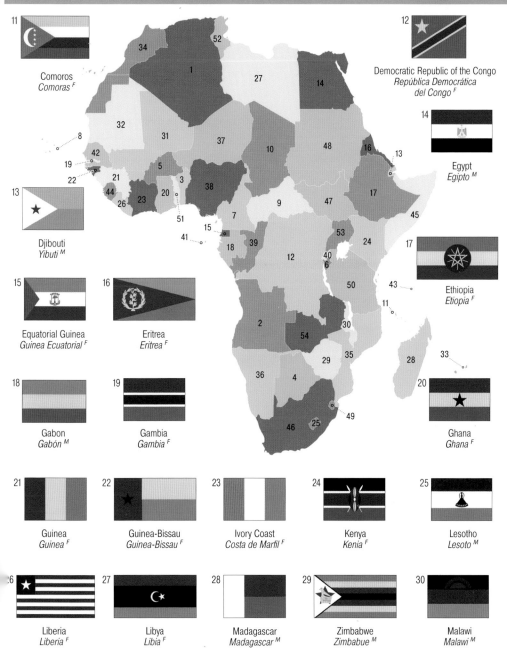

11 Comoros
Comoras F

12 Democratic Republic of the Congo
República Democrática del Congo F

14 Egypt
Egipto M

13 Djibouti
Yibuti M

15 Equatorial Guinea
Guinea Ecuatorial F

16 Eritrea
Eritrea F

17 Ethiopia
Etiopía F

18 Gabon
Gabón M

19 Gambia
Gambia F

20 Ghana
Ghana F

21 Guinea
Guinea F

22 Guinea-Bissau
Guinea-Bissau F

23 Ivory Coast
Costa de Marfil F

24 Kenya
Kenia F

25 Lesotho
Lesoto M

26 Liberia
Liberia F

27 Libya
Libia F

28 Madagascar
Madagascar M

29 Zimbabwe
Zimbabue M

30 Malawi
Malawi M

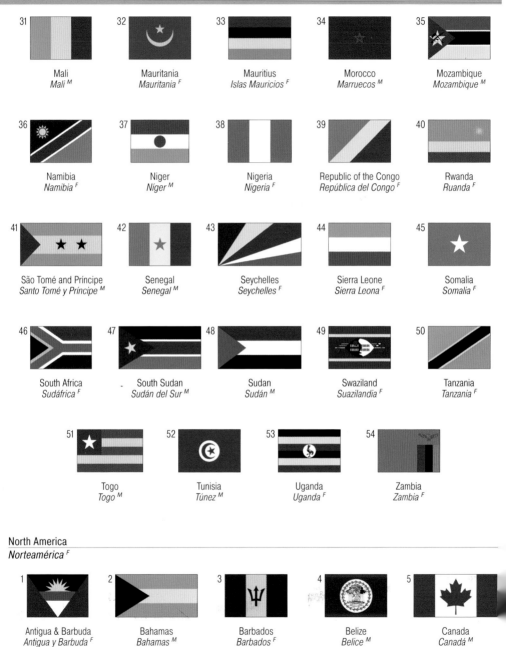

31 Mali
Mali ᴹ

32 Mauritania
Mauritania ᶠ

33 Mauritius
Islas Mauricios ᶠ

34 Morocco
Marruecos ᴹ

35 Mozambique
Mozambique ᴹ

36 Namibia
Namibia ᶠ

37 Niger
Níger ᴹ

38 Nigeria
Nigeria ᶠ

39 Republic of the Congo
República del Congo ᶠ

40 Rwanda
Ruanda ᶠ

41 São Tomé and Príncipe
Santo Tomé y Príncipe ᴹ

42 Senegal
Senegal ᴹ

43 Seychelles
Seychelles ᶠ

44 Sierra Leone
Sierra Leona ᶠ

45 Somalia
Somalia ᶠ

46 South Africa
Sudáfrica ᶠ

47 South Sudan
Sudán del Sur ᴹ

48 Sudan
Sudán ᴹ

49 Swaziland
Suazilandia ᶠ

50 Tanzania
Tanzania ᶠ

51 Togo
Togo ᴹ

52 Tunisia
Túnez ᴹ

53 Uganda
Uganda ᶠ

54 Zambia
Zambia ᶠ

North America
Norteamérica ᶠ

1 Antigua & Barbuda
Antigua y Barbuda ᶠ

2 Bahamas
Bahamas ᴹ

3 Barbados
Barbados ᶠ

4 Belize
Belice ᴹ

5 Canada
Canadá ᴹ

6

Costa Rica
Costa Rica ᶠ

7

Cuba
Cuba ᶠ

8

Dominica
Dominica ᶠ

9

Dominican Republic
República Dominicana ᶠ

10

El Salvador
El Salvador ᴹ

11

Grenada
Granada ᶠ

12

Guatemala
Guatemala ᶠ

13

Haiti
Haití ᴹ

14

Honduras
Honduras ᶠ

15

Jamaica
Jamaica ᶠ

16

Mexico
México ᴹ

17

Nicaragua
Nicaragua ᶠ

18

Panama
Panamá ᶠ

19

Saint Kitts-Nevis
San Cristóbal ᴹ _y Nieves_ ᶠ

20

Saint Lucia
Santa Lucía ᶠ

21

Saint Vincent and
the Grenadines
San Vicente y las Granadinas ᴹ

22

United States of America
Estados Unidos de
América ᴹ

South America
Sudamérica [F]

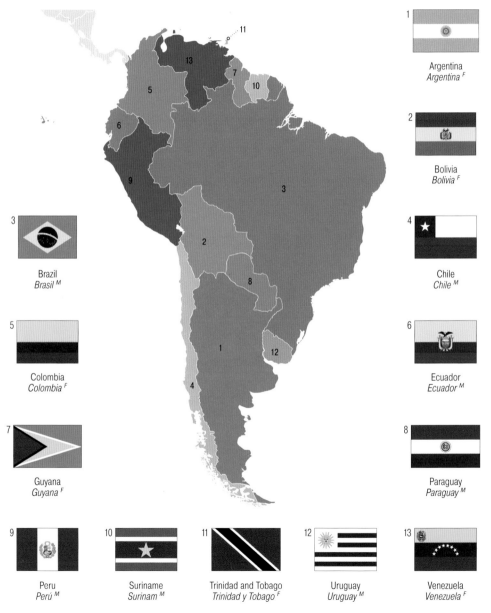

1
Argentina
Argentina [F]

2
Bolivia
Bolivia [F]

3
Brazil
Brasil [M]

4
Chile
Chile [M]

5
Colombia
Colombia [F]

6
Ecuador
Ecuador [M]

7
Guyana
Guyana [F]

8
Paraguay
Paraguay [M]

9
Peru
Perú [M]

10
Suriname
Surinam [M]

11
Trinidad and Tobago
Trinidad y Tobago [F]

12
Uruguay
Uruguay [M]

13
Venezuela
Venezuela [F]

Australia and Oceania
Australia y Oceanía [F]

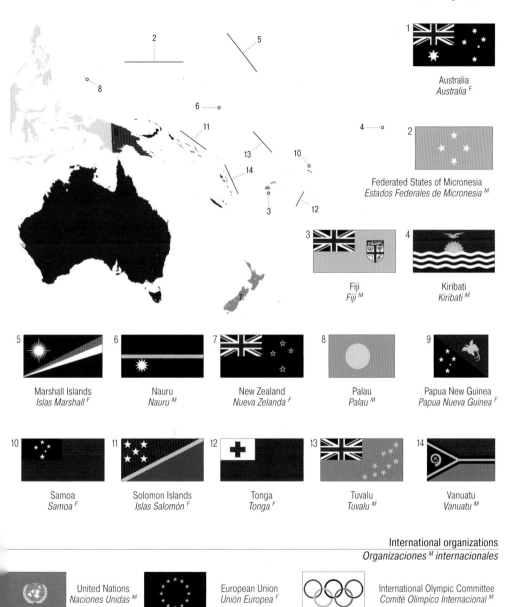

Australia
Australia [F]

Federated States of Micronesia
Estados Federales de Micronesia [M]

Fiji
Fiji [M]

Kiribati
Kiribati [M]

Marshall Islands
Islas Marshall [F]

Nauru
Nauru [M]

New Zealand
Nueva Zelanda [F]

Palau
Palau [M]

Papua New Guinea
Papua Nueva Guinea [F]

Samoa
Samoa [F]

Solomon Islands
Islas Salomón [F]

Tonga
Tonga [F]

Tuvalu
Tuvalu [M]

Vanuatu
Vanuatu [M]

International organizations
Organizaciones [M] *internacionales*

United Nations
Naciones Unidas [M]

European Union
Unión Europea [F]

International Olympic Committee
Comité Olímpico Internacional [M]

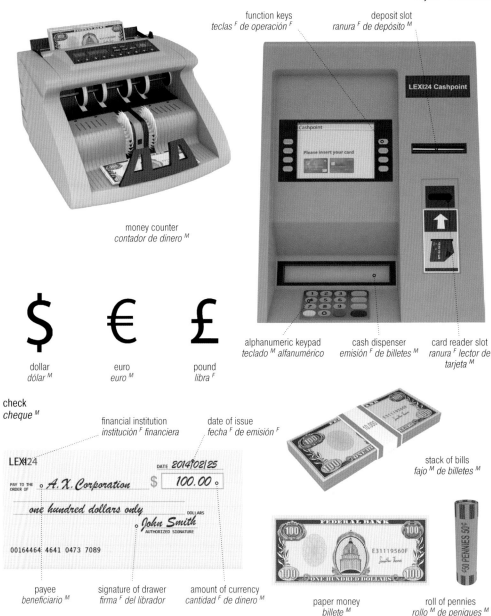

automatic teller machine (ATM)
cajero M automático

function keys
teclas F de operación F

deposit slot
ranura F de depósito M

LEXI24 Cashpoint

Cashpoint

Please insert your card

money counter
contador de dinero M

$ € £

dollar
dólar M

euro
euro M

pound
libra F

alphanumeric keypad
teclado M alfanumérico

cash dispenser
emisión F de billetes M

card reader slot
ranura F lector de tarjeta M

check
cheque M

financial institution
institución F financiera

date of issue
fecha F de emisión F

LEXI24

PAY TO THE ORDER OF · A. X. Corporation $ 100.00

DATE 2014/02/25

one hundred dollars only

DOLLARS

John Smith
AUTHORIZED SIGNATURE

00164464: 4641 0473 7089

stack of bills
fajo M de billetes M

payee
beneficiario M

signature of drawer
firma F del librador

amount of currency
cantidad F de dinero M

FEDERAL BANK
100
E31119560F
100
ONE HUNDRED DOLLARS

50 PENNIES 50¢

paper money
billete M

roll of pennies
rollo M de peniques M

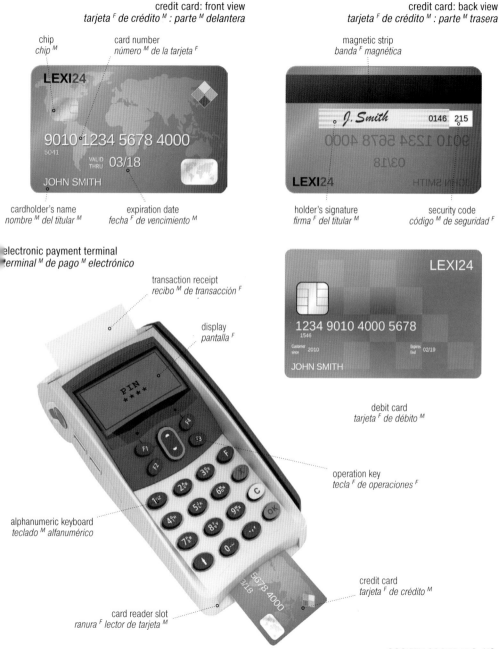

credit card: front view
tarjeta ^F de crédito ^M : parte ^M delantera

credit card: back view
tarjeta ^F de crédito ^M : parte ^M trasera

chip
chip ^M

card number
número ^M de la tarjeta ^F

magnetic strip
banda ^F magnética

LEXI24

9010 1234 5678 4000
5041
VALID THRU 03/18
JOHN SMITH

cardholder's name
nombre ^M del titular ^M

expiration date
fecha ^F de vencimiento ^M

holder's signature
firma ^F del titular ^M

security code
código ^M de seguridad ^F

electronic payment terminal
terminal ^M de pago ^M electrónico

transaction receipt
recibo ^M de transacción ^F

display
pantalla ^F

debit card
tarjeta ^F de débito ^M

operation key
tecla ^F de operaciones ^F

alphanumeric keyboard
teclado ^M alfanumérico

credit card
tarjeta ^F de crédito ^M

card reader slot
ranura ^F lector de tarjeta ^M

pistol
pistola ^F

front sight
punto ^M *de mira* ^F

barrel
barril ^M

takedown lever
palanca ^F *para desmontar*

rear sight
alza ^F *de mira* ^F *trasera*

hammer
martillo ^M

muzzle
boca ^F

safety catch
seguro ^M

trigger
gatillo ^M

slide
estructura ^F

magazine
cargador ^M

trigger guard
guardamontes ^M

magazine catch
retén ^M *del cargador* ^M

butt
mango ^M

grip panel
panel ^M *de empuñadura*

cartridge case
envoltura ^F

magazine
cargador ^M

bullet
bala ^F

cylinder
cilindro ^M

barrel
cañón ^M

front sight
mira ^F *delantera*

revolver
revólver ^M

hammer
martillo ^M

muzzle
boca ^F

butt
empuñadura ^F

trigger guard
guardamonte ^M

trigger
gatillo ^M

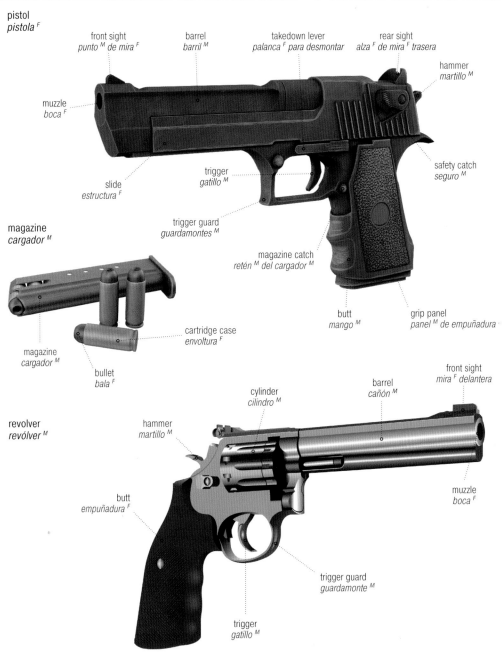

assault rifle
fusil ^M *automático de asalto* ^M

gas tube
respiradero ^M

front sight housing
punto ^M *de mira* ^F

rear sight
alza ^F *de mira* ^F

trigger
gatillo ^M

safety lever
bloqueo ^M *de seguridad* ^F *y selector* ^M *de disparos* ^M

barrel
cañón ^M

handguard
cazoleta ^F

stock
culata ^F

pistol grip
empuñadura ^F *de la pistola* ^F

magazine
cargador ^M

cartridge
cartucho ^M

bullet
bala ^F

cartridge case
cartuchera ^F

primer
pistón ^M

assault rifle with folding stock
rifle ^M *de asalto* ^M *con culata* ^F *plegable*

light machine gun
ametralladora ^F *ligera*

rocket-propelled grenade (RPG) and launcher
granada [F] *propulsada por cohete* [M] *y lanzacohetes* [M]

breech
culata [F]

optical sight
alza [F] *de mira* [F] *mecánico*

barrel
cañón [M]

front sight
punto [M] *de mira* [F]

rear grip
mango [M] *adicional*

grenade
granada [F]

front grip
mango [M]

trigger
gatillo [M]

shotgun
escopeta [F]

sniper rifle
rifle [M] *de francotirador* [M]

optical sight
alza [M] *de mira* [F] *óptico*

rear sight
alza [M] *de mira* [F] *mecánico*

barrel
cañón [M]

front sight
punto [M] *de mira* [F]

handguard
cazoleta [F]

flash hider
soporte [M] *del punto* [M] *de mira*

stock
culata [F]

trigger
gatillo [M]

magazine
cargador [M]

combat submachine gun
subfusil ^M *de combate* ^M

submachine gun
subfusil ^M

stun grenade
granada ^F *de aturdimiento* ^M

primary pull ring
anilla ^F *de tiro* ^M *principal*

aerial bomb
bomba ^F *aérea*

secondary pull ring
anilla ^F *de tiro* ^M *secundaria*

safety lever
palanca ^F *de seguridad* ^F

body
cuerpo ^M

charge
carga ^F

mine
mina ^F

missile
misil ^M

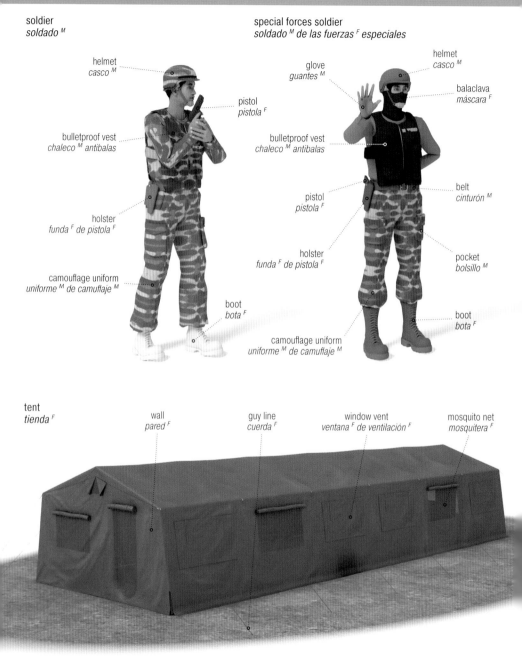

soldier
soldado ^M

special forces soldier
soldado ^M *de las fuerzas* ^F *especiales*

helmet
casco ^M

glove
guantes ^M

helmet
casco ^M

pistol
pistola ^F

balaclava
máscara ^F

bulletproof vest
chaleco ^M *antibalas*

bulletproof vest
chaleco ^M *antibalas*

belt
cinturón ^M

holster
funda ^F *de pistola* ^F

pistol
pistola ^F

holster
funda ^F *de pistola* ^F

pocket
bolsillo ^M

camouflage uniform
uniforme ^M *de camuflaje* ^M

boot
bota ^F

camouflage uniform
uniforme ^M *de camuflaje* ^M

boot
bota ^F

tent
tienda ^F

wall
pared ^F

guy line
cuerda ^F

window vent
ventana ^F *de ventilación* ^F

mosquito net
mosquitera ^F

main battle tank (MBT)
tanque M *de batalla* F

turret
torreta F

periscope
periscopio M

armor
blindaje M

cannon
cañón M

headlight
faro M *delantero*

hatch
escotilla F

wheel
rueda F

track
eslabones M *modulares de oruga* F

infantry fighting vehicle (IFV)
vehículo M *de combate* M *de infantería* F

heavy tank
tanque M *pesado*

high mobility multipurpose wheeled vehicle (humvee)
vehículo ^M *todoterreno multiuso*

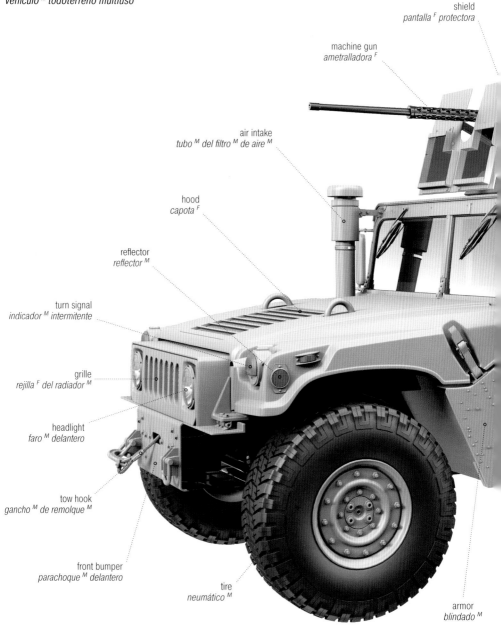

shield
pantalla ^F *protectora*

machine gun
ametralladora ^F

air intake
tubo ^M *del filtro* ^M *de aire* ^M

hood
capota ^F

reflector
reflector ^M

turn signal
indicador ^M *intermitente*

grille
rejilla ^F *del radiador* ^M

headlight
faro ^M *delantero*

tow hook
gancho ^M *de remolque* ^M

front bumper
parachoque ^M *delantero*

tire
neumático ^M

armor
blindado ^M

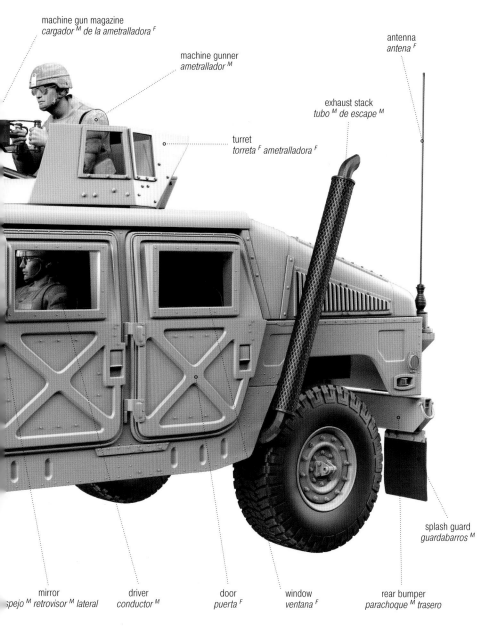

machine gun magazine
cargador ^M *de la ametralladora* ^F

machine gunner
ametrallador ^M

antenna
antena ^F

exhaust stack
tubo ^M *de escape* ^M

turret
torreta ^F *ametralladora* ^F

splash guard
guardabarros ^M

mirror
spejo ^M *retrovisor* ^M *lateral*

driver
conductor ^M

door
puerta ^F

window
ventana ^F

rear bumper
parachoque ^M *trasero*

humvee: bottom view
vehículo ^M *todoterreno multiuso: vista* ^F *inferior*

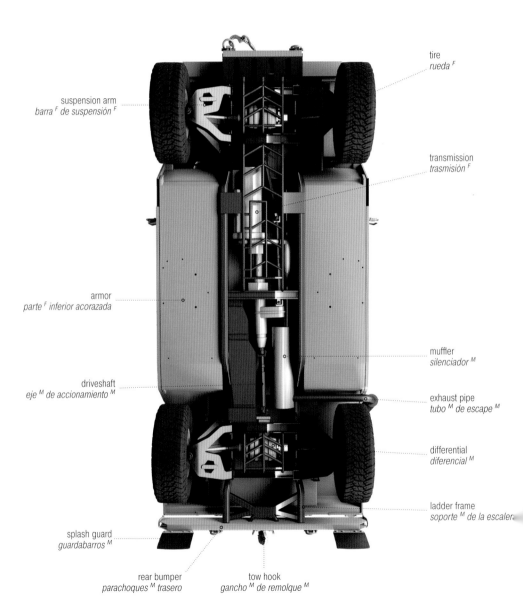

tire
rueda ^F

suspension arm
barra ^F *de suspensión* ^F

transmission
trasmisión ^F

armor
parte ^F *inferior acorazada*

muffler
silenciador ^M

driveshaft
eje ^M *de accionamiento* ^M

exhaust pipe
tubo ^M *de escape* ^M

differential
diferencial ^M

ladder frame
soporte ^M *de la escalera*

splash guard
guardabarros ^M

rear bumper
parachoques ^M *trasero*

tow hook
gancho ^M *de remolque* ^M

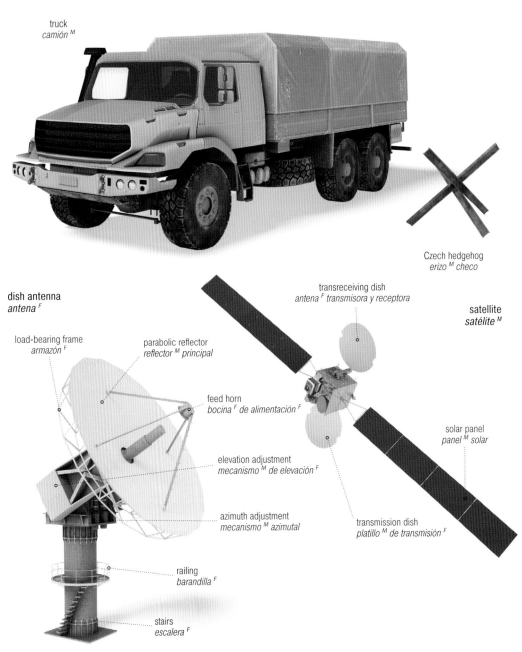

truck
camión [M]

Czech hedgehog
erizo [M] *checo*

dish antenna
antena [F]

transreceiving dish
antena [F] *transmisora y receptora*

satellite
satélite [M]

load-bearing frame
armazón [F]

parabolic reflector
reflector [M] *principal*

feed horn
bocina [F] *de alimentación* [F]

solar panel
panel [M] *solar*

elevation adjustment
mecanismo [M] *de elevación* [F]

azimuth adjustment
mecanismo [M] *azimutal*

transmission dish
platillo [M] *de transmisión* [F]

railing
barandilla [F]

stairs
escalera [F]

Airplanes
Aviones ^M

interceptor
interceptor ^M

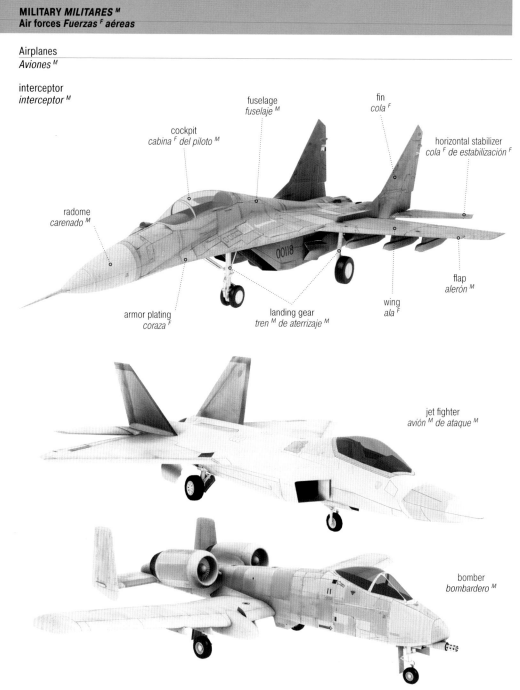

cockpit
cabina ^F *del piloto* ^M

fuselage
fuselaje ^M

fin
cola ^F

horizontal stabilizer
cola ^F *de estabilización* ^F

radome
carenado ^M

00118

flap
alerón ^M

armor plating
coraza ^F

landing gear
tren ^M *de aterrizaje* ^M

wing
ala ^F

jet fighter
avión ^M *de ataque* ^M

bomber
bombardero ^M

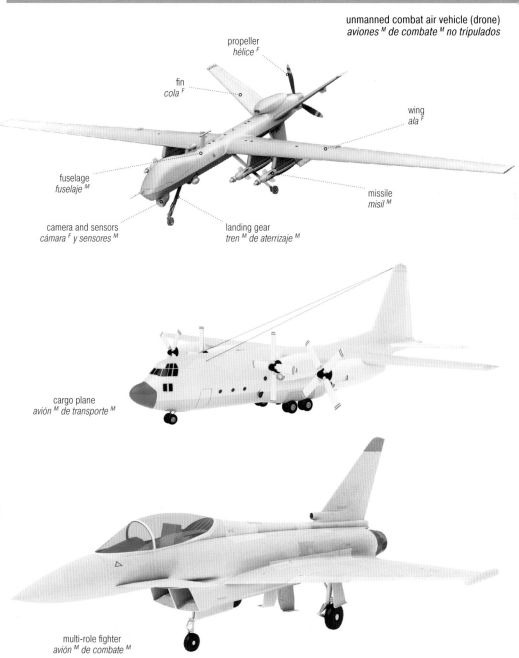

unmanned combat air vehicle (drone)
aviones ^M *de combate* ^M *no tripulados*

propeller
hélice ^F

fin
cola ^F

wing
ala ^F

fuselage
fuselaje ^M

missile
misil ^M

camera and sensors
cámara ^F *y sensores* ^M

landing gear
tren ^M *de aterrizaje* ^M

cargo plane
avión ^M *de transporte* ^M

multi-role fighter
avión ^M *de combate* ^M

Helicopter
Helicóptero [M]

utility helicopter: side view
helicóptero [M] *multi función* [F]*: vista* [F] *lateral*

rotor hub
mecanismo [M] de control [M] de aspas [F] automático

engine
motor [M]

window
ventanilla [F]

rotor blade
hoja [F] del rotor [M]

fuselage
fuselaje [M]

cockpit
cabina [F] del piloto [M]

cockpit door
puerta [F] de la cabina [F]

landing window
ventana [F] de aterrizaje [M]

landing gear
tren [M] de aterrizaje [M]

light
luz ^F *intermitente*

tail rotor
rotor ^M *de cola* ^F

tail boom
estructura ^F *de cola* ^F

tail rotor pylon
pilón ^M *de la estructura* ^F *de cola* ^F

horizontal stabilizer
estabilizador ^M *horizontal*

step
escalón ^M

wheel
rueda ^F

helicopter: front view
helicóptero ^M : *vista* ^F *delantera*

cockpit
cabina ^F de vuelo

windshield
parabrisas ^M

windshield wiper
limpiaparabrisas ^M

control stick
palanca ^F de control ^M

display
pantalla ^F

anti-torque pedal
pedal ^M de control ^M

gauge
manómetro ^M

center console
unidad ^F de control ^M central

instrument panel
panel ^M de instrumentos

passenger cabin
compartimento ^M de pasajeros

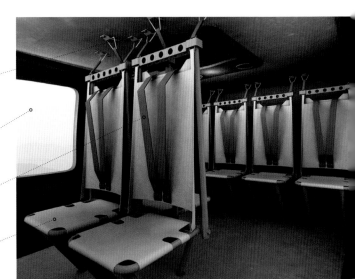

anchor point
*enganche ^M del cinturón ^M de
seguridad ^F*

window
ventanilla ^F

safety belt
cinturón ^M de seguridad ^F

seat
asiento ^M

search and rescue (SAR) helicopter
helicóptero M de búsqueda F y rescate M

transport helicopter
helicóptero M de pasajeros M

attack helicopter
helicóptero M de combate M

patrol coastal ship
buque ^M *de patrulla* ^F *costera*

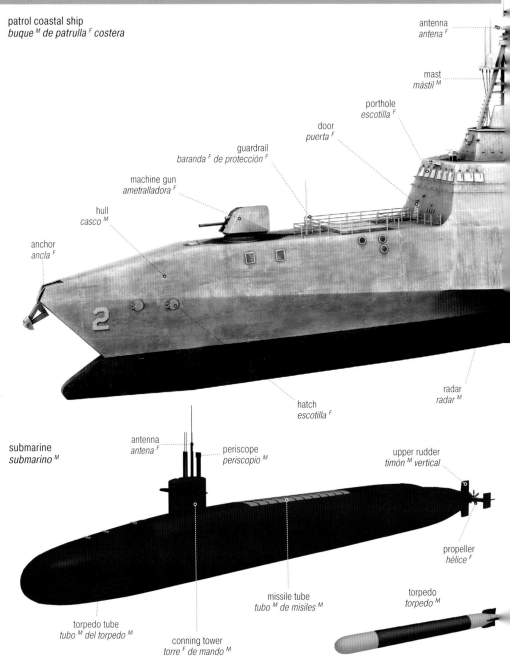

antenna
antena ^F

mast
mástil ^M

porthole
escotilla ^F

door
puerta ^F

guardrail
baranda ^F *de protección* ^F

machine gun
ametralladora ^F

hull
casco ^M

anchor
ancla ^F

radar
radar ^M

hatch
escotilla ^F

submarine
submarino ^M

antenna
antena ^F

periscope
periscopio ^M

upper rudder
timón ^M *vertical*

propeller
hélice ^F

missile tube
tubo ^M *de misiles* ^M

torpedo
torpedo ^M

torpedo tube
tubo ^M *del torpedo* ^M

conning tower
torre ^F *de mando* ^M

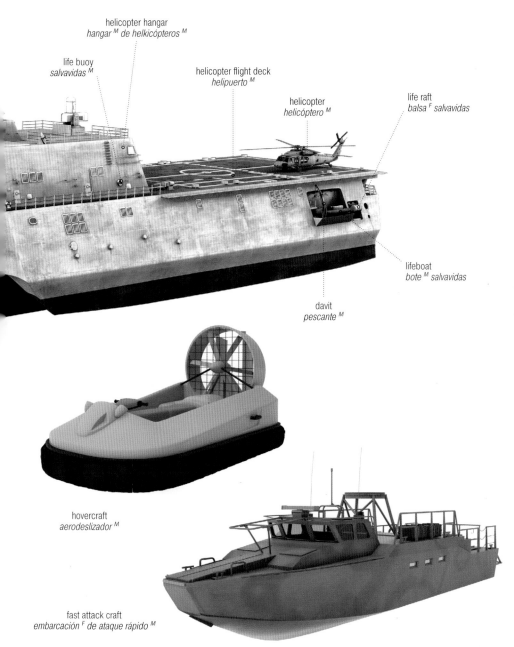

helicopter hangar
hangar ^M *de helkicópteros* ^M

life buoy
salvavidas ^M

helicopter flight deck
helipuerto ^M

helicopter
helicóptero ^M

life raft
balsa ^F *salvavidas*

lifeboat
bote ^M *salvavidas*

davit
pescante ^M

hovercraft
aerodeslizador ^M

fast attack craft
embarcación ^F *de ataque rápido* ^M

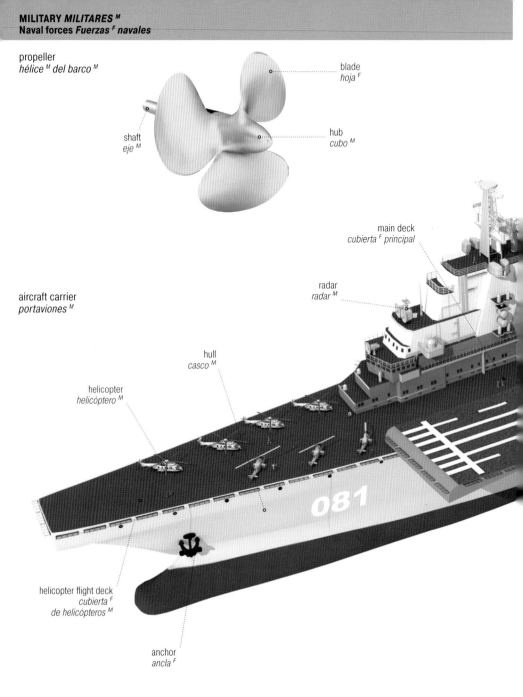

propeller
hélice ^M *del barco* ^M

blade
hoja ^F

shaft
eje ^M

hub
cubo ^M

main deck
cubierta ^F *principal*

radar
radar ^M

aircraft carrier
portaviones ^M

hull
casco ^M

helicopter
helicóptero ^M

helicopter flight deck
cubierta ^F
de helicópteros ^M

anchor
ancla ^F

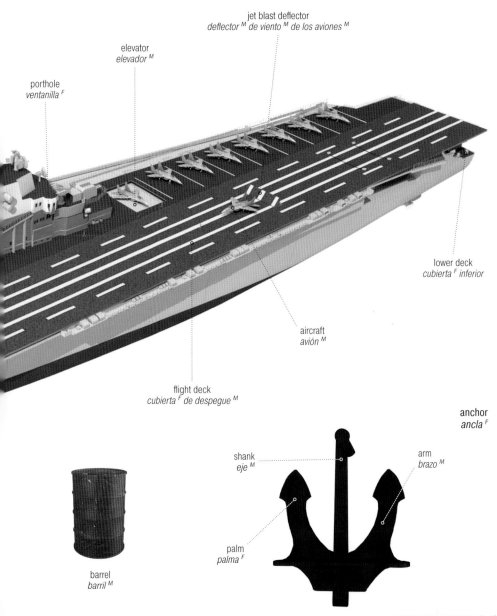

jet blast deflector
deflector M *de viento* M *de los aviones* M

elevator
elevador M

porthole
ventanilla F

lower deck
cubierta F *inferior*

aircraft
avión M

flight deck
cubierta F *de despegue* M

anchor
ancla F

shank
eje M

arm
brazo M

palm
palma F

barrel
barril M

ARTS AND ARCHITECTURE

ARTES Y ARQUITECTURA

band
grupo M *musical*

block of lights
panel M *de iluminación* F

parabolic aluminized reflector light
reflector parabólico M *aluminizado*

guitarist
guitarrista M

electric guitar
guitarra F *eléctrica*

loudspeaker
altavoces M

cable
cable M

monitor
monitor M

synthesizer
sintetizador M

keyboardist
tecladista M

audio enginee
técnico M *de sonido* N

singer
cantante ᴹ

drummer
baterista ᴹ

drum kit
batería ᶠ

bassist
bajista ᴹ

trussing
andamiaje ᴹ

console
consola ᶠ

chair
silla ᶠ

laptop computer
computadora ᶠ *portátil*

table
mesa ᶠ

bass guitar
bajo ᴹ

stage
escenario ᴹ

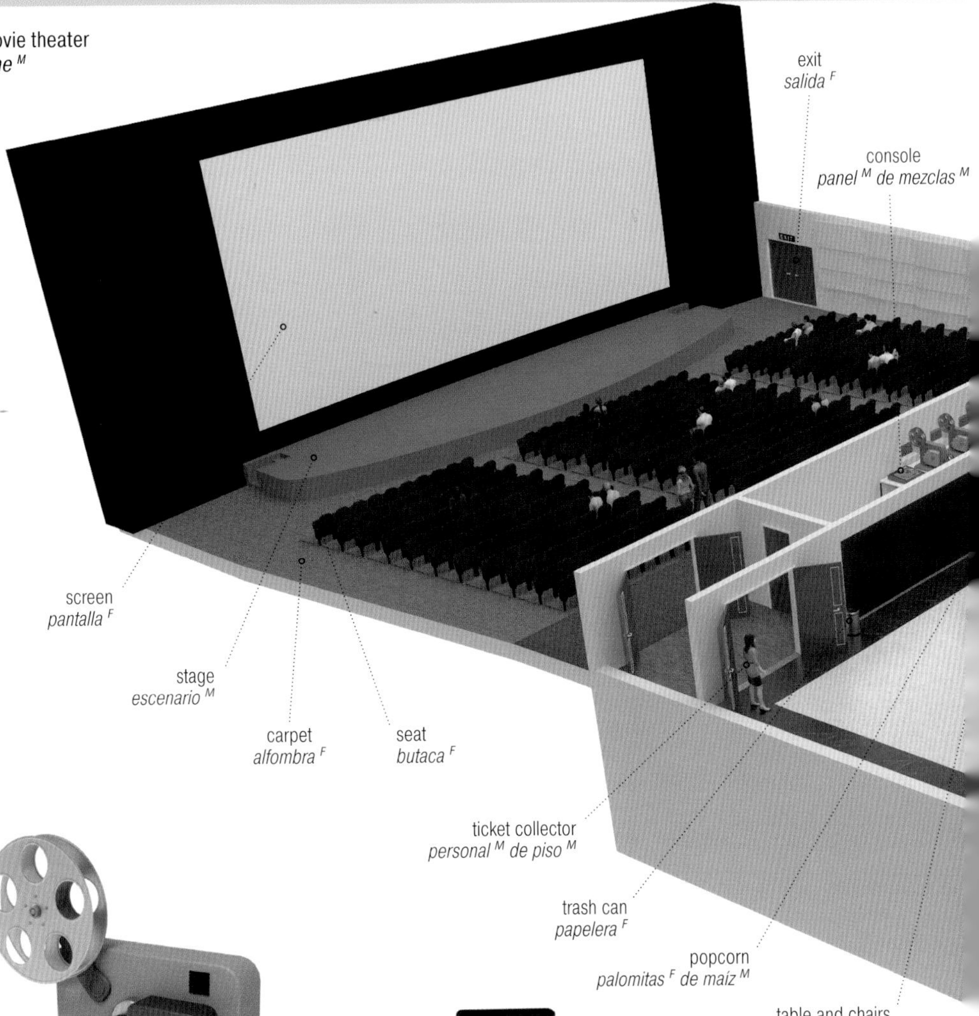

movie theater
cine M

exit
salida F

console
panel M *de mezclas* M

screen
pantalla F

stage
escenario M

carpet
alfombra F

seat
butaca F

ticket collector
personal M *de piso* M

trash can
papelera F

popcorn
palomitas F *de maíz* M

table and chairs
mesa F *con sillas* F

counter
mostrador M

film projector
proyector M *de cine* M

digital projector
proyector M *digital*

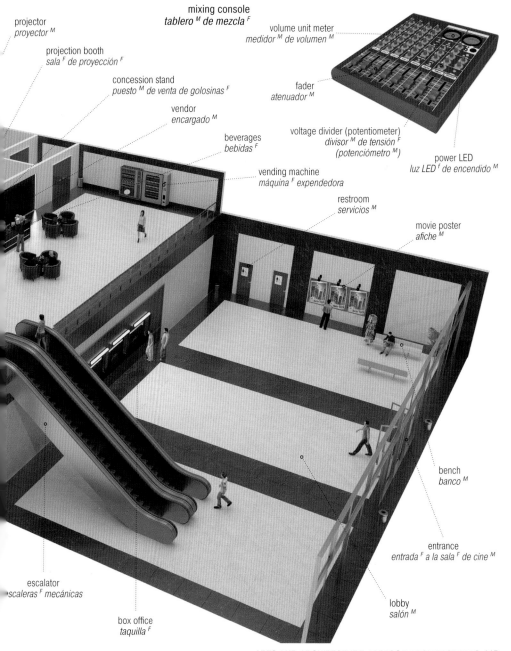

projector
proyector M

projection booth
sala F *de proyección* F

concession stand
puesto M *de venta de golosinas* F

vendor
encargado M

beverages
bebidas F

vending machine
máquina F *expendedora*

mixing console
tablero M *de mezcla* F

volume unit meter
medidor M *de volumen* M

fader
atenuador M

voltage divider (potentiometer)
divisor M *de tensión* F
(potenciómetro M*)*

power LED
luz LED f *de encendido* M

restroom
servicios M

movie poster
afiche M

bench
banco M

entrance
entrada F *a la sala* F *de cine* M

lobby
salón M

escalator
escaleras F *mecánicas*

box office
taquilla F

television show
programa M *de televisión* F

stage	desk	scenery	host	monitor
escena F	*mesa* F	*decorado* M	*presentador* M	*monitor* M

guest
invitado M

chair
silla F

electric guitar
guitarra F *eléctrica*

drum kit
batería F

microphone
micrófono M

television studio
estudio ᴹ de televisión ᶠ

scenery
decorado ᴹ

light
luz ᶠ

monitor
monitor ᴹ

truss
entramado ᴹ

host
presentador ᴹ

cable
cable ᴹ

microphone
micrófono ᴹ

cameraman
camarógrafo ᴹ

script
guión ᴹ

stage
escena ᶠ

guest
invitado ^M

singer
cantante ^M

musician
músico ^M

director
director ^M

camera
cámara ^F *de televisión* ^F

audience member
espectador ^M

stage
escenario M

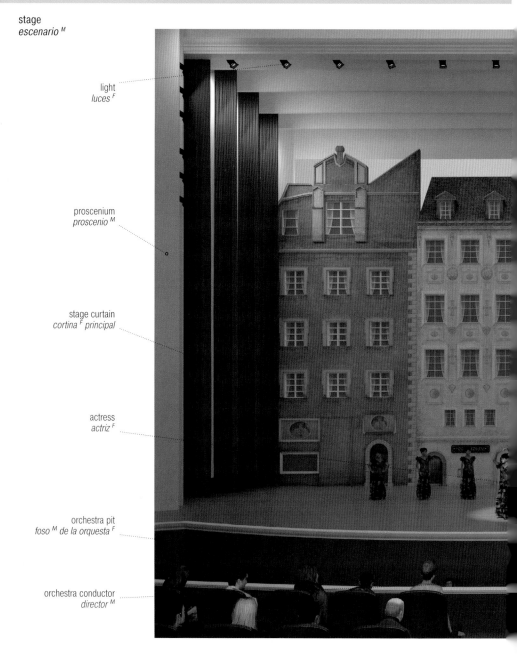

light
luces F

proscenium
proscenio M

stage curtain
cortina F *principal*

actress
actriz F

orchestra pit
foso M *de la orquesta* F

orchestra conductor
director M

beam
tela ᴹ

backdrop
telón ᴹ *de fondo* ᴹ

actor
actor ᴹ

stage
escenario ᴹ

audience
público ᴹ

theater
teatro ^M

mezzanine
palco ^M *de honor* ^M

balcony
palco ^M

seat
butaca ^F

orchestra
platea ^F

opera glasses
binoculares ᴹ *de ópera* ᶠ

lens
lente ᶠ

focusing wheel
perilla ᶠ *de enfoque* ᴹ

body
cuerpo ᴹ

handle
mango ᴹ

flamenco dancer
bailarina ᶠ *de flamenco* ᴹ

ruffled sleeve
mangas ᶠ *con volantes* ᴹ

ruffled skirt
falda ᶠ *con faralaos* ᴹ

Indian dancer
bailarina ᶠ *india*

maang tikka
accesorio ᴹ *para el pelo* ᴹ *maang tikka*

bindi
bindi ᴹ

nose ring
pendiente ᴹ *de nariz* ᶠ *nath*

actor
actor ᴹ

costume
traje ᴹ

panja bracelet
pulsera ᶠ *panja*

choli
blusa ᶠ *choli*

bangle
brazaletes ᴹ

dupatta
chal ᴹ *dupatta*

lehenga
falda ᶠ *lehenga*

first position of the arms
primera posición F *de brazos* M

leotard
maillot M

tights
mallas F

ballet shoes
zapatillas F *de ballet* M

arabesque on pointe
arabesco M *en punta* F

jeté
jeté F

front attitude on pointe
attitude F *hacia adelante en punta* F

grand jeté
grand jeté F

second position of the arms
segunda posición F *de los brazos* M

third position of the arms
tercera posición F *de los brazos* M

fourth position of the arms
cuarta posición ᶠ de los brazos ᴹ

backward attitude on pointe
attitude ᶠ hacia atrás en punta ᶠ

fifth position of the arms
quinta posición ᶠ de los brazos ᴹ

retiré on pointe
retiré ᴹ en punta ᶠ

pas de bourrée
pas ᴹ *de bourrée* ᶠ

arabesque
arabesque ᴹ

ballet moves
pasos ᴹ *de ballet* ᴹ

back bend
cambré ᴹ / *cuerpo* ᴹ *inclinado hacia atrás*

entrechat
entrechat ᴹ

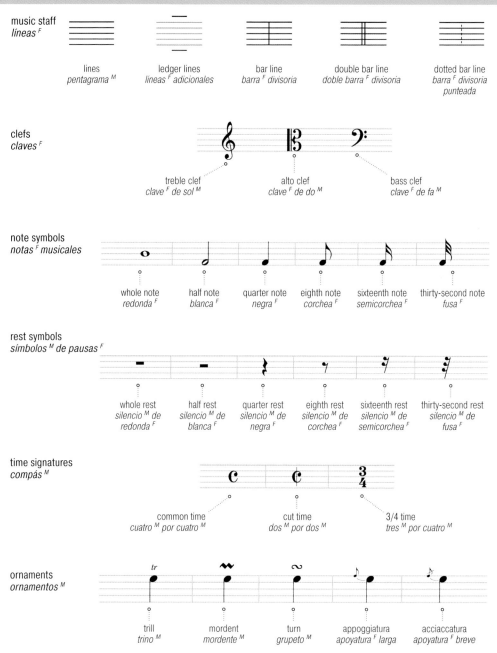

music staff
líneas ^F

lines
pentagrama ^M

ledger lines
líneas ^F *adicionales*

bar line
barra ^F *divisoria*

double bar line
doble barra ^F *divisoria*

dotted bar line
barra ^F *divisoria punteada*

clefs
claves ^F

treble clef
clave ^F *de sol* ^M

alto clef
clave ^F *de do* ^M

bass clef
clave ^F *de fa* ^M

note symbols
notas ^F *musicales*

whole note
redonda ^F

half note
blanca ^F

quarter note
negra ^F

eighth note
corchea ^F

sixteenth note
semicorchea ^F

thirty-second note
fusa ^F

rest symbols
símbolos ^M *de pausas* ^F

whole rest
silencio ^M *de redonda* ^F

half rest
silencio ^M *de blanca* ^F

quarter rest
silencio ^M *de negra* ^F

eighth rest
silencio ^M *de corchea* ^F

sixteenth rest
silencio ^M *de semicorchea* ^F

thirty-second rest
silencio ^M *de fusa* ^F

time signatures
compás ^M

common time
cuatro ^M *por cuatro* ^M

cut time
dos ^M *por dos* ^M

3/4 time
tres ^M *por cuatro* ^M

ornaments
ornamentos ^M

trill
trino ^M

mordent
mordente ^M

turn
grupeto ^M

appoggiatura
apoyatura ^F *larga*

acciaccatura
apoyatura ^F *breve*

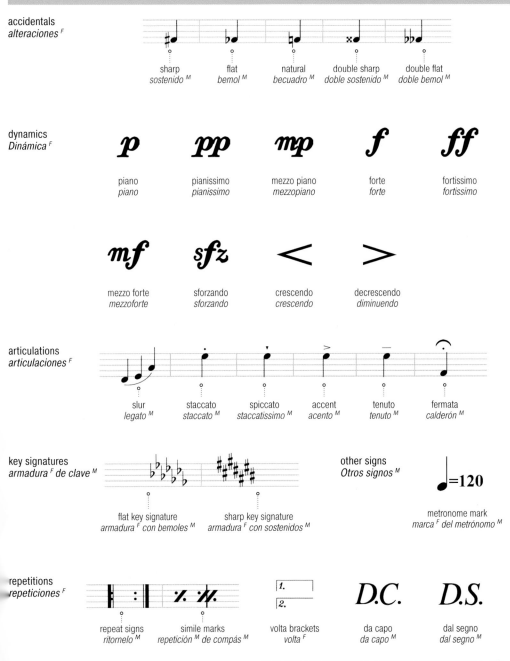

accidentals
alteraciones F

sharp	flat	natural	double sharp	double flat
sostenido M	*bemol* M	*becuadro* M	*doble sostenido* M	*doble bemol* M

dynamics
Dinámica F

piano	pianissimo	mezzo piano	forte	fortissimo
piano	*pianissimo*	*mezzopiano*	*forte*	*fortissimo*

mezzo forte	sforzando	crescendo	decrescendo
mezzoforte	*sforzando*	*crescendo*	*diminuendo*

articulations
articulaciones F

slur	staccato	spiccato	accent	tenuto	fermata
legato M	*staccato* M	*staccatissimo* M	*acento* M	*tenuto* M	*calderón* M

key signatures
armadura F *de clave* M

flat key signature	sharp key signature
armadura F *con bemoles* M	*armadura* F *con sostenidos* M

other signs
Otros signos M

♩=120

metronome mark
marca F *del metrónomo* M

repetitions
repeticiones F

repeat signs	simile marks	volta brackets	da capo	dal segno
ritornelo M	*repetición* M *de compás* M	*volta* F	*da capo* M	*dal segno* M

upright piano
piano M vertical

cabinet
caja F

upper panel
panel M superior

lid
cubierta F

music stand
atril M

fallboard
tapa F

key
teclado M

keybed
soporte M del teclado M

leg
pata F

keyblock
bloque M del teclado M

lower panel
panel M inferior

synthesizer
sintetizador M

cursor buttons
botones M del cursor F

soft pedal
pedal M de sordina F

damper pedal
pedal M de resonancia F

toe block
traviesa F

muffler pedal
pedal M de amortiguación F

liquid-crystal display (LCD)
pantalla F de cristal M líquido

dial
dial M de datos M

system buttons
panel M de control M

sequencer buttons
control M de entrada F de datos M

pitch switch
rueda F de modulación F

function buttons
botones M de función F y subfunción F

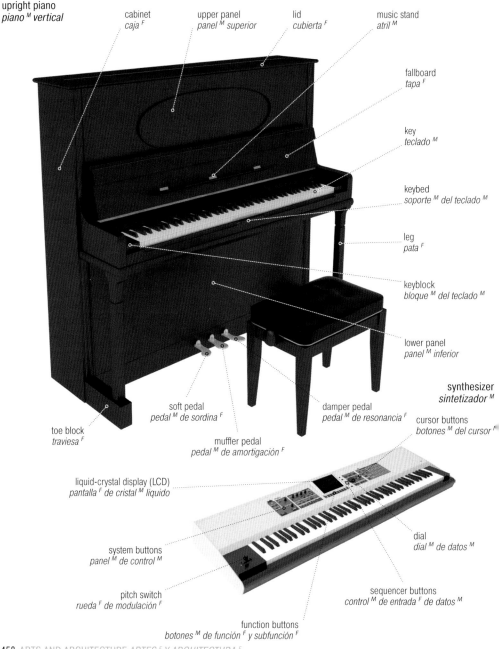

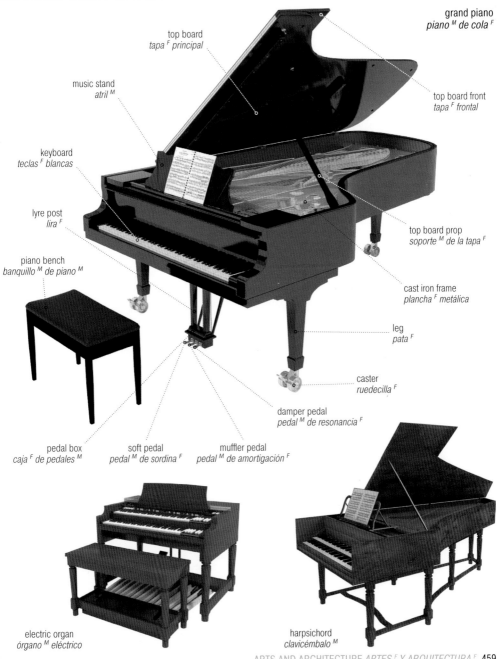

grand piano
piano M *de cola* F

top board
tapa F *principal*

music stand
atril M

top board front
tapa F *frontal*

keyboard
teclas F *blancas*

lyre post
lira F

top board prop
soporte M *de la tapa* F

piano bench
banquillo M *de piano* M

cast iron frame
plancha F *metálica*

leg
pata F

caster
ruedecilla F

damper pedal
pedal M *de resonancia* F

pedal box
caja F *de pedales* M

soft pedal
pedal M *de sordina* F

muffler pedal
pedal M *de amortigación* F

electric organ
órgano M *eléctrico*

harpsichord
clavicémbalo M

drum kit
batería [F]

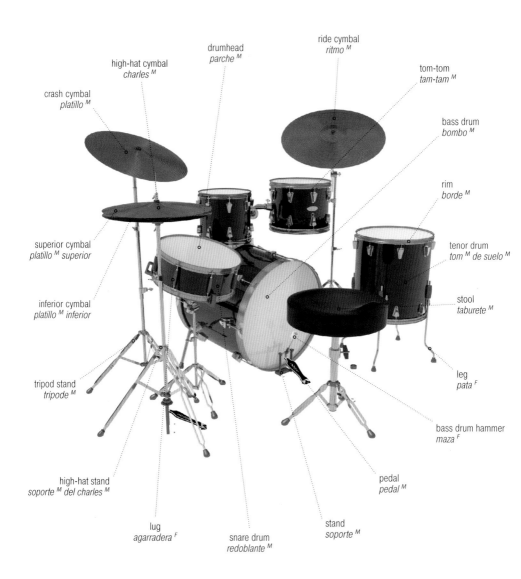

crash cymbal
platillo [M]

high-hat cymbal
charles [M]

drumhead
parche [M]

ride cymbal
ritmo [M]

tom-tom
tam-tam [M]

bass drum
bombo [M]

rim
borde [M]

superior cymbal
platillo [M] *superior*

tenor drum
tom [M] *de suelo* [M]

inferior cymbal
platillo [M] *inferior*

stool
taburete [M]

tripod stand
tripode [M]

leg
pata [F]

bass drum hammer
maza [F]

high-hat stand
soporte [M] *del charles* [M]

pedal
pedal [M]

lug
agarradera [F]

snare drum
redoblante [M]

stand
soporte [M]

cymbals
platillos M

triangle
triángulo M

tambourine
pandereta F

gong
gong M

drumsticks
baquetas F

sleigh bells
cascabeles M

wire brush
cepillos M de batería F

castanets
castañuelas F

tubular bells
campanas F tubulares

xylophone
xilófono M

vibraphone
vibráfono M

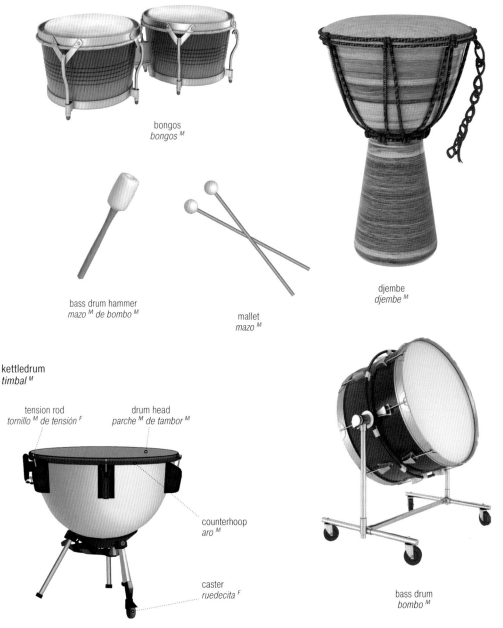

bongos
bongos M

djembe
djembe M

bass drum hammer
mazo M *de bombo* M

mallet
mazo M

kettledrum
timbal M

tension rod
tornillo M *de tensión* F

drum head
parche M *de tambor* M

counterhoop
aro M

caster
ruedecita F

bass drum
bombo M

Brass instruments
Instrumentos M _de metal_ M

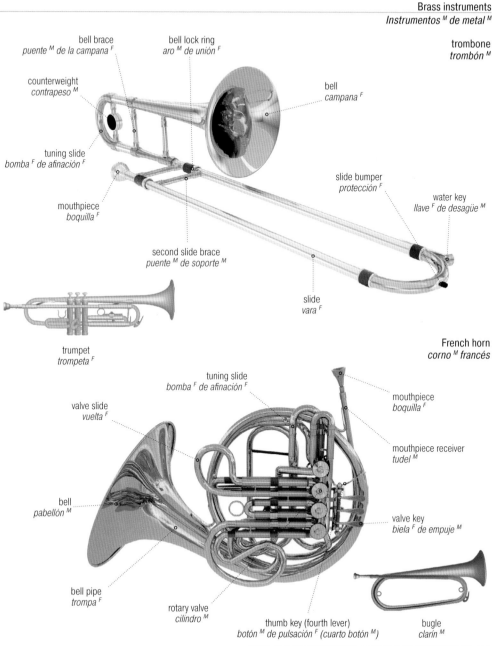

bell brace
puente M _de la campana_ F

bell lock ring
aro M _de unión_ F

trombone
trombón M

counterweight
contrapeso M

bell
campana F

tuning slide
bomba F _de afinación_ F

slide bumper
protección F

water key
llave F _de desagüe_ M

mouthpiece
boquilla F

second slide brace
puente M _de soporte_ M

slide
vara F

trumpet
trompeta F

French horn
corno M _francés_

tuning slide
bomba F _de afinación_ F

mouthpiece
boquilla F

valve slide
vuelta F

mouthpiece receiver
tudel M

bell
pabellón M

valve key
biela F _de empuje_ M

bell pipe
trompa F

rotary valve
cilindro M

thumb key (fourth lever)
botón M _de pulsación_ F _(cuarto botón_ M)

bugle
clarín M

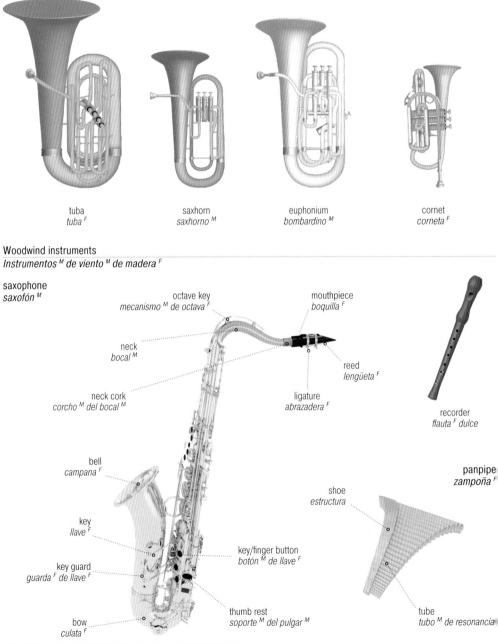

tuba
tuba ^F

saxhorn
saxhorno ^M

euphonium
bombardino ^M

cornet
corneta ^F

Woodwind instruments
Instrumentos ^M *de viento* ^M *de madera* ^F

saxophone
saxofón ^M

octave key
mecanismo ^M *de octava* ^F

mouthpiece
boquilla ^F

neck
bocal ^M

reed
lengüeta ^F

neck cork
corcho ^M *del bocal* ^M

ligature
abrazadera ^F

recorder
flauta ^F *dulce*

bell
campana ^F

panpipe
zampoña ^F

shoe
estructura

key
llave ^F

key/finger button
botón ^M *de llave* ^F

key guard
guarda ^F *de llave* ^F

thumb rest
soporte ^M *del pulgar* ^M

bow
culata ^F

tube
tubo ^M *de resonancia*

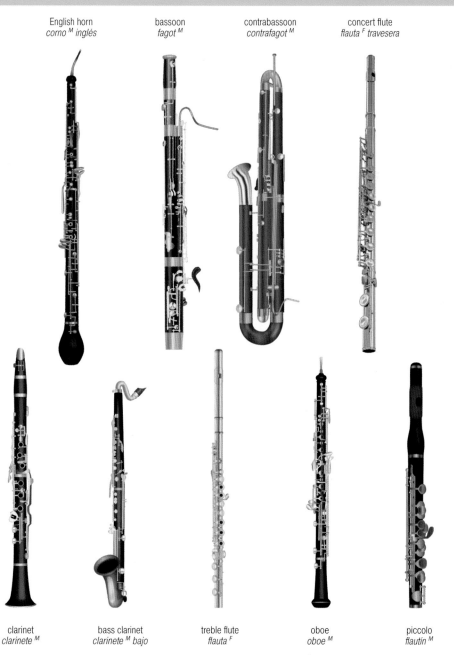

English horn
corno ^M *inglés*

bassoon
fagot ^M

contrabassoon
contrafagot ^M

concert flute
flauta ^F *travesera*

clarinet
clarinete ^M

bass clarinet
clarinete ^M *bajo*

treble flute
flauta ^F

oboe
oboe ^M

piccolo
flautín ^M

cello
violoncello [M]

violin and bow
violín [M] *y arco* [M]

head
cabeza [F]

tip
punta [F]

scroll
voluta [F]

nut
cejilla [F]

hair
cerdas [F]

pegbox
clavijero [M]

ribs
aro [M]

belly
vientre [M]

peg
clavija [F]

string
cuerda [F]

top bout
cuerpo [M] *inferior*

purfling
filete [M]

stick
vara [F]

fingerboard
diapasón [M]

handle
talón [M]

waist
escotadura [F]

frog
nuez [F]

C string
cuerda [F] *de do* [M]

G string
cuerda [F] *de sol* [M]

screw
tornillo [M]

D string
cuerda [F] *de re* [M]

chin rest
mentonera [F]

bridge
puente [M]

A string
cuerda [F] *de la* [M]

F hole
oído [M]

tailpiece
cordal [M]

bottom bout
cuerpo [M] *superior*

end spike
pica [F]

tailpiece
afinador [M]

bow
arco [M]

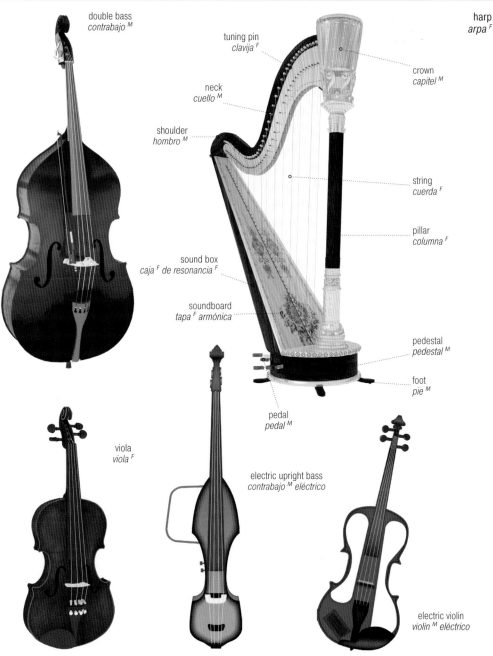

double bass
contrabajo M

harp
arpa F

tuning pin
clavija F

crown
capitel M

neck
cuello M

shoulder
hombro M

string
cuerda F

pillar
columna F

sound box
caja F de resonancia F

soundboard
tapa F armónica

pedestal
pedestal M

foot
pie M

pedal
pedal M

viola
viola F

electric upright bass
contrabajo M eléctrico

electric violin
violín M eléctrico

bass guitar
bajo M *eléctrico*

electric guitar
guitarra F *eléctrica*

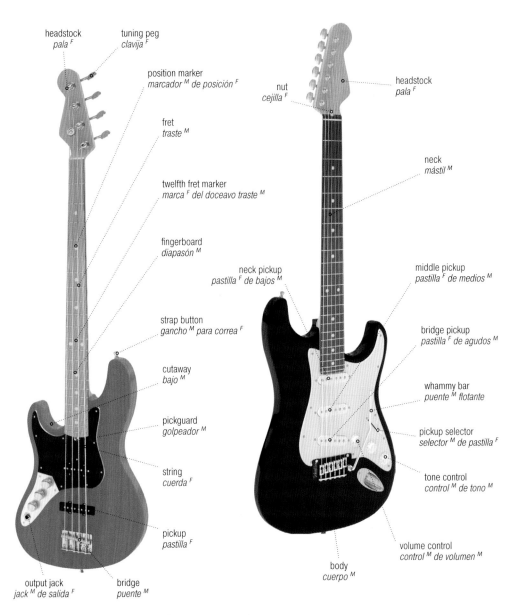

headstock
pala F

tuning peg
clavija F

position marker
marcador M *de posición* F

nut
cejilla F

headstock
pala F

fret
traste M

neck
mástil M

twelfth fret marker
marca F *del doceavo traste* M

fingerboard
diapasón M

neck pickup
pastilla F *de bajos* M

middle pickup
pastilla F *de medios* M

strap button
gancho M *para correa* F

bridge pickup
pastilla F *de agudos* M

cutaway
bajo M

whammy bar
puente M *flotante*

pickguard
golpeador M

pickup selector
selector M *de pastilla* F

string
cuerda F

tone control
control M *de tono* M

pickup
pastilla F

volume control
control M *de volumen* M

output jack
jack M *de salida* F

bridge
puente M

body
cuerpo M

acoustic guitar
guitarra F *acústica*

peg
clavija F

headstock
clavijero M

nut
cejilla F

fret
traste M

neck
mástil M *y diapasón* M

heel
cuello M

ribs
aro M

rosette
roseta F

distortion pedal
pedal M *de distorsión* F

sound hole
boca F

semi-acoustic guitar
guitarra F *semi-acústica*

purfling
ribete M

string
cuerda F

bridge
montura F

soundboard
tapa F *armónica*

amplifier
amplificador M *de guitarra* F

guitar case
estuche M *de guitarra* F

concertina
concertina ^F

harmonium
armonio ^M

melodica
melódica ^F

harmonica
armónica ^F

accordion
acordeón ^M

bayan
bayán ^M

Australian instruments
Instrumentos M *australianos*

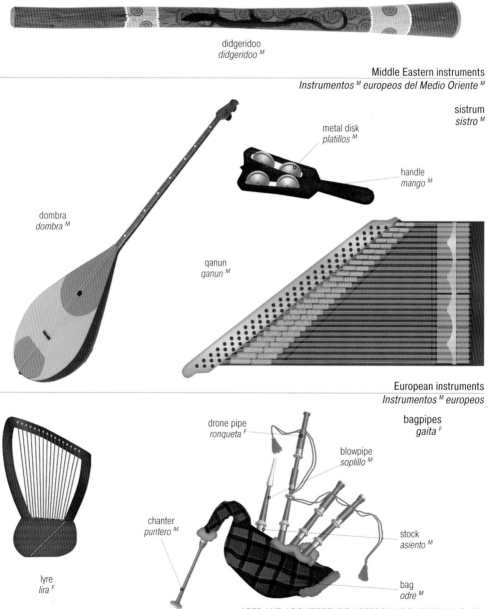

didgeridoo
didgeridoo M

Middle Eastern instruments
Instrumentos M *europeos del Medio Oriente* M

sistrum
sistro M

metal disk
platillos M

handle
mango M

dombra
dombra M

qanun
qanun M

European instruments
Instrumentos M *europeos*

drone pipe
ronqueta F

bagpipes
gaita F

blowpipe
soplillo M

chanter
puntero M

stock
asiento M

lyre
lira F

bag
odre M

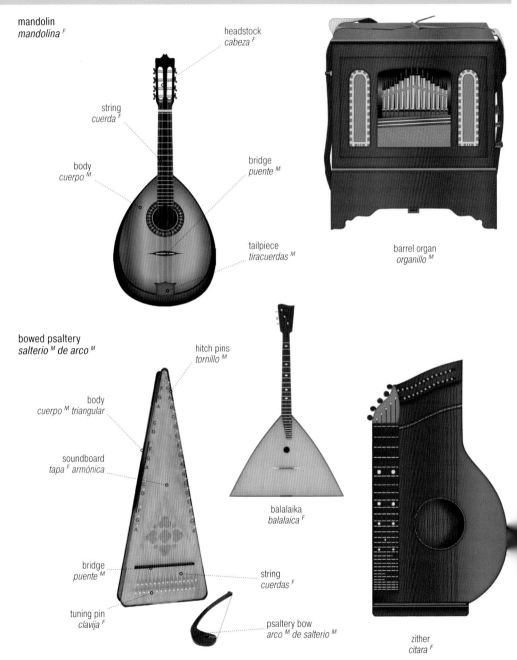

mandolin
mandolina F

headstock
cabeza F

string
cuerda F

body
cuerpo M

bridge
puente M

tailpiece
tiracuerdas M

barrel organ
organillo M

bowed psaltery
salterio M *de arco* M

hitch pins
tornillo M

body
cuerpo M *triangular*

soundboard
tapa F *armónica*

balalaika
balalaica F

bridge
puente M

string
cuerdas F

tuning pin
clavija F

psaltery bow
arco M *de salterio* M

zither
citara F

African instruments
Instrumentos ^M *africanos*

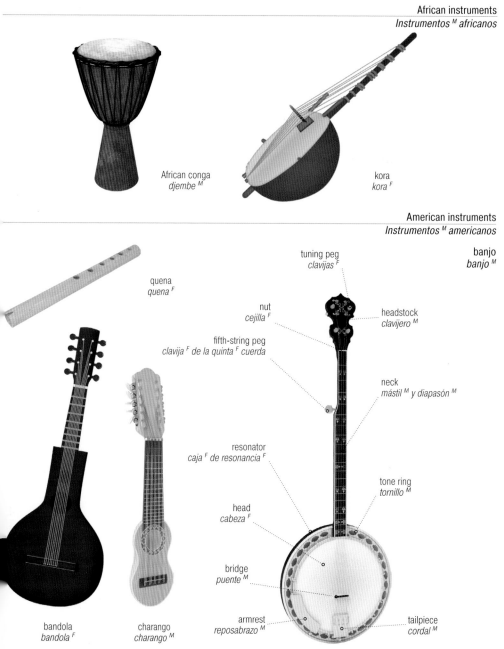

African conga
djembe ^M

kora
kora ^F

American instruments
Instrumentos ^M *americanos*

banjo
banjo ^M

tuning peg
clavijas ^F

quena
quena ^F

nut
cejilla ^F

headstock
clavijero ^M

fifth-string peg
clavija ^F *de la quinta* ^F *cuerda*

neck
mástil ^M *y diapasón* ^M

resonator
caja ^F *de resonancia* ^F

tone ring
tornillo ^M

head
cabeza ^F

bridge
puente ^M

bandola
bandola ^F

charango
charango ^M

armrest
reposabrazo ^M

tailpiece
cordal ^M

Asian instruments
Instrumentos M *asiáticos*

guzheng
guzheng M

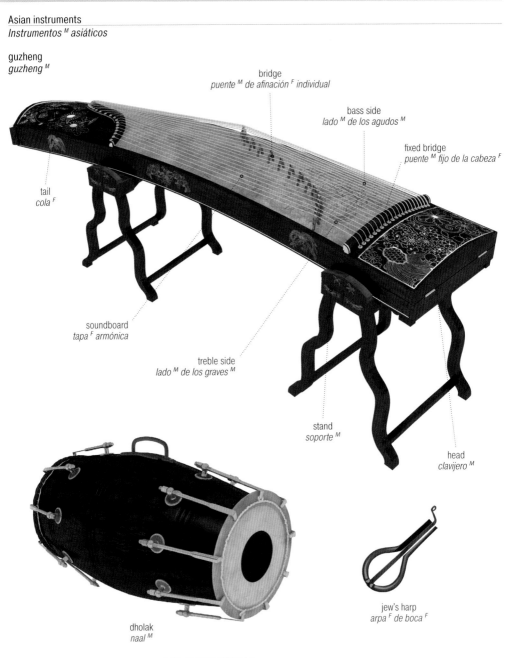

bridge
puente M *de afinación* F *individual*

bass side
lado M *de los agudos* M

fixed bridge
puente M *fijo de la cabeza* F

tail
cola F

soundboard
tapa F *armónica*

treble side
lado M *de los graves* M

stand
soporte M

head
clavijero M

dholak
naal M

jew's harp
arpa F *de boca* F

guqin
qugin ^M

shehnai
shenai ^M

double reed
lengüeta ^F *doble*

staple
cabezal ^M

ivory needle
aguja ^F *de marfil* ^M

finger hole
agujero ^M

bell
campana ^F

huqin
huqin ^M

pipa
pipa ^F

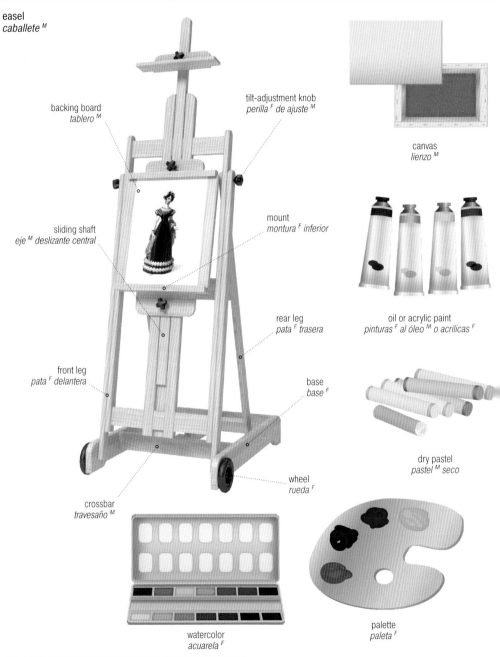

easel
caballete M

backing board
tablero M

tilt-adjustment knob
perilla F *de ajuste* M

canvas
lienzo M

sliding shaft
eje M *deslizante central*

mount
montura F *inferior*

rear leg
pata F *trasera*

oil or acrylic paint
pinturas F *al óleo* M *o acrílicas* F

front leg
pata F *delantera*

base
base F

dry pastel
pastel M *seco*

crossbar
travesaño M

wheel
rueda F

watercolor
acuarela F

palette
paleta F

airbrush
aerógrafo ᴹ

wax crayon
lápiz ᴹ de cera ᶠ

brush
pincel ᴹ

flat brush
pincel ᴹ plano

gouache
gouache ᴹ

turpentine
trementina ᶠ

colored pencil
lápices ᴹ de colorear

oil pastel
pastel ᴹ al aceite ᴹ

Mosaic work
Trabajo ᴹ de mosaico ᴹ

glue
cola ᶠ

tessera
piedra ᶠ de mosaico ᴹ

mosaic
mosaico ᴹ

Embroidery
Bordado ^M

satin stitch
punto ^M *de satén* ^M

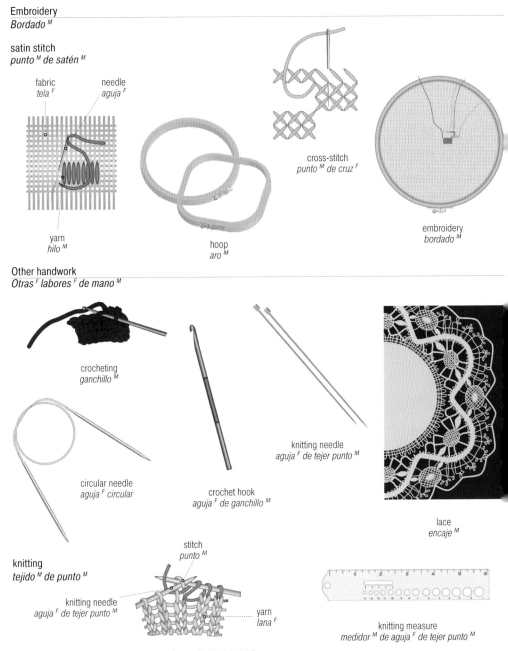

fabric
tela ^F

needle
aguja ^F

cross-stitch
punto ^M *de cruz* ^F

embroidery
bordado ^M

yarn
hilo ^M

hoop
aro ^M

Other handwork
Otras ^F *labores* ^F *de mano* ^M

crocheting
ganchillo ^M

knitting needle
aguja ^F *de tejer punto* ^M

circular needle
aguja ^F *circular*

crochet hook
aguja ^F *de ganchillo* ^M

lace
encaje ^M

knitting
tejido ^M *de punto* ^M

stitch
punto ^M

knitting needle
aguja ^F *de tejer punto* ^M

yarn
lana ^F

knitting measure
medidor ^M *de aguja* ^F *de tejer punto* ^M

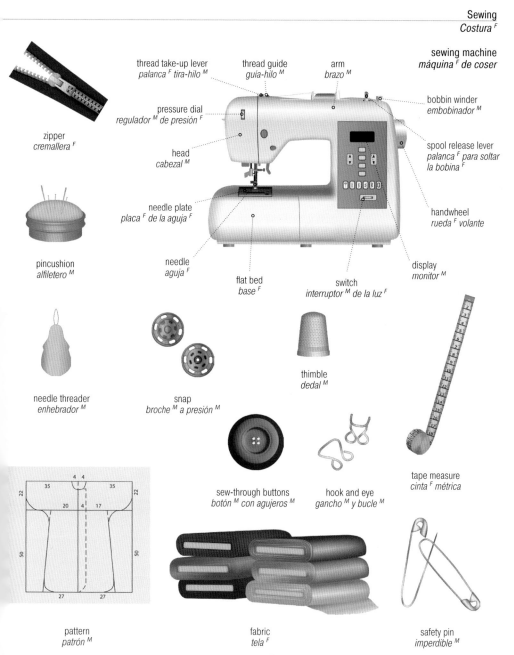

Sewing
Costura ^F

sewing machine
máquina ^F *de coser*

thread take-up lever
palanca ^F *tira-hilo* ^M

thread guide
guía-hilo ^M

arm
brazo ^M

bobbin winder
embobinador ^M

pressure dial
regulador ^M *de presión* ^F

zipper
cremallera ^F

head
cabezal ^M

spool release lever
palanca ^F *para soltar*
la bobina ^F

handwheel
rueda ^F *volante*

needle plate
placa ^F *de la aguja* ^F

pincushion
alfiletero ^M

needle
aguja ^F

flat bed
base ^F

switch
interruptor ^M *de la luz* ^F

display
monitor ^M

thimble
dedal ^M

needle threader
enhebrador ^M

snap
broche ^M *a presión* ^M

sew-through buttons
botón ^M *con agujeros* ^M

hook and eye
gancho ^M *y bucle* ^M

tape measure
cinta ^F *métrica*

pattern
patrón ^M

fabric
tela ^F

safety pin
imperdible ^M

cathedral
catedral F

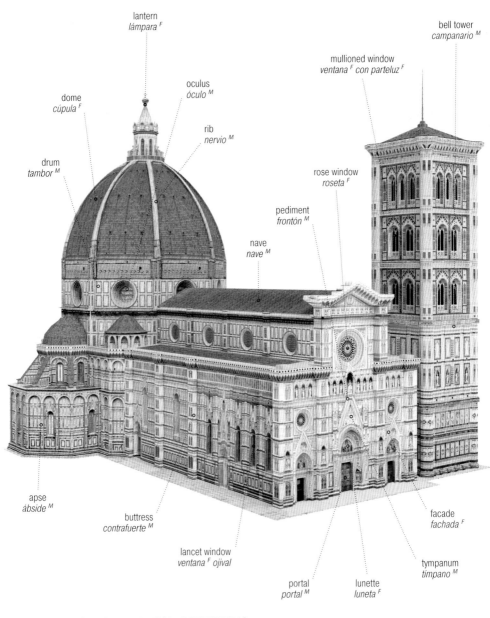

lantern
lámpara F

bell tower
campanario M

mullioned window
ventana F *con parteluz* F

oculus
óculo M

dome
cúpula F

rib
nervio M

drum
tambor M

rose window
roseta F

pediment
frontón M

nave
nave M

apse
ábside M

buttress
contrafuerte M

facade
fachada F

lancet window
ventana F *ojival*

tympanum
tímpano M

portal
portal M

lunette
luneta F

mosque
mezquita ^F

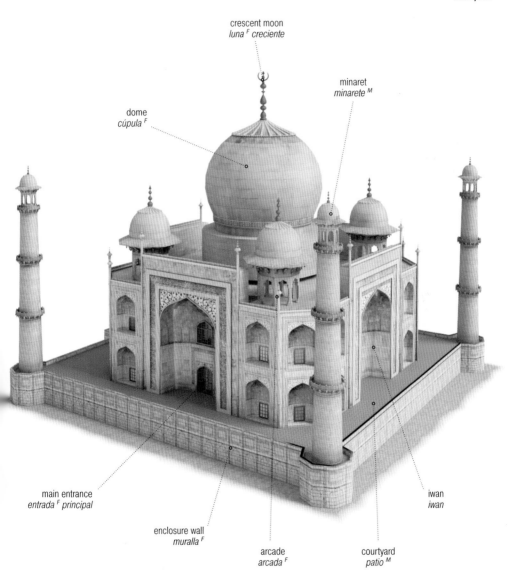

crescent moon
luna ^F *creciente*

minaret
minarete ^M

dome
cúpula ^F

main entrance
entrada ^F *principal*

iwan
iwan

enclosure wall
muralla ^F

arcade
arcada ^F

courtyard
patio ^M

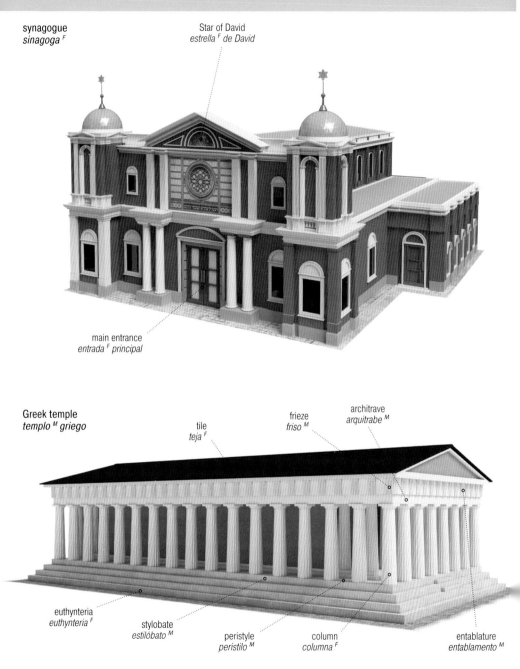

synagogue
sinagoga F

Star of David
estrella F *de David*

main entrance
entrada F *principal*

Greek temple
templo M *griego*

tile
teja F

frieze
friso M

architrave
arquitrabe M

euthynteria
euthynteria F

stylobate
estilóbato M

peristyle
peristilo M

column
columna F

entablature
entablamento M

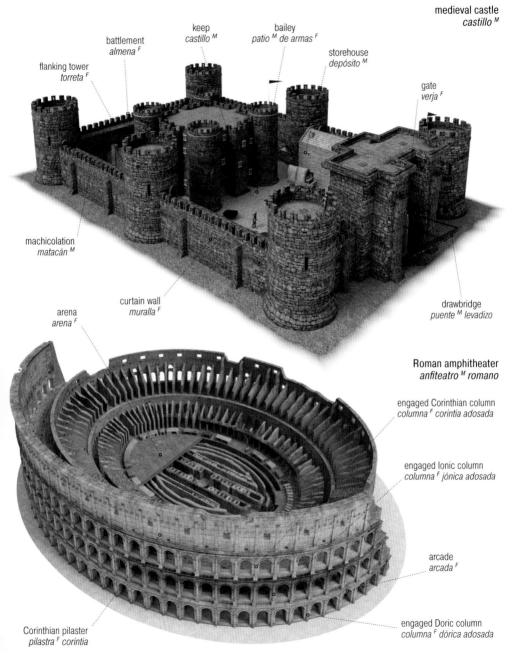

medieval castle
castillo M

flanking tower
torreta F

battlement
almena F

keep
castillo M

bailey
patio M *de armas* F

storehouse
depósito M

gate
verja F

machicolation
matacán M

curtain wall
muralla F

drawbridge
puente M *levadizo*

arena
arena F

Roman amphitheater
anfiteatro M *romano*

engaged Corinthian column
columna F *corintia adosada*

engaged Ionic column
columna F *jónica adosada*

arcade
arcada F

Corinthian pilaster
pilastra F *corintia*

engaged Doric column
columna F *dórica adosada*

SPORTS

DEPORTES

soccer field
campo M *de futbol* M

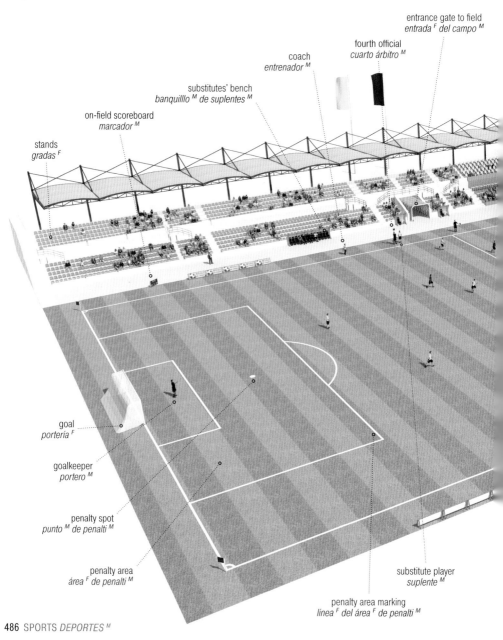

entrance gate to field
entrada F *del campo* M

fourth official
cuarto árbitro M

coach
entrenador M

substitutes' bench
banquilllo M *de suplentes* M

on-field scoreboard
marcador M

stands
gradas F

goal
portería F

goalkeeper
portero M

penalty spot
punto M *de penalti* M

penalty area
área F *de penalti* M

substitute player
suplente M

penalty area marking
línea F *del área* F *de penalti* M

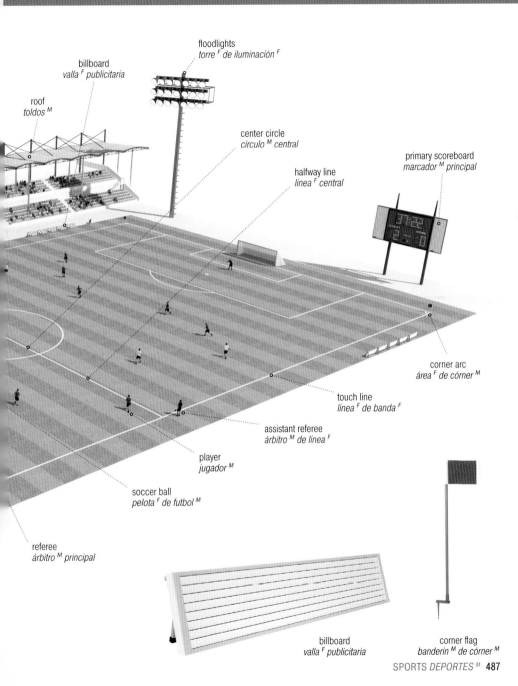

floodlights
torre ᶠ de iluminación ᶠ

billboard
valla ᶠ publicitaria

roof
toldos ᴹ

center circle
círculo ᴹ central

primary scoreboard
marcador ᴹ principal

halfway line
línea ᶠ central

corner arc
área ᶠ de córner ᴹ

touch line
línea ᶠ de banda ᶠ

assistant referee
árbitro ᴹ de línea ᶠ

player
jugador ᴹ

soccer ball
pelota ᶠ de futbol ᴹ

referee
árbitro ᴹ principal

billboard
valla ᶠ publicitaria

corner flag
banderín ᴹ de córner ᴹ

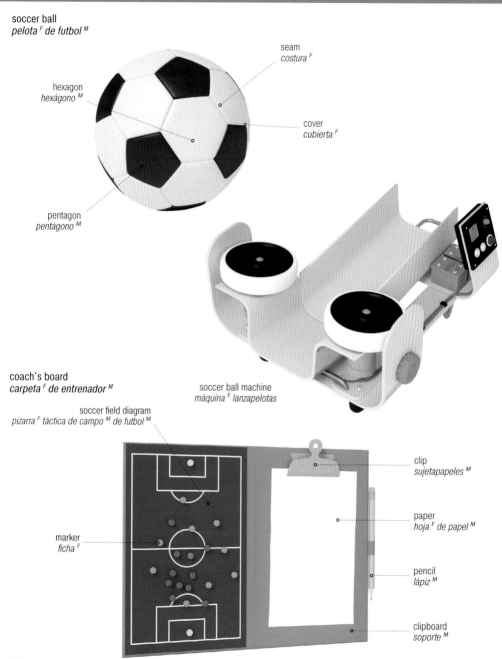

soccer ball
pelota ^F *de futbol* ^M

seam
costura ^F

hexagon
hexágono ^M

cover
cubierta ^F

pentagon
pentágono ^M

coach's board
carpeta ^F *de entrenador* ^M

soccer ball machine
máquina ^F *lanzapelotas*

soccer field diagram
pizarra ^F *táctica de campo* ^M *de futbol* ^M

clip
sujetapapeles ^M

paper
hoja ^F *de papel* ^M

marker
ficha ^F

pencil
lápiz ^M

clipboard
soporte ^M

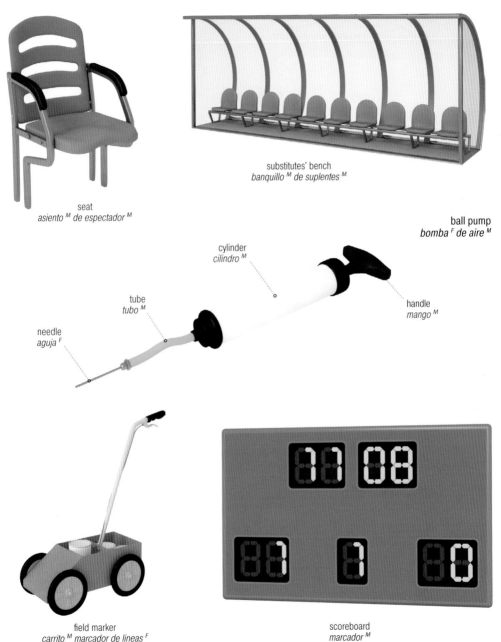

seat
asiento ^M *de espectador* ^M

substitutes' bench
banquillo ^M *de suplentes* ^M

ball pump
bomba ^F *de aire* ^M

cylinder
cilindro ^M

tube
tubo ^M

needle
aguja ^F

handle
mango ^M

field marker
carrito ^M *marcador de líneas* ^F

scoreboard
marcador ^M

Referee's equipment
Equipo M *del árbitro* M

referee's shelter
caseta F *de árbitro* M

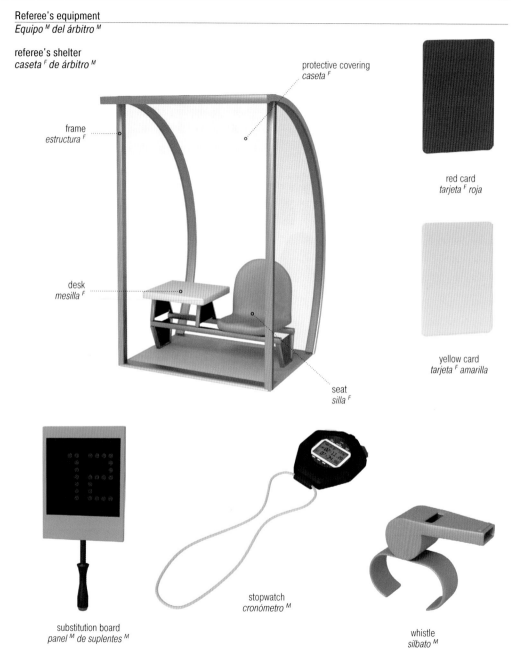

frame
estructura F

protective covering
caseta F

desk
mesilla F

seat
silla F

red card
tarjeta F *roja*

yellow card
tarjeta F *amarilla*

substitution board
panel M *de suplentes* M

stopwatch
cronómetro M

whistle
silbato M

Soccer player and equipment
Jugador ᴹ y equipo ᴹ de futbol ᴹ

shin guard
espinilleras ᶠ

soccer player
jugador ᴹ de futbol ᴹ

jersey
camiseta ᶠ

shorts
pantalón ᴹ corto

goalkeeper's glove
guantes ᴹ de portero ᴹ

soccer cleats
zapatos ᴹ de futbol ᴹ

tongue
lengüeta ᶠ

lace
cordones ᴹ

stud
taco ᴹ

heel
talón ᴹ

toe
puntera ᴹ

American football field
campo ^M *de futbol* ^M *americano*

referee
árbitro ^M *principal*

team area
área ^F *de equipo* ^M

line judge
árbitro ^M *de línea* ^F

end zone
zona ^F *de anotación* ^F

billboard
valla ^F *publicitaria*

concession stand
punto ^M *de venta* ^F

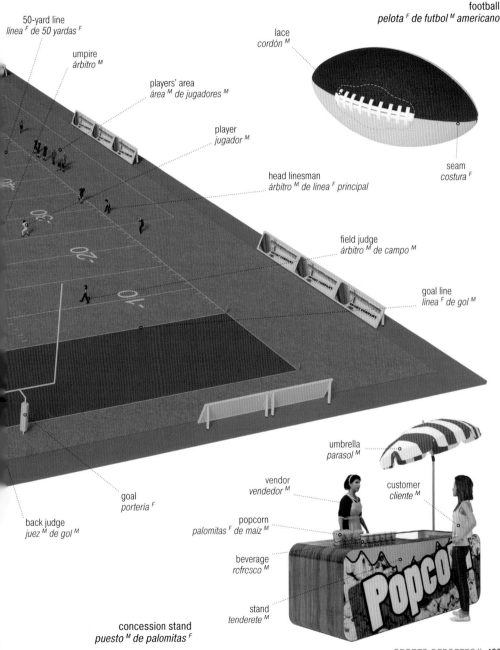

50-yard line
línea F *de 50 yardas* F

umpire
árbitro M

players' area
área M *de jugadores* M

player
jugador M

head linesman
árbitro M *de línea* F *principal*

field judge
árbitro M *de campo* M

goal line
línea F *de gol* M

goal
portería F

back judge
juez M *de gol* M

football
pelota F *de futbol* M *americano*

lace
cordón M

seam
costura F

umbrella
parasol M

vendor
vendedor M

customer
cliente M

popcorn
palomitas F *de maíz* M

beverage
rcfrcsco M

stand
tenderete M

concession stand
puesto M *de palomitas* F

basketball arena
cancha ᶠ *de baloncesto* ᴹ

three-point line
línea ᶠ *de tres puntos* ᴹ

restraining circle
círculo ᴹ *de restricción* ᶠ

players' bench
banquillo ᴹ *de jugadores* ᴹ

backboard
tablero ᴹ

basket
aro ᴹ

stands
gradas ᶠ

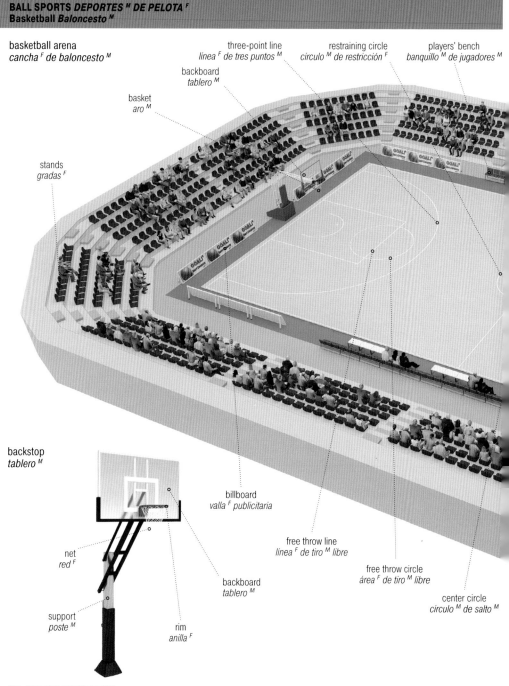

backstop
tablero ᴹ

billboard
valla ᶠ *publicitaria*

net
red ᶠ

free throw line
línea ᶠ *de tiro* ᴹ *libre*

free throw circle
área ᶠ *de tiro* ᴹ *libre*

backboard
tablero ᴹ

center circle
círculo ᴹ *de salto* ᴹ

support
poste ᴹ

rim
anilla ᶠ

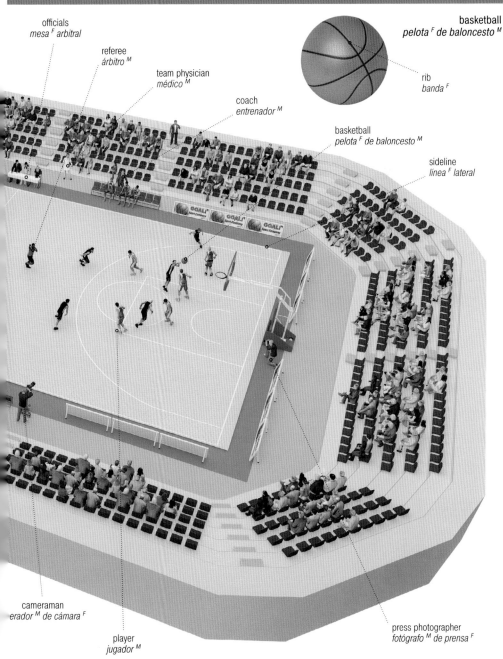

officials
mesa *F* *arbitral*

referee
árbitro *M*

team physician
médico *M*

coach
entrenador *M*

basketball
pelota *F* *de baloncesto* *M*

basketball
pelota *F* *de baloncesto* *M*

rib
banda *F*

sideline
línea *F* *lateral*

cameraman
erador *M* *de cámara* *F*

player
jugador *M*

press photographer
fotógrafo *M* *de prensa* *F*

Basketball moves
Movimientos ^M *de baloncesto* ^M

layup
tiro ^M *con una mano* ^F

hook shot
tiro ^M *libre*

holding
aguantar ^M *la pelota* ^F

dribbling
dribleo ^M

pump fake
tiro ^M *falso*

baseball glove: bottom view
guante ᴹ *de béisbol* ᴹ *: vista posterior*

thumb
sección ᶠ *del pulgar* ᴹ

palm
palma ᶠ

lace
cordón ᴹ

strap
correa ᶠ

finger
sección ᶠ *de los dedos* ᴹ

cross section of a baseball
corte ᴹ *de la pelota* ᴹ *de béisbol* ᴹ

yarn ball
bola ᶠ *de hilo* ᴹ

cork center
centro ᴹ *de corcho* ᴹ

baseball glove: top view
guante ᴹ *de beisbol: vista* ᶠ *superior*

stitches
costura ᶠ

cover
forro ᴹ

bat
bate ᴹ

baseball field (baseball diamond)
campo M *de béisbol* M

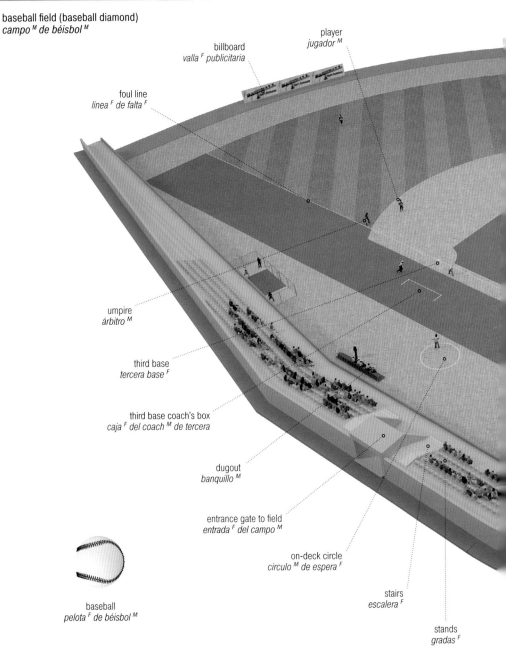

player
jugador M

billboard
valla F *publicitaria*

foul line
línea F *de falta* F

umpire
árbitro M

third base
tercera base F

third base coach's box
caja F *del coach* M *de tercera*

dugout
banquillo M

entrance gate to field
entrada F *del campo* M

on-deck circle
círculo M *de espera* F

stairs
escalera F

stands
gradas F

baseball
pelota F *de béisbol* M

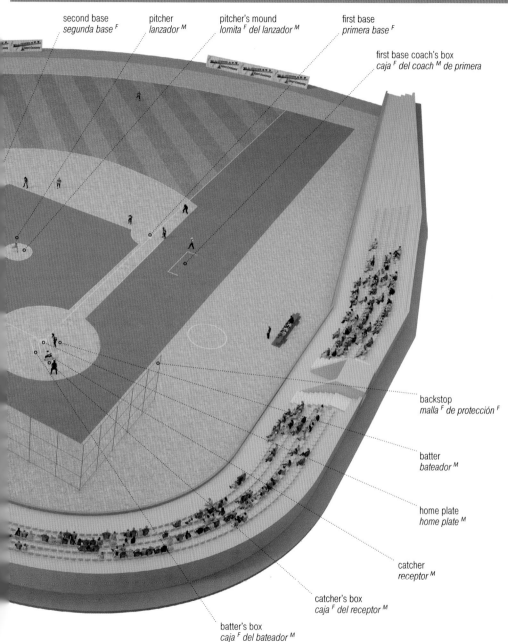

second base
segunda base ^F

pitcher
lanzador ^M

pitcher's mound
lomita ^F *del lanzador* ^M

first base
primera base ^F

first base coach's box
caja ^F *del coach* ^M *de primera*

backstop
malla ^F *de protección* ^F

batter
bateador ^M

home plate
home plate ^M

catcher
receptor ^M

catcher's box
caja ^F *del receptor* ^M

batter's box
caja ^F *del bateador* ^M

volleyball court
campo ^M *de vóleibol* ^M

center attacker
atacante ^M *central*

left attacker
atacante ^M *izquierdo*

right attacker
atacante ^M *derecho*

vertical side band
banda ^F *lateral de la red* ^F

right back
defensor ^M *derecho*

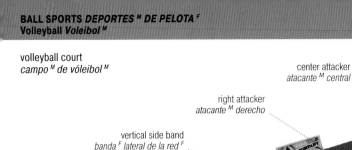

umpire
árbitro ^M

scorekeeper
marcador ^M

net
red ^F

post
poste ^M

coach
entrenador ^M

players' bench
banquillo ^M

attack zone
zona ^F *de ataque*

players' bench
banquillo ^M *de suplentes* ^M

volleyball
pelota ^F *de voleibol* ^M

back
respaldo ^M

towel
toalla ^F

water bottle
botella ^F *de agua* ^F

seat
asiento ^M

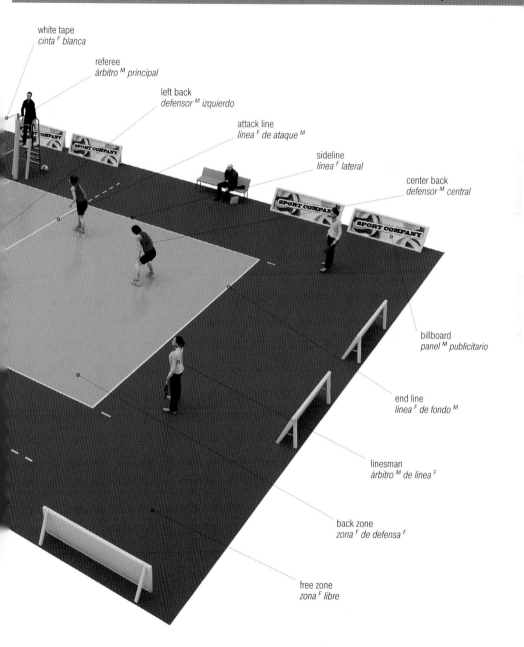

white tape
cinta ᶠ *blanca*

referee
árbitro ᴹ *principal*

left back
defensor ᴹ *izquierdo*

attack line
línea ᶠ *de ataque* ᴹ

sideline
línea ᶠ *lateral*

center back
defensor ᴹ *central*

billboard
panel ᴹ *publicitario*

end line
línea ᶠ *de fondo* ᴹ

linesman
árbitro ᴹ *de línea* ᶠ

back zone
zona ᶠ *de defensa* ᶠ

free zone
zona ᶠ *libre*

beach volleyball court
campo M *de voleibol* M *playero* M

umbrella
sombrilla F

players' chairs
sillas F *de los jugadores* M

cooler
nevera F

first referee
primer árbitro M

umpire's chair
silla F *del árbitro* M

stand
poste M

net
red F

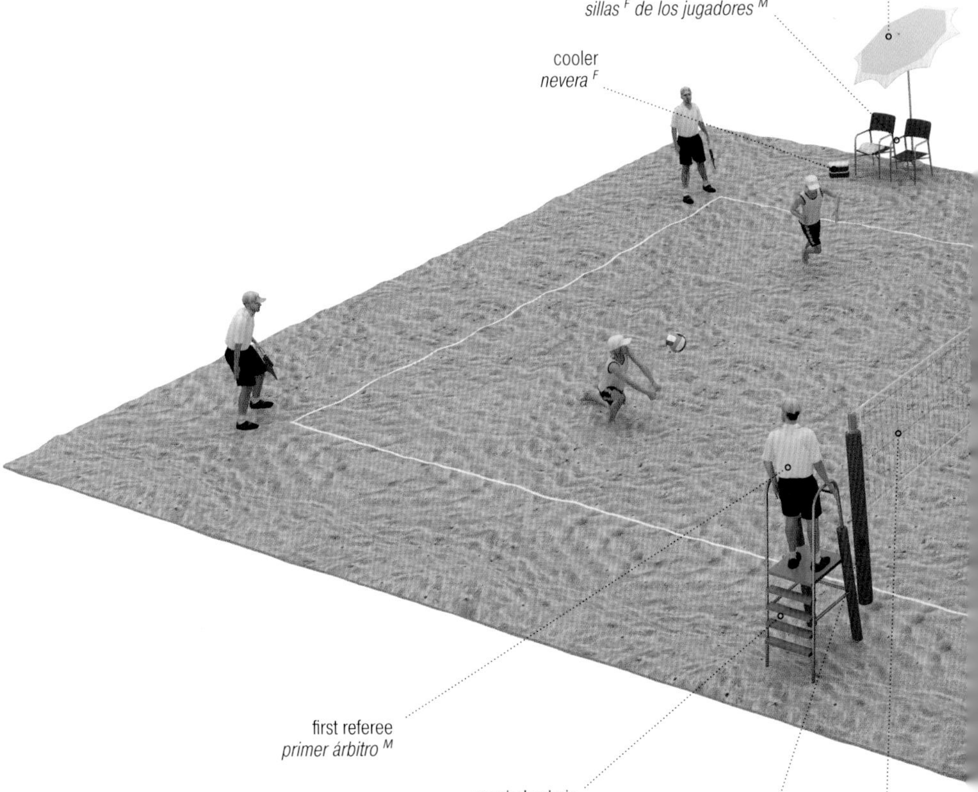

beach volleyball
balón M *de voleibol* M *playero* M

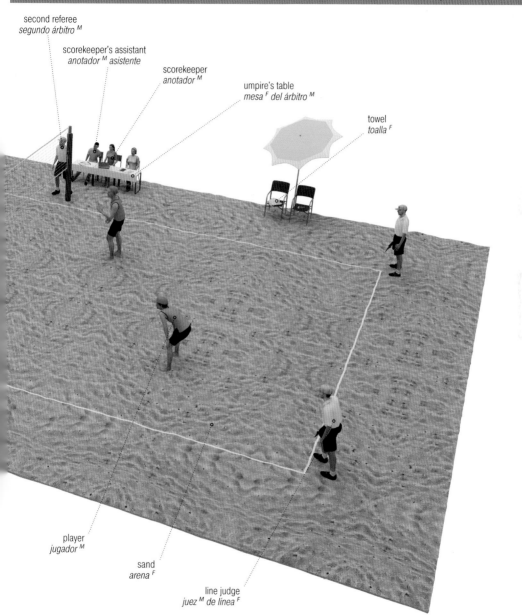

second referee
segundo árbitro *M*

scorekeeper's assistant
anotador *M* *asistente*

scorekeeper
anotador *M*

umpire's table
mesa *F* *del árbitro* *M*

towel
toalla *F*

player
jugador *M*

sand
arena *F*

line judge
juez *M* *de línea* *F*

badminton court
cancha [F] *de bádminton* [M]

umpire
árbitro [M] *principal*

towel
toalla [F]

water bottle
botella [F] *de agua* [F]

racket bag
funda [F] *de raquetas* [F]

long service line
línea [F] *de servicio* [M] *larga*

billboard
valla [F] *publicitaria*

center line
línea [F] *central*

doubles sideline
línea [F] *lateral*

short service line
línea [F] *de servicio* [M] *corto*

singles sideline
línea [F] *lateral de individuales* [M]

back boundary line
línea [F] *de fondo* [M]

linesman
árbitro [M] *de línea* [F]

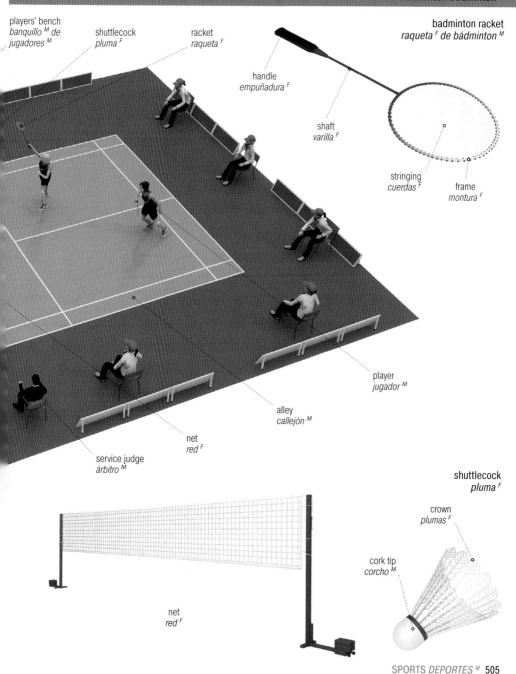

players' bench
banquillo M *de jugadores* M

shuttlecock
pluma F

racket
raqueta F

badminton racket
raqueta F *de bádminton* M

handle
empuñadura F

shaft
varilla F

stringing
cuerdas F

frame
montura F

player
jugador M

alley
callejón M

net
red F

service judge
árbitro M

net
red F

shuttlecock
pluma F

crown
plumas F

cork tip
corcho M

tennis court
cancha [F] *de tenis* [M]

cameraman
operador [M] *de cámara* [F]

player's bench
banquillo [M] *de jugadores* [M]

chair umpire
juez [M] *de silla* [F]

service line
línea [F] *de servicio* [M]

alley
callejón [M]

tennis racket
raqueta [F] *de tenis* [M]

ball boy
recogepelotas [M]

billboard
valla [F] *publicitaria*

stairs
escalera [F]

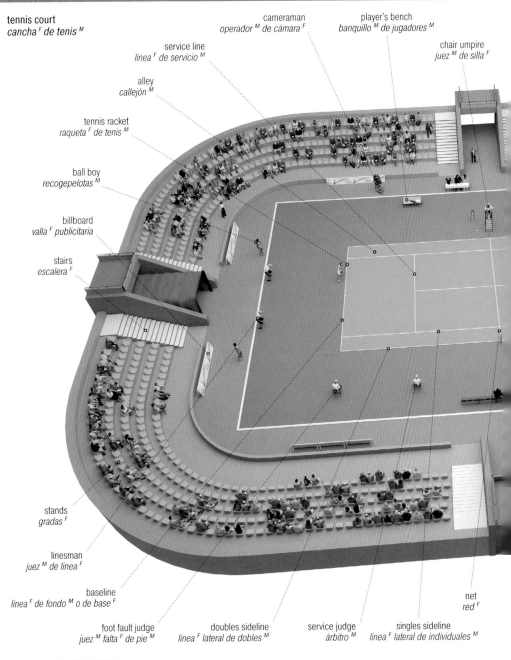

stands
gradas [F]

linesman
juez [M] *de línea* [F]

baseline
línea [F] *de fondo* [M] *o de base* [F]

foot fault judge
juez [M] *falta* [F] *de pie* [M]

doubles sideline
línea [F] *lateral de dobles* [M]

service judge
árbitro [M]

singles sideline
línea [F] *lateral de individuales* [M]

net
red [F]

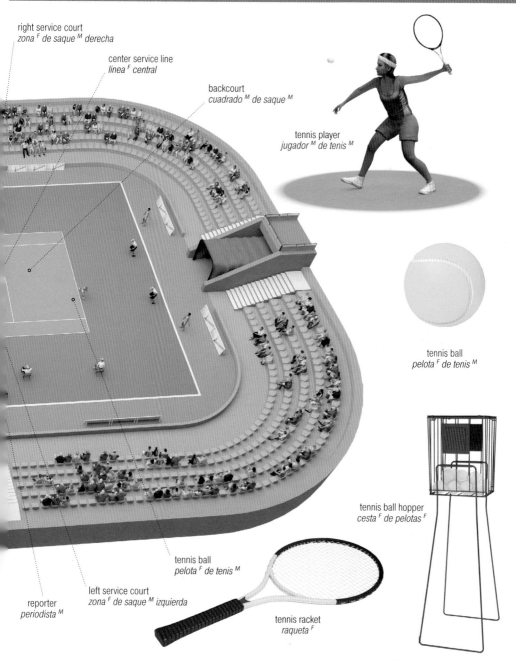

right service court
zona ᶠ *de saque* ᴹ *derecha*

center service line
línea ᶠ *central*

backcourt
cuadrado ᴹ *de saque* ᴹ

tennis player
jugador ᴹ *de tenis* ᴹ

tennis ball
pelota ᶠ *de tenis* ᴹ

tennis ball
pelota ᶠ *de tenis* ᴹ

tennis ball hopper
cesta ᶠ *de pelotas* ᶠ

reporter
periodista ᴹ

left service court
zona ᶠ *de saque* ᴹ *izquierda*

tennis racket
raqueta ᶠ

table tennis court
sala F *de tenis* M *de mesa* F

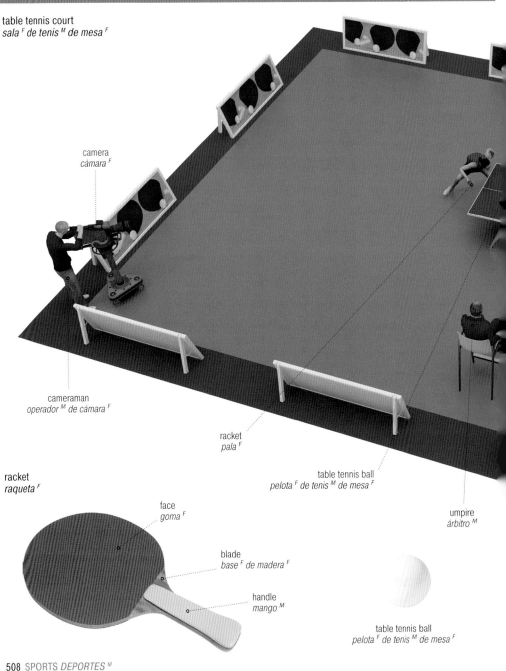

camera
cámara F

cameraman
operador M *de cámara* F

racket
pala F

racket
raqueta F

table tennis ball
pelota F *de tenis* M *de mesa* F

umpire
árbitro M

face
goma F

blade
base F *de madera* F

handle
mango M

table tennis ball
pelota F *de tenis* M *de mesa* F

scorekeeper
árbitro [M] *principal*

scoreboard
marcador [M]

billboard
valla [F] *publicitaria*

net
red [F]

tennis table
tenis [M] *de mesa* [F]

player
jugador [M]

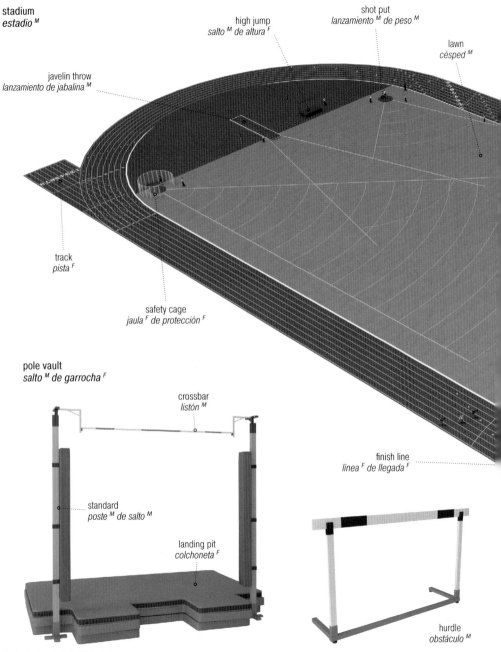

stadium
estadio ^M

high jump
salto ^M *de altura* ^F

shot put
lanzamiento ^M *de peso* ^M

lawn
césped ^M

javelin throw
lanzamiento de jabalina ^M

track
pista ^F

safety cage
jaula ^F *de protección* ^F

pole vault
salto ^M *de garrocha* ^F

crossbar
listón ^M

standard
poste ^M *de salto* ^M

landing pit
colchoneta ^F

finish line
línea ^F *de llegada* ^F

hurdle
obstáculo ^M

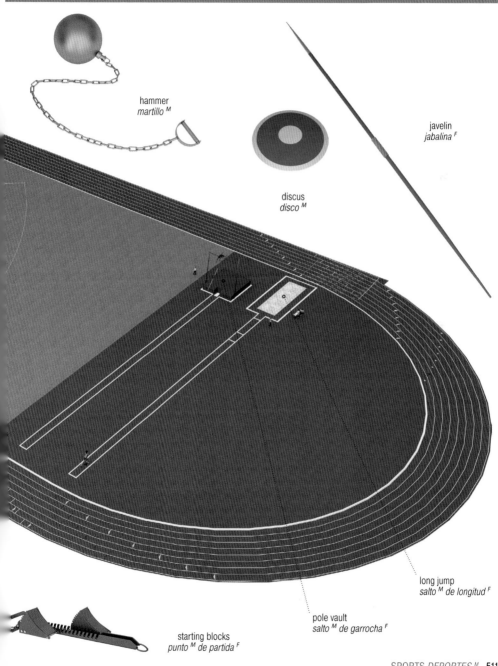

hammer
martillo ^M

discus
disco ^M

javelin
jabalina ^F

long jump
salto ^M *de longitud* ^F

pole vault
salto ^M *de garrocha* ^F

starting blocks
punto ^M *de partida* ^F

artistic gymnastics
gimnasia F *artística*

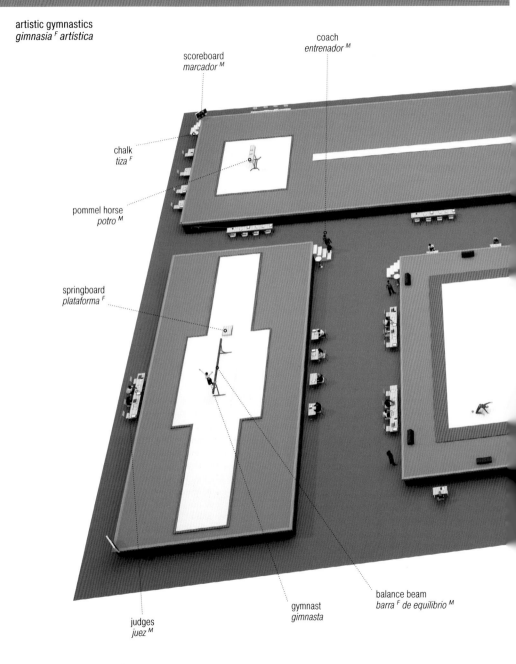

coach
entrenador M

scoreboard
marcador M

chalk
tiza F

pommel horse
potro M

springboard
plataforma F

judges
juez M

gymnast
gimnasta

balance beam
barra F *de equilibrio* M

vault
potro ^M

parallel bars
barras ^F *paralelas*

uneven parallel bars
barras ^F *asimétricas*

rings
anillas ^F

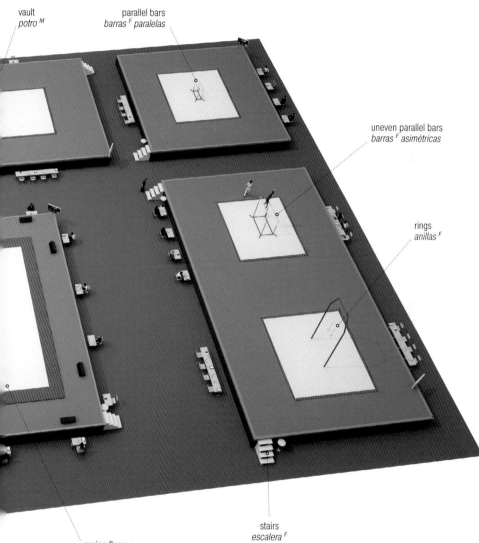

stairs
escalera ^F

spring floor
moqueta ^F

Artistic gymnastics equipment
Aparatos ^M de la gimnasia ^F artística

uneven bars
barras ^F paralelas asimétricas

upper bar
barra ^F alta

lower bar
barra ^F baja

guy cable
cable ^M de tirante ^M

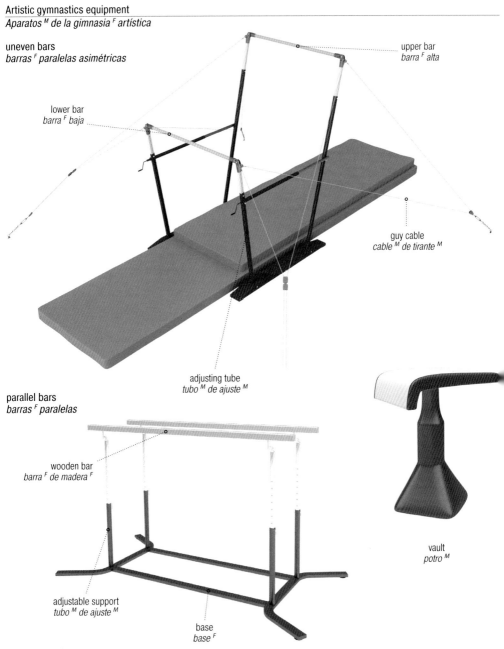

adjusting tube
tubo ^M de ajuste ^M

parallel bars
barras ^F paralelas

wooden bar
barra ^F de madera ^F

vault
potro ^M

adjustable support
tubo ^M de ajuste ^M

base
base ^F

pommel horse
caballo [M] *con arcos* [M]

neck
cabeza [F]

saddle
silla [F]

pommel
arzón [M]

horse
caballo [M]

croup
grupa [F]

base
base [F]

height adjustment
regulador [M] *de altura* [F]

chalk bowl
bol [M] *para talco* [M]

anti-slip shoe
zapata [F] *antideslizante*

springboard
tabla [F] *de balanceo* [M]

balance beam
barra [F] *de equilibrio* [M]

vaulting horse
plinto [M]

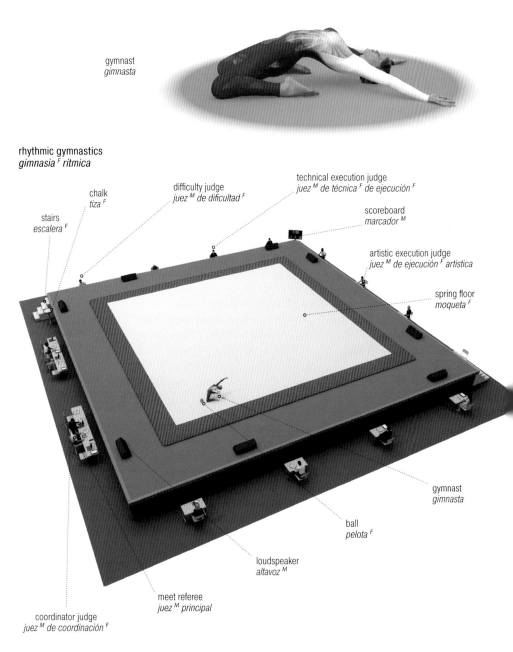

gymnast
gimnasta

rhythmic gymnastics
gimnasia ᶠ *rítmica*

difficulty judge
juez ᴹ *de dificultad* ᶠ

technical execution judge
juez ᴹ *de técnica* ᶠ *de ejecución* ᶠ

chalk
tiza ᶠ

scoreboard
marcador ᴹ

stairs
escalera ᶠ

artistic execution judge
juez ᴹ *de ejecución* ᶠ *artística*

spring floor
moqueta ᶠ

gymnast
gimnasta

ball
pelota ᶠ

loudspeaker
altavoz ᴹ

meet referee
juez ᴹ *principal*

coordinator judge
juez ᴹ *de coordinación* ᶠ

golf cart: front view
carrito ^M *de golf* ^M *: vista delantera* ^F

roof
lona ^F

back
respaldo ^M

seat
asiento ^M

tire
ruedas ^F

golf cart: back view
carrito ^M *de golf* ^M *: vista trasera* ^F

club
palo ^M *de golf* ^M

steering wheel
volante ^M

strap
correa ^F

cup holder
portavasos ^M

golf bag
bolsa ^F *de palos* ^M *de golf* ^M

storage compartment
compartimiento ^M

armrest
reposabrazos ^M

basket
cesto ^M

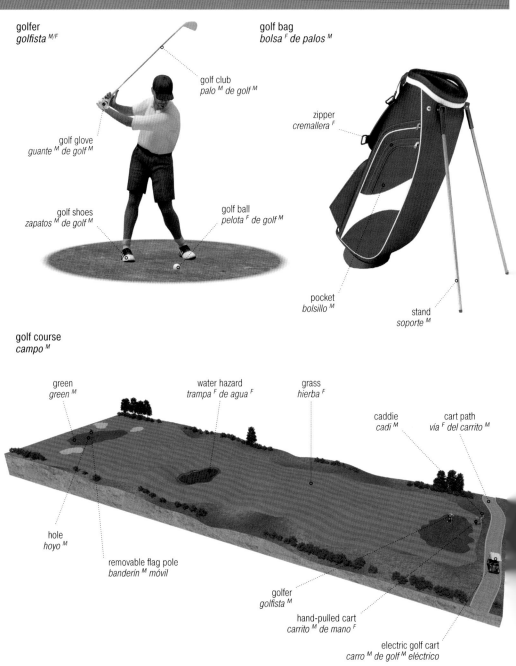

golfer
golfista ^{M/F}

golf bag
bolsa ^F *de palos* ^M

golf club
palo ^M *de golf* ^M

zipper
cremallera ^F

golf glove
guante ^M *de golf* ^M

golf shoes
zapatos ^M *de golf* ^M

golf ball
pelota ^F *de golf* ^M

pocket
bolsillo ^M

stand
soporte ^M

golf course
campo ^M

green
green ^M

water hazard
trampa ^F *de agua* ^F

grass
hierba ^F

caddie
cadi ^M

cart path
vía ^F *del carrito* ^M

hole
hoyo ^M

removable flag pole
banderín ^M *móvil*

golfer
golfista ^M

hand-pulled cart
carrito ^M *de mano* ^F

electric golf cart
carro ^M *de golf* ^M *eléctrico*

clubhead
cabeza ^F *de palo* ^M *de golf* ^M

golf ball
pelota ^F *de golf* ^M

cover
revestimiento ^M

dimple
hoyuelo ^M

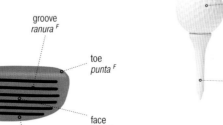

ferrule
cuello ^M

groove
ranura ^F

toe
punta ^F

tee
tee ^M

hosel
boquilla ^F

face
cara ^F

heel
talón ^M

sole
base ^F

tee
tee ^M

wood
madera ^F

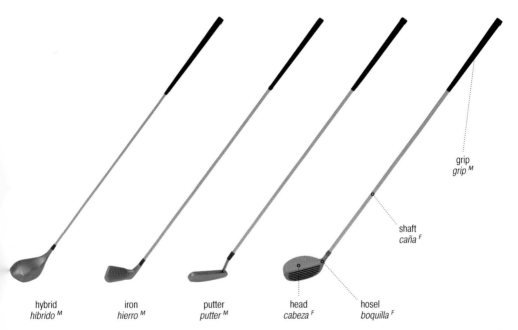

grip
grip ^M

shaft
caña ^F

hybrid
híbrido ^M

iron
hierro ^M

putter
putter ^M

head
cabeza ^F

hosel
boquilla ^F

boxing ring
ring ^M *de boxeo* ^M

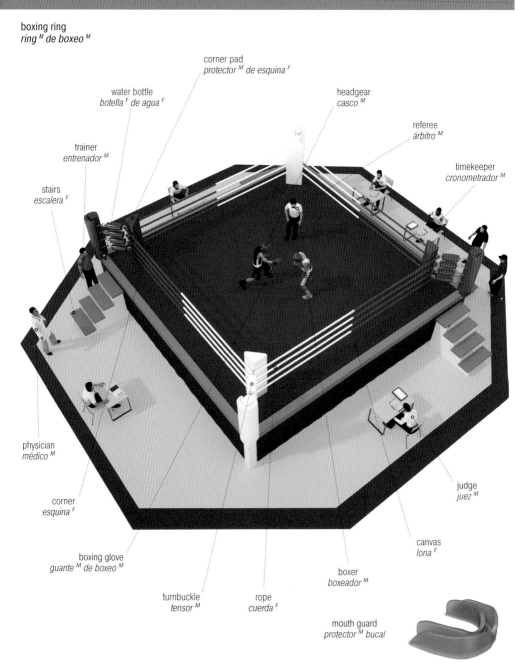

corner pad
protector ^M *de esquina* ^F

water bottle
botella ^F *de agua* ^F

headgear
casco ^M

referee
árbitro ^M

trainer
entrenador ^M

timekeeper
cronometrador ^M

stairs
escalera ^F

physician
médico ^M

judge
juez ^M

corner
esquina ^F

canvas
lona ^F

boxing glove
guante ^M *de boxeo* ^M

boxer
boxeador ^M

turnbuckle
tensor ^M

rope
cuerda ^F

mouth guard
protector ^M *bucal*

heavy bag
saco ^M *de boxeo* ^M *colgante*

shock-absorbing spring
amortiguador ^M

stand
soporte ^M

freestanding heavy bag
saco ^M *de boxeo* ^M *con base* ^F

chain
cadena ^F

punching bag
saco ^M *de boxeo* ^M

stitching
costura ^F

base
pedestal ^M

rubber foot
pie ^M *de goma* ^F

boxing gloves
guantes ^M *de boxeo* ^M

strap
tira ^F

laces
cordones ^M

speed bag
pera ^F *de boxeo* ^M

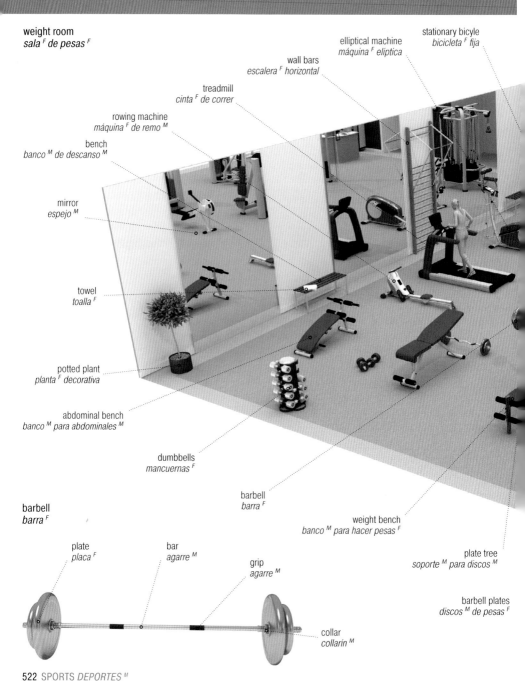

weight room
sala ^F *de pesas* ^F

stationary bicycle
bicicleta ^F *fija*

elliptical machine
máquina ^F *elíptica*

wall bars
escalera ^F *horizontal*

treadmill
cinta ^F *de correr*

rowing machine
máquina ^F *de remo* ^M

bench
banco ^M *de descanso* ^M

mirror
espejo ^M

towel
toalla ^F

potted plant
planta ^F *decorativa*

abdominal bench
banco ^M *para abdominales* ^M

dumbbells
mancuernas ^F

barbell
barra ^F

weight bench
banco ^M *para hacer pesas* ^F

plate tree
soporte ^M *para discos* ^M

barbell
barra ^F

plate
placa ^F

bar
agarre ^M

grip
agarre ^M

barbell plates
discos ^M *de pesas* ^F

collar
collarín ^M

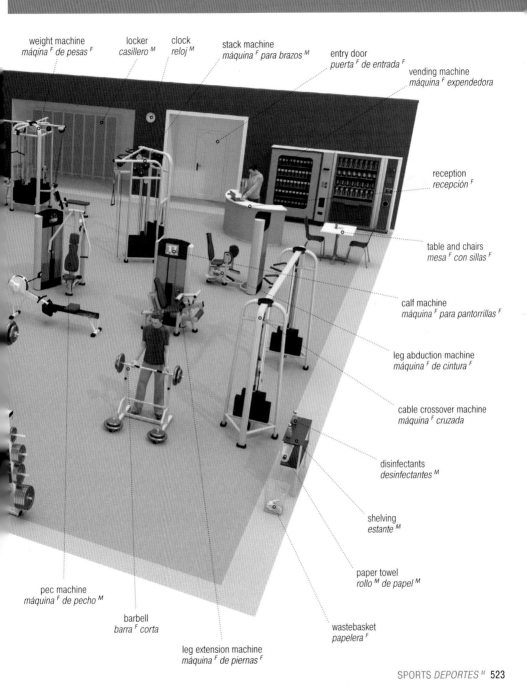

weight machine
máquina ^F *de pesas* ^F

locker
casillero ^M

clock
reloj ^M

stack machine
máquina ^F *para brazos* ^M

entry door
puerta ^F *de entrada* ^F

vending machine
máquina ^F *expendedora*

reception
recepción ^F

table and chairs
mesa ^F *con sillas* ^F

calf machine
máquina ^F *para pantorrillas* ^F

leg abduction machine
máquina ^F *de cintura* ^F

cable crossover machine
máquina ^F *cruzada*

disinfectants
desinfectantes ^M

shelving
estante ^M

paper towel
rollo ^M *de papel* ^M

pec machine
máquina ^F *de pecho* ^M

barbell
barra ^F *corta*

leg extension machine
máquina ^F *de piernas* ^F

wastebasket
papelera ^F

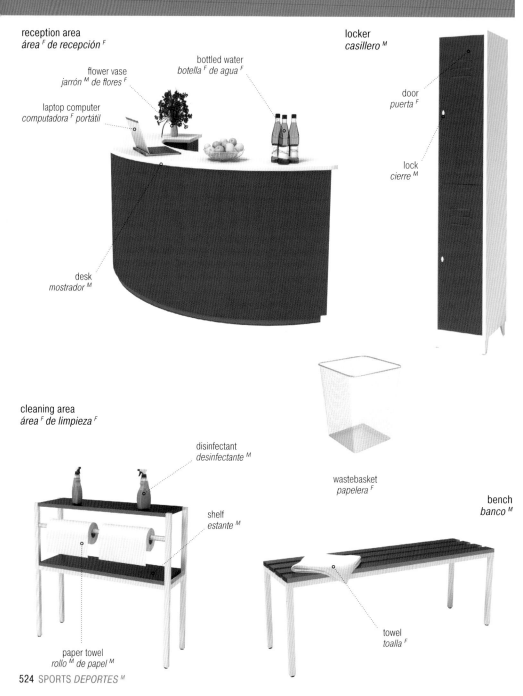

reception area
área ^F *de recepción* ^F

flower vase
jarrón ^M *de flores* ^F

bottled water
botella ^F *de agua* ^F

laptop computer
computadora ^F *portátil*

desk
mostrador ^M

locker
casillero ^M

door
puerta ^F

lock
cierre ^M

cleaning area
área ^F *de limpieza* ^F

disinfectant
desinfectante ^M

shelf
estante ^M

wastebasket
papelera ^F

bench
banco ^M

paper towel
rollo ^M *de papel* ^M

towel
toalla ^F

fixed dumbbells
mancuernas [F] *fijas*

cable crossover machine
máquina [F] *de brazos* [M] *uso* [M] *general*

electronic console
panel [M] *electrónico*

handlebars
manillar [M]

stationary bicyle
bicicleta [F] *fija*

frame
estructura [F]

saddle
sillín [M]

pedal
pedal [M]

anti-slip feet
patas [F] *antideslizantes*

stair-climber
elíptica [F]

height adjustment
mecanismo [M] *de ajuste* [M] *de altura* [F]

treadmill
cinta [F] *de correr*

display
pantalla [F]

electronic console
panel [M] *de control* [M]

grip
manillar [M]

running surface
cinta [F]

base
base [F]

barbell plates and tree
discos [M] *y árbol* [M] *de pesas* [F]

rowing machine
máquina [F] *de remo* [M]

handle
mango [M]

footrest
reposapiés [M]

display
pantalla [F]

anti-slip foot
superficie [F] *antideslizante*

adjustable dumbbell
mancuerna [F] *ajustable*

frame
estructura [F]

strap
agarre [M]

resistance adjustment
control [M] *de esfuerzo* [M]

sliding seat
asiento [M] *deslizante*

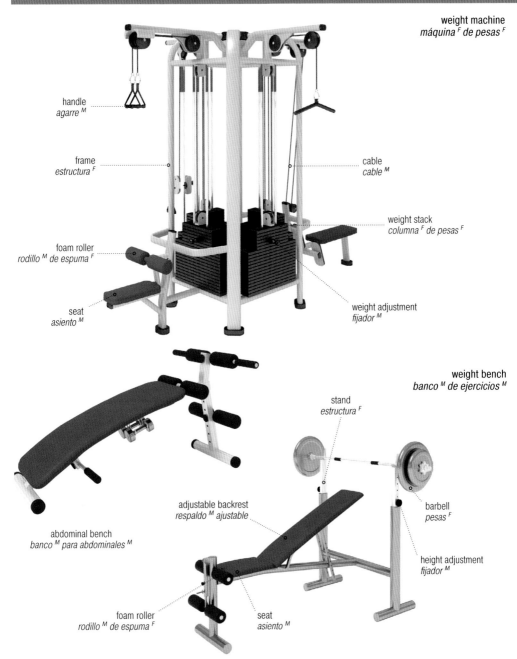

weight machine
máquina ^F *de pesas* ^F

handle
agarre ^M

frame
estructura ^F

cable
cable ^M

weight stack
columna ^F *de pesas* ^F

foam roller
rodillo ^M *de espuma* ^F

weight adjustment
fijador ^M

seat
asiento ^M

weight bench
banco ^M *de ejercicios* ^M

stand
estructura ^F

adjustable backrest
respaldo ^M *ajustable*

barbell
pesas ^F

abdominal bench
banco ^M *para abdominales* ^M

height adjustment
fijador ^M

foam roller
rodillo ^M *de espuma* ^F

seat
asiento ^M

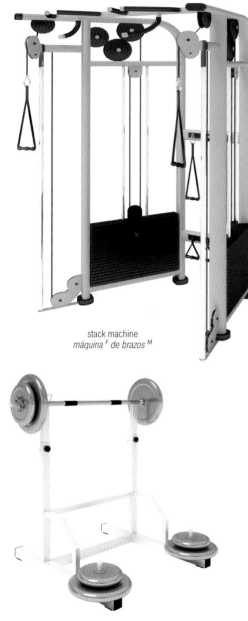

stack machine
máquina F *de brazos* M

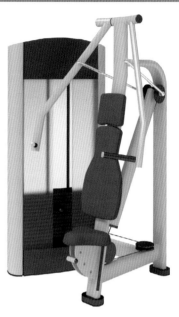

pec machine
máquina F *de hombros* M

barbell stand
barra F *de soporte* M

leg extension machine
máquina F *de piernas* F

tanning bed
cama ᶠ *bronceadora*

fluorescent lamps
luces ᶠ *fluorescentes*

on/off button
botón ᴹ *de encendido* ᴹ

exercise ball
pelota ᶠ *de gimnasia* ᶠ

hand grips
pinzas ᶠ *de mano* ᶠ

rubber hand grip
mango ᴹ *de goma* ᶠ

yoga mat
colchoneta ᶠ *de yoga* ᴹ

aerobics step
escalón ᴹ *para ejercicio* ᴹ *aeróbico*

shoulder stand
estiramiento M *de piernas* F
sobre los hombros M

standing leg lift
elevación F *sobre una pierna* F

push-up
flexiones F

scissors
tijeras F

forward bend
estiramiento M *para adelante*

side lunge
estiramientos M *laterales*

bra top
sostén M *deportivo*

sweatpants
pantalones M *de deporte* M

sneakers
zapatillas F *deportivas*

seated forward bend
estiramiento M *para adelante sentada en el suelo* M

shoulder stand scissors
tijereta F *en posición* F *supina*

forward lunge
estiramiento M *de piernas* F

Skateboarding
Deporte ^M de patineta ^F

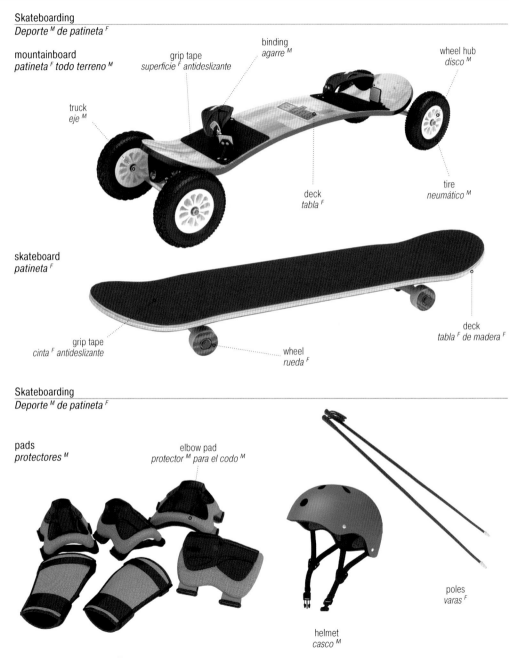

mountainboard
patineta ^F todo terreno ^M

grip tape
superficie ^F antideslizante

binding
agarre ^M

wheel hub
disco ^M

truck
eje ^M

deck
tabla ^F

tire
neumático ^M

skateboard
patineta ^F

grip tape
cinta ^F antideslizante

wheel
rueda ^F

deck
tabla ^F de madera ^F

Skateboarding
Deporte ^M de patineta ^F

pads
protectores ^M

elbow pad
protector ^M para el codo ^M

poles
varas ^F

helmet
casco ^M

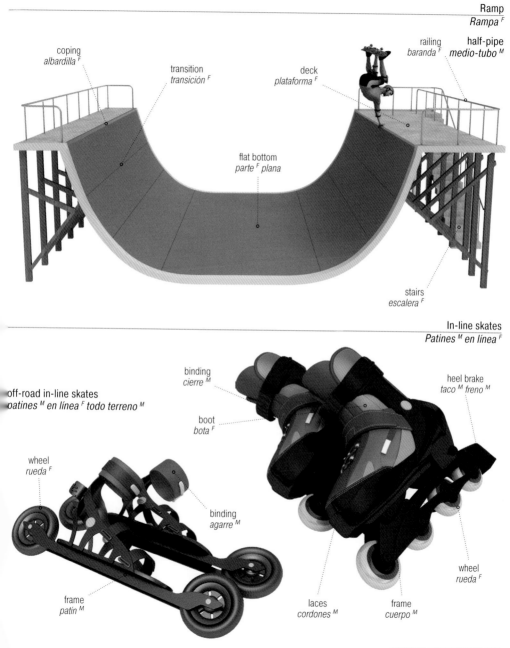

Ramp
Rampa ^F

coping
albardilla ^F

transition
transición ^F

deck
plataforma ^F

railing
baranda ^F

half-pipe
medio-tubo ^M

flat bottom
parte ^F *plana*

stairs
escalera ^F

In-line skates
Patines ^M *en línea* ^F

binding
cierre ^M

heel brake
taco ^M *freno* ^M

off-road in-line skates
patines ^M *en línea* ^F *todo terreno* ^M

boot
bota ^F

wheel
rueda ^F

binding
agarre ^M

wheel
rueda ^F

frame
patín ^M

laces
cordones ^M

frame
cuerpo ^M

SPORTS *DEPORTES* ^M 533

mountain bicycle
bicicleta ^F *de montaña* ^F

handlebars
manillar ^M

front brake lever
palanca ^F *de freno* ^M *delantero*

shifter
palanca ^F *de cambio* ^M

rear brake lever
palanca ^F *de freno* ^M *trasero*

front fork
horquilla ^F *de suspensión* ^F

front brake
freno ^M *delantero*

hub
eje ^M

tire
neumático ^M

rim
llanta ^F

spoke
radio ^M

seat
sillín ^M

frame
armazón ^M

road-racing bicycle
bicicleta ^F _de carreras_ ^F

rear brake
freno ^M _trasero_

rear derailleur
desviador ^M _trasero_

chain
cadena ^F

front derailleur
desviador ^M _delantero_

pedal
pedal ^M

stand
caballete ^M

crankset
piñón ^M

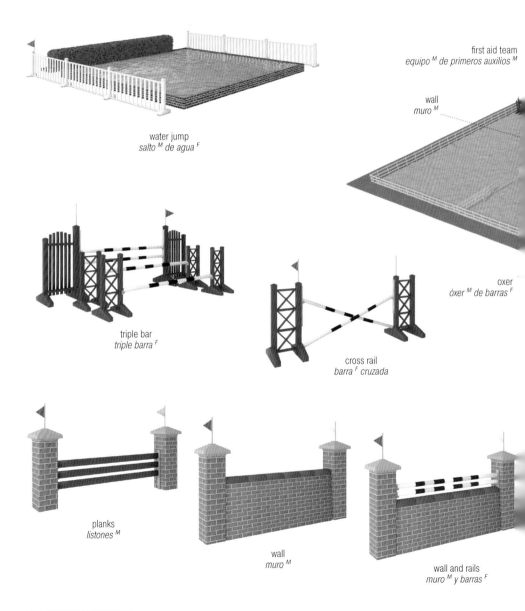

first aid team
equipo ᴹ *de primeros auxilios* ᴹ

wall
muro ᴹ

water jump
salto ᴹ *de agua* ᶠ

oxer
óxer ᴹ *de barras* ᶠ

triple bar
triple barra ᶠ

cross rail
barra ᶠ *cruzada*

planks
listones ᴹ

wall
muro ᴹ

wall and rails
muro ᴹ *y barras* ᶠ

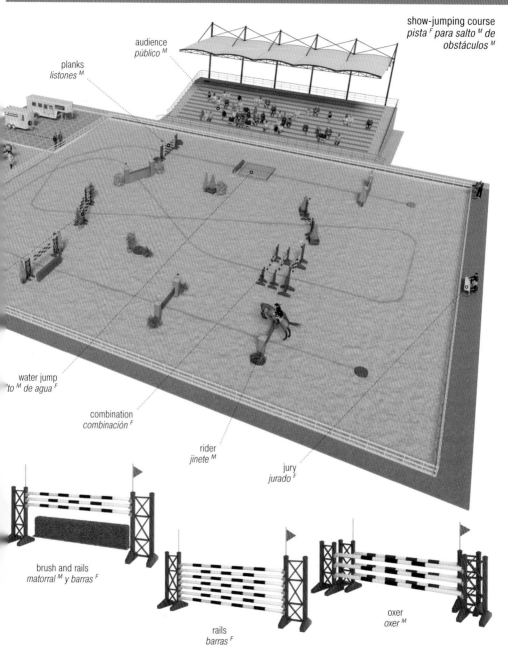

show-jumping course
pista ᶠ *para salto* ᴹ *de*
obstáculos ᴹ

audience
público ᴹ

planks
listones ᴹ

water jump
'to ᴹ *de agua* ᶠ

combination
combinación ᶠ

rider
jinete ᴹ

jury
jurado ᶠ

brush and rails
matorral ᴹ *y barras* ᶠ

rails
barras ᶠ

oxer
oxer ᴹ

English saddle
silla ^F *de montar inglesa*

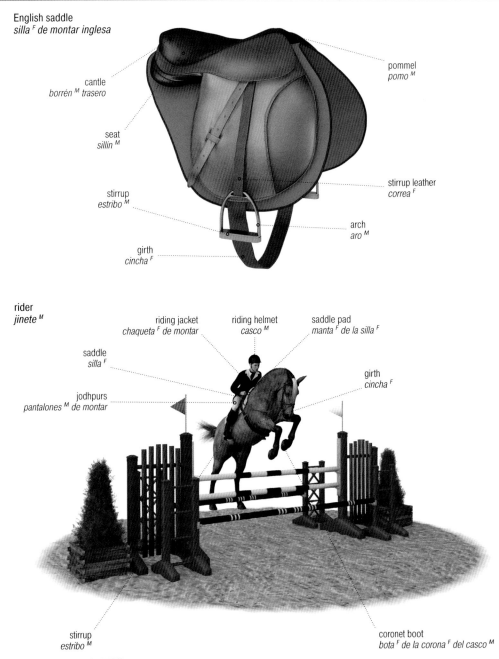

cantle
borrén ^M *trasero*

seat
sillín ^M

stirrup
estribo ^M

girth
cincha ^F

pommel
pomo ^M

stirrup leather
correa ^F

arch
aro ^M

rider
jinete ^M

riding jacket
chaqueta ^F *de montar*

riding helmet
casco ^M

saddle pad
manta ^F *de la silla* ^F

saddle
silla ^F

jodhpurs
pantalones ^M *de montar*

girth
cincha ^F

stirrup
estribo ^M

coronet boot
bota ^F *de la corona* ^F *del casco* ^M

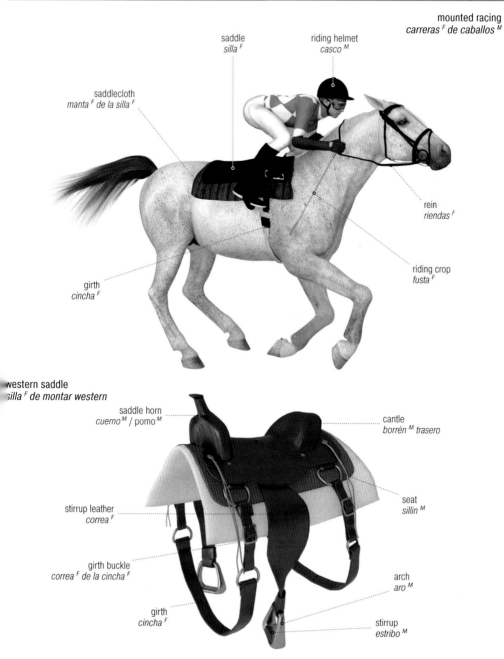

mounted racing
carreras ᶠ de caballos ᴹ

saddle
silla ᶠ

riding helmet
casco ᴹ

saddlecloth
manta ᶠ de la silla ᶠ

rein
riendas ᶠ

girth
cincha ᶠ

riding crop
fusta ᶠ

western saddle
silla ᶠ de montar western

saddle horn
cuerno ᴹ / pomo ᴹ

cantle
borrén ᴹ trasero

stirrup leather
correa ᶠ

seat
sillín ᴹ

girth buckle
correa ᶠ de la cincha ᶠ

arch
aro ᴹ

girth
cincha ᶠ

stirrup
estribo ᴹ

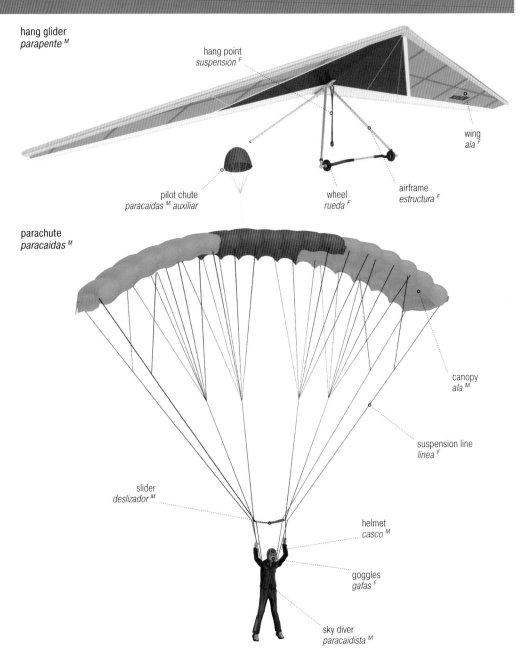

hang glider
parapente ᴹ

hang point
suspensión ᶠ

wing
ala ᶠ

pilot chute
paracaídas ᴹ *auxiliar*

wheel
rueda ᶠ

airframe
estructura ᶠ

parachute
paracaídas ᴹ

canopy
ala ᴹ

suspension line
línea ᶠ

slider
deslizador ᴹ

helmet
casco ᴹ

goggles
gafas ᶠ

sky diver
paracaidista ᴹ

powerboat
lancha ᶠ

engine compartment
compartimiento ᴹ del motor ᴹ

seat
asiento ᴹ

windshield
parabrisas ᴹ

hull
casco ᴹ

power racing catamaran
catamarán ᴹ motorizado de carreras ᶠ

Rowing *Remo ᴹ*

whitewater raft
kayak ᴹ de río ᴹ

seat back
respaldo ᴹ

ring
anilla ᶠ

handle
asa ᶠ

seat
silla ᶠ

paddle
remo ᴹ

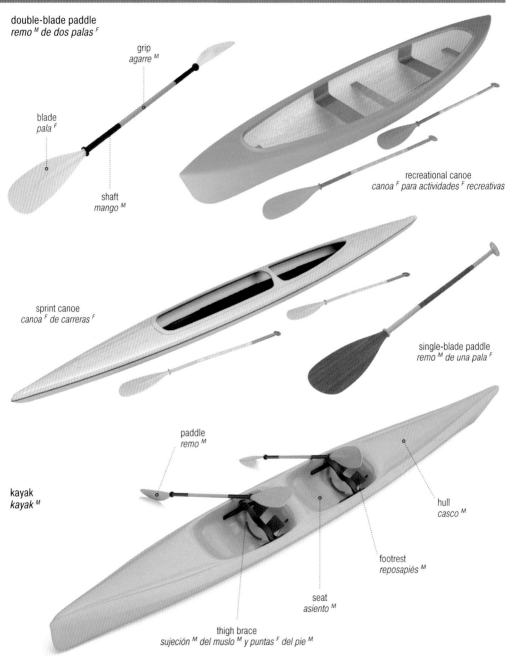

double-blade paddle
remo ^M *de dos palas* ^F

grip
agarre ^M

blade
pala ^F

shaft
mango ^M

recreational canoe
canoa ^F *para actividades* ^F *recreativas*

sprint canoe
canoa ^F *de carreras* ^F

single-blade paddle
remo ^M *de una pala* ^F

paddle
remo ^M

kayak
kayak ^M

hull
casco ^M

footrest
reposapiés ^M

seat
asiento ^M

thigh brace
sujeción ^M *del muslo* ^M *y puntas* ^F *del pie* ^M

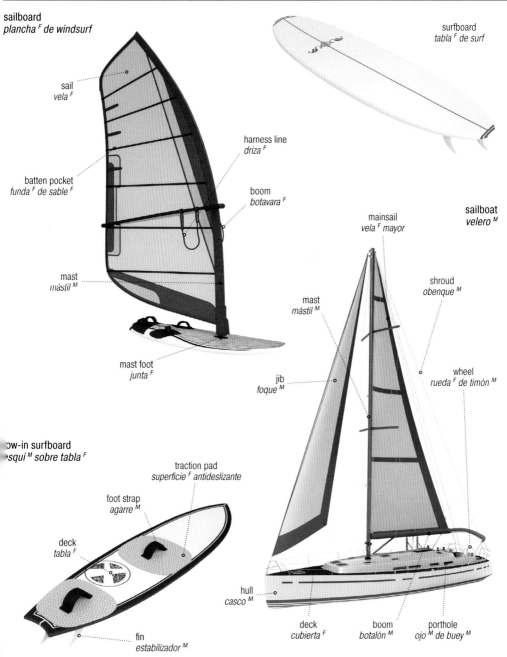

sailboard
plancha ^F de windsurf

surfboard
tabla ^F de surf

sail
vela ^F

harness line
driza ^F

batten pocket
funda ^F de sable ^F

boom
botavara ^F

sailboat
velero ^M

mainsail
vela ^F mayor

shroud
obenque ^M

mast
mástil ^M

mast
mástil ^M

wheel
rueda ^F de timón ^M

jib
foque ^M

mast foot
junta ^F

tow-in surfboard
esquí ^M sobre tabla ^F

traction pad
superficie ^F antideslizante

foot strap
agarre ^M

deck
tabla ^F

hull
casco ^M

fin
estabilizador ^M

deck
cubierta ^F

boom
botalón ^M

porthole
ojo ^M de buey ^M

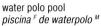

water polo pool
piscina ᶠ *de waterpolo* ᴹ

goal judge
juez ᴹ *de gol* ᴹ

goal
portería ᶠ

goal line
línea ᶠ *de meta* ᶠ

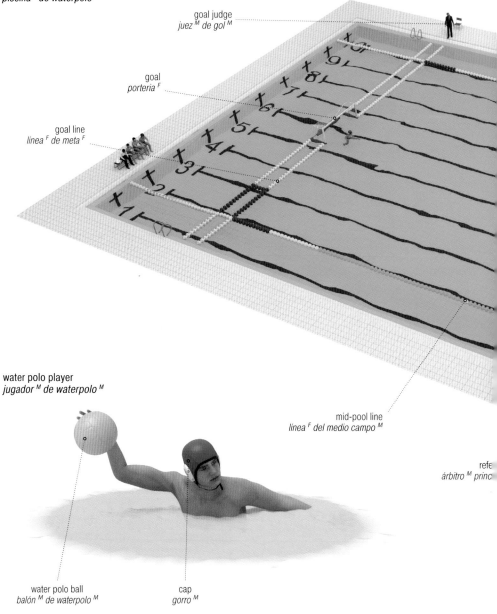

water polo player
jugador ᴹ *de waterpolo* ᴹ

mid-pool line
línea ᶠ *del medio campo* ᴹ

refe
árbitro ᴹ *princ*

water polo ball
balón ᴹ *de waterpolo* ᴹ

cap
gorro ᴹ

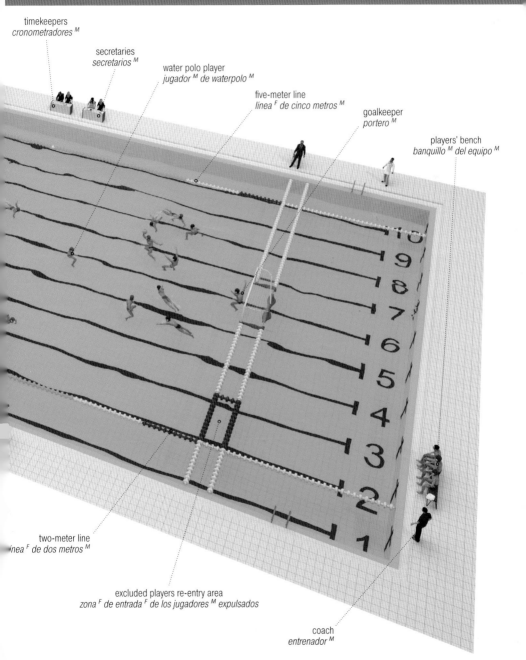

timekeepers
cronometradores ^M

secretaries
secretarios ^M

water polo player
jugador ^M *de waterpolo* ^M

five-meter line
línea ^F *de cinco metros* ^M

goalkeeper
portero ^M

players' bench
banquillo ^M *del equipo* ^M

two-meter line
línea ^F *de dos metros* ^M

excluded players re-entry area
zona ^F *de entrada* ^F *de los jugadores* ^M *expulsados*

coach
entrenador ^M

Olympic-sized pool
piscina ^F *olímpica* ^F

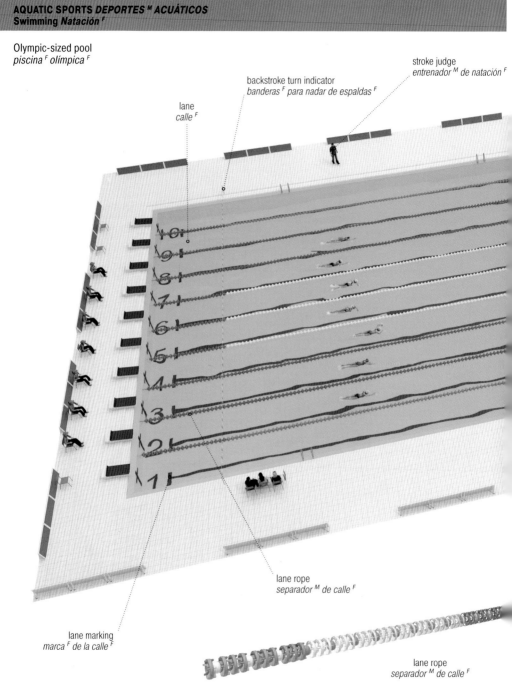

stroke judge
entrenador ^M *de natación* ^F

backstroke turn indicator
banderas ^F *para nadar de espaldas* ^F

lane
calle ^F

lane rope
separador ^M *de calle* ^F

lane marking
marca ^F *de la calle* ^F

lane rope
separador ^M *de calle* ^F

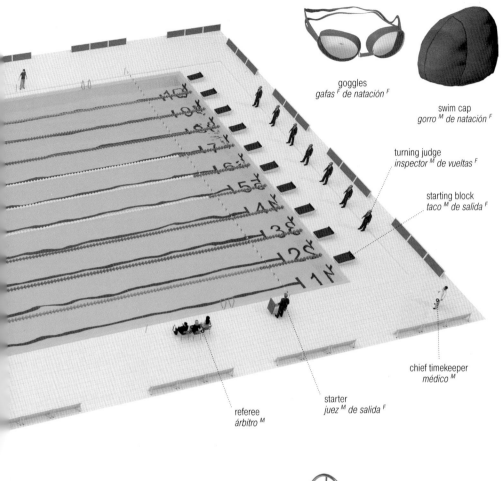

goggles
gafas ᶠ *de natación* ᶠ

swim cap
gorro ᴹ *de natación* ᶠ

turning judge
inspector ᴹ *de vueltas* ᶠ

starting block
taco ᴹ *de salida* ᶠ

chief timekeeper
médico ᴹ

starter
juez ᴹ *de salida* ᶠ

referee
árbitro ᴹ

starting block
taco ᴹ *de salida* ᶠ

lane rope storage reel
bobina ᶠ *de cuerda* ᶠ

handrails
barandillas ᶠ

diving positions
fases ᶠ *del salto* ᴹ

starting position
posición ᶠ *de salida* ᶠ

platform
plataforma ᶠ

flight
fase ᶠ *del salto* ᴹ

entry
entrada ᶠ *al agua* ᶠ

surface of the water
superficie ᶠ *del agua* ᶠ

diving installations
torre ᶠ *de trampolín* ᴹ

platform
plataforma ᶠ

diving tower
plataforma ᶠ

surface of the water
superficie ᶠ *del agua* ᶠ

diver
saltador ᴹ *de trampolín* ᴹ

referee
árbitro ᴹ

springboard
trampolín ᴹ

coach
entrenador ᴹ

stairs
escalera ᶠ *al trampolín* ᴹ

whirlpool
piscina ᶠ *de hidromasaje* ᴹ

shower
ducha ᶠ

judge
juez ᴹ

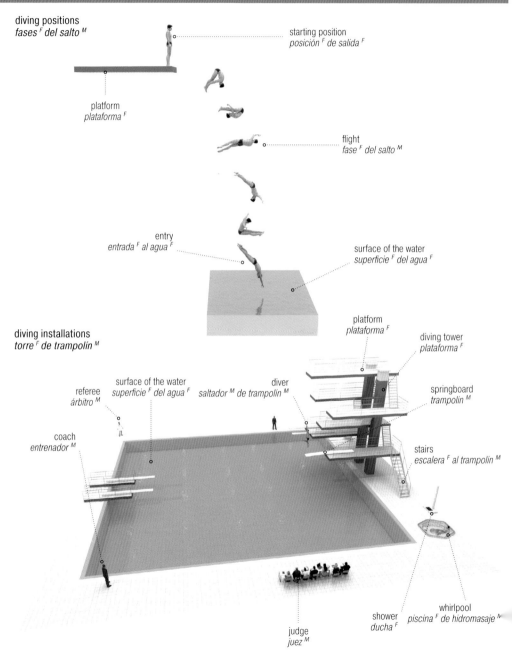

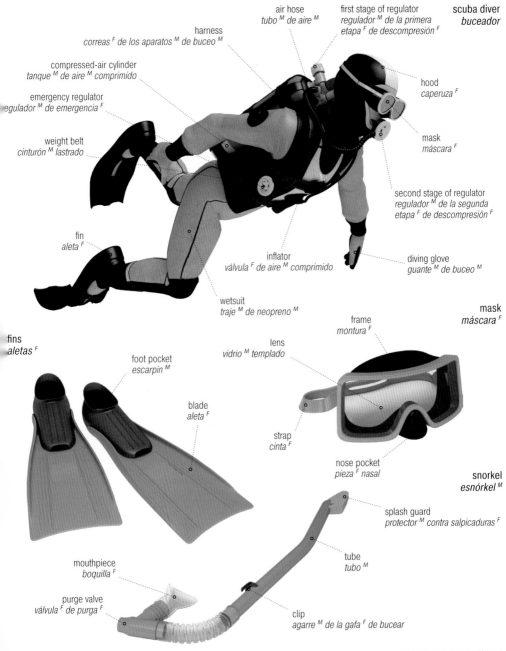

air hose
tubo ^M de aire ^M

first stage of regulator
regulador ^M de la primera
etapa ^F de descompresión ^F

scuba diver
buceador

harness
correas ^F de los aparatos ^M de buceo ^M

compressed-air cylinder
tanque ^M de aire ^M comprimido

hood
caperuza ^F

emergency regulator
regulador ^M de emergencia ^F

mask
máscara ^F

weight belt
cinturón ^M lastrado

second stage of regulator
regulador ^M de la segunda
etapa ^F de descompresión ^F

fin
aleta ^F

inflator
válvula ^F de aire ^M comprimido

diving glove
guante ^M de buceo ^M

wetsuit
traje ^M de neopreno ^M

mask
máscara ^F

frame
montura ^F

fins
aletas ^F

lens
vidrio ^M templado

foot pocket
escarpín ^M

blade
aleta ^F

strap
cinta ^F

nose pocket
pieza ^F nasal

snorkel
esnórkel ^M

splash guard
protector ^M contra salpicaduras ^F

tube
tubo ^M

mouthpiece
boquilla ^F

purge valve
válvula ^F de purga ^F

clip
agarre ^M de la gafa ^F de bucear

rink
pista F *de hielo* M

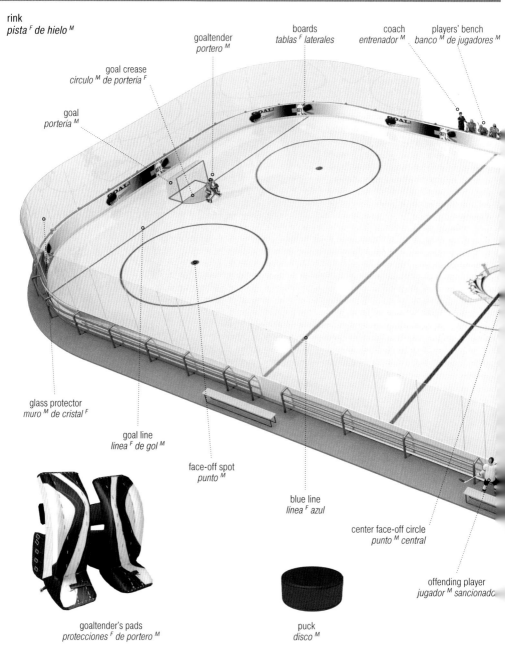

goaltender
portero M

boards
tablas F *laterales*

coach
entrenador M

players' bench
banco M *de jugadores* M

goal crease
círculo M *de portería* F

goal
portería M

glass protector
muro M *de cristal* F

goal line
línea F *de gol* M

face-off spot
punto M

blue line
línea F *azul*

center face-off circle
punto M *central*

offending player
jugador M *sancionado*

goaltender's pads
protecciones F *de portero* M

puck
disco M

center line
línea F *roja*

officials' bench
banco M *de árbitros* M

linesman
juez M *de línea* F

player
jugador M

ice
hielo M

camera
cámara F

penalty box
banquillo M

referee
árbitro M *principal*

cameraman
operador M *de cámara* F

helmet
casco M

vent
agujero M *de ventilación* F

chin strap
correa F

hockey player
jugador M *de hockey* M

glove
guante M

player's stick
palo M *de hockey* M

hockey skates
patines M *de hockey* M

tongue
lengüeta F

blade
cuchilla F

lace
cordón M

shaft
mango M

toe
punta F

blade
pala F

edge
filo M

figure skates
patines ^M *de patinaje* ^M *artístico*

figure skater
patinador ^M *artístico*

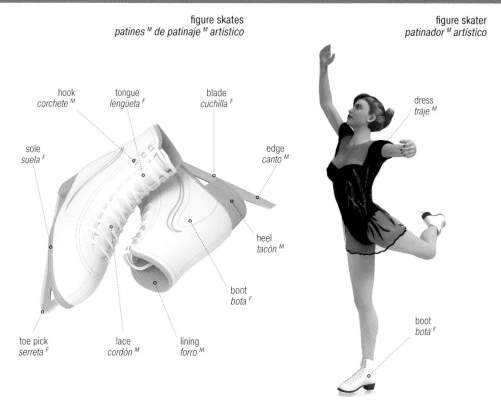

hook
corchete ^M

tongue
lengüeta ^F

blade
cuchilla ^F

dress
traje ^M

sole
suela ^F

edge
canto ^M

heel
tacón ^M

boot
bota ^F

boot
bota ^F

toe pick
serreta ^F

lace
cordón ^M

lining
forro ^M

Bobsled *Bobsleigh* ^M

sled
trineo ^M *de bobsleigh* ^M

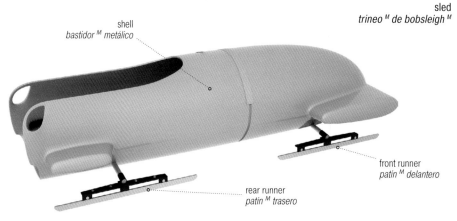

shell
bastidor ^M *metálico*

front runner
patín ^M *delantero*

rear runner
patín ^M *trasero*

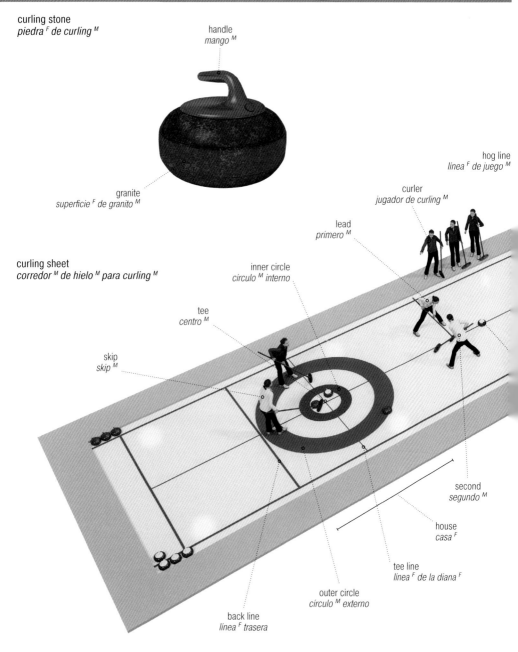

curling stone
piedra ^F *de curling* ^M

handle
mango ^M

hog line
línea ^F *de juego* ^M

granite
superficie ^F *de granito* ^M

curler
jugador de curling ^M

lead
primero ^M

curling sheet
corredor ^M *de hielo* ^M *para curling* ^M

inner circle
círculo ^M *interno*

tee
centro ^M

skip
skip ^M

second
segundo ^M

house
casa ^F

tee line
línea ^F *de la diana* ^F

outer circle
círculo ^M *externo*

back line
línea ^F *trasera*

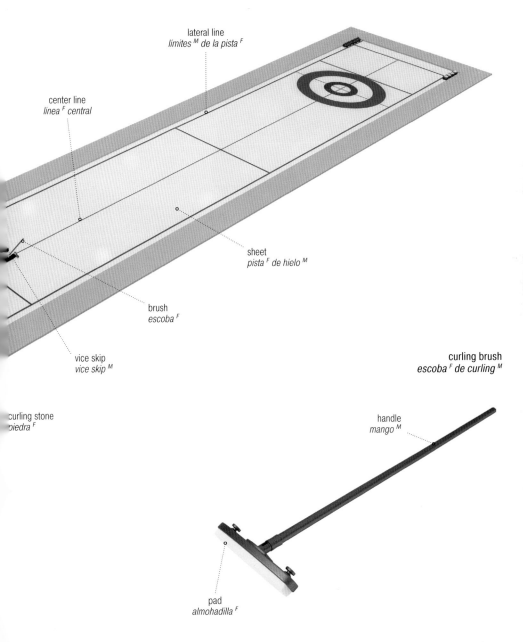

lateral line
límites ^M *de la pista* ^F

center line
línea ^F *central*

sheet
pista ^F *de hielo* ^M

brush
escoba ^F

vice skip
vice skip ^M

curling brush
escoba ^F *de curling* ^M

curling stone
piedra ^F

handle
mango ^M

pad
almohadilla ^F

alpine skier
esquiador ^M

ski boots
botas ^F *de esquí* ^M

ski goggles
gafas ^F *de esquí* ^M

strap
correa ^F

strap
tira ^F

upper shell
cubierta ^F *superior*

buckle
hebilla ^F

adjustable catch
gancho ^M *ajustable*

lower shell
cubierta ^F *inferior*

lens
cristal ^M

frame
montura ^F

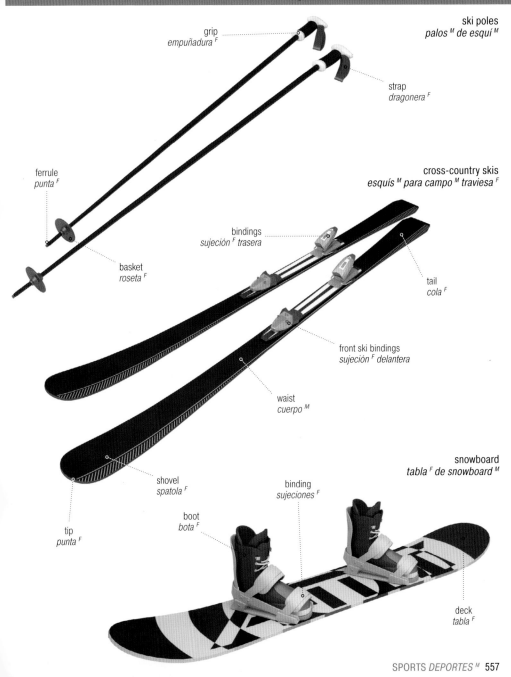

ski poles
palos M *de esquí* M

grip
empuñadura F

strap
dragonera F

ferrule
punta F

cross-country skis
esquís M *para campo* M *traviesa* F

bindings
sujeción F *trasera*

basket
roseta F

tail
cola F

front ski bindings
sujeción F *delantera*

waist
cuerpo M

snowboard
tabla F *de snowboard* M

shovel
spatola F

binding
sujeciones F

boot
bota F

tip
punta F

deck
tabla F

LEISURE AND ENTERTAINMENT

OCIO Y ENTRETENIMIENTO

plush block
dado ᴹ *de peluche* ᴹ

interactive toy
juguete ᴹ *interactivo*

blocks
bloques ᴹ *de peluche* ᶠ

activity gym
gimnasio ᴹ *para bebé* ᴹ

mobile
móvil ᴹ

stuffed animal
animal ᴹ *de peluche* ᴹ

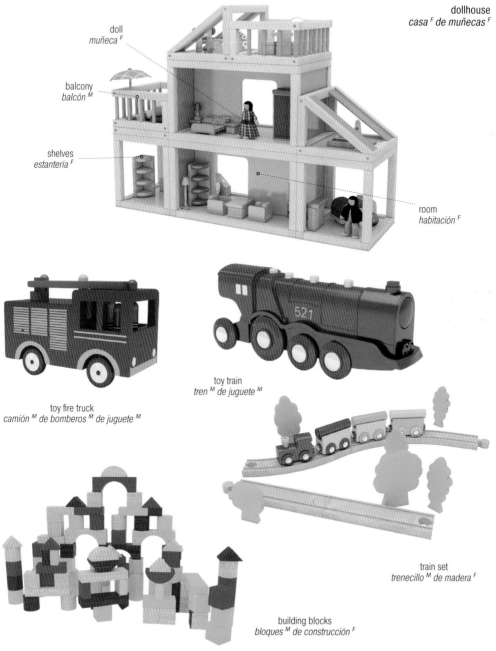

dollhouse
casa ᶠ *de muñecas* ᶠ

doll
muñeca ᶠ

balcony
balcón ᴹ

shelves
estantería ᶠ

room
habitación ᶠ

toy fire truck
camión ᴹ *de bomberos* ᴹ *de juguete* ᴹ

toy train
tren ᴹ *de juguete* ᴹ

train set
trenecillo ᴹ *de madera* ᶠ

building blocks
bloques ᴹ *de construcción* ᶠ

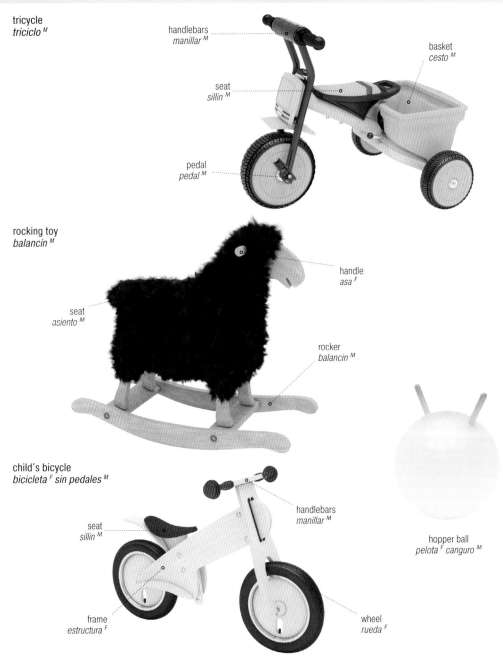

tricycle
triciclo M

handlebars
manillar M

basket
cesto M

seat
sillín M

pedal
pedal M

rocking toy
balancín M

handle
asa F

seat
asiento M

rocker
balancín M

child's bicycle
bicicleta F *sin pedales* M

seat
sillín M

handlebars
manillar M

hopper ball
pelota F *canguro* M

frame
estructura F

wheel
rueda F

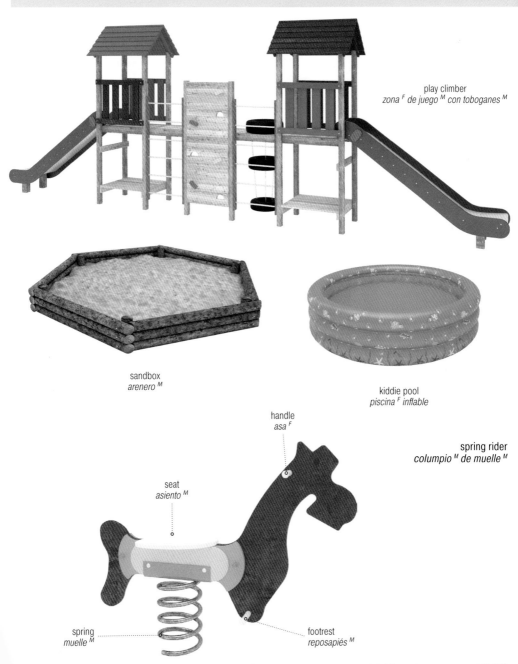

play climber
zona ᶠ de juego ᴹ con toboganes ᴹ

sandbox
arenero ᴹ

kiddie pool
piscina ᶠ inflable

spring rider
columpio ᴹ de muelle ᴹ

handle
asa ᶠ

seat
asiento ᴹ

spring
muelle ᴹ

footrest
reposapiés ᴹ

swing set
columpios ᴹ

top rail
travesaño ᴹ

post
soporte ᴹ

seat
asiento ᴹ

chain
cadena ᶠ

jungle gym
parque infantil ᴹ

monkey bars
barra ᶠ *fija*

top rail
viga ᶠ

ring
anilla ᶠ

post
soporte ᴹ

rope ladder
escalera ᶠ *de cuerda* ᶠ

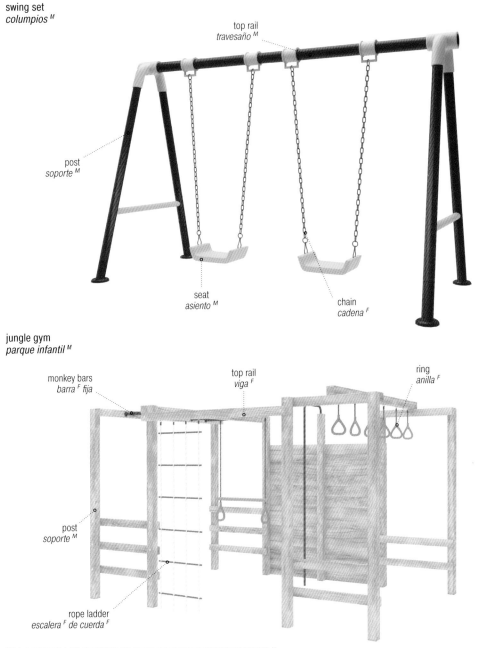

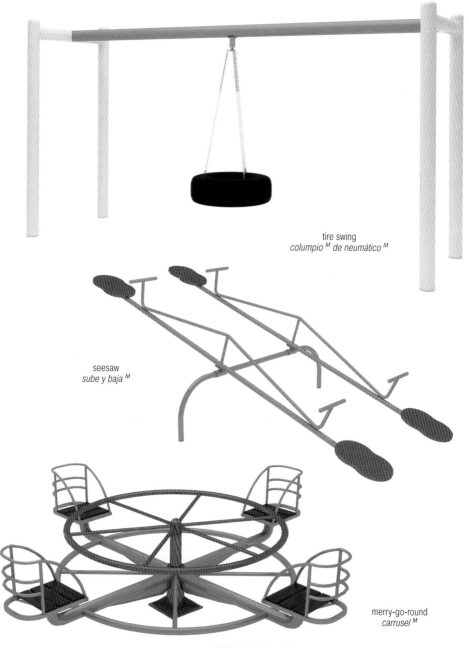

tire swing
columpio ᴹ de neumático ᴹ

seesaw
sube y baja ᴹ

merry-go-round
carrusel ᴹ

amusement park rides
atracciones F

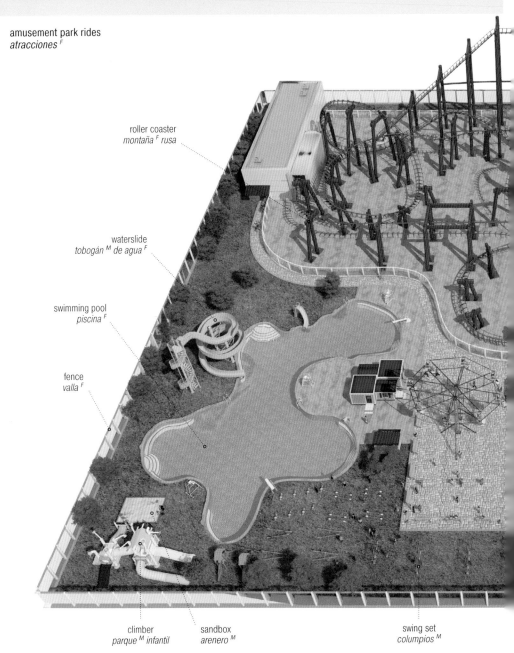

roller coaster
montaña F *rusa*

waterslide
tobogán M *de agua* F

swimming pool
piscina F

fence
valla F

climber
parque M *infantil*

sandbox
arenero M

swing set
columpios M

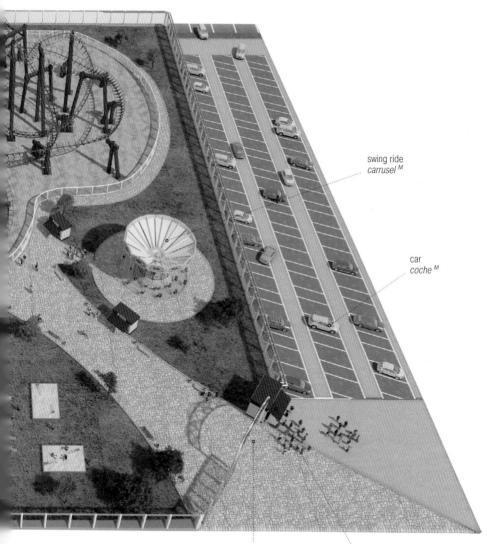

swing ride
carrusel ^M

car
coche ^M

entrance
entrada ^F

ticket office
taquilla ^F

Chess
Ajedrez ᴹ

black square
escaque ᴹ *negro*

chessboard
tablero ᴹ

white square
escaque ᴹ *blanco*

chess piece
ficha ꟳ *de ajedrez* ᴹ

pawn
peón ᴹ

knight
caballo ᴹ

rook
torre ꟳ

bishop
alfil ᴹ

king
rey ᴹ

queen
reina ꟳ

Checkers
Damas ᶠ

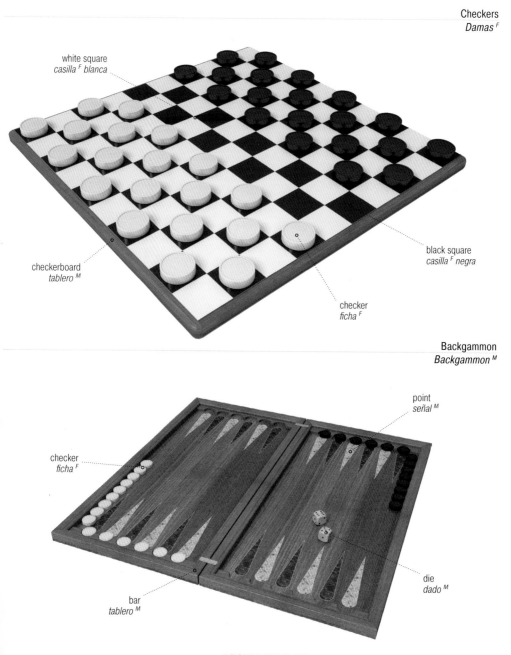

white square
casilla ᶠ *blanca*

black square
casilla ᶠ *negra*

checkerboard
tablero ᴹ

checker
ficha ᶠ

Backgammon
Backgammon ᴹ

point
señal ᴹ

checker
ficha ᶠ

die
dado ᴹ

bar
tablero ᴹ

bowling
bolo ᴹ */ boliche* ᴹ

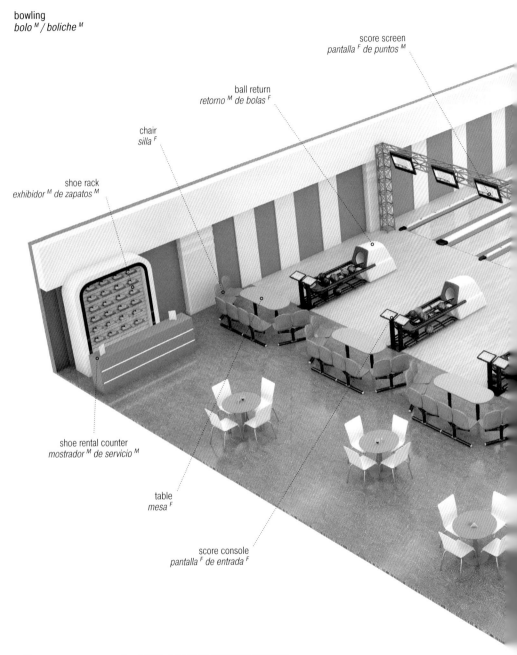

score screen
pantalla ꜰ *de puntos* ᴹ

ball return
retorno ᴹ *de bolas* ꜰ

chair
silla ꜰ

shoe rack
exhibidor ᴹ *de zapatos* ᴹ

shoe rental counter
mostrador ᴹ *de servicio* ᴹ

table
mesa ꜰ

score console
pantalla ꜰ *de entrada* ꜰ

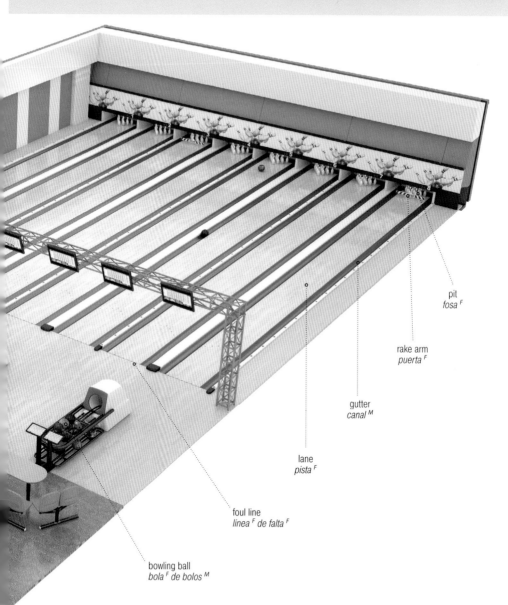

pit
fosa ᶠ

rake arm
puerta ᶠ

gutter
canal ᴹ

lane
pista ᶠ

foul line
línea ᶠ *de falta* ᶠ

bowling ball
bola ᶠ *de bolos* ᴹ

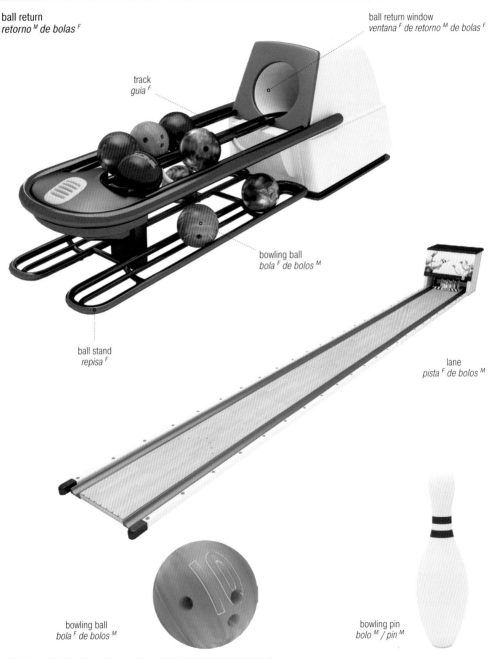

ball return
retorno M de bolas F

ball return window
ventana F de retorno M de bolas F

track
guía F

bowling ball
bola F de bolos M

ball stand
repisa F

lane
pista F de bolos M

bowling ball
bola F de bolos M

bowling pin
bolo M / pin M

billiard table
mesa F de billar M

pocket
buchaca F

pool cue
taco M

table leg
pata F de mesa F

ball
bola F de billar M

rail
banda F

felt
fieltro M

billiards rack
soporte M de billar

billiards chalk
tiza F de billar

snooker table
mesa F de snooker M

electronic dartboard
tablero ^M *de dardos* ^M *electrónico*

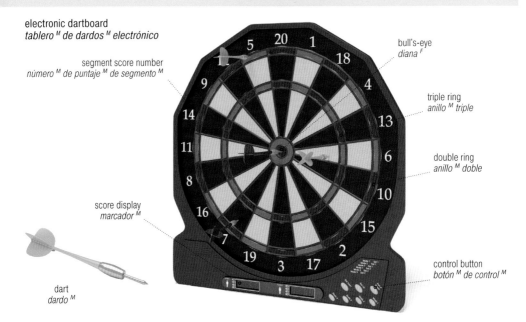

bull's-eye
diana ^F

segment score number
número ^M *de puntaje* ^M *de segmento* ^M

triple ring
anillo ^M *triple*

double ring
anillo ^M *doble*

score display
marcador ^M

control button
botón ^M *de control* ^M

dart
dardo ^M

ARCADE GAMES *VIDEOJUEGOS* ^M

bowling game
simulador ^M *de bolos* ^M

claw crane machine
máquina ^F *atrapa peluches* ^M

maze game
videojuego ^M

score display
marcador ^M

air hockey table
mesa ^F *de hockey* ^M *de aire* ^M

goal
portería ^F

face-off spot
área ^M *de saque* ^M

goalie mallet
mazo ^M *de portero* ^M

playing surface
campo ^M *de juego* ^M

center face-off circle
círculo ^M *de saque* ^M *central*

puck return
retorno ^M *de disco* ^M

soccer table
futbolito ^M

fighting game
simulador ^M *de combate* ^M

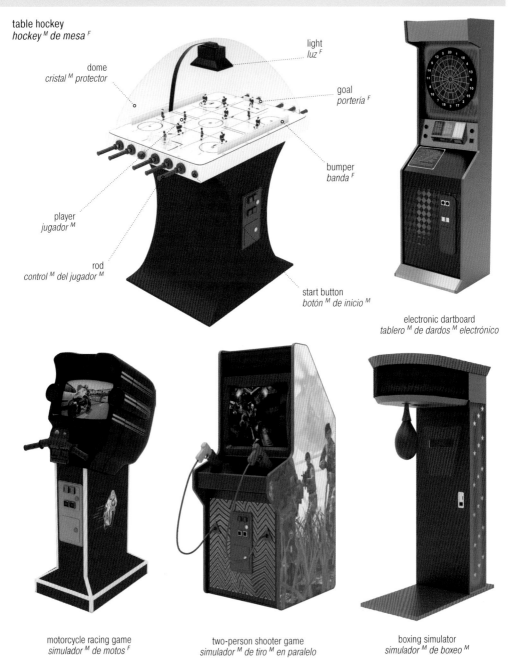

table hockey
hockey ^M *de mesa* ^F

dome
cristal ^M *protector*

light
luz ^F

goal
portería ^F

bumper
banda ^F

player
jugador ^M

rod
control ^M *del jugador* ^M

start button
botón ^M *de inicio* ^M

electronic dartboard
tablero ^M *de dardos* ^M *electrónico*

motorcycle racing game
simulador ^M *de motos* ^F

two-person shooter game
simulador ^M *de tiro* ^M *en paralelo*

boxing simulator
simulador ^M *de boxeo* ^M

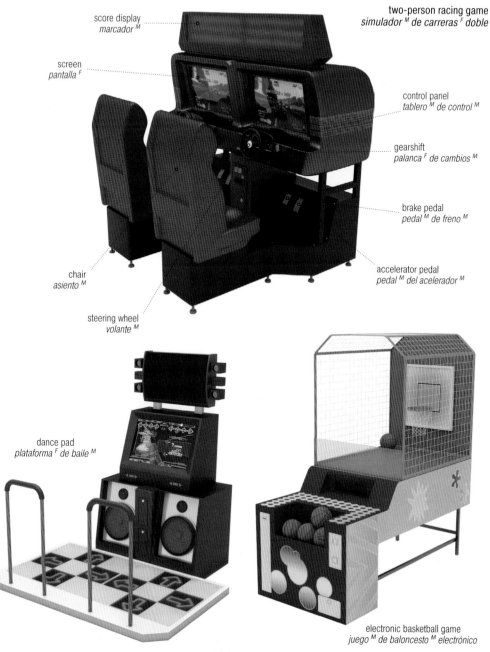

two-person racing game
simulador ^M *de carreras* ^F *doble*

score display
marcador ^M

screen
pantalla ^F

control panel
tablero ^M *de control* ^M

gearshift
palanca ^F *de cambios* ^M

brake pedal
pedal ^M *de freno* ^M

chair
asiento ^M

accelerator pedal
pedal ^M *del acelerador* ^M

steering wheel
volante ^M

dance pad
plataforma ^F *de baile* ^M

electronic basketball game
juego ^M *de baloncesto* ^M *electrónico*

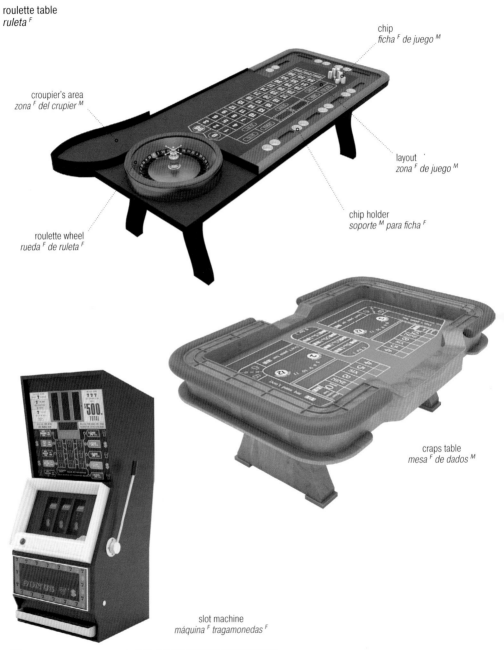

roulette table
ruleta F

chip
ficha F *de juego* M

croupier's area
zona F *del crupier* M

layout
zona F *de juego* M

chip holder
soporte M *para ficha* F

roulette wheel
rueda F *de ruleta* F

craps table
mesa F *de dados* M

slot machine
máquina F *tragamonedas* F

casino poker table
mesa F *de blackjack* M

poker table
mesa F *de póquer* M

card table
mesa F *de cartas* F

Suits
Palos M

hearts
corazones M

diamonds
diamantes M

clubs
tréboles M

spades
picas F

Face cards and special cards
Cartas F *de números* M *y cartas* F *de figuras* F

jack
sota F

queen
reina F

king
rey M

ace
as M

joker
joker M

Standard poker hands
Manos M *de póquer* M *estándar*

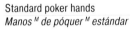

one pair
par M

two pairs
dos pares M

three of a kind
trío M

straight
escalera F

flush
color M

full house
full M

four of a kind
póquer M

straight flush
escalera F *de color* M

royal flush
escalera F *real*

tent
tienda ᶠ *de campaña* ᶠ

patio umbrella
sombrilla ᶠ *de terraza* ᶠ

pole
vara ᶠ

guy line
viento ᴹ

cooler
nevera ᶠ

antern
ámpara ᶠ

wall
tela ᶠ *de tienda* ᶠ

floor
suelo ᴹ

hook
gancho ᶠ

handle
mango ᴹ

lamp
lámpara ᶠ

folding camp stool
silla ᶠ *plegable*

globe
cristal ᴹ

seat
asiento ᴹ

leg
pata ᶠ

on/off button
botón ᴹ *de encendido* ᴹ

housing
cuerpo ᴹ

skid-proof foot
banda ᶠ *antideslizante*

backpack
mochila ᶠ

pocket knife
navaja ᶠ

flashlight
linterna ᶠ

sleeping bag
saco ᴹ *de dormir*

thermal jug
termo ᴹ

lounge chair
tumbona ᶠ

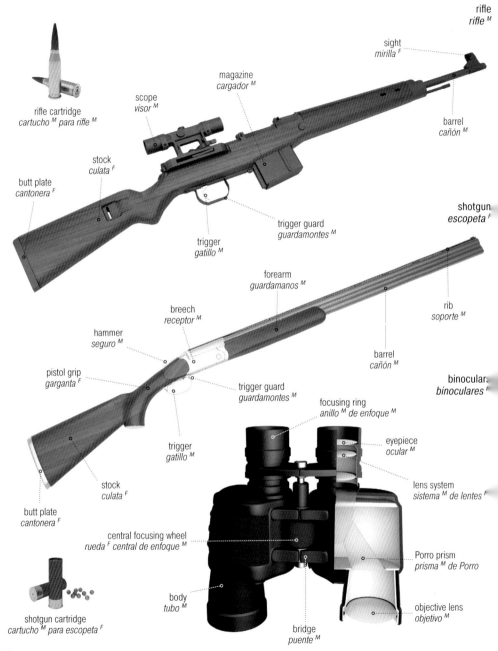

rifle
rifle M

sight
mirilla F

magazine
cargador M

scope
visor M

barrel
cañón M

rifle cartridge
cartucho M *para rifle* M

stock
culata F

butt plate
cantonera F

shotgun
escopeta F

trigger guard
guardamontes M

trigger
gatillo M

forearm
guardamanos M

breech
receptor M

rib
soporte M

hammer
seguro M

barrel
cañón M

pistol grip
garganta F

trigger guard
guardamontes M

binocular
binoculares F

focusing ring
anillo M *de enfoque* M

eyepiece
ocular M

trigger
gatillo M

lens system
sistema M *de lentes* F

stock
culata F

butt plate
cantonera F

central focusing wheel
rueda F *central de enfoque* M

Porro prism
prisma M *de Porro*

body
tubo M

objective lens
objetivo M

shotgun cartridge
cartucho M *para escopeta* F

bridge
puente M

reel
carrete M *de pesca* F

seat
asiento M *del rodillo* M

handle
manivela F

line spool nut
freno M *delantero*

spool
bobina F

bail
pick-up M

gear housing
caja F *del carrete* M

fishhook
anzuelo M

triple fishhook
anzuelo M *triple*

leg
brazo M

anti-reverse lever
palanca F *antirretroceso*

float
flotador M

bead
plomo M

fly fishing rod
caña F *de mosca* F

rod
caña F *de pescar*

float
flotador M

leader
quilla F

keeper ring
anilla F *destorcedora*

guide
anillo M *guía*

fly reel
carrete M *de mosca* F

fly line
línea F *de mosca* F

fishing line
línea F *de pescar*

spool
carrete M

handgrip
mango M

reel
carrete M

fishing lure
señuelo M

OFFICE

OFICINA

cubicles
cubículos ᴹ

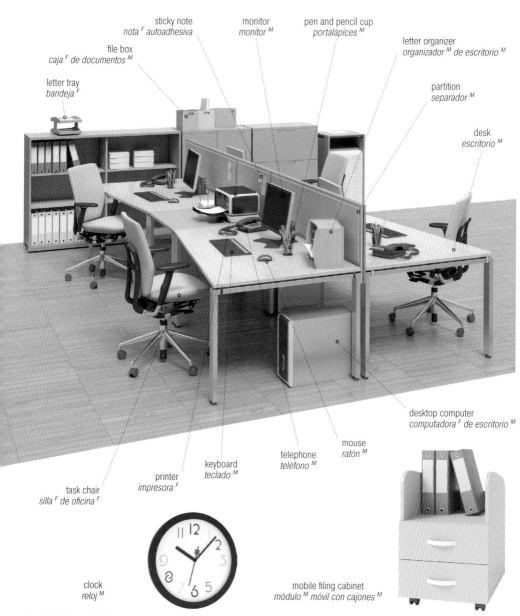

sticky note
nota ᶠ autoadhesiva

monitor
monitor ᴹ

pen and pencil cup
portalápices ᴹ

letter organizer
organizador ᴹ de escritorio ᴹ

file box
caja ᶠ de documentos ᴹ

letter tray
bandeja ᶠ

partition
separador ᴹ

desk
escritorio ᴹ

desktop computer
computadora ᶠ de escritorio ᴹ

mouse
ratón ᴹ

telephone
teléfono ᴹ

keyboard
teclado ᴹ

printer
impresora ᶠ

task chair
silla ᶠ de oficina ᶠ

clock
reloj ᴹ

mobile filing cabinet
módulo ᴹ móvil con cajones ᴹ

call center
centro M de atención telefónica F

storage cabinet
estante M

task chair
silla F de oficina F

headset
auriculares M

partition
separador M

monitor
monitor M

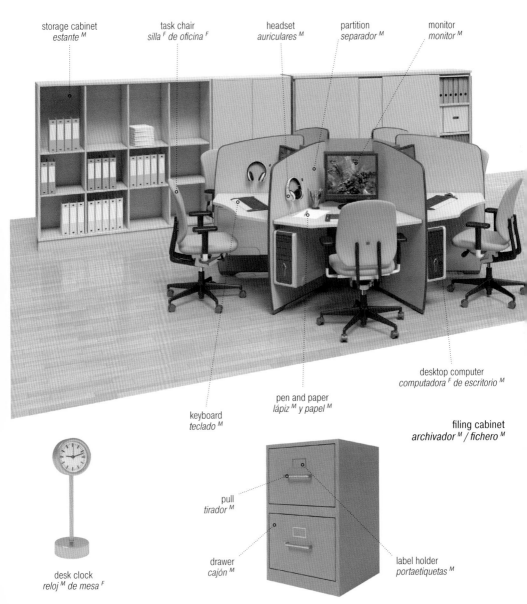

keyboard
teclado M

pen and paper
lápiz M y papel M

desktop computer
computadora F de escritorio M

filing cabinet
archivador M / fichero M

pull
tirador M

drawer
cajón M

label holder
portaetiquetas M

desk clock
reloj M de mesa F

reception
recepción ᶠ

binder
carpeta ᶠ *archivadora*

storage cabinet
estante ᴹ

paper
documento ᴹ

armchair
sillón ᴹ

cup
taza ᶠ

coffee table
mesa ᶠ *de café* ᴹ

executive armchair
silla ᶠ *ejecutiva*

bookcase
librero ᴹ

armrest
reposabrazos ᴹ

backrest
respaldo ᴹ

seat
asiento ᴹ

base
base ᶠ

height adjustment lever
regulador ᴹ *de altura* ᶠ

wheel
rueda ᶠ

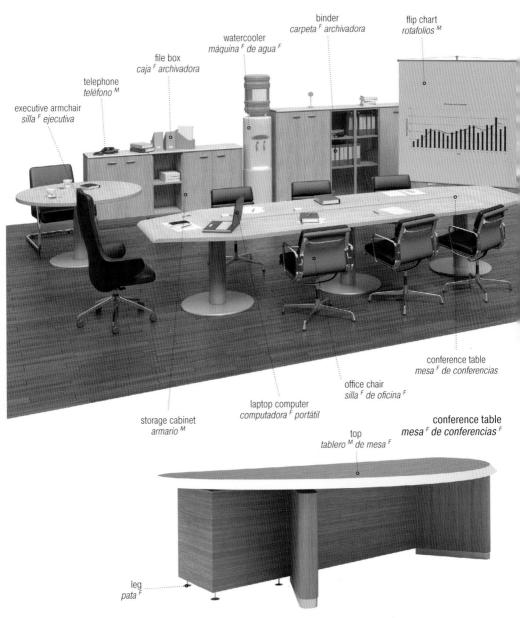

conference room
salón ^M *de conferencias*

binder
carpeta ^F *archivadora*

flip chart
rotafolios ^M

watercooler
máquina ^F *de agua* ^F

file box
caja ^F *archivadora*

telephone
teléfono ^M

executive armchair
silla ^F *ejecutiva*

conference table
mesa ^F *de conferencias*

office chair
silla ^F *de oficina* ^F

storage cabinet
armario ^M

laptop computer
computadora ^F *portátil*

conference table
mesa ^F *de conferencias* ^F

top
tablero ^M *de mesa* ^F

leg
pata ^F

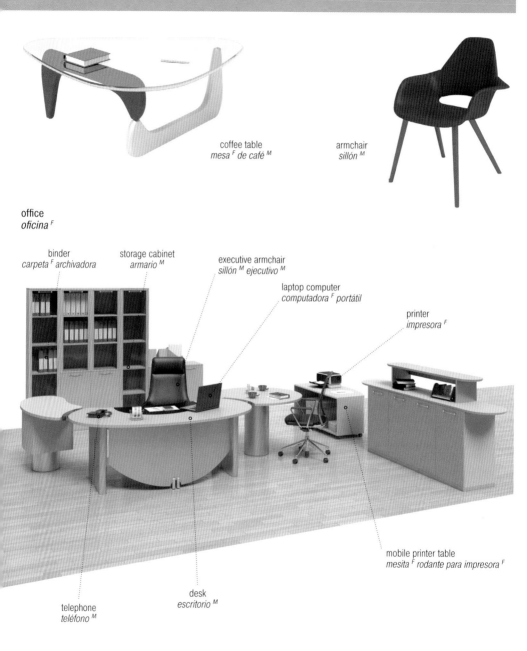

coffee table
mesa ^F *de café* ^M

armchair
sillón ^M

office
oficina ^F

binder
carpeta ^F *archivadora*

storage cabinet
armario ^M

executive armchair
sillón ^M *ejecutivo* ^M

laptop computer
computadora ^F *portátil*

printer
impresora ^F

mobile printer table
mesita ^F *rodante para impresora* ^F

desk
escritorio ^M

telephone
teléfono ^M

break room
salón ^M *de descanso* ^M

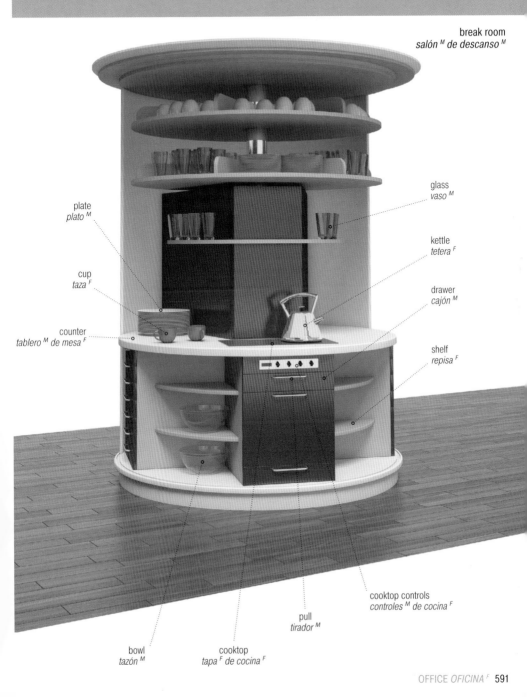

glass
vaso ^M

plate
plato ^M

kettle
tetera ^F

cup
taza ^F

drawer
cajón ^M

counter
tablero ^M *de mesa* ^F

shelf
repisa ^F

cooktop controls
controles ^M *de cocina* ^F

pull
tirador ^M

bowl
tazón ^M

cooktop
tapa ^F *de cocina* ^F

filing cabinet
archivero ᴹ

stationary cabinet
vitrina ᶠ *para documentos* ᴹ

Vending machines
Máquinas ᶠ *expendedoras*

coffeemaker
cafetera ᶠ

coffee hopper
tolva ᶠ *para el café* ᴹ

control panel
panel ᴹ *de control* ᴹ

drip tray
bandeja ᶠ *de goteo* ᴹ

nozzle
boquilla ᶠ

snack food vending machine
máquina ᶠ *expendedora*

coffee machine
máquina ᶠ *de café* ᴹ

hot and cold beverage vending machine
máquina ᶠ *expendedora con bebidas* ᶠ *frías y calientes*

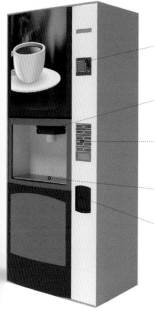

bill acceptor
ranura ᶠ *para dinero* ᴹ

nozzle
boquilla ᶠ

drink selection keypad
teclado ᴹ *para*
seleccionar bebidas ᶠ

drip tray
bandeja ᶠ *de goteo* ᴹ

change return slot
ventana ᶠ *de entrega* ᶠ
de cambio ᴹ

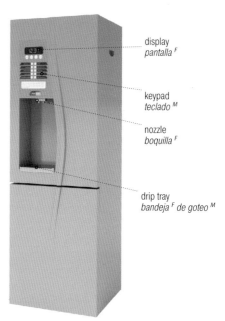

display
pantalla ᶠ

keypad
teclado ᴹ

nozzle
boquilla ᶠ

drip tray
bandeja ᶠ *de goteo* ᴹ

beverage vending machine
máquina ᶠ *expendedora*

display
expositor ᴹ

beverage bottle
botella ᶠ

bill acceptor
ranura ᶠ *para dinero* ᴹ

keypad
teclado ᴹ

laptop computer
computadora [F] *portátil*

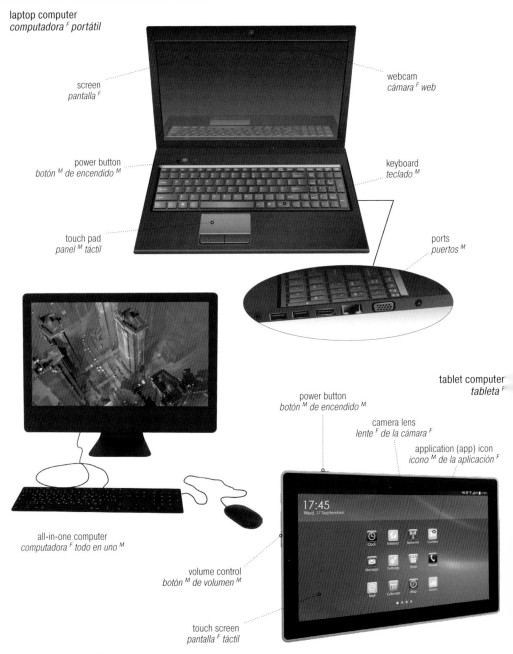

screen
pantalla [F]

webcam
cámara [F] *web*

power button
botón [M] *de encendido* [M]

keyboard
teclado [M]

touch pad
panel [M] *táctil*

ports
puertos [M]

tablet computer
tableta [F]

power button
botón [M] *de encendido* [M]

camera lens
lente [F] *de la cámara* [F]

application (app) icon
icono [M] *de la aplicación* [F]

all-in-one computer
computadora [F] *todo en uno* [M]

volume control
botón [M] *de volumen* [M]

touch screen
pantalla [F] *táctil*

17:45
Wed, 17 September

Clock   Internet   Network   Camera

Message   Settings   Shop   Phone

Mail   Calendar   Map   Stocks

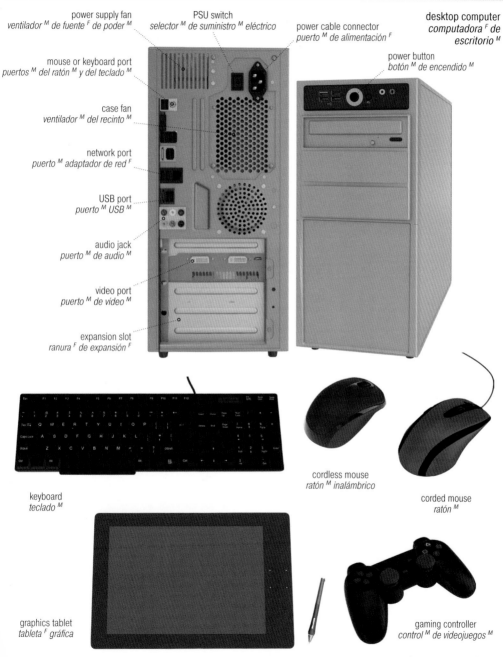

power supply fan
ventilador ᴹ *de fuente* ᶠ *de poder* ᴹ

PSU switch
selector ᴹ *de suministro* ᴹ *eléctrico*

power cable connector
puerto ᴹ *de alimentación* ᶠ

desktop computer
computadora ᶠ *de escritorio* ᴹ

power button
botón ᴹ *de encendido* ᴹ

mouse or keyboard port
puertos ᴹ *del ratón* ᴹ *y del teclado* ᴹ

case fan
ventilador ᴹ *del recinto* ᴹ

network port
puerto ᴹ *adaptador de red* ᶠ

USB port
puerto ᴹ *USB* ᴹ

audio jack
puerto ᴹ *de audio* ᴹ

video port
puerto ᴹ *de video* ᴹ

expansion slot
ranura ᶠ *de expansión* ᶠ

keyboard
teclado ᴹ

cordless mouse
ratón ᴹ *inalámbrico*

corded mouse
ratón ᴹ

graphics tablet
tableta ᶠ *gráfica*

gaming controller
control ᴹ *de videojuegos* ᴹ

Printers, copiers and scanners
Impresoras, [F] *fotocopiadoras* [F] *y escáneres* [M]

laser printer
impresora [F] *láser*

plotter
trazador [M] *de gráficos*

ink cartridge
cartucho [M] *de tinta* [F] *de impresora* [F]

toner cartridge
cartucho [M] *de impresora* [F] *láser*

flatbed scanner
escáner [M] *plano* [M]

sheetfed scanner
escáner [M] *de alimentación* [F] *vertical*

paper tray
bandeja [F] *para papeles* [M]

cover
tapa [F]

belt
cinta [F]

scan head
cabezal [M] *de escaneo*

platen glass
cristal [M]

control panel
panel [M] *de control* [M]

power button
botón [M] *de encendido* [M]/*apagado* [M]

output tray
bandeja [F] *de salida*

ink-jet printer
impresora ^F *de chorro* ^M *de tinta* ^F

control panel
panel ^M *de control* ^M

display
pantalla ^F

copier
fotocopiadora ^F

power button
botón ^M *de encendido* ^M

memory card
tarjeta ^F *de memoria* ^F

Other electronic devices *Otros aparatos* ^M *electrónicos*

headset
auriculares ^M

headband
banda ^F *de la cabeza* ^F

smartphone
teléfono ^M *inteligente*

power button
botón ^M *de encendido* ^M

receiver
receptor ^M

camera lens
lente ^F *de la cámara* ^F

earpiece
auricular ^M

volume control
botón ^M *de volumen* ^M

touch screen
pantalla ^F *táctil*

application (app) icon
icono ^M *de la aplicación* ^F

back button
botón ^M *atrás*

microphone
micrófono ^M

cable
cable ^M

menu button
botón ^M *del menú* ^M

home button
botón ^M *de inicio* ^M

microphone
micrófono M

webcam
cámara F *web*

fax
fax M

Internet stick
módem M *USB* M

display
pantalla F

handset cord
cable M *del auricular* M

handset
auricular M

speed dial button
botón M *de marcado* M *rápido*

keypad
teclado M

telephone
teléfono M

push button
botón M

speed dial directory
directorio M *de marcado* M *rápido*

automatic document feeder
alimentador M *de documentos* M

power button
botón M *de encendido* M

handset
auricular M

start button
botón M *de enviar fax* M

display
pantalla F

handset cord
cable M *del auricular* M

wireless router
router M *inalámbrico*

indicator light
indicador M

antenna
antena F

power button
botón M *de encendido* M

printing calculator
calculadora F *con función* F *de impresión* M

calculator
calculadora F

paper roll
rollo M *de papel* M

key
tecla F

screen
pantalla F

shredder
trituradora F

control button
botón M *de control* M

cutting head
cabezal M *de corte* M

lid
tapa F

pocket calculator
calculadora F *de bolsillo* M

waste basket
cesto M *de basura* F

monitor
monitor M

label maker
etiquetadora ᶠ

external hard drive
disco ᴹ *duro externo*

display
pantalla ᶠ

navigation buttons
botones ᴹ *de navegación* ᶠ

USB flash drive
memoria ᶠ *USB* ᴹ

connector
enchufe ᴹ

keypad
teclado ᴹ

case
cuerpo ᴹ

control button
botón ᴹ *de control* ᴹ

cap
tapón ᴹ

digital voice recorder
grabadora ᶠ *digital*

display
pantalla ᶠ

02/02

01.28:05

control button
botón ᴹ *de control* ᴹ

loudspeaker
altavoz ᴹ

e-reader
lector ᴹ *de libros* ᴹ *electrónicos*

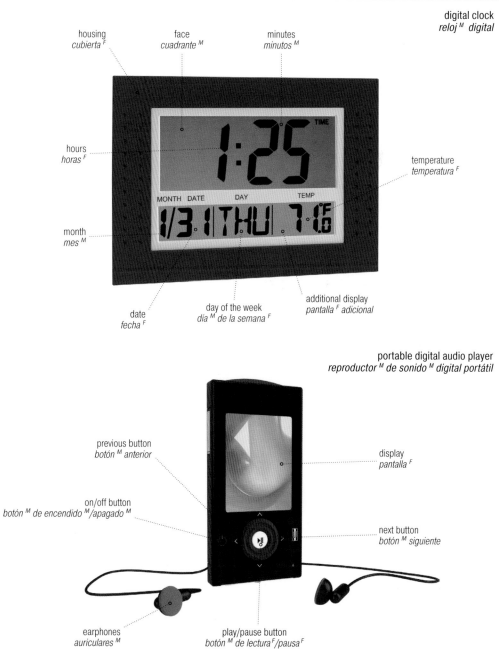

digital clock
reloj ᴹ *digital*

housing
cubierta ᶠ

face
cuadrante ᴹ

minutes
minutos ᴹ

hours
horas ᶠ

temperature
temperatura ᶠ

month
mes ᴹ

date
fecha ᶠ

day of the week
día ᴹ *de la semana* ᶠ

additional display
pantalla ᶠ *adicional*

portable digital audio player
reproductor ᴹ *de sonido* ᴹ *digital portátil*

previous button
botón ᴹ *anterior*

display
pantalla ᶠ

on/off button
botón ᴹ *de encendido* ᴹ*/apagado* ᴹ

next button
botón ᴹ *siguiente*

earphones
auriculares ᴹ

play/pause button
botón ᴹ *de lectura* ᶠ*/pausa* ᶠ

single-lens reflex (SLR) digital camera: front view
cámara ᶠ *digital reflex de lente* ᶠ *única: vista* ᶠ *frontal*

accessory shoe
zapata ᶠ *para accesorios* ᴹ

data display
panel ᴹ *de datos* ᴹ

hot-shoe contact
zapata ᶠ *de contacto* ᴹ *para flash* ᴹ

shutter release button
botón ᴹ *disparador*

mode dial
selector de modos ᴹ

focus setting ring
anillo ᴹ *para ajustar el enfoque* ᴹ

neckstrap eyelet
anilla ᶠ *para correa* ᶠ

lens
objetivos ᴹ

camery body
cámara ᶠ

single-lens reflex (SLR) digital camera: back view
cámara ᶠ *digital reflex de lente* ᶠ *única: vista trasera*

lens aperture scale
escala ᶠ *de abertura* ᶠ *de objetivos* ᴹ

viewfinder
visor ᴹ

menu button
botón ᴹ *menú* ᴹ

settings display button
botón ᴹ *de funciones* ᶠ *de visualización* ᶠ

image review button
botón ᴹ *de revisión* ᶠ *de imagen* ᶠ

erase button
botón ᴹ *de eliminar*

display
pantalla ᶠ

enlarge button
botón ᴹ *de ampliar*

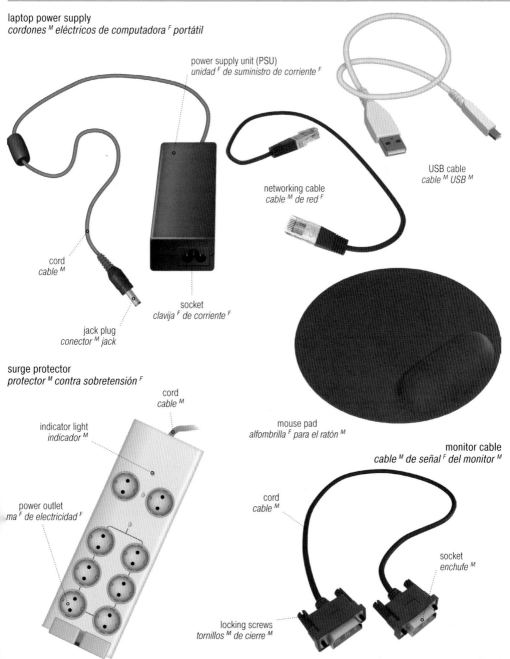

laptop power supply
cordones ^M *eléctricos de computadora* ^F *portátil*

power supply unit (PSU)
unidad ^F *de suministro de corriente* ^F

USB cable
cable ^M *USB* ^M

networking cable
cable ^M *de red* ^F

cord
cable ^M

socket
clavija ^F *de corriente* ^F

jack plug
conector ^M *jack*

surge protector
protector ^M *contra sobretensión* ^F

cord
cable ^M

indicator light
indicador ^M

mouse pad
alfombrilla ^F *para el ratón* ^M

monitor cable
cable ^M *de señal* ^F *del monitor* ^M

power outlet
ma ^F *de electricidad* ^F

cord
cable ^M

socket
enchufe ^M

locking screws
tornillos ^M *de cierre* ^M

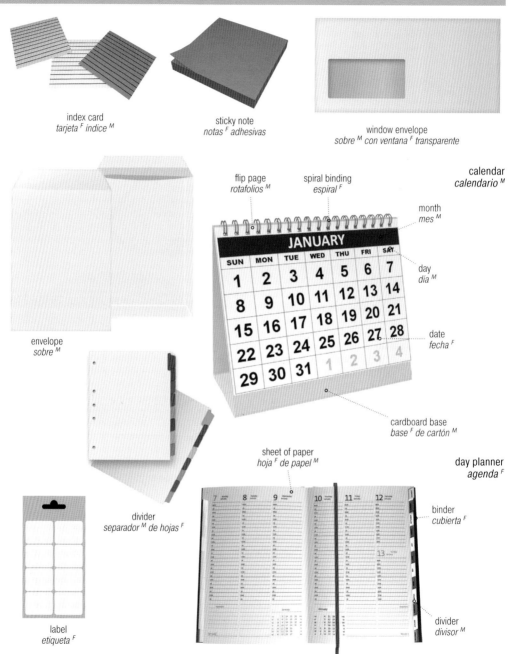

index card
tarjeta F *índice* M

sticky note
notas F *adhesivas*

window envelope
sobre M *con ventana* F *transparente*

envelope
sobre M

flip page
rotafolios M

spiral binding
espiral F

calendar
calendario M

month
mes M

JANUARY

day
día M

date
fecha F

cardboard base
base F *de cartón* M

sheet of paper
hoja F *de papel* M

day planner
agenda F

binder
cubierta F

divider
separador M *de hojas* F

divider
divisor M

label
etiqueta F

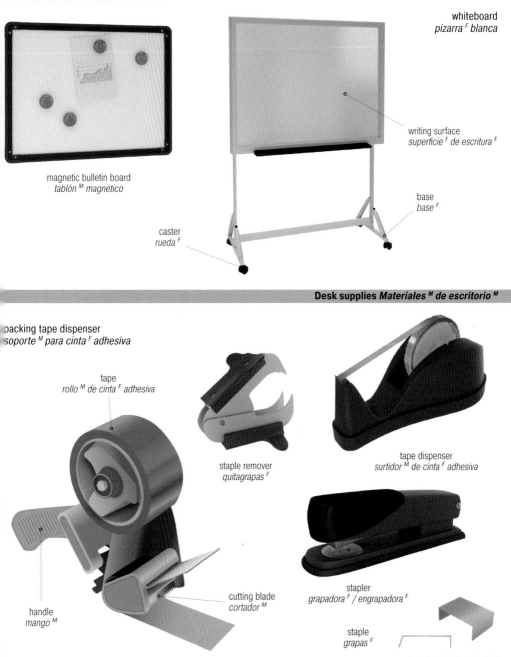

whiteboard
pizarra [F] *blanca*

writing surface
superficie [F] *de escritura* [F]

magnetic bulletin board
tablón [M] *magnético*

base
base [F]

caster
rueda [F]

Desk supplies *Materiales* [M] *de escritorio* [M]

packing tape dispenser
soporte [M] *para cinta* [F] *adhesiva*

tape
rollo [M] *de cinta* [F] *adhesiva*

staple remover
quitagrapas [F]

tape dispenser
surtidor [M] *de cinta* [F] *adhesiva*

cutting blade
cortador [M]

handle
mango [M]

stapler
grapadora [F] / *engrapadora* [F]

staple
grapas [F]

set square
transportador ^M

pencil sharpener
sacapuntas ^M

blade
hoja ^F

paper punch
perforadora ^F *de papel* ^M

glue stick
pegamento ^M *en barra* ^F

box cutter
cúter ^M / *cuchillo* ^M *de trabajo* ^M

slide lock
marco ^M *limitador*

correction tape
cinta ^F *correctora*

blade
hoja ^F

handle
mango ^M

paper clip
clip ^M

eraser
goma ^F *de borrar*

ruler
regla ^F

handle
manivela ^F

pushpin
chincheta ^F

paper cutter
guillotina ^F

paper guide
guía ^F *para el papel* ^M

clamp lock
regulador ^M

base
base ^F

wastebasket
papelera ^F

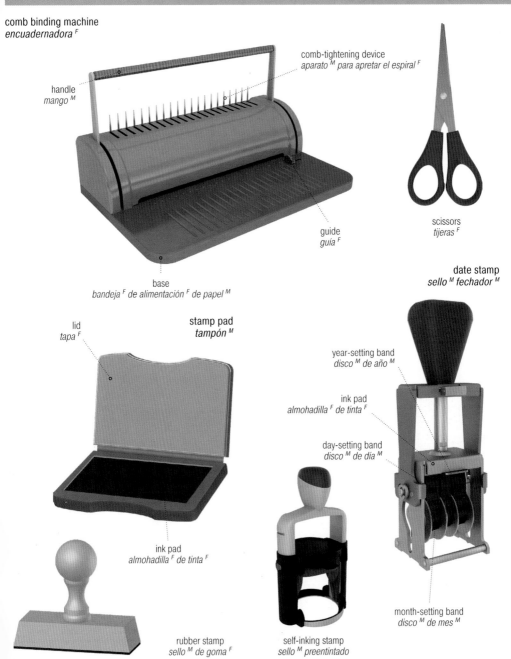

comb binding machine
encuadernadora ^F

handle
mango ^M

comb-tightening device
aparato ^M *para apretar el espiral* ^F

guide
guía ^F

base
bandeja ^F *de alimentación* ^F *de papel* ^M

scissors
tijeras ^F

date stamp
sello ^M *fechador* ^M

lid
tapa ^F

stamp pad
tampón ^M

year-setting band
disco ^M *de año* ^M

ink pad
almohadilla ^F *de tinta* ^F

day-setting band
disco ^M *de día* ^M

ink pad
almohadilla ^F *de tinta* ^F

rubber stamp
sello ^M *de goma* ^F

self-inking stamp
sello ^M *preentintado*

month-setting band
disco ^M *de mes* ^M

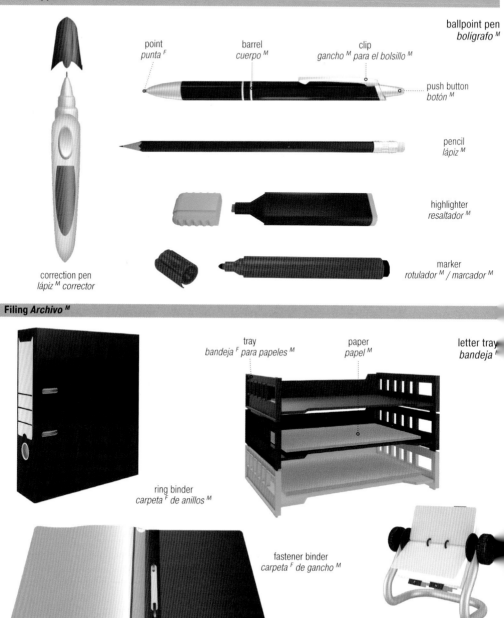

ballpoint pen
bolígrafo M

point
punta F

barrel
cuerpo M

clip
gancho M *para el bolsillo* M

push button
botón M

pencil
lápiz M

highlighter
resaltador M

marker
rotulador M / *marcador* M

correction pen
lápiz M *corrector*

Filing *Archivo* M

tray
bandeja F *para papeles* M

paper
papel M

letter tray
bandeja F

ring binder
carpeta F *de anillos* M

fastener binder
carpeta F *de gancho* M

rotary file
tarjetero M *giratorio*

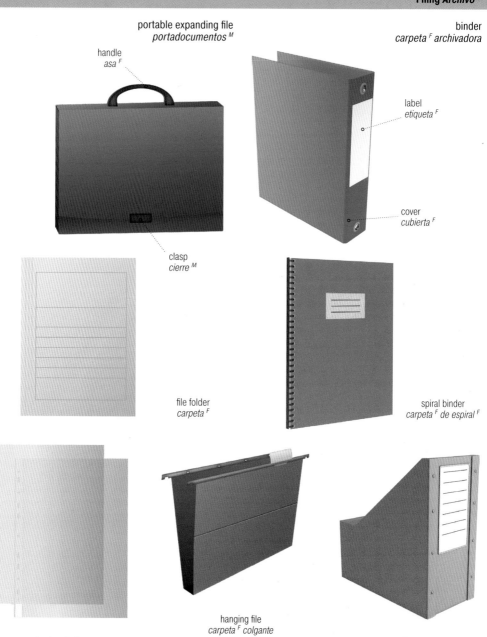

portable expanding file
portadocumentos M

handle
asa F

binder
carpeta F *archivadora*

label
etiqueta F

cover
cubierta F

clasp
cierre M

file folder
carpeta F

spiral binder
carpeta F *de espiral* F

sheet protector
funda F *de plástico* M

hanging file
carpeta F *colgante*

file box
revistero M

diacritics
signos ^M *diacríticos*

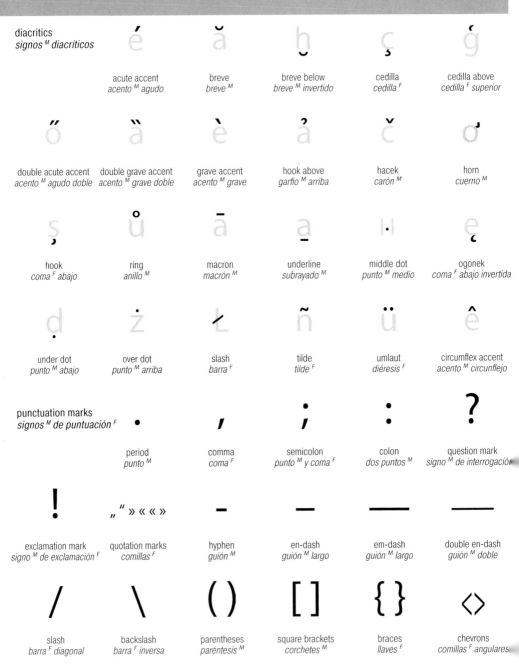

acute accent *acento* ^M *agudo*	breve *breve* ^M	breve below *breve* ^M *invertido*	cedilla *cedilla* ^F	cedilla above *cedilla* ^F *superior*
double acute accent *acento* ^M *agudo doble*	double grave accent *acento* ^M *grave doble*	grave accent *acento* ^M *grave*	hook above *garfio* ^M *arriba*	hacek *carón* ^M	horn *cuerno* ^M
hook *coma* ^F *abajo*	ring *anillo* ^M	macron *macrón* ^M	underline *subrayado* ^M	middle dot *punto* ^M *medio*	ogonek *coma* ^F *abajo invertida*
under dot *punto* ^M *abajo*	over dot *punto* ^M *arriba*	slash *barra* ^F	tilde *tilde* ^F	umlaut *diéresis* ^F	circumflex accent *acento* ^M *circunflejo*

punctuation marks
signos ^M *de puntuación* ^F

period *punto* ^M	comma *coma* ^F	semicolon *punto* ^M *y coma* ^F	colon *dos puntos* ^M	question mark *signo* ^M *de interrogación*
exclamation mark *signo* ^M *de exclamación* ^F	quotation marks *comillas* ^F	hyphen *guión* ^M	en-dash *guión* ^M *largo*	em-dash *guión* ^M *largo*	double en-dash *guión* ^M *doble*
slash *barra* ^F *diagonal*	backslash *barra* ^F *inversa*	parentheses *paréntesis* ^M	square brackets *corchetes* ^M	braces *llaves* ^F	chevrons *comillas* ^F *angulares*

ellipsis
puntos [M] suspensivos

apostrophe
apóstrofe [F]

double hyphen
guión [M] doble

interrobang
interrobang [M]

tilde
acento [M]

bullet
viñeta [F]

pound
almohadilla [F]

number sign
signo [M] de número [M]

section sign
símbolo [M] de sección [F]

pilcrow
calderón [M]

at
arroba [F]

ampersand
signo & [M] / ampersand [M]

other marks
Otros signos [M]

prime
primo [M]

double dagger
daga [F] doble

asterisk
asterisco [M]

asterism
asterismo [M]

dagger
daga [F]

double prime
primo [M] doble

vertical line
línea [F] vertical

degree sign
signo [M] de grado

typesetting
composición [F] tipográfica

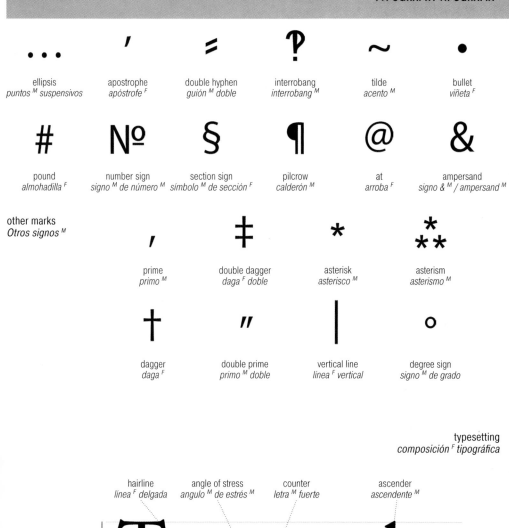

hairline
línea [F] delgada

angle of stress
ángulo [M] de estrés [M]

counter
letra [M] fuerte

ascender
ascendente [M]

capital letter height
*altura [F] de una
letra [F] mayúscula*

baseline
línea [F] principal

descender
descendente [M]

serif
serif [M]

width
ancho [M]

x-height
tamaño [M] del corpus [M]

TRANSPORTATION

TRANSPORTE

interchange
intercambio ᴹ *vial*

car
coche ᴹ

arch bridge
puente ᴹ *de arco* ᴹ

road marking
líneas ꟳ *de carretera* ꟳ

traffic sign
señal ꟳ *de tráfico* ᴹ

roadway
carretera ꟳ

billboard (back view)
valla ꟳ *publicitaria* ꟳ *(vista* ꟳ *posterior)*

safety railing
barandilla ꟳ

road worker
trabajador ᴹ *de carreteras* ꟳ

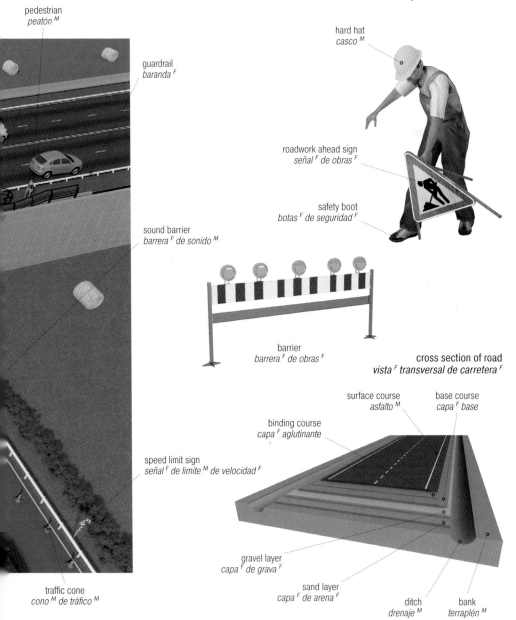

road worker
trabajador ^F *de carreteras* ^F

pedestrian
peatón ^M

hard hat
casco ^M

guardrail
baranda ^F

roadwork ahead sign
señal ^F *de obras* ^F

safety boot
botas ^F *de seguridad* ^F

sound barrier
barrera ^F *de sonido* ^M

barrier
barrera ^F *de obras* ^F

cross section of road
vista ^F *transversal de carretera* ^F

surface course
asfalto ^M

base course
capa ^F *base*

binding course
capa ^F *aglutinante*

speed limit sign
señal ^F *de límite* ^M *de velocidad* ^F

gravel layer
capa ^F *de grava* ^F

sand layer
capa ^F *de arena* ^F

traffic cone
cono ^M *de tráfico* ^M

ditch
drenaje ^M

bank
terraplén ^M

arch bridge
puente M *en arco* M

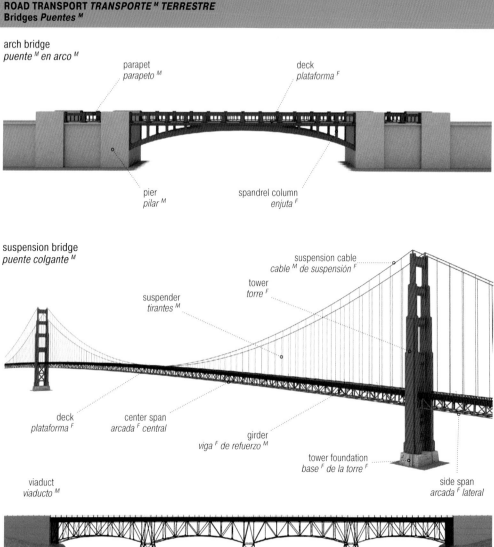

parapet
parapeto M

deck
plataforma F

pier
pilar M

spandrel column
enjuta F

suspension bridge
puente colgante M

suspension cable
cable M *de suspensión* F

tower
torre F

suspender
tirantes M

deck
plataforma F

center span
arcada F *central*

girder
viga F *de refuerzo* M

tower foundation
base F *de la torre* F

side span
arcada F *lateral*

viaduct
viaducto M

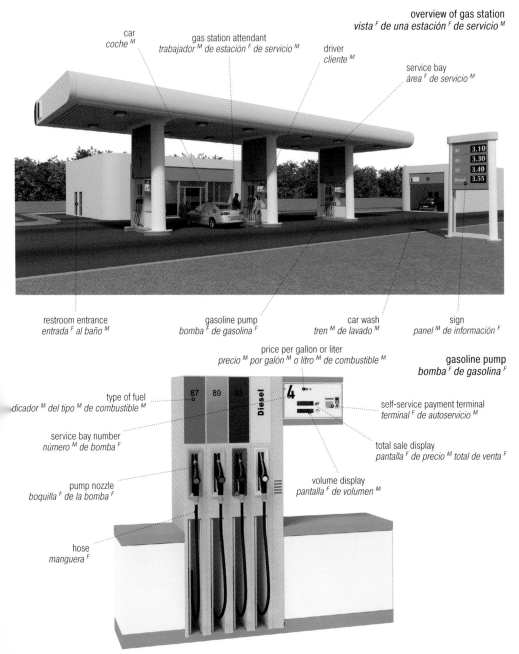

overview of gas station
vista ^F *de una estación* ^F *de servicio* ^M

car
coche ^M

gas station attendant
trabajador ^M *de estación* ^F *de servicio* ^M

driver
cliente ^M

service bay
área ^F *de servicio* ^M

restroom entrance
entrada ^F *al baño* ^M

gasoline pump
bomba ^F *de gasolina* ^F

car wash
tren ^M *de lavado* ^M

sign
panel ^M *de información* ^F

price per gallon or liter
precio ^M *por galón* ^M *o litro* ^M *de combustible* ^M

gasoline pump
bomba ^F *de gasolina* ^F

type of fuel
indicador ^M *del tipo* ^M *de combustible* ^M

self-service payment terminal
terminal ^F *de autoservicio* ^M

service bay number
número ^M *de bomba* ^F

total sale display
pantalla ^F *de precio* ^M *total de venta* ^F

pump nozzle
boquilla ^F *de la bomba* ^F

volume display
pantalla ^F *de volumen* ^M

hose
manguera ^F

Car accessories
Accesorios ^M *de automóvil* ^M

jack
gato ^M

jumper cables
cables ^M *puente*

fire extinguisher
extintor ^M

bicycle rack
portabicicletas ^M

sun visor
parasol ^M

floor mat
alfombrilla ^F

snow brush with scraper
cepillo ^M *para nieve* ^F *con raspador* ^M

ski rack
portaesquís ^M

trailer hitch
gancho ^M *de remolque* ^M

scraper
rasqueta ^F

roller shade
cortinillas ^F

infant car seat
silla ^F *de seguridad* ^F *para bebés* ^M

booster car seat
asiento ^M *elevador* ^M

child car seat
silla ^F *de seguridad* ^F *para niños* ^N

emergency warning triangle
triángulo ^M *de seguridad* ^F

first-aid kit
botiquín ^M *de primeros auxilios* ^M

reflective vest
chaleco ^M *reflector*

lug wrench
llave ^F *de cruz* ^F

Car systems
Sistemas ^M *del coche* ^M

cooling system
sistema ^M *de refrigeración* ^F

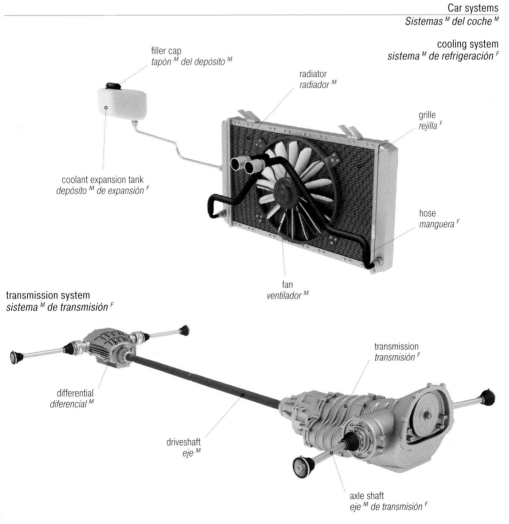

filler cap
tapón ^M *del depósito* ^M

radiator
radiador ^M

grille
rejilla ^F

coolant expansion tank
depósito ^M *de expansión* ^F

hose
manguera ^F

fan
ventilador ^M

transmission system
sistema ^M *de transmisión* ^F

transmission
transmisión ^F

differential
diferencial ^M

driveshaft
eje ^M

axle shaft
eje ^M *de transmisión* ^F

braking system
sistema M *de frenado* M

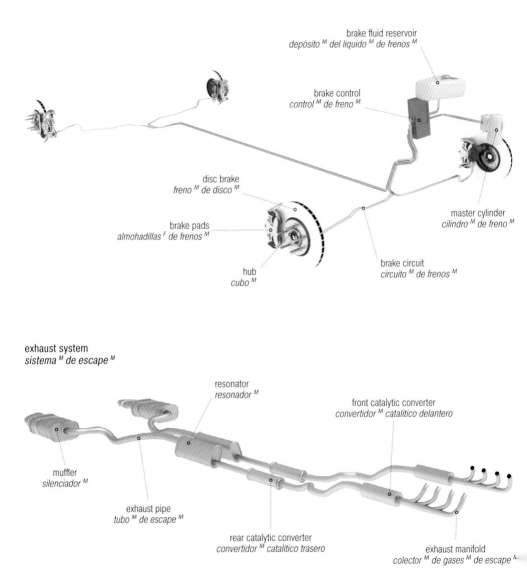

brake fluid reservoir
depósito M *del líquido* M *de frenos* M

brake control
control M *de freno* M

disc brake
freno M *de disco* M

brake pads
almohadillas F *de frenos* M

master cylinder
cilindro M *de freno* M

hub
cubo M

brake circuit
circuito M *de frenos* M

exhaust system
sistema M *de escape* M

resonator
resonador M

front catalytic converter
convertidor M *catalítico delantero*

muffler
silenciador M

exhaust pipe
tubo M *de escape* M

rear catalytic converter
convertidor M *catalítico trasero*

exhaust manifold
colector M *de gases* M *de escape* M

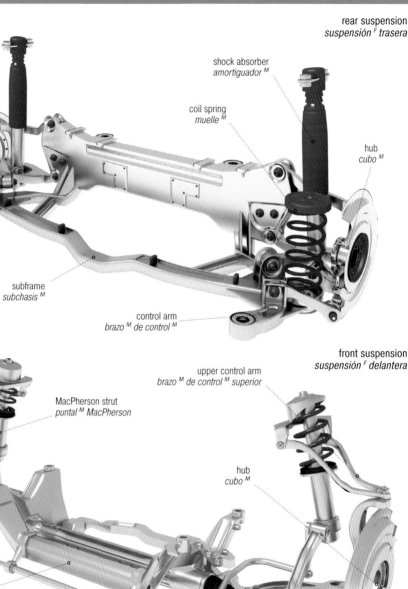

rear suspension
suspensión ^F *trasera*

shock absorber
amortiguador ^M

coil spring
muelle ^M

hub
cubo ^M

subframe
subchasis ^M

control arm
brazo ^M *de control* ^M

front suspension
suspensión ^F *delantera*

upper control arm
brazo ^M *de control* ^M *superior*

MacPherson strut
puntal ^M *MacPherson*

hub
cubo ^M

subframe
subchasis ^M

sway bar
estabilizador ^M *transversal*

engine
motor ^M

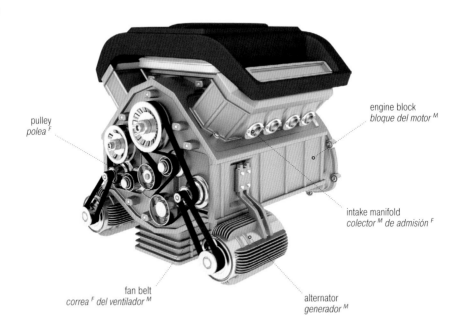

pulley
polea ^F

engine block
bloque del motor ^M

intake manifold
colector ^M *de admisión* ^F

fan belt
correa ^F *del ventilador* ^M

alternator
generador ^M

four-stroke engine cycle
ciclo ^M *de un motor* ^M *de cuatro tiempos* ^M

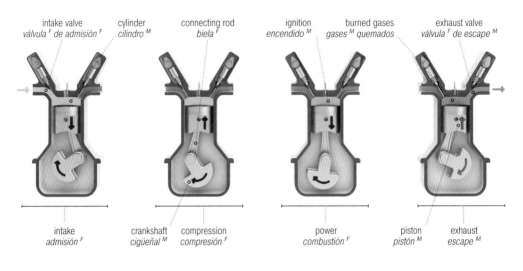

intake valve
válvula ^F *de admisión* ^F

cylinder
cilindro ^M

connecting rod
biela ^F

ignition
encendido ^M

burned gases
gases ^M *quemados*

exhaust valve
válvula ^F *de escape* ^M

intake
admisión ^F

crankshaft
cigüeñal ^M

compression
compresión ^F

power
combustión ^F

piston
pistón ^M

exhaust
escape ^M

rear fascia
parte ᶠ *trasera*

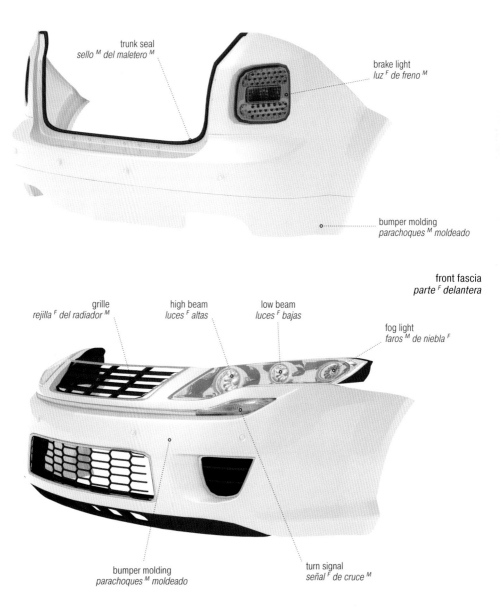

trunk seal
sello ᴹ *del maletero* ᴹ

brake light
luz ᶠ *de freno* ᴹ

bumper molding
parachoques ᴹ *moldeado*

front fascia
parte ᶠ *delantera*

grille
rejilla ᶠ *del radiador* ᴹ

high beam
luces ᶠ *altas*

low beam
luces ᶠ *bajas*

fog light
faros ᴹ *de niebla* ᶠ

bumper molding
parachoques ᴹ *moldeado*

turn signal
señal ᶠ *de cruce* ᴹ

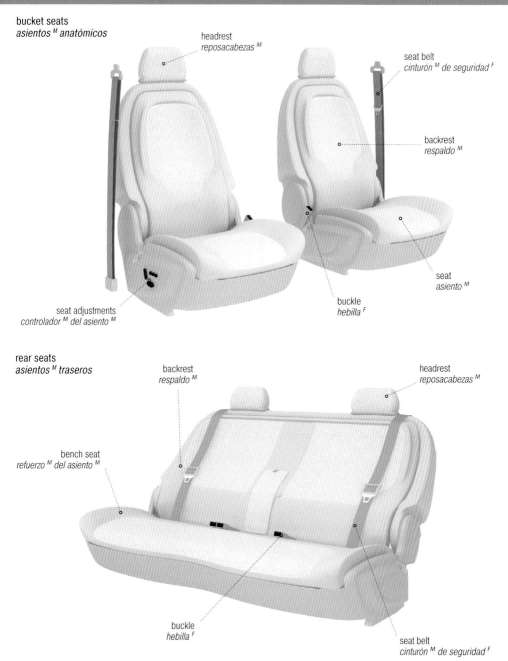

bucket seats
asientos ᴹ *anatómicos*

headrest
reposacabezas ᴹ

seat belt
cinturón ᴹ *de seguridad* ꜰ

backrest
respaldo ᴹ

seat
asiento ᴹ

buckle
hebilla ꜰ

seat adjustments
controlador ᴹ *del asiento* ᴹ

rear seats
asientos ᴹ *traseros*

backrest
respaldo ᴹ

headrest
reposacabezas ᴹ

bench seat
refuerzo ᴹ *del asiento* ᴹ

buckle
hebilla ꜰ

seat belt
cinturón ᴹ *de seguridad* ꜰ

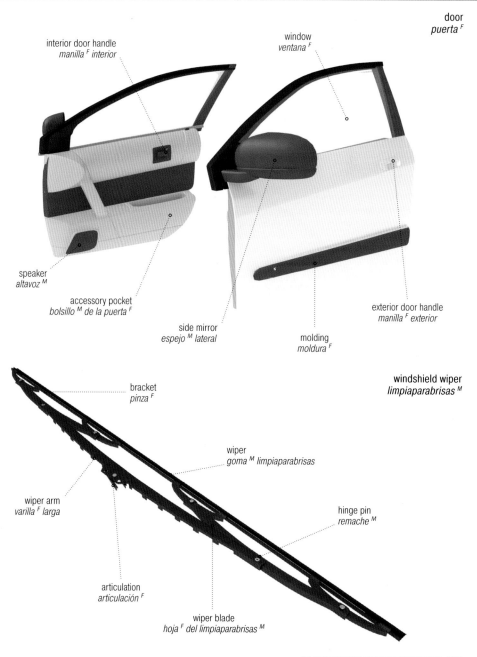

door
puerta ᶠ

interior door handle
manilla ᶠ *interior*

window
ventana ᶠ

speaker
altavoz ᴹ

accessory pocket
bolsillo ᴹ *de la puerta* ᶠ

side mirror
espejo ᴹ *lateral*

molding
moldura ᶠ

exterior door handle
manilla ᶠ *exterior*

windshield wiper
limpiaparabrisas ᴹ

bracket
pinza ᶠ

wiper
goma ᴹ *limpiaparabrisas*

wiper arm
varilla ᶠ *larga*

hinge pin
remache ᴹ

articulation
articulación ᶠ

wiper blade
hoja ᶠ *del limpiaparabrisas* ᴹ

instrument panel
tablero [M] *de control* [M]

left turn signal indicator
señal [F] *de cruce* [M] *a la izquierda* [F]

alternator warning light
alerta [F] *de carga* [F] *del alternador* [M]

warning light
indicador [M] *de alerta* [F]

tachometer
tacómetro [M]

scale
escala [F]

needle
aguja [F]

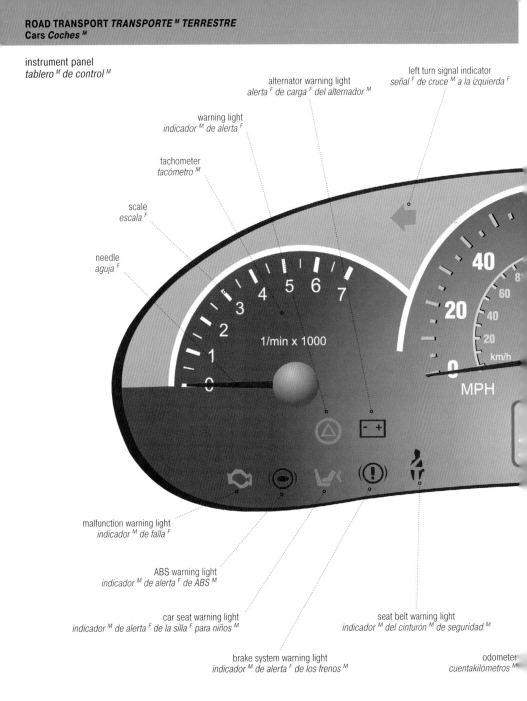

malfunction warning light
indicador [M] *de falla* [F]

ABS warning light
indicador [M] *de alerta* [F] *de ABS* [M]

car seat warning light
indicador [M] *de alerta* [F] *de la silla* [F] *para niños* [M]

seat belt warning light
indicador [M] *del cinturón* [M] *de seguridad* [M]

brake system warning light
indicador [M] *de alerta* [F] *de los frenos* [M]

odometer
cuentakilómetros [M]

speedometer
velocímetro ^M

temperature indicator
indicador ^M *de temperatura* ^F

right turn signal indicator
señal ^F *de cruce* ^M *a la derecha* ^F

parking brake indicator light
indicador ^M *de freno* ^M *de mano* ^M

fuel indicator
indicador ^M *de combustible* ^M

low fuel warning light
indicador ^M *de alerta* ^F *de combustible* ^M *bajo*

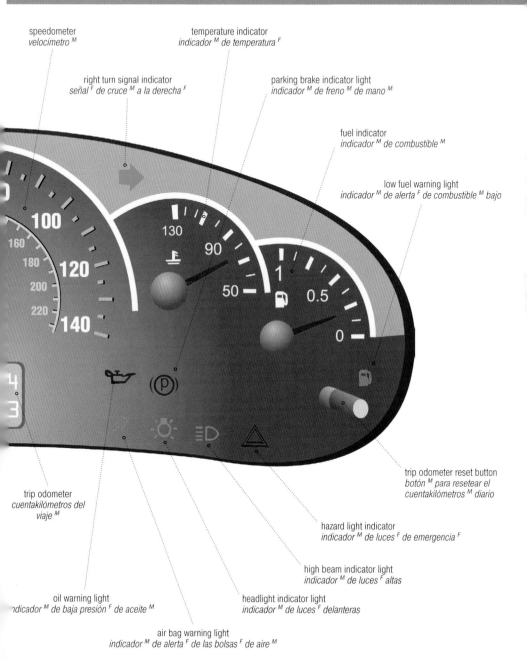

trip odometer reset button
botón ^M *para resetear el*
cuentakilómetros ^M *diario*

trip odometer
cuentakilómetros del
viaje ^M

hazard light indicator
indicador ^M *de luces* ^F *de emergencia* ^F

high beam indicator light
indicador ^M *de luces* ^F *altas*

oil warning light
indicador ^M *de baja presión* ^F *de aceite* ^M

headlight indicator light
indicador ^M *de luces* ^F *delanteras*

air bag warning light
indicador ^M *de alerta* ^F *de las bolsas* ^F *de aire* ^M

tires
neumáticos M

tread
huella F

hubcap
tapacubos M

bolt
tornillo M

brake pads
pastillas F *de freno* M

shock absorber
amortiguador M

suspension coil spring
muelle M *de suspensión* F

disc brake
freno M *de disco* M

leaf spring
muelle M

tire
neumático M

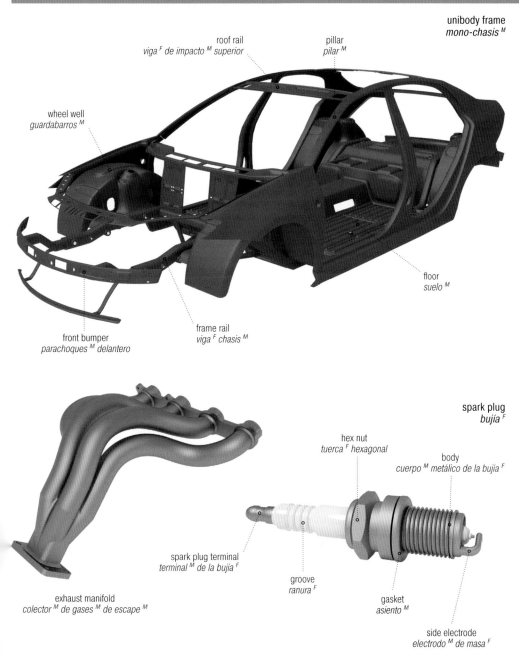

unibody frame
mono-chasis ^M

roof rail
viga ^F *de impacto* ^M *superior*

pillar
pilar ^M

wheel well
guardabarros ^M

floor
suelo ^M

front bumper
parachoques ^M *delantero*

frame rail
viga ^F *chasis* ^M

spark plug
bujía ^F

hex nut
tuerca ^F *hexagonal*

body
cuerpo ^M *metálico de la bujía* ^F

spark plug terminal
terminal ^M *de la bujía* ^F

groove
ranura ^F

gasket
asiento ^M

exhaust manifold
colector ^M *de gases* ^M *de escape* ^M

side electrode
electrodo ^M *de masa* ^F

radiator
radiador ^M

muffler
silenciador ^M

catalytic converter
convertidor ^M *catalítico*

air filter
filtro ^M *de aire* ^M

fuel filter
filtro ^M *de combustible* ^M

cabin air filter
filtro ^M *de cabina* ^F

oil filter
filtro ^M *de aceite* ^M

battery
batería ^F

dashboard
tablero *M* *de instrumentos* *M*

ignition switch
interruptor *M* *de encendido* *M*

onboard computer
computadora *F* *de a bordo* *M*

instrument panel
tablero *M* *de mandos* *M*

audio system
reproductor *M* *de audio* *M*

rearview mirror
espejo *M* *retrovisor*

vanity mirror
espejo *M*

steering wheel
volante *M*

sun visor
parasol *M*

clutch pedal
pedal *M* *de embrague* *M*

vent
rejilla *F* *de ventilación* *F*

brake pedal
pedal *M* *de freno* *M*

panel
panel *M* *frontal*

windshield wiper
escobilla *F* *de limpiaparabrisa* *M*

gas pedal
pedal *M* *del acelerador* *M*

glove compartment
guantera *F*

parking brake button
botón *M* *de freno* *M* *de mano* *M*

driving mode selector
selección *M* *de tipo* *M* *de conducción* *F*

gearshift lever
palanca *F* *de cambio* *M*

center console
guantera *F* *central*

exterior
exterior M

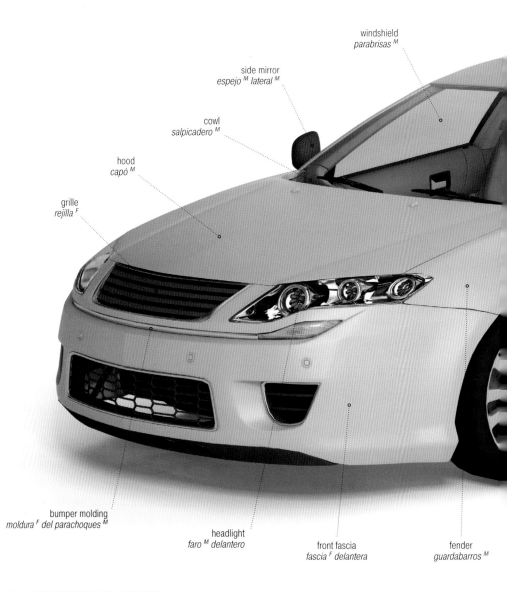

windshield
parabrisas M

side mirror
espejo M *lateral* M

cowl
salpicadero M

hood
capó M

grille
rejilla F

bumper molding
moldura F *del parachoques* M

headlight
faro M *delantero*

front fascia
fascia F *delantera*

fender
guardabarros M

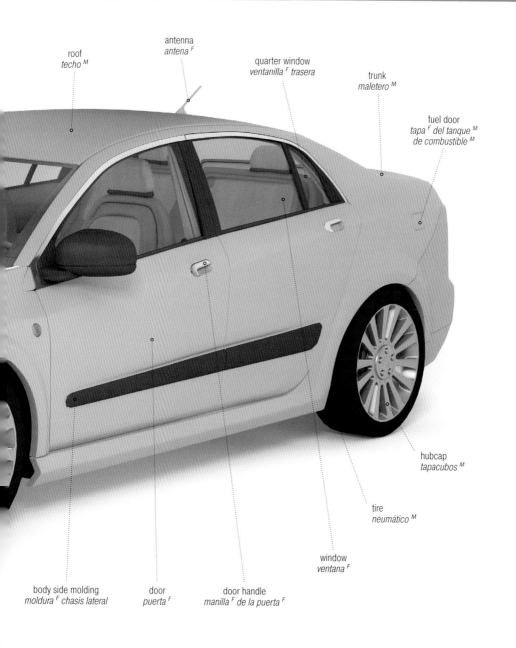

roof
techo M

antenna
antena F

quarter window
ventanilla F *trasera*

trunk
maletero M

fuel door
tapa F *del tanque* M
de combustible M

hubcap
tapacubos M

tire
neumático M

window
ventana F

body side molding
moldura F *chasis lateral*

door
puerta F

door handle
manilla F *de la puerta* F

Types of cars
Tipos ᴹ de coche ᴹ

electric car
coche ᴹ eléctrico

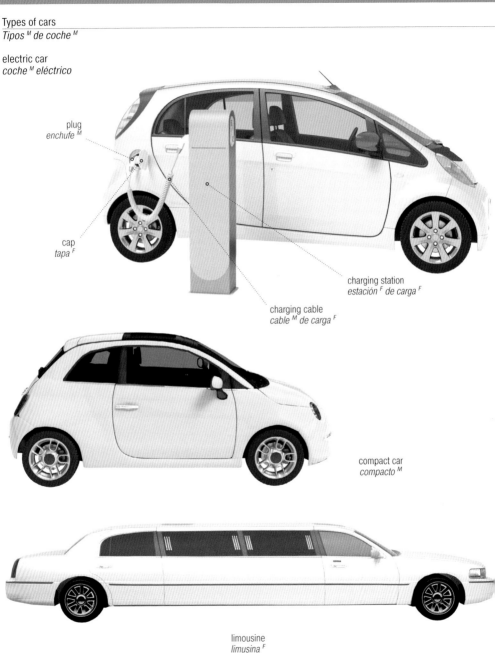

plug
enchufe ᴹ

cap
tapa ꟳ

charging station
estación ꟳ de carga ꟳ

charging cable
cable ᴹ de carga ꟳ

compact car
compacto ᴹ

limousine
limusina ꟳ

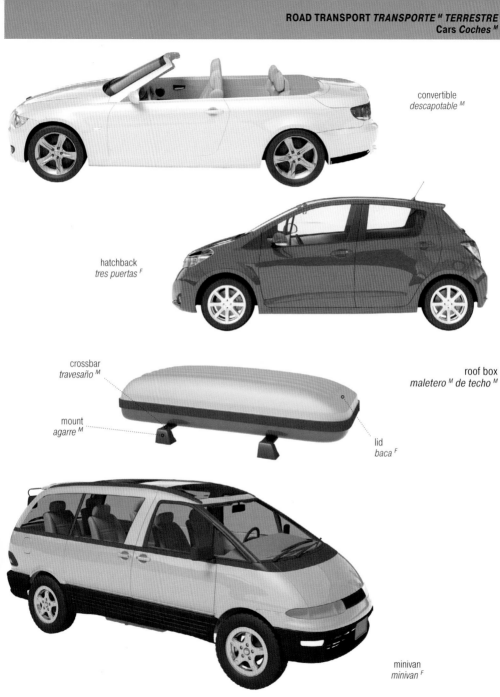

convertible
descapotable ^M

hatchback
tres puertas ^F

crossbar
travesaño ^M

roof box
maletero ^M *de techo* ^M

mount
agarre ^M

lid
baca ^F

minivan
minivan ^F

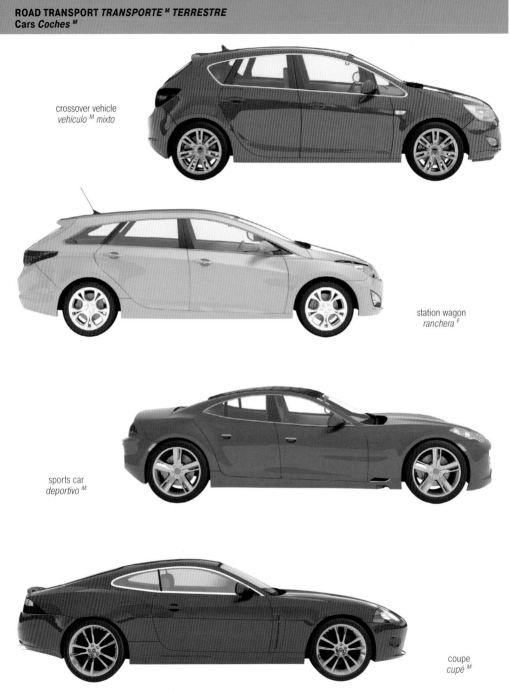

crossover vehicle
vehículo ᴹ *mixto*

station wagon
ranchera ᶠ

sports car
deportivo ᴹ

coupe
cupé ᴹ

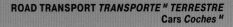

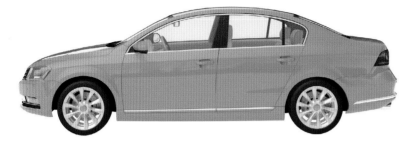

sedan
sedán ^M

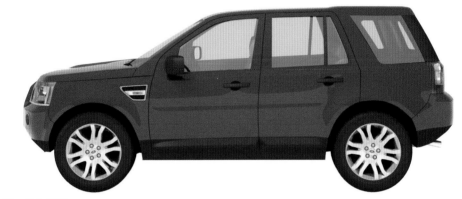

sport utility vehicle (SUV)
todoterreno ^M

pickup truck
camioneta ^F

full-size van
camión M *de reparto* M

Recreational vehicles
Vehículos M *recreativos*

motor home
casa F *rodante*

mirror
espejo M *retrovisor*

windshield
parabrisas M

door to living area
puerta F *al remolque* M

window
ventana F

door to cab
puerta F *del conductor* M

turn signal
señal F *de cruce* M

hood
capó M

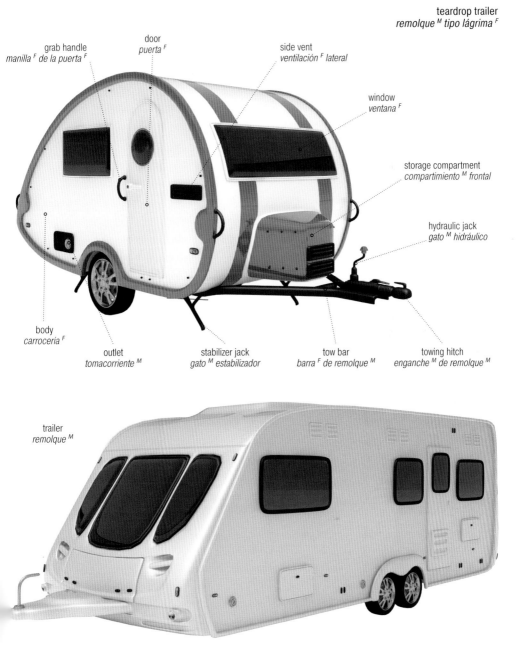

teardrop trailer
remolque ^M *tipo lágrima* ^F

grab handle
manilla ^F *de la puerta* ^F

door
puerta ^F

side vent
ventilación ^F *lateral*

window
ventana ^F

storage compartment
compartimiento ^M *frontal*

hydraulic jack
gato ^M *hidráulico*

body
carrocería ^F

outlet
tomacorriente ^M

stabilizer jack
gato ^M *estabilizador*

tow bar
barra ^F *de remolque* ^M

towing hitch
enganche ^M *de remolque* ^M

trailer
remolque ^M

sport bike
motocicleta ^F *deportiva*

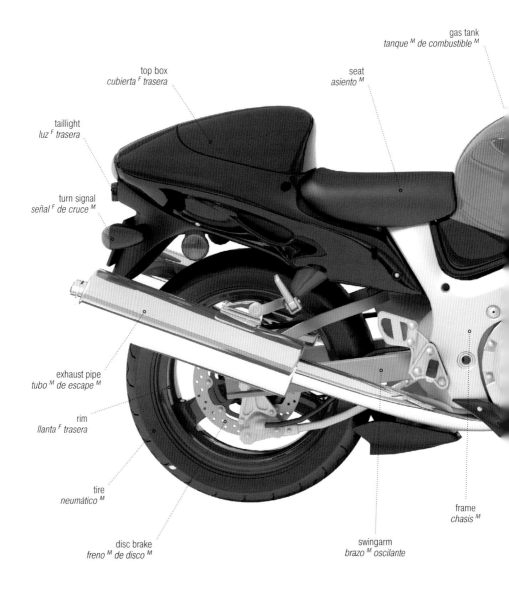

gas tank
tanque ^M *de combustible* ^M

top box
cubierta ^F *trasera*

seat
asiento ^M

taillight
luz ^F *trasera*

turn signal
señal ^F *de cruce* ^M

exhaust pipe
tubo ^M *de escape* ^M

rim
llanta ^F *trasera*

tire
neumático ^M

frame
chasis ^M

disc brake
freno ^M *de disco* ^M

swingarm
brazo ^M *oscilante*

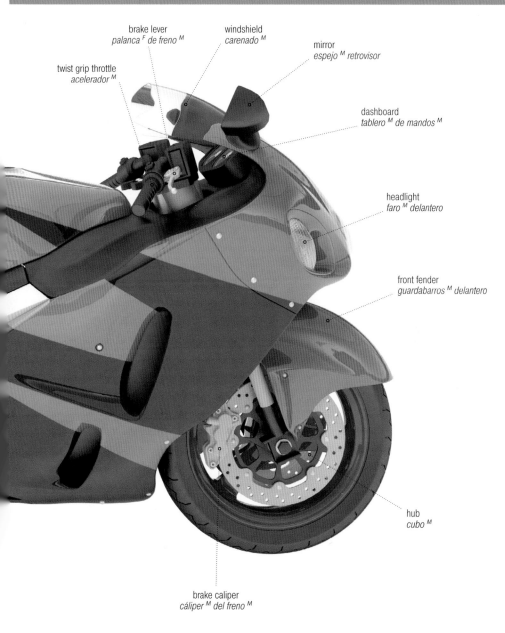

brake lever
palanca *F* *de freno* *M*

windshield
carenado *M*

mirror
espejo *M* *retrovisor*

twist grip throttle
acelerador *M*

dashboard
tablero *M* *de mandos* *M*

headlight
faro *M* *delantero*

front fender
guardabarros *M* *delantero*

hub
cubo *M*

brake caliper
cáliper *M* *del freno* *M*

touring motorcycle
motocicleta ᶠ *de turismo* ᴹ

driver's seat
asiento ᴹ *del conductor* ᴹ

passenger's seat
asiento ᴹ *del pasajero* ᴹ

windshield
parabrisas ᴹ

backrest
respaldo ᴹ

top box
maletero ᴹ

saddlebag
alforja ᶠ

passenger's grab handle
agarre ᴹ *para el pasajero* ᴹ

passenger's footrest
reposapiés ᴹ *del pasajero* ᴹ

driver's footrest
reposapiés ᴹ *del conductor* ᴹ

brake pedal
pedal ᴹ *de freno* ᴹ

motor scooter
motoneta ᶠ

off-road motorcycle
moto ᶠ *de enduro* ᴹ

all-terrain vehicle (ATV)
vehículo ᴹ *todo-terreno* ᴹ

headlight
carenado ᴹ

handlebars
manillar ᴹ

brake lever
palanca ᶠ *de freno* ᴹ

gas tank
depósito ᴹ *de combustible* ᴹ

handgrip
empuñadura ᶠ

front cargo rack
portapaquetes ᴹ *delantero*

seat
asiento ᴹ

rear cargo rack
portapaquetes ᴹ *trasero*

rear fender
guardabarros ᴹ *trasero*

front bumper
parachoques ᴹ *delantero*

footrest
escalón ᴹ

tire
neumático ᴹ

shock absorber
amortiguador ᴹ

front fender
guardabarros ᴹ *delantero*

motocross motorcycle
moto ᶠ *de motocross*

standard motorcycle
motocicleta F

mirror
espejo M *retrovisor*

brake lever
palanca F *de freno* M

clutch lever
palanca F *de embrague* M

handgrip
empuñadura F

seat
asiento M

fuel tank
depósito M *de combustible* M

dashboard
tablero M *de mandos* M

turn signal
señal F *de cruce* M

headlight
faro M *delantero*

front fender
guardabarros M *delantero*

muffler
silenciador M

frame
chasis M

disc brake
freno M *de disco* M

exhaust pipe
tubo M *de escape* M

V-twin engine
motor M *en V*

front fork
horquilla F *delantera*

brake caliper
pinza F *de freno* M

cruiser motorcycle
motocicleta F *cruiser*

chopper
chopper F

balance bicycle
bicicleta ᶠ de equilibrio ᴹ

tricycle
triciclo ᴹ

scooter
patinete ᴹ

child carrier
sillita ᶠ de niños ᴹ para bicis ᶠ

backpack
mochilla ᶠ

BMX bicycle
bicicleta ᶠ BMX

mountain bicycle
bicicleta ᶠ de montaña ᶠ

touring bicycle
bicicleta ᶠ de paseo ᴹ

tandem bicycle
tándem ᴹ

child bike trailer
remolque ᴹ de bicicleta ᶠ para niños ᴹ

cruiser bicycle
bicicleta ᶠ *urbana*

seat
sillín ᴹ

brake cable
cable ᴹ *del freno* ᴹ

rear brake
freno ᴹ *trasero*

carrier
transportador ᴹ

lock
candado ᴹ *de bicicleta* ᶠ

rear fender
guardabarro ᴹ *trasero*

mudguard
guardabarro ᴹ

spoke
radio ᴹ

rim
llanta ᶠ

tire
neumático ᴹ

chain
cadena ᶠ

chain wheel
piñón ᴹ

pedal
pedal ᴹ

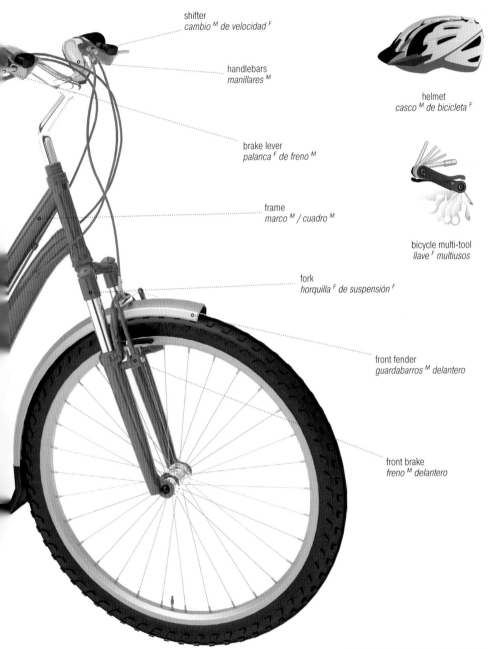

shifter
cambio ^M *de velocidad* ^F

handlebars
manillares ^M

helmet
casco ^M *de bicicleta* ^F

brake lever
palanca ^F *de freno* ^M

frame
marco ^M / *cuadro* ^M

bicycle multi-tool
llave ^F *multiusos*

fork
horquilla ^F *de suspensión* ^F

front fender
guardabarros ^M *delantero*

front brake
freno ^M *delantero*

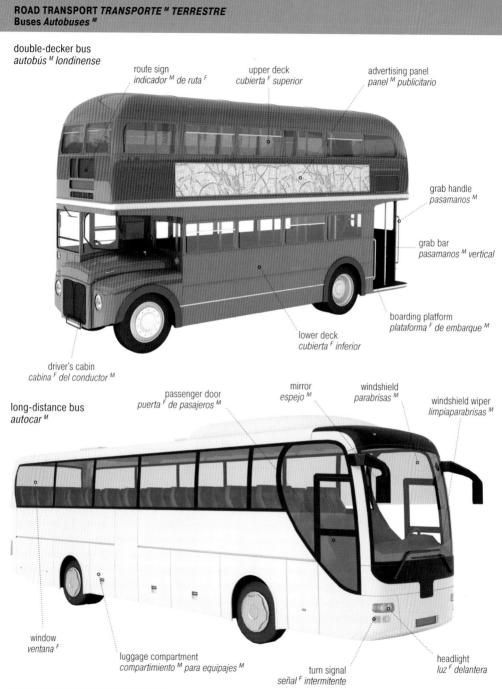

double-decker bus
autobús ^M *londinense*

route sign
indicador ^M *de ruta* ^F

upper deck
cubierta ^F *superior*

advertising panel
panel ^M *publicitario*

grab handle
pasamanos ^M

grab bar
pasamanos ^M *vertical*

boarding platform
plataforma ^F *de embarque* ^M

lower deck
cubierta ^F *inferior*

driver's cabin
cabina ^F *del conductor* ^M

mirror
espejo ^M

windshield
parabrisas ^M

windshield wiper
limpiaparabrisas ^M

passenger door
puerta ^F *de pasajeros* ^M

long-distance bus
autocar ^M

window
ventana ^F

luggage compartment
compartimiento ^M *para equipajes* ^M

turn signal
señal ^F *intermitente*

headlight
luz ^F *delantera*

city bus
autobús ^M *urbano*

minibus
minibús ^M

double-decker long-distance bus
autobús ^M *de viaje* ^M *de dos pisos* ^M

articulated bus
bus M *articulado*

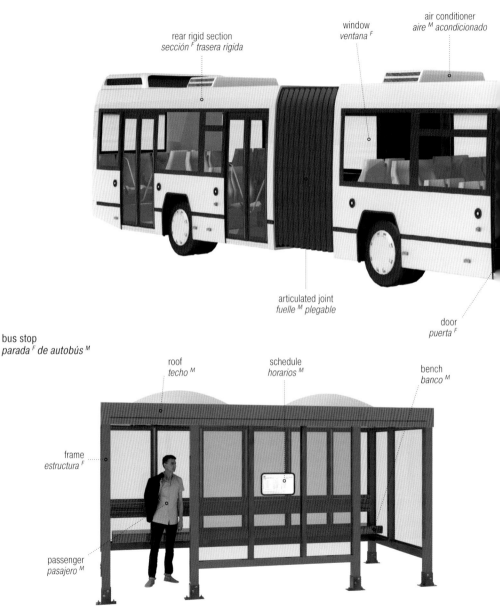

rear rigid section
sección F *trasera rigida*

window
ventana F

air conditioner
aire M *acondicionado*

articulated joint
fuelle M *plegable*

door
puerta F

bus stop
parada F *de autobús* M

roof
techo M

schedule
horarios M

bench
banco M

frame
estructura F

passenger
pasajero M

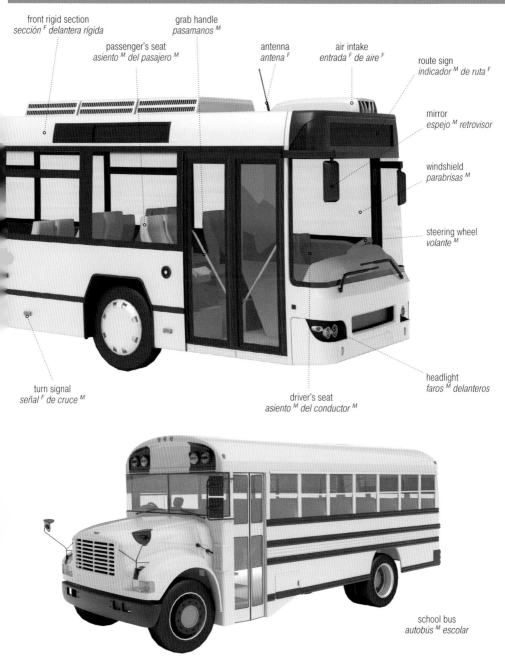

front rigid section
sección ᶠ *delantera rígida*

grab handle
pasamanos ᴹ

passenger's seat
asiento ᴹ *del pasajero* ᴹ

antenna
antena ᶠ

air intake
entrada ᶠ *de aire* ᶠ

route sign
indicador ᴹ *de ruta* ᶠ

mirror
espejo ᴹ *retrovisor*

windshield
parabrisas ᴹ

steering wheel
volante ᴹ

turn signal
señal ᶠ *de cruce* ᴹ

driver's seat
asiento ᴹ *del conductor* ᴹ

headlight
faros ᴹ *delanteros*

school bus
autobús ᴹ *escolar*

semitrailer
semirremolque ᴹ

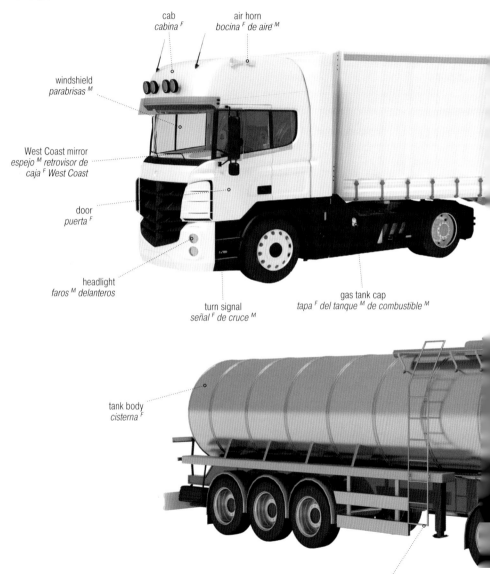

cab
cabina ᶠ

air horn
bocina ᶠ *de aire* ᴹ

windshield
parabrisas ᴹ

West Coast mirror
espejo ᴹ *retrovisor de
caja* ᶠ *West Coast*

door
puerta ᶠ

headlight
faros ᴹ *delanteros*

turn signal
señal ᶠ *de cruce* ᴹ

gas tank cap
tapa ᶠ *del tanque* ᴹ *de combustible* ᴹ

tank body
cisterna ᶠ

ladder
escalera ᶠ

semitrailer
semirremolque ^M

tank trailer
camión ^M *cisterna* ^F

step
escalón ^M

cab
cabina ^F

West Coast mirror
espejo ^M *retrovisor de caja* ^F
West Coast

radiator grille
rejilla ^F *del radiador* ^M

headlight
faros ^M *delanteros*

fuel tank
depósito ^M *de combustible* ^M

turn signal
señal ^F *de cruce* ^M

semitrailer cab
cabina ^F *de semirremolque* ^M

steering wheel
volante ^M

speaker
altavoz ^M

gearshift lever
palanca ^F *de cambio* ^M

armrest
reposabrazos ^M

sleeper cab
camarín ^M

clutch pedal
pedal ^M *de embrague* ^M

brake pedal
pedal ^M *de freno* ^M

gas pedal
pedal ^M *del acelerador* ^M

instrument panel
tablero ^M *de mandos* ^M

seat
asiento ^M

dump truck
camión ^M *volteo*

cement truck
hormigonera ^F

truck and tandem trailer
camión ^M *y remolque* ^M *tándem*

semitrailer with sleeper cab
semirremolque ^M *con camarín* ^M

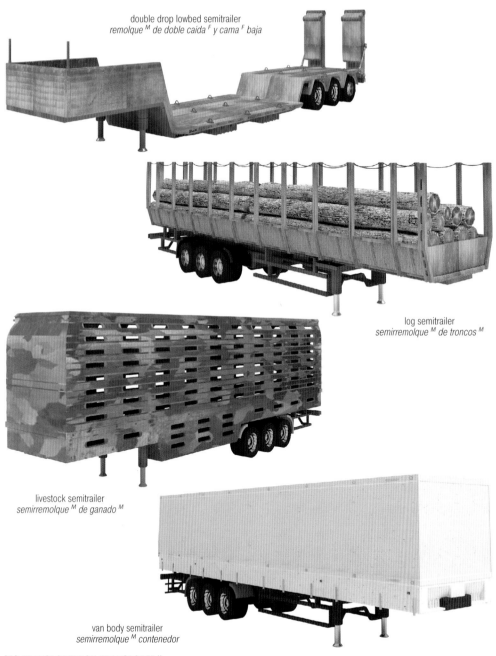

double drop lowbed semitrailer
remolque M *de doble caída* F *y cama* F *baja*

log semitrailer
semirremolque M *de troncos* M

livestock semitrailer
semirremolque M *de ganado* M

van body semitrailer
semirremolque M *contenedor*

tank trailer
cisterna F *de remolque*

automobile transport semitrailer
semirremolque M *de vehículos* M

truck tractor
camión M *tractor* M

box van
furgoneta F

police van
furgoneta ^F *de policía* ^F

police officer
mujer ^F *policía*

fire truck
camión ^M *de bomberos* ^M

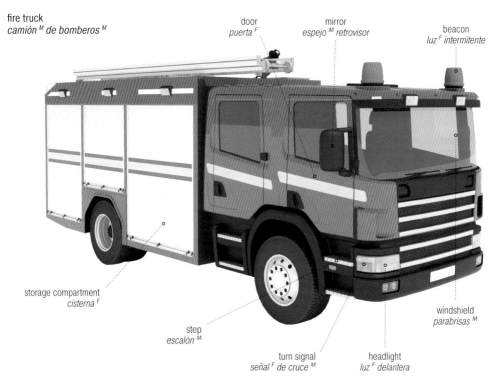

door
puerta ^F

mirror
espejo ^M *retrovisor*

beacon
luz ^F *intermitente*

storage compartment
cisterna ^F

step
escalón ^M

turn signal
señal ^F *de cruce* ^M

headlight
luz ^F *delantera*

windshield
parabrisas ^M

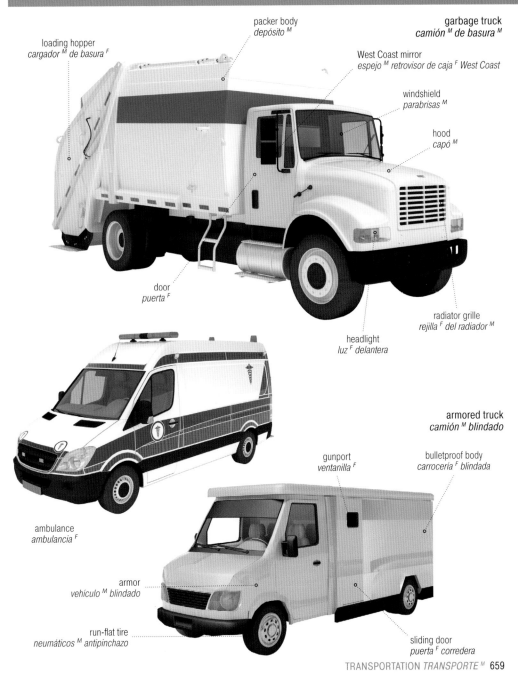

packer body
depósito ^M

garbage truck
camión ^M *de basura* ^M

loading hopper
cargador ^M *de basura* ^F

West Coast mirror
espejo ^M *retrovisor de caja* ^F *West Coast*

windshield
parabrisas ^M

hood
capó ^M

door
puerta ^F

radiator grille
rejilla ^F *del radiador* ^M

headlight
luz ^F *delantera*

armored truck
camión ^M *blindado*

gunport
ventanilla ^F

bulletproof body
carrocería ^F *blindada*

ambulance
ambulancia ^F

armor
vehículo ^M *blindado*

run-flat tire
neumáticos ^M *antipinchazo*

sliding door
puerta ^F *corredera*

street cleaner
camión ^M *limpia calles* ^F

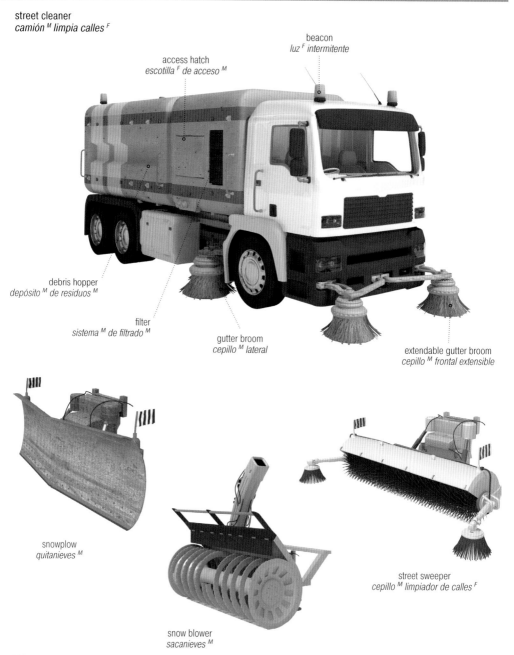

beacon
luz ^F *intermitente*

access hatch
escotilla ^F *de acceso* ^M

debris hopper
depósito ^M *de residuos* ^M

filter
sistema ^M *de filtrado* ^M

gutter broom
cepillo ^M *lateral*

extendable gutter broom
cepillo ^M *frontal extensible*

snowplow
quitanieves ^M

snow blower
sacanieves ^M

street sweeper
cepillo ^M *limpiador de calles* ^F

bulldozer
excavadora F

compact excavator
excavadora F sobre orugas F compacta

skid-steer loader
minicargadora F

portable concrete mixer
hormigonera F móvil

mini road roller
apisonadora ᶠ compacta

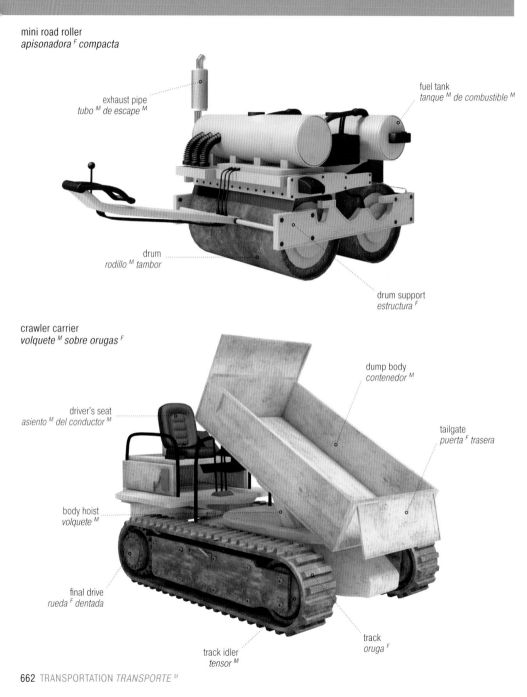

exhaust pipe
tubo ᴹ de escape ᴹ

fuel tank
tanque ᴹ de combustible ᴹ

drum
rodillo ᴹ tambor

drum support
estructura ᶠ

crawler carrier
volquete ᴹ sobre orugas ᶠ

dump body
contenedor ᴹ

driver's seat
asiento ᴹ del conductor ᴹ

tailgate
puerta ᶠ trasera

body hoist
volquete ᴹ

final drive
rueda ᶠ dentada

track
oruga ᶠ

track idler
tensor ᴹ

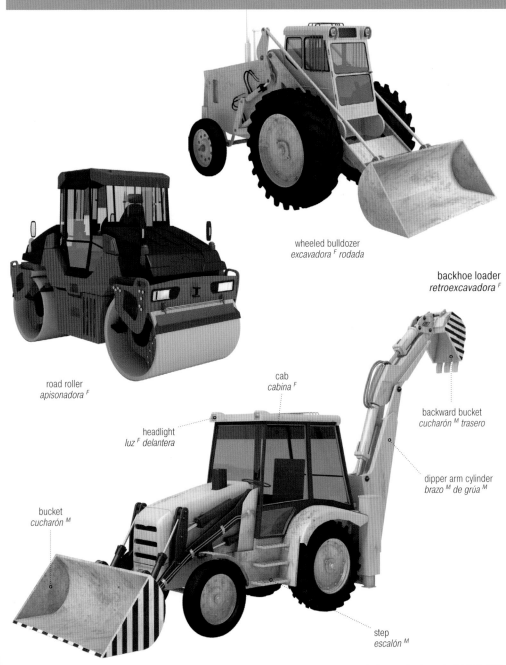

wheeled bulldozer
excavadora F rodada

backhoe loader
retroexcavadora F

road roller
apisonadora F

cab
cabina F

headlight
luz F delantera

backward bucket
cucharón M trasero

dipper arm cylinder
brazo M de grúa M

bucket
cucharón M

step
escalón M

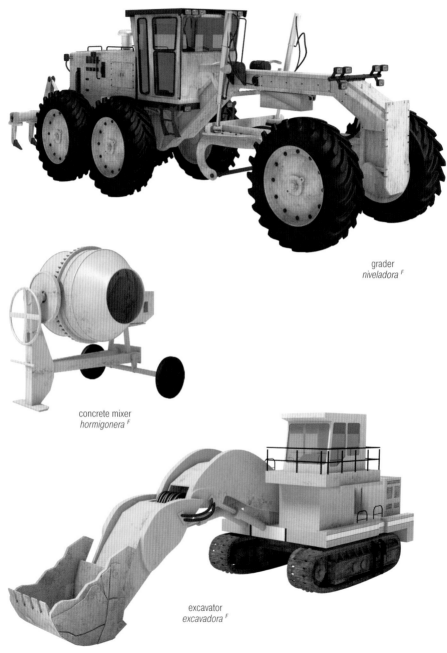

grader
niveladora F

concrete mixer
hormigonera F

excavator
excavadora F

haul truck
camión ^M de volteo ^M

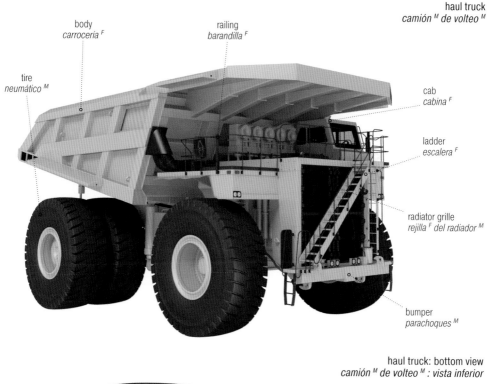

body
carrocería ^F

railing
barandilla ^F

tire
neumático ^M

cab
cabina ^F

ladder
escalera ^F

radiator grille
rejilla ^F del radiador ^M

bumper
parachoques ^M

haul truck: bottom view
camión ^M de volteo ^M : vista inferior

tire
neumático ^M

transmission
transmisión ^F

axle shaft
eje ^M trasero

driveshaft
eje ^M de transmisión ^M

bumper
parachoques ^M

crankcase
cárter ^M

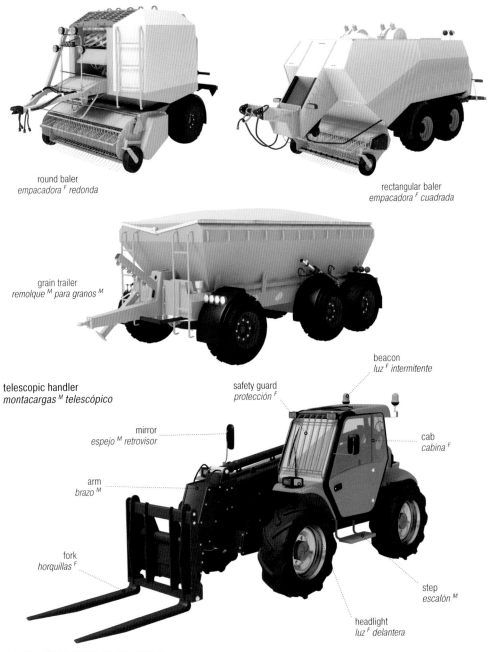

round baler
empacadora F redonda

rectangular baler
empacadora F cuadrada

grain trailer
remolque M para granos M

telescopic handler
montacargas M telescópico

beacon
luz F intermitente

safety guard
protección F

mirror
espejo M retrovisor

cab
cabina F

arm
brazo M

fork
horquillas F

step
escalón M

headlight
luz F delantera

harvester
agavilladora F

tractor
tractor M

horse trailer
remolque M *para caballos* M

combine harvester
cosechadora F *combinada*

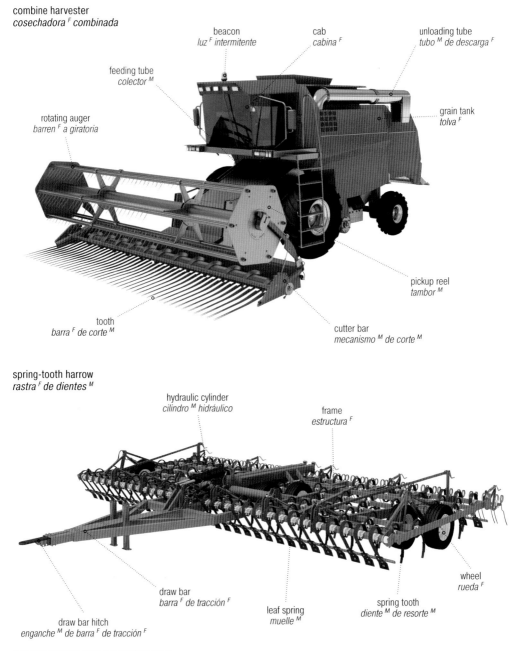

beacon
luz F *intermitente*

cab
cabina F

unloading tube
tubo M *de descarga* F

feeding tube
colector M

rotating auger
barren F *a giratoria*

grain tank
tolva F

pickup reel
tambor M

tooth
barra F *de corte* M

cutter bar
mecanismo M *de corte* M

spring-tooth harrow
rastra F *de dientes* M

hydraulic cylinder
cilindro M *hidráulico*

frame
estructura F

wheel
rueda F

draw bar
barra F *de tracción* F

leaf spring
muelle M

spring tooth
diente M *de resorte* M

draw bar hitch
enganche M *de barra* F *de tracción* F

air seeder
sembradora ^F *neumática*

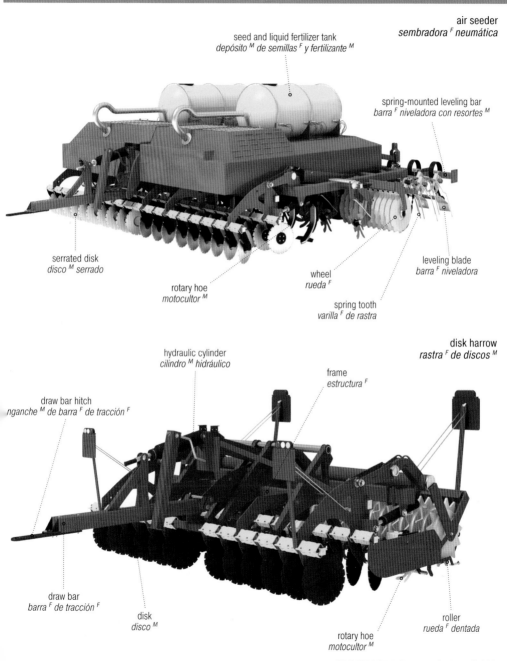

seed and liquid fertilizer tank
depósito ^M *de semillas* ^F *y fertilizante* ^M

spring-mounted leveling bar
barra ^F *niveladora con resortes* ^M

serrated disk
disco ^M *serrado*

rotary hoe
motocultor ^M

wheel
rueda ^F

spring tooth
varilla ^F *de rastra*

leveling blade
barra ^F *niveladora*

disk harrow
rastra ^F *de discos* ^M

hydraulic cylinder
cilindro ^M *hidráulico*

frame
estructura ^F

draw bar hitch
enganche ^M *de barra* ^F *de tracción* ^F

draw bar
barra ^F *de tracción* ^F

disk
disco ^M

rotary hoe
motocultor ^M

roller
rueda ^F *dentada*

fallen rocks
desprendimeinto M *de rocas* F

pavement ends
fin de pavimento M

loose gravel
gravilla F

no passing zone
zona F *de no rebasar*

signal ahead
semáforo M *más adelante*

road narrows
estrechamiento M *de vía* F

truck crossing
cruce M *de camiones* M

two-way traffic
tráfico M *en ambas direcciones*

advisory speed
velocidad F *aconsejable*

metric speed limit
límite M *de velocidad* F *metrica*

speed limit
límite M *de velocidad* F

night speed limit
límite M *de velocidad* F
nocturna

divided highway crossing
cruce M *de autopista* F

left or through
izquierda F *o recto* M

bicycle and pedestrian detour
desvio M *de bicicletas* F *y*
peatones M

exit closed
salida F *cerrada*

school zone or area
zona F *escolar*

bicycle crossing with share
the road warning
advertencia F *de cruce* M *de*
bicicletas, F *carretera compartida* F

handicapped crossing
paso de peatones M
discapacitados

pedestrian crossing
paso M *de peatones* M

obstruction to be passed on left
obstrucción, *F pase por la*
izquierda *F*

obstruction to be passed on right or left
obstrucción, *F pase por la izquierda o*
la derecha *F*

obstruction to be passed on right
obstrucción, *F pase por la*
derecha *F*

right turn only
giro *M a la derecha* *F*
únicamente

intersection lane control
control *M de carril* *F*
de intersección *F*

two-way left turn only
giro *M a la izquierda* *F*
en ambos sentidos

straight ahead only
sentido *M obligatorio*

truck weight limit
límite *M de peso* *M*
de camiones *M*

railroad crossing
cruce *M de ferrocarril* *M*

reserved for handicapped parking
estacionamiento *M reservado para*
discapacitados *M*

HOV lane ahead
carril VAO *M más adelante*

road ending at T intersection
carretera *F termina en*
intersección *F en T*

sharp curve to left (arrow)
curva *F cerrada a la*
izquierda *F (flecha* *F)*

sharp curve to left (chevron)
curva *F cerrada a la izquierda* *F*
(cheurón *M)*

detour
desvío *M*

do not enter
prohibido el paso *M*

wrong way
dirección *F prohibida*

yield
ceda el paso *M*

stop
alto *M*

270-degree loop
curva F *de 270 grados* M

curve
curva F

hairpin curve
curva F *de volteo* M

curve with speed advisory
curva F *con límite* M
de velocidad F

circular intersection ahead
redoma F *más adelante*

side road (right)
carretera F *secundaria*
a la derecha F

winding road
carretera F *sinuosa*

reverse turns
curvas F *peligrosas*

right curve and minor road
curva F *a la derecha* F *con*
carretera F *secundaria*

cross road ahead
cruce M *de carretera* F *más*
adelante

limited vehicle storage space
espacio M *de almacenamiento* M
de vehículos M *limitado*

T intersection ahead
intersección F *en T más adelante*

merging traffic
incorporación F *de tráfico* M

added lane
incorporación F *de carril* M

merge
incorporación F

added lane
incorporación F *de carril* M

divided highway ahead
autovía F *más adelante*

road narrows
estrechamiento M
de carretera F

flagger ahead
señalizador M *más adelante*

road works
obras F

cattle crossing
cruce ^M *de ganado* ^M

trucks rollover warning with speed advisory
peligro ^M *de volcamiento* ^M *con límite* ^M
de velocidad ^F

low clearance ahead
altura ^F *baja más adelante*

no bicycles
prohibido ^M *bicicletas* ^F

no pedestrian crossing
prohibido ^M *el paso de peatones* ^M

no large trucks
prohibido ^M *camiones* ^M

no parking
prohibido ^M *estacionar* ^M

no left turn
giro ^M *a la izquierda* ^F *prohibido*

no right turn
giro ^M *a la derecha* ^F
prohibido

no left or u turns
giro ^M *a la izquierda* ^F *y media*
vuelta ^F *prohibida*

no straight through
prohibido ^M *seguir recto*

no U turn
media vuelta ^F *prohibida*

slippery when wet
peligroso ^M *al humedecerse*

railroad crossing
cruce ^M *de ferrocarril* ^M

deer crossing
cruce ^M *de venado* ^M

tow away zone
zona ^F *de remolque* ^M

keep left
mantenerse ^M *a la izquierda* ^F

one way traffic
tráfico ^M *en un solo sentido* ^M

Airport exterior
*Exterior*ᴹ *del aeropuerto*ᴹ

maintenance hangar
*hangar*ᴹ *de mantenimiento*ᴹ

runway
*pista*ᶠ *de aterrizaje o despegue*ᴹ

road
*carretera*ᶠ

parking lot
*playa*ᶠ *de estacionamiento*ᴹ

passenger terminal
*terminal*ᶠ *de pasajeros*ᴹ

taxiway
pista [F] *de rodaje* [M]

control tower
torre [F] *de control* [M]

control tower cab
sala [F] *de control* [M]

maneuvering area
área [M] *de maniobras* [F]

service road
vía [F] *de servicio* [M]

taxiway line
líneas [F] *de pista* [F]

boarding area
terminal M *de abordaje* M

satellite terminal
terminal F *satélite*

airplane
avión M

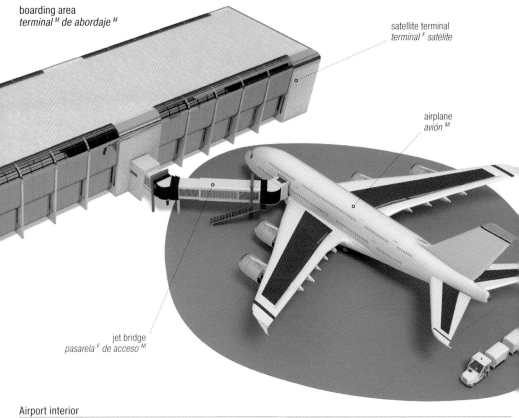

jet bridge
pasarela F *de acceso* M

Airport interior
Interior M *del aeropuerto* M

baggage carousel
cinta M *transportadora del equipaje* M

baggage cart
carrito M *para equipaje* M

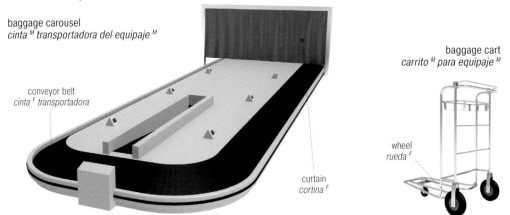

conveyor belt
cinta F *transportadora*

curtain
cortina F

wheel
rueda F

security checkpoint
punto ^M *de control* ^M *de seguridad* ^F

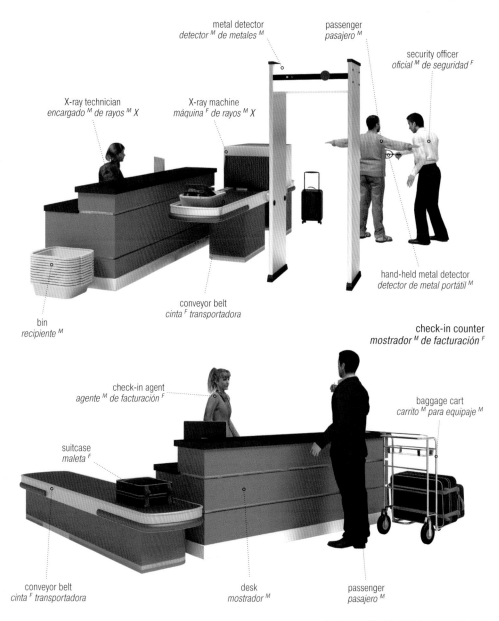

metal detector
detector ^M *de metales* ^M

passenger
pasajero ^M

security officer
oficial ^M *de seguridad* ^F

X-ray technician
encargado ^M *de rayos* ^M *X*

X-ray machine
máquina ^F *de rayos* ^M *X*

hand-held metal detector
detector de metal portátil ^M

bin
recipiente ^M

conveyor belt
cinta ^F *transportadora*

check-in counter
mostrador ^M *de facturación* ^F

check-in agent
agente ^M *de facturación* ^F

baggage cart
carrito ^M *para equipaje* ^M

suitcase
maleta ^F

conveyor belt
cinta ^F *transportadora*

desk
mostrador ^M

passenger
pasajero ^M

departure area
área ᴹ *de salida* ᶠ

coffee shop
cafetería ᶠ

restroom
baños ᴹ

baggage check-in counter
facturación ᶠ *de equipajes* ᴹ

flight information board
panel ᴹ *de información* ᴹ *de vuelos* ᴹ

escalator
escalera ᶠ *mecánica*

self-service check-in kiosk
quiosco ᴹ *de auto-facturación* ᶠ

display
pantalla ᶠ

document scanner
escáner ᴹ *de documentos* ᴹ

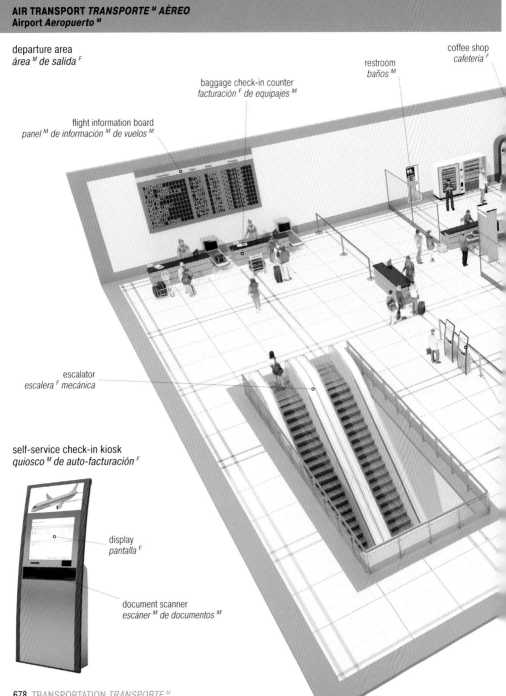

gate agent
asistente ^M *de embarque* ^M

Gate 2

Gate 1

gate
puerta ^F *de embarque* ^M

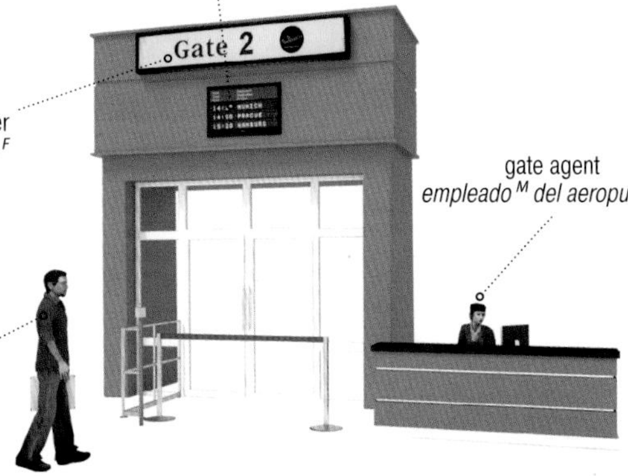

flight number board
tablero ^M *de información* ^F *de vuelos* ^M

gate number
número ^M *de puerta* ^F

Gate 2

gate agent
empleado ^M *del aeropuerto* ^M

self-service check-in kiosk
quiosco ^M *de auto-facturación* ^F

passenger
pasajero ^M

arrival area
área ᴹ *de llegada* ᶠ

suitcase
maleta ᶠ

flight number board
tablero ᴹ *de información* ᶠ *de vuelos* ᴹ

baggage carousel
cinta ᶠ *de equipaje* ᴹ

passenger
pasajero ᴹ

lost baggage desk
servicio ᴹ *de equipajes* ᴹ
perdidos

baggage cart
carrito ᴹ *de equipaje* ᴹ

baggage claim area
patio ᴹ *de equipaje* ᴹ

overview of departure and arrival areas
vista ᶠ *de las áreas* ᴹ *de salida* ᶠ *y llegada* ᶠ

departure area
zona ᶠ *de salidas* ᶠ

arrival area
zona ᶠ *de llegadas* ᶠ

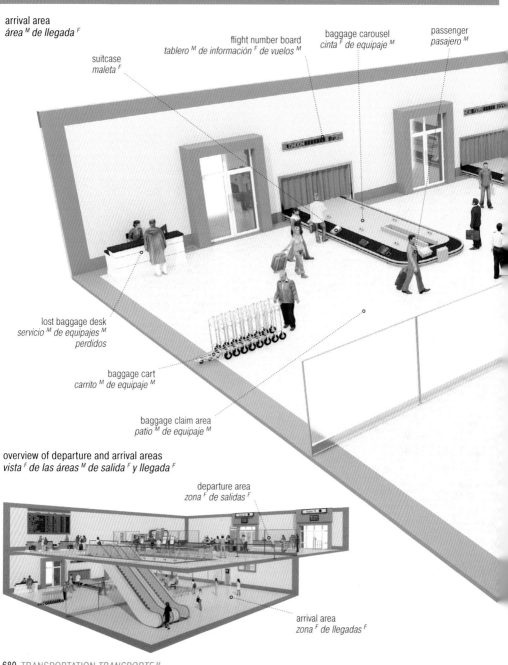

security officer
agente M *de seguridad* F

customs officer
oficial M *de aduanas* F

restroom
baños M

flight information board
panel M *de horarios* M *de los vuelos* M

flight information board
panel M *de horarios* M

frame
estructura F

screen
pantalla F

ARRIVALS				11:34am
DESTINATION	TIME	FLIGHT	GATE	STATUS
NEW YORK	13:12 am	1256	D12	On Time
NEW YORK	11:44 am	656	E34	On Time
NEW YORK	10:46 am	857	A13	On Time
ORLANDO, FL	09:32 am	2584	C27	On Time
ORLANDO, FL	15:17 am	3674	B32	On Time
ORLANDO, FL	17:22 am	1854	A7	On Time
PHILADELPHIA	13:05 am	3110	C22	On Time
PHILADELPHIA	12:14 am	2504	A18	On Time
PHILADELPHIA	11:04 am	654	D29	On Time
PHOENIX	11:37 am	548	E11	Canceled
CHICAGO	07:48 am	1458	D31	On Time
PHOENIX	06:55 am	1684	B38	Canceled
PHOENIX	08:48 am	3561	E17	On Time
NEW YORK	07:14 am	3541	E22	On Time
NEW YORK	09:58 am	2547	D21	On Time

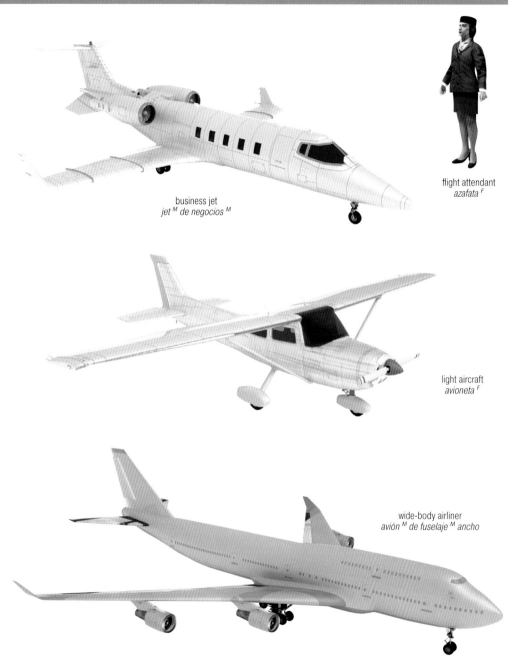

flight attendant
azafata ᶠ

business jet
jet ᴹ *de negocios* ᴹ

light aircraft
avioneta ᶠ

wide-body airliner
avión ᴹ *de fuselaje* ᴹ *ancho*

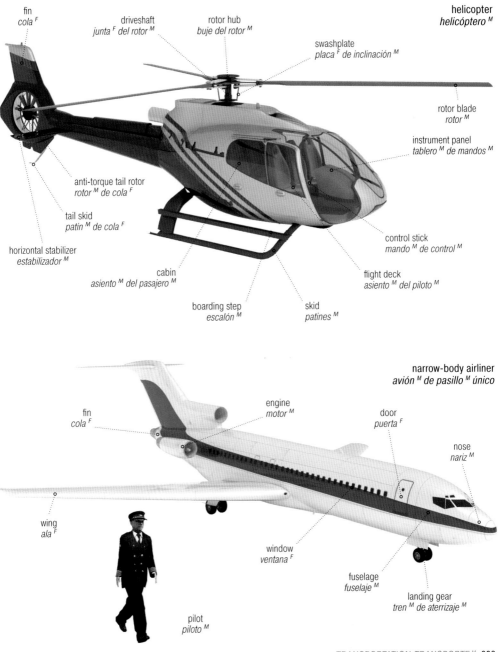

helicopter
helicóptero ᴹ

fin
cola ᶠ

driveshaft
junta ᶠ *del rotor* ᴹ

rotor hub
buje del rotor ᴹ

swashplate
placa ᶠ *de inclinación* ᴹ

rotor blade
rotor ᴹ

instrument panel
tablero ᴹ *de mandos* ᴹ

anti-torque tail rotor
rotor ᴹ *de cola* ᶠ

tail skid
patín ᴹ *de cola* ᶠ

horizontal stabilizer
estabilizador ᴹ

cabin
asiento ᴹ *del pasajero* ᴹ

boarding step
escalón ᴹ

skid
patines ᴹ

flight deck
asiento ᴹ *del piloto* ᴹ

control stick
mando ᴹ *de control* ᴹ

narrow-body airliner
avión ᴹ *de pasillo* ᴹ *único*

fin
cola ᶠ

engine
motor ᴹ

door
puerta ᶠ

nose
nariz ᴹ

wing
ala ᶠ

window
ventana ᶠ

fuselage
fuselaje ᴹ

landing gear
tren ᴹ *de aterrizaje* ᴹ

pilot
piloto ᴹ

catering vehicle
camión ᴹ de catering ᴹ

box
caja ꜰ

guardrail
barandilla ꜰ

platform
plataforma ꜰ

beacon
luz ꜰ intermitente

jet refueler
reabastecedor ᴹ de combustible ᴹ

baggage conveyor
cinta F *transportadora* F *de equipaje* M

mobile closed passenger stairs
pasillo M *cerrado*

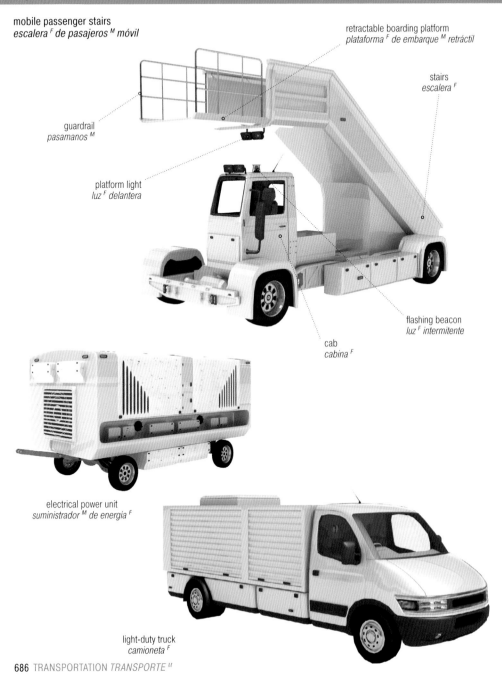

mobile passenger stairs
escalera ^F *de pasajeros* ^M *móvil*

retractable boarding platform
plataforma ^F *de embarque* ^M *retráctil*

stairs
escalera ^F

guardrail
pasamanos ^M

platform light
luz ^F *delantera*

flashing beacon
luz ^F *intermitente*

cab
cabina ^F

electrical power unit
suministrador ^M *de energía* ^F

light-duty truck
camioneta ^F

escort vehicle
coche ᴹ *escolta*

service vehicle
vehículo ᴹ *de servicio* ᴹ

mobile loading platform
plataforma ᶠ *de carga* ᶠ *móvil*

baggage vehicle
vehículo ^M *de equipajes* ^M

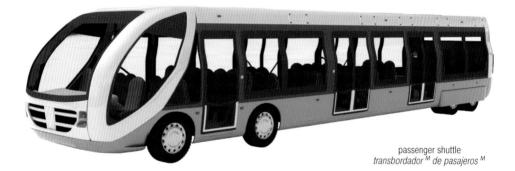

passenger shuttle
transbordador ^M *de pasajeros* ^M

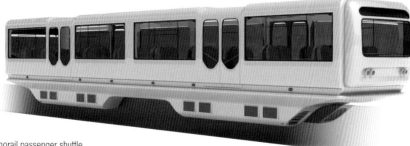

monorail passenger shuttle
transbordador ^M *monorriel* ^M

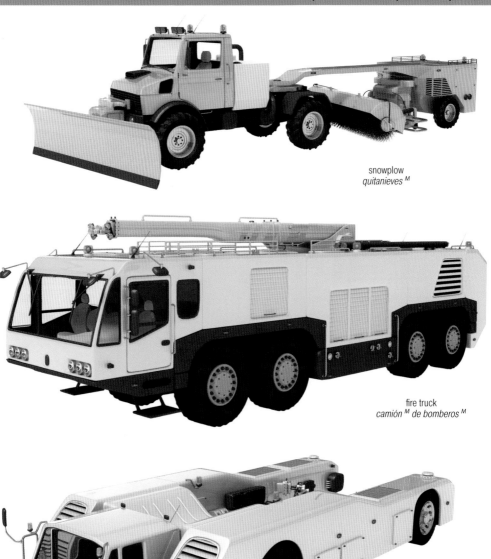

snowplow
quitanieves ᴹ

fire truck
camión ᴹ *de bomberos* ᴹ

pushback tug
remolcador ᴹ

passenger station
estación ᶠ *de tren* ᴹ

clock
reloj ᴹ

exit
salida ᶠ

store
tienda ᶠ

ticket office
oficina ᶠ *de venta* ᶠ *de billetes* ᴹ

schedules information board
panel ᴹ *de horarios* ᴹ

platform
andén ᴹ

bench
asiento ᴹ

stairs
escaleras ᶠ

escalator
escalera ᶠ *mecánica*

ticket vending machine
máquina ᶠ *de venta* ᶠ *de billete*

train
tren ^M

coffee shop
cafetería ^F

train information board
cartel ^M *de información* ^M

commuter train
tren ^M *suburbano*

newsstand
kiosco ^M

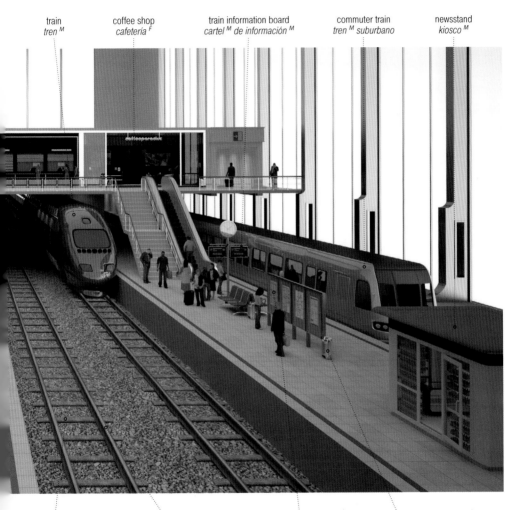

tie
durmiente ^M

track
vías ^F

schedules board
panel ^M *de horarios* ^M

trash can
papelera ^F

junction
empalme ^M

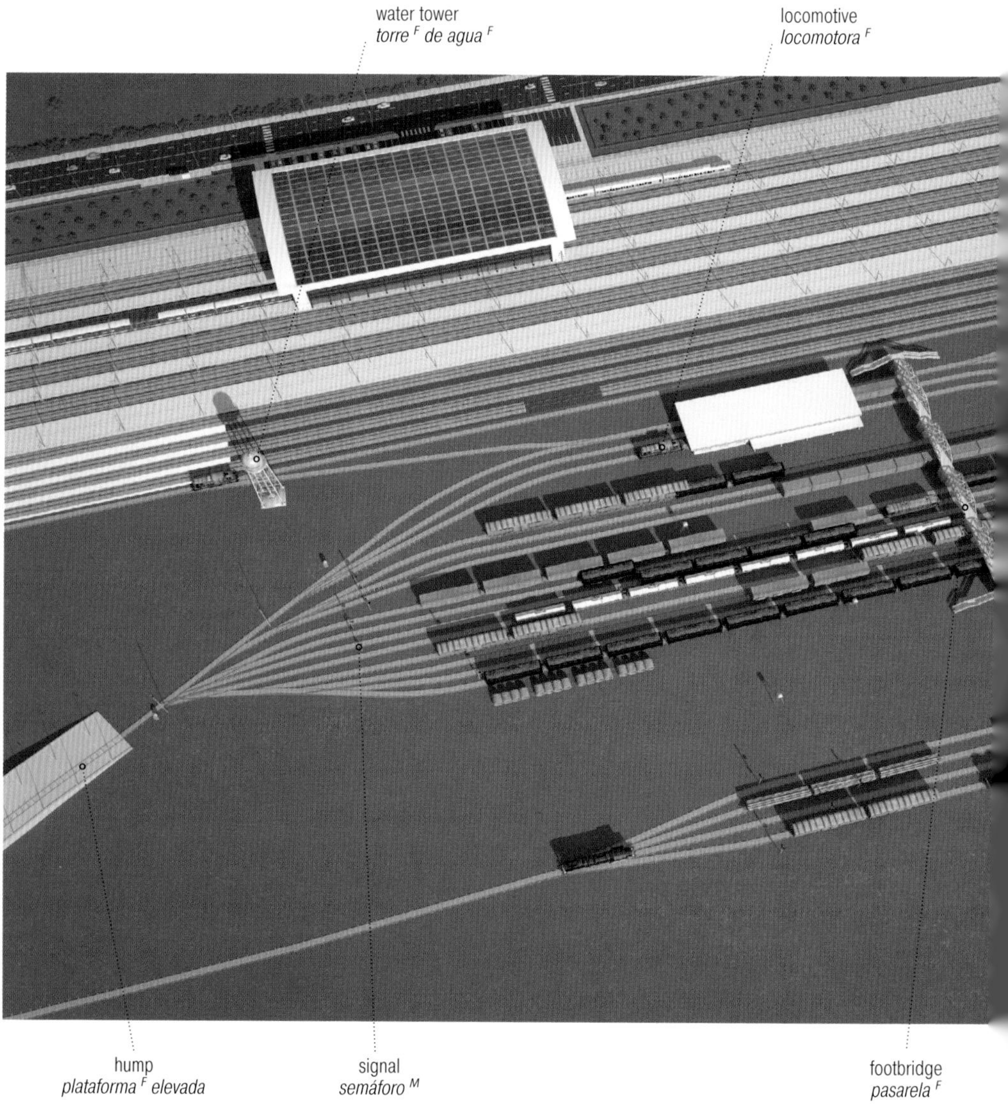

water tower
torre ^F *de agua* ^F

locomotive
locomotora ^F

hump
plataforma ^F *elevada*

signal
semáforo ^M

footbridge
pasarela ^F

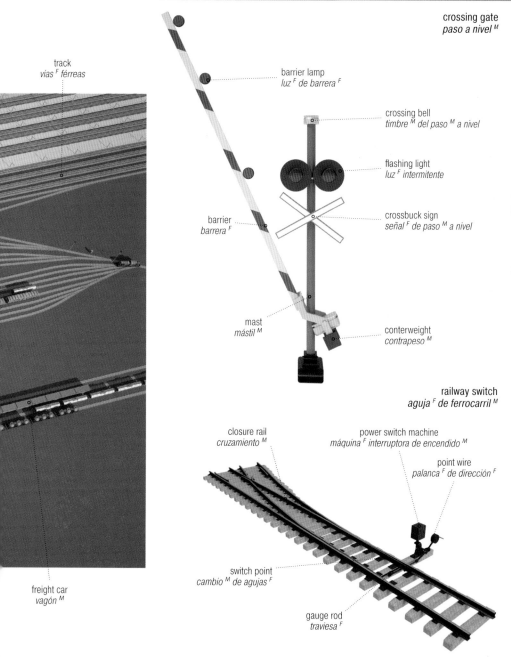

crossing gate
paso a nivel ^M

track
vías ^F *férreas*

barrier lamp
luz ^F *de barrera* ^F

crossing bell
timbre ^M *del paso* ^M *a nivel*

flashing light
luz ^F *intermitente*

crossbuck sign
señal ^F *de paso* ^M *a nivel*

barrier
barrera ^F

mast
mástil ^M

conterweight
contrapeso ^M

railway switch
aguja ^F *de ferrocarril* ^M

closure rail
cruzamiento ^M

power switch machine
máquina ^F *interruptora de encendido* ^M

point wire
palanca ^F *de dirección* ^F

switch point
cambio ^M *de agujas* ^F

gauge rod
traviesa ^F

freight car
vagón ^M

Urban rail transit
Transporte M *ferroviario urbano*

articulated streetcar
tranvía M *articulado*

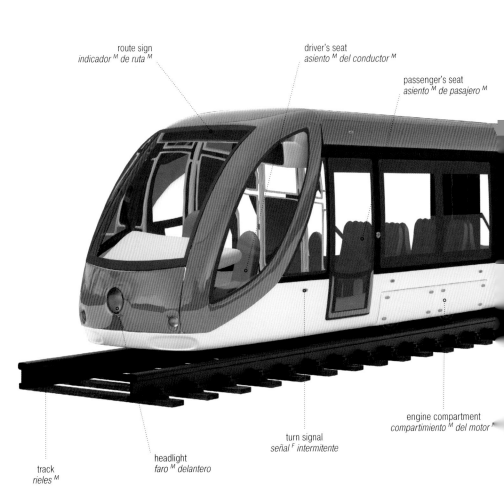

route sign
indicador M *de ruta* M

driver's seat
asiento M *del conductor* M

passenger's seat
asiento M *de pasajero* M

engine compartment
compartimiento M *del motor* M

turn signal
señal F *intermitente*

headlight
faro M *delantero*

track
rieles M

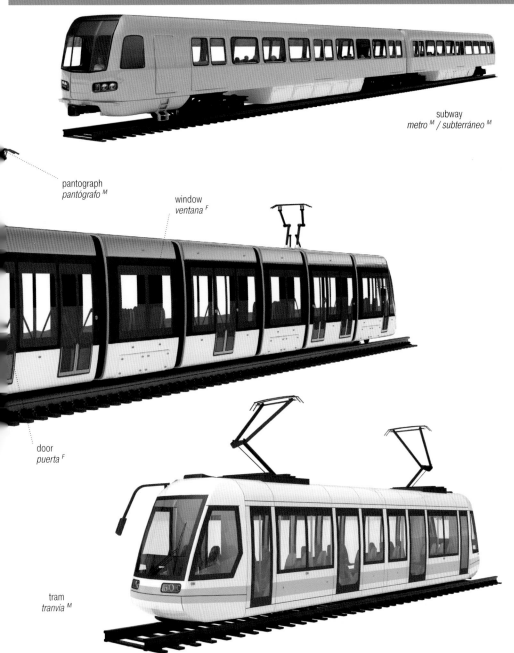

subway
metro ᴹ / *subterráneo* ᴹ

pantograph
pantógrafo ᴹ

window
ventana ᶠ

door
puerta ᶠ

tram
tranvía ᴹ

Intercity transport
Transporte ^{M} interurbano

steam locomotive
locomotora ^{F} de vapor ^{M}

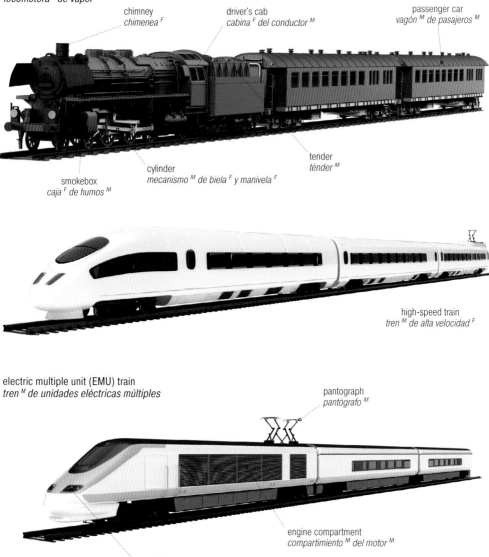

chimney
chimenea ^{F}

driver's cab
cabina ^{F} del conductor ^{M}

passenger car
vagón ^{M} de pasajeros ^{M}

tender
ténder ^{M}

cylinder
mecanismo ^{M} de biela ^{F} y manivela ^{F}

smokebox
caja ^{F} de humos ^{M}

high-speed train
tren ^{M} de alta velocidad ^{F}

electric multiple unit (EMU) train
tren ^{M} de unidades eléctricas múltiples

pantograph
pantógrafo ^{M}

engine compartment
compartimiento ^{M} del motor ^{M}

headlight
luz ^{F} delantera

Locomotives
Locomotoras ^F

diesel locomotive
locomotora ^F *diesel*

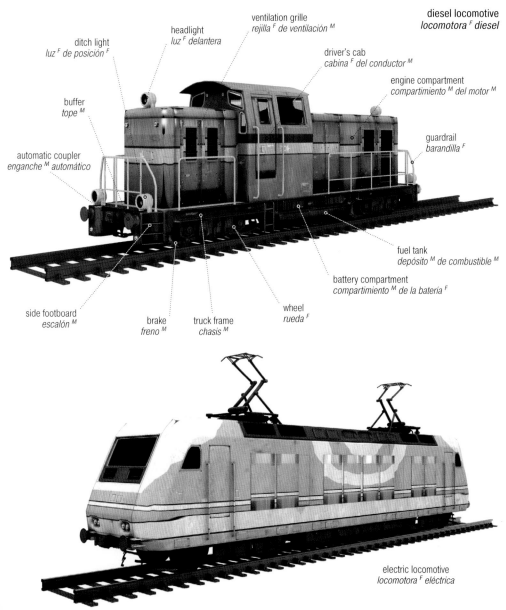

ventilation grille
rejilla ^F *de ventilación* ^M

headlight
luz ^F *delantera*

ditch light
luz ^F *de posición* ^F

driver's cab
cabina ^F *del conductor* ^M

engine compartment
compartimiento ^M *del motor* ^M

buffer
tope ^M

guardrail
barandilla ^F

automatic coupler
enganche ^M *automático*

fuel tank
depósito ^M *de combustible* ^M

battery compartment
compartimiento ^M *de la batería* ^F

side footboard
escalón ^M

brake
freno ^M

truck frame
chasis ^M

wheel
rueda ^F

electric locomotive
locomotora ^F *eléctrica*

double-ended locomotive
locomotora ᶠ *bidireccional*

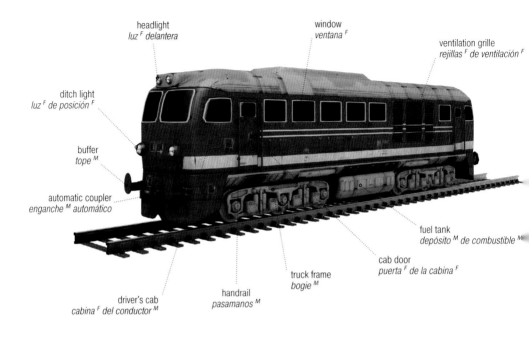

headlight
luz ᶠ *delantera*

window
ventana ᶠ

ventilation grille
rejillas ᶠ *de ventilación* ᶠ

ditch light
luz ᶠ *de posición* ᶠ

buffer
tope ᴹ

automatic coupler
enganche ᴹ *automático*

fuel tank
depósito ᴹ *de combustible* ᴹ

cab door
puerta ᶠ *de la cabina* ᶠ

truck frame
bogie ᴹ

handrail
pasamanos ᴹ

driver's cab
cabina ᶠ *del conductor* ᴹ

Freight cars *Vagones* ᴹ *de carga* ᴹ

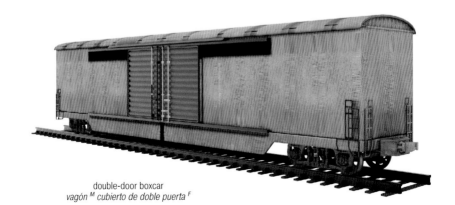

double-door boxcar
vagón ᴹ *cubierto de doble puerta* ᶠ

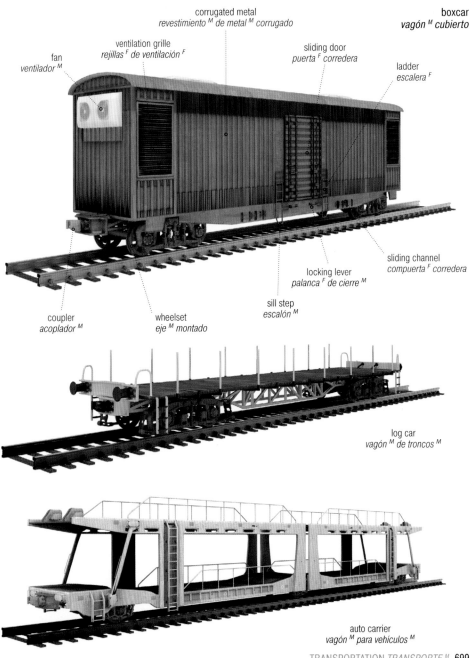

corrugated metal
revestimiento M *de metal* M *corrugado*

boxcar
vagón M *cubierto*

ventilation grille
rejillas F *de ventilación* F

sliding door
puerta F *corredera*

fan
ventilador M

ladder
escalera F

sliding channel
compuerta F *corredera*

locking lever
palanca F *de cierre* M

sill step
escalón M

coupler
acoplador M

wheelset
eje M *montado*

log car
vagón M *de troncos* M

auto carrier
vagón M *para vehículos* M

tank car
vagón ᴹ *cisterna* ᶠ

tank
cisterna ᴹ

automatic coupler
enganche ᴹ *automático*

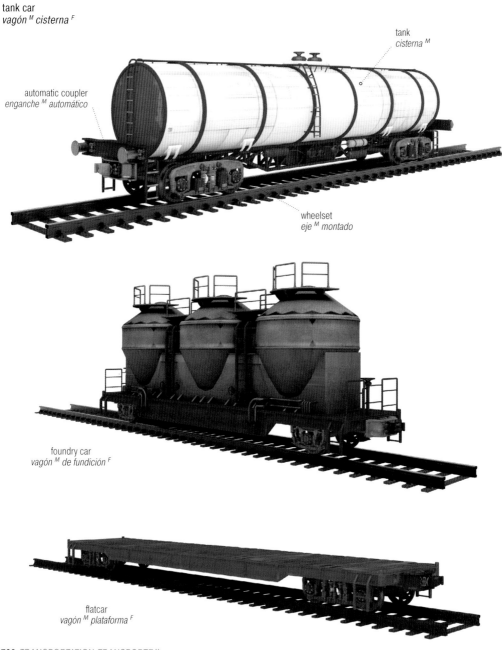

wheelset
eje ᴹ *montado*

foundry car
vagón ᴹ *de fundición* ᶠ

flatcar
vagón ᴹ *plataforma* ᶠ

crane car
grúa ᶠ

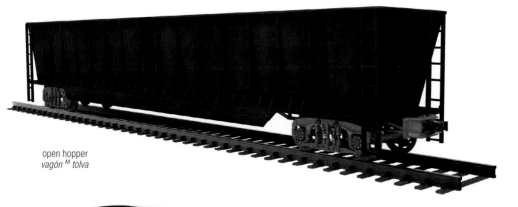

open hopper
vagón ᴹ *tolva*

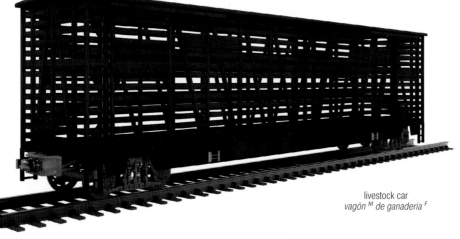

livestock car
vagón ᴹ *de ganadería* ᶠ

subway station
estación F *de metro* F

ticket collector's booth
puesto M *del colector* M *de billetes* M

subway map
plano M *del metro* M

advertisement
anuncio M *publicitario*

ticket office
oficina F *de venta* F *de billetes* M

city map
mapa M *de la ciudad* F

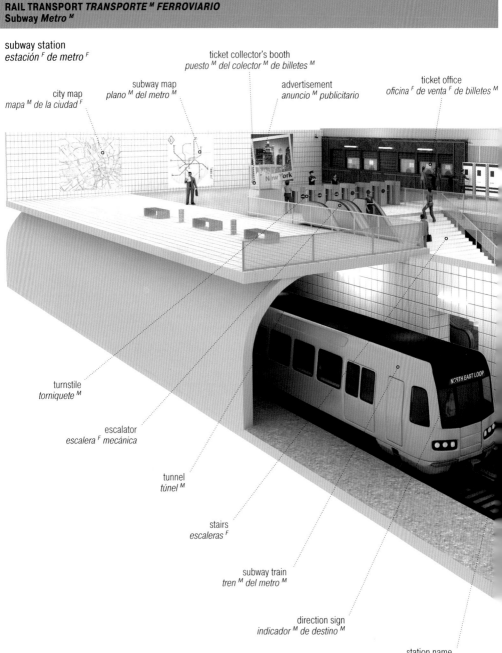

turnstile
torniquete M

escalator
escalera F *mecánica*

tunnel
túnel M

stairs
escaleras F

subway train
tren M *del metro* M

direction sign
indicador M *de destino* M

station name
nombre M *de la estación* F

ticket vending machine
máquina ᶠ *de venta* ᶠ *de billetes* ᴹ

automatic teller machine (ATM)
cajero ᴹ *automático*

coffee shop
cafetería ᶠ

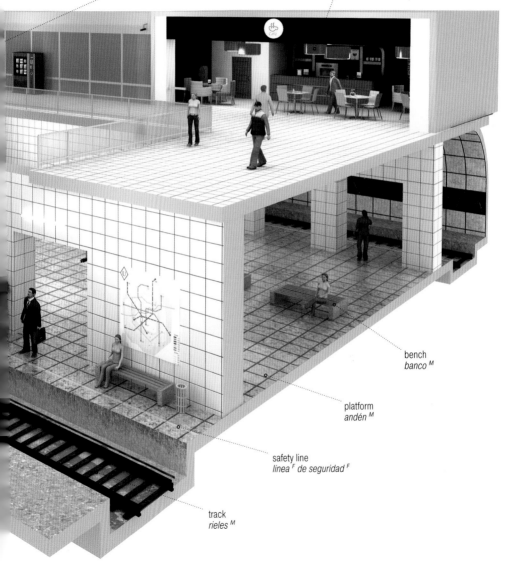

bench
banco ᴹ

platform
andén ᴹ

safety line
línea ᶠ *de seguridad* ᶠ

track
rieles ᴹ

port
puerto ^M

transit shed
almacén ^M *de productos* ^M *en tránsito* ^M

tanker
buque ^M *petrolero*

fuel tank
depósito ^M *de combustible* ^M

train
locomotora ^F

slipway
gradas ^F

railroad tracks
vías ^F *del ferrocarril* ^M

tugboat
remolcador ^M

gantry crane
grúa ^F *para contenedores* ^M

customs house
aduana ^F

lighthouse
faro ^M

lantern
faro ^M

gallery
galería ^F

container
contenedor ^M

container ship
buque ^M *carguero*

container terminal
muelle ^M *de contenedores* ^M

tower
torre ^F

Passenger vessels
Barcos M *de pasajeros* M

cruise ship
crucero M

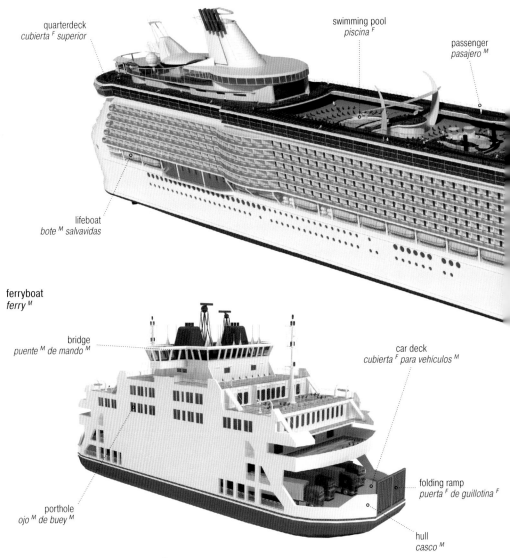

quarterdeck
cubierta F *superior*

swimming pool
piscina F

passenger
pasajero M

lifeboat
bote M *salvavidas*

ferryboat
ferry M

bridge
puente M *de mando* M

car deck
cubierta F *para vehículos* M

folding ramp
puerta F *de guillotina* F

porthole
ojo M *de buey* M

hull
casco M

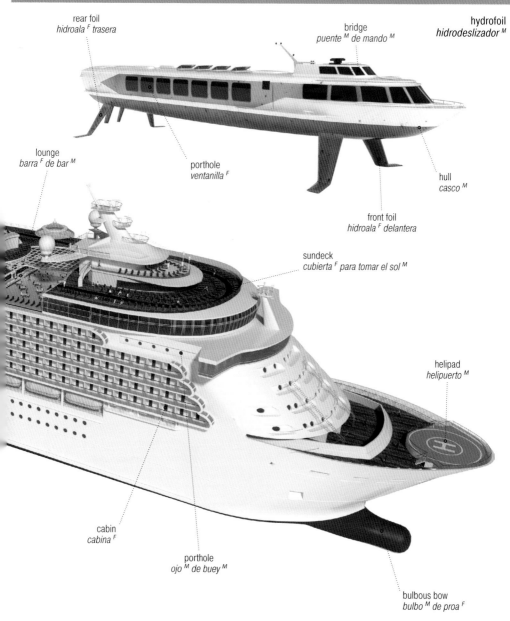

rear foil
hidroala ᶠ *trasera*

bridge
puente ᴹ *de mando* ᴹ

hydrofoil
hidrodeslizador ᴹ

lounge
barra ᶠ *de bar* ᴹ

porthole
ventanilla ᶠ

hull
casco ᴹ

front foil
hidroala ᶠ *delantera*

sundeck
cubierta ᶠ *para tomar el sol* ᴹ

helipad
helipuerto ᴹ

cabin
cabina ᶠ

porthole
ojo ᴹ *de buey* ᴹ

bulbous bow
bulbo ᴹ *de proa* ᶠ

Ancillary vessels
Barcos M *auxiliares*

tugboat
remolcador M

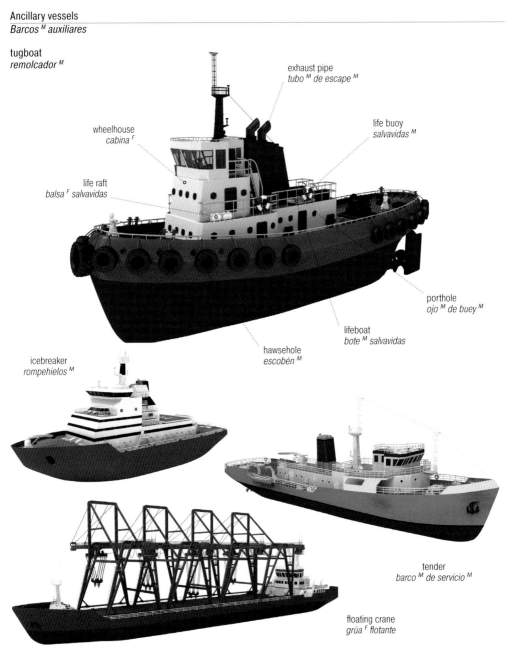

exhaust pipe
tubo M *de escape* M

wheelhouse
cabina F

life buoy
salvavidas M

life raft
balsa F *salvavidas*

porthole
ojo M *de buey* M

lifeboat
bote M *salvavidas*

hawsehole
escobén M

icebreaker
rompehielos M

tender
barco M *de servicio* M

floating crane
grúa F *flotante*

Cargo and fishing vessels
Barcos ᴹ cargueros ᴹ y de pesca ᶠ

container ship
buque ᴹ de carga ᶠ

bridge
puente ᴹ de mando ᴹ

container
contenedor ᴹ

deck
cubierta ᶠ

lifeboat
bote ᴹ salvavidas

hull
casco ᴹ

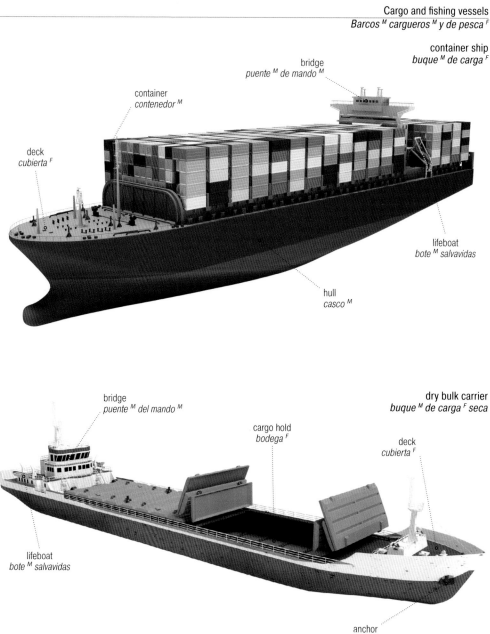

dry bulk carrier
buque ᴹ de carga ᶠ seca

bridge
puente ᴹ del mando ᴹ

cargo hold
bodega ᶠ

deck
cubierta ᶠ

lifeboat
bote ᴹ salvavidas

anchor
ancla ᶠ

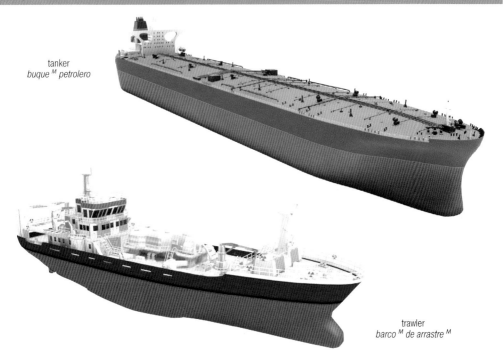

tanker
buque M *petrolero*

trawler
barco M *de arrastre* M

Recreational vessels
Barcos M *recreativos*

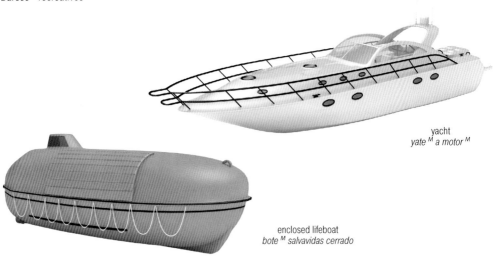

yacht
yate M *a motor* M

enclosed lifeboat
bote M *salvavidas cerrado*

schooner
barco ᴹ de vela ꟻ

mainmast
mástil ᴹ principal

sailboat
bote ᴹ de vela ꟻ

sail
vela ꟻ

bowsprit
bauprés ᴹ

hull
casco ᴹ

foremast
palo ᴹ de trinquete ᴹ

mizzenmast
mástil ᴹ de mesana ꟻ

personal watercraft: front view
moto ^{F} *acuática: vista delantera*

personal watercraft: rear view
moto ^{F} *acuática: vista trasera*

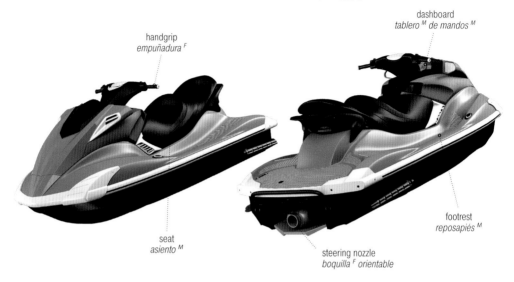

dashboard
tablero ^{M} *de mandos* ^{M}

handgrip
empuñadura ^{F}

footrest
reposapiés ^{M}

seat
asiento ^{M}

steering nozzle
boquilla ^{F} *orientable*

snowcat
tractor ^{M} *para nieve* ^{F}

headlight
faro ^{M} *delantero*

windshield
parabrisas ^{M}

cab
cabina ^{F}

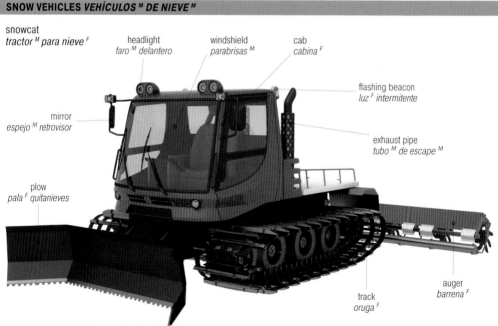

flashing beacon
luz ^{F} *intermitente*

mirror
espejo ^{M} *retrovisor*

exhaust pipe
tubo ^{M} *de escape* ^{M}

plow
pala ^{F} *quitanieves*

track
oruga ^{F}

auger
barrena ^{F}

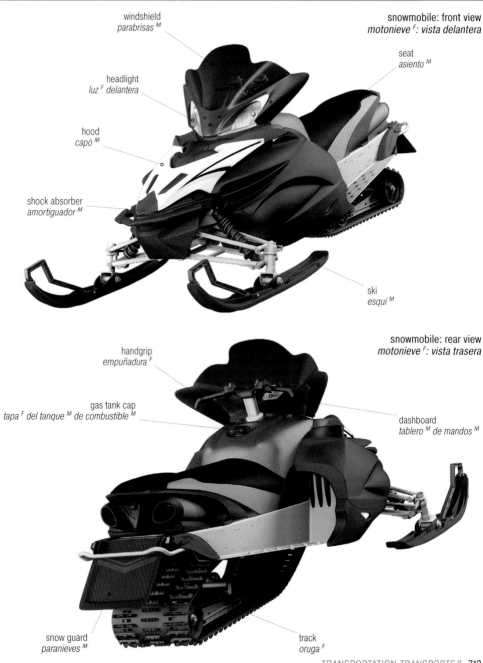

snowmobile: front view
motonieve *F*: *vista delantera*

windshield
parabrisas *M*

seat
asiento *M*

headlight
luz *F delantera*

hood
capó *M*

shock absorber
amortiguador *M*

ski
esquí *M*

snowmobile: rear view
motonieve *F*: *vista trasera*

handgrip
empuñadura *F*

gas tank cap
tapa *F del tanque* *M de combustible* *M*

dashboard
tablero *M de mandos* *M*

snow guard
paranieves *M*

track
oruga *F*

cable car
teleférico M

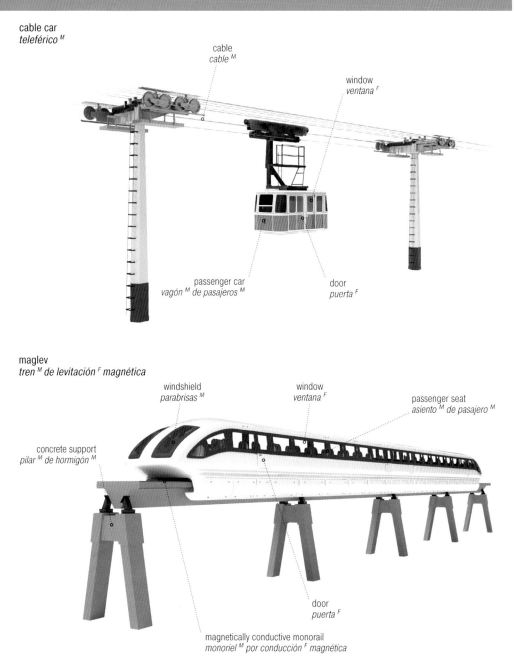

cable
cable M

window
ventana F

passenger car
vagón M *de pasajeros* M

door
puerta F

maglev
tren M *de levitación* F *magnética*

windshield
parabrisas M

window
ventana F

passenger seat
asiento M *de pasajero* M

concrete support
pilar M *de hormigón* M

door
puerta F

magnetically conductive monorail
monoriel M *por conducción* F *magnética*

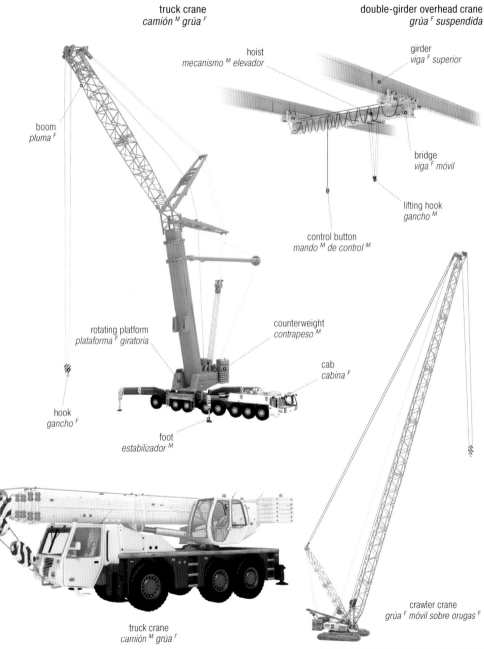

truck crane
camión M *grúa* F

double-girder overhead crane
grúa F *suspendida*

hoist
mecanismo M *elevador*

girder
viga F *superior*

boom
pluma F

bridge
viga F *móvil*

lifting hook
gancho M

control button
mando M *de control* M

rotating platform
plataforma F *giratoria*

counterweight
contrapeso M

cab
cabina F

hook
gancho F

foot
estabilizador M

truck crane
camión M *grúa* F

crawler crane
grúa F *móvil sobre orugas* F

harbor gantry crane
grúa F *de puerto* M

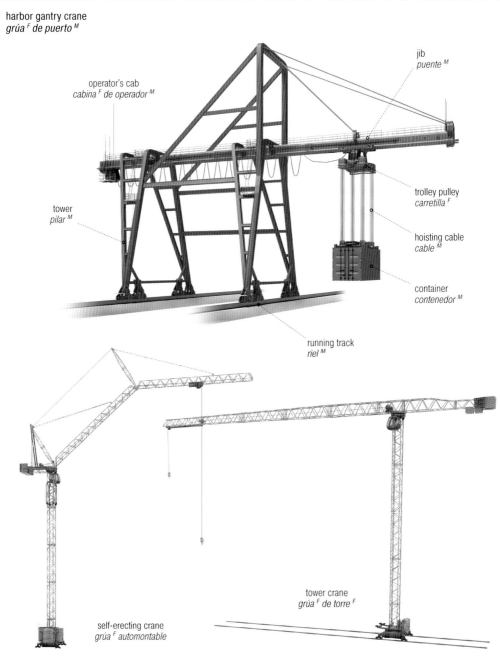

jib
puente M

operator's cab
cabina F *de operador* M

trolley pulley
carretilla F

tower
pilar M

hoisting cable
cable M

container
contenedor M

running track
riel M

self-erecting crane
grúa F *automontable*

tower crane
grúa F *de torre* F

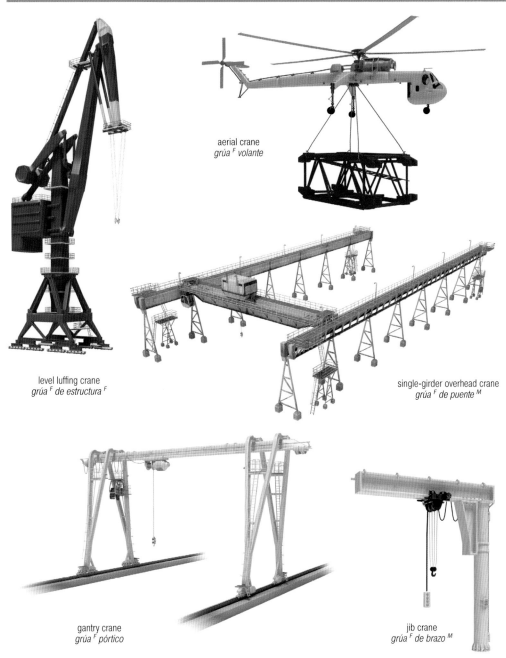

aerial crane
grúa F volante

level luffing crane
grúa F de estructura F

single-girder overhead crane
grúa F de puente M

gantry crane
grúa F pórtico

jib crane
grúa F de brazo M

SCIENCE

CIENCIA

CHEMISTRY *QUÍMICA* F
Chemical elements *Elementos* M *químicos*

periodic table
tabla F *periódica*

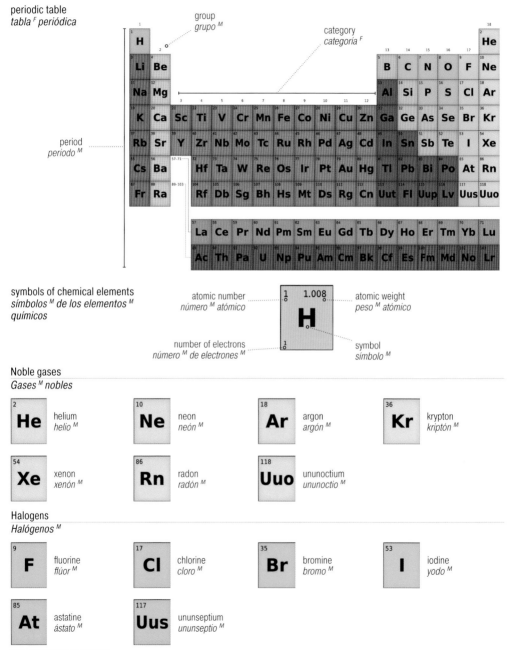

symbols of chemical elements
símbolos M *de los elementos* M
químicos

atomic number
número M *atómico*

atomic weight
peso M *atómico*

number of electrons
número M *de electrones* M

symbol
símbolo M

Noble gases
Gases M *nobles*

He helium *helio* M	**Ne** neon *neón* M	**Ar** argon *argón* M	**Kr** krypton *kriptón* M
Xe xenon *xenón* M	**Rn** radon *radón* M	**Uuo** ununoctium *ununoctio* M	

Halogens
Halógenos M

F fluorine *flúor* M	**Cl** chlorine *cloro* M	**Br** bromine *bromo* M	**I** iodine *yodo* M
At astatine *ástato* M	**Uus** ununseptium *ununseptio* M		

Transition metals
Metales M *de transición* F

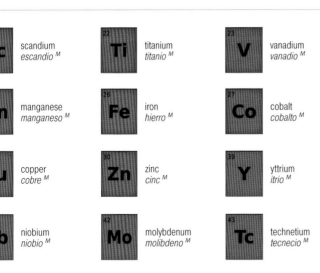

Sc 21 scandium *escandio* M	**Ti** 22 titanium *titanio* M	**V** 23 vanadium *vanadio* M	**Cr** 24 chromium *cromo* M
Mn 25 manganese *manganeso* M	**Fe** 26 iron *hierro* M	**Co** 27 cobalt *cobalto* M	**Ni** 28 nickel *níquel* M
Cu 29 copper *cobre* M	**Zn** 30 zinc *cinc* M	**Y** 39 yttrium *itrio* M	**Zr** 40 zirconium *circonio* M
Nb 41 niobium *niobio* M	**Mo** 42 molybdenum *molibdeno* M	**Tc** 43 technetium *tecnecio* M	**Ru** 44 ruthenium *rutenio* M
Rh 45 rhodium *rodio* M	**Pd** 46 palladium *paladio* M	**Ag** 47 silver *plata* F	**Cd** 48 cadmium *cadmio* M
Hf 72 hafnium *hafnio* M	**Ta** 73 tantalum *tantalio* M	**W** 74 tungsten *tungsteno* M	**Re** 75 rhenium *renio* M
Os 76 osmium *osmio* M	**Ir** 77 iridium *iridio* M	**Pt** 78 platinum *platino* M	**Au** 79 gold *oro* M
Hg 80 mercury *mercurio* M	**Rf** 104 rutherfordium *rutherfordio* M	**Db** 105 dubnium *dubnio* M	**Sg** 106 seaborgium *seaborgio* M
Bh 107 bohrium *bohrio* M	**Hs** 108 hassium *hassio* M	**Mt** 109 meitnerium *meitnerio* M	**Ds** 110 darmstadtium *darmstadio* M
Rg 111 roentgenium *roentgenio* M	**Cn** 112 copernicium *copernicio* M		

Alkali metals
Metales ^M *alcalinos*

 Li lithium
litio ^M

 Na sodium
sodio ^M

 K potassium
potasio ^M

 Rb rubidium
rubidio ^M

 Cs cesium
cesio ^M

 Fr francium
francio ^M

Post-transition metals
Metales ^M *del bloque* ^M *P*

 Al aluminum
aluminio ^M

 Ga gallium
galio ^M

 In indium
indio ^M

 Sn tin
estaño ^M

 Tl thallium
talio ^M

 Pb lead
plomo ^M

 Bi bismuth
bismuto ^M

 Po polonium
polonio ^M

 Uut ununtrium
ununtrio ^M

 Fl flerovium
flerovio ^M

 Uup ununpentium
unumpentio ^M

 Lv livermorium
livermorio ^M

Metalloids
Metaloides ^M

 B boron
boro ^M

Si silicon
silicio ^M

Ge germanium
germanio ^M

As arsenic
arsénico ^M

Sb antimony
antimonio ^M

Te tellurium
telurio ^M

Nonmetals
No metales ^M

 H hydrogen
hidrógeno ^M

 C carbon
carbón ^M

 N nitrogen
nitrógeno ^M

O oxygen
oxigeno ^M

 P phosphorus
fósforo ^M

S sulfur
azufre ^M

Se selenium
selenio ^M

Lanthanides
Lantánidos M

57 **La**	lanthanum *lantano* M	58 **Ce**	cerium *cerio* M	59 **Pr**	praseodymium *praseodimio* M	60 **Nd**	neodymium *neodimio* M
61 **Pm**	promethium *prometio* M	62 **Sm**	samarium *samario* M	63 **Eu**	europium *europio* M	64 **Gd**	gadolinium *gadolinio* M
65 **Tb**	terbium *terbio* M	66 **Dy**	dysprosium *disprosio* M	67 **Ho**	holmium *holmio* M	68 **Er**	erbium *erbio* M
69 **Tm**	thulium *tulio* M	70 **Yb**	ytterbium *iterbio* M	71 **Lu**	lutetium *lutecio* M		

Actinides
Actínidos M

89 **Ac**	actinium *actinio* M	90 **Th**	thorium *torio* M	91 **Pa**	protactinium *protactinio* M	92 **U**	uranium *uranio* M
93 **Np**	neptunium *neptunio* M	94 **Pu**	plutonium *plutonio* M	95 **Am**	americium *americio* M	96 **Cm**	curium *curio* M
97 **Bk**	berkelium *berkelio* M	98 **Cf**	californium *californio* M	99 **Es**	einsteinium *einstenio* M	100 **Fm**	fermium *fermio* M
101 **Md**	mendelevium *mendelevio* M	102 **No**	nobelium *nobelio* M	103 **Lr**	lawrencium *laurencio* M		

Alkaline earth metals
Metales M alcalinotérreos

| 4 **Be** | beryllium *berilio* M | 12 **Mg** | magnesium *magnesio* M | 20 **Ca** | calcium *calcio* M | 38 **Sr** | strontium *estroncio* M |
| 56 **Ba** | barium *bario* M | 88 **Ra** | radium *radio* M | | | | |

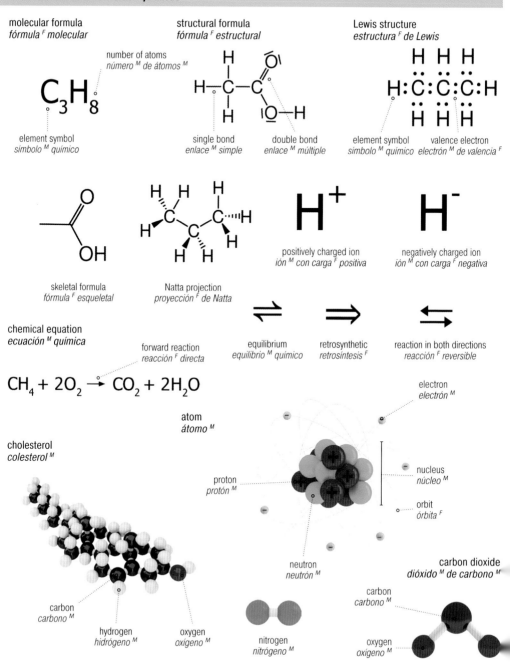

molecular formula
fórmula F *molecular*

number of atoms
número M *de átomos* M

C_3H_8

element symbol
símbolo M *químico*

structural formula
fórmula F *estructural*

single bond
enlace M *simple*

double bond
enlace M *múltiple*

Lewis structure
estructura F *de Lewis*

H H H

H:C:C:C:H

H H H

element symbol
símbolo M *químico*

valence electron
electrón M *de valencia* F

skeletal formula
fórmula F *esqueletal*

Natta projection
proyección F *de Natta*

H^+

positively charged ion
ión M *con carga* F *positiva*

H^-

negatively charged ion
ión M *con carga* F *negativa*

chemical equation
ecuación M *química*

forward reaction
reacción F *directa*

equilibrium
equilíbrio M *químico*

retrosynthetic
retrosintesis F

reaction in both directions
reacción F *reversible*

$$CH_4 + 2O_2 \rightarrow CO_2 + 2H_2O$$

electron
electrón M

atom
átomo M

cholesterol
colesterol M

proton
protón M

nucleus
núcleo M

orbit
órbita F

neutron
neutrón M

carbon dioxide
dióxido M *de carbono* M

carbon
carbono M

carbon
carbono M

hydrogen
hidrógeno M

oxygen
oxígeno M

nitrogen
nitrógeno M

oxygen
oxígeno M

Kinematics
Cinemática ^F

v

velocity
velocidad ^F

a

acceleration
aceleración ^F

g

gravitational acceleration
aceleración ^F *gravitacional*

f

frequency
frecuencia ^F

n

rotational frequency
revoluciones ^M *por minuto* ^M

λ

wavelength
longitud ^F *de onda* ^F

v

kinematic viscosity
viscosidad ^F *cinemática*

t

time
tiempo ^M

T

period duration
periodo ^M *de duración* ^F

ω

angular velocity
velocidad ^F *angular*

Mechanics
Mecánica ^F

m

mass
masa ^F

F

force
fuerza ^F

J

impulse
impulso ^M

p

linear momentum
momento ^M *lineal*

I

moment of inertia
momento ^M *de inercia* ^F

M

moment of force
momento ^M *de fuerza* ^F

L

angular momentum
momento ^M *angular*

σ

normal tension
tensión ^F *normal*

τ

shear stress
tensión ^F *cortante*

P

power
potencia ^F

W

work
trabajo ^M

ρ

density
densidad ^F

I

intensity
intensidad ^F

η

efficiency
eficiencia ^F

S

entropy
entropía ^F

F_{R}

frictional force
fuerza ^F *de fricción* ^F

γ

specific weight
peso ^M *específico*

V

specific volume
volumen ^M *específico*

Photometry and optics
Fotometría ^F *y óptica* ^F

D

diameter
diámetro ^M

I_{V}

luminous intensity
luminosidad ^F

Φ_{v}

luminous flux
flujo ^M *luminoso*

η

luminous efficacy
eficacia ^F *luminosa*

L_{v}

luminance
luminancia ^F

E_{v}

illuminance
iluminancia ^F

M_{v}

luminous exitance
emitancia ^F *luminosa*

H_{v}

luminous exposure
exposición ^F *luminosa*

f

focal length
distancia ^F *focal*

Q_{v}

luminous energy
energía ^F *luminosa*

Thermodynamics
Termodinámica ^F

λ

thermal conductivity
conductividad ^F *térmica*

T

absolute temperature
temperatura ^F *absoluta*

ϑ

Celsius temperature
temperatura ^F *celsius*

Q

heat
calor ^M

U

internal energy
energía ^F *interna*

E_{th}

thermal energy
energía ^F *térmica*

μ

chemical potential
potencial ^M *quimico*

H

enthalpy
entalpia ^F

Φ_{th}

heat flux
flujo ^M *de calor* ^M

S

entropy
entropia ^F

C_{th}

thermal capacity
capacidad ^F *calorífica*

Electricity
Electricidad ^F

Y

admittance
conductancia ^F *falsa*

I

electric current
corriente ^F *eléctrica*

J

electric current density
densidad ^F *de transmisión* ^F *eléctrica*

Q

electric charge
carga ^F *eléctrica*

U

electric tension
tensión ^F *eléctrica*

φ

phase shift
cambio ^M *de fase* ^F

R

resistance
resistencia ^F

X

reactance
reactancia ^F

Z

impedance
impedancia ^F

ρ

specific resistance
resistividad ^F

B

susceptance
conductancia ^F *ciega*

F_{L}

Lorentz force
fuerza ^F *de Lorentz*

E

electric field
campo ^M *eléctrico*

Ψ

water potential
potencial ^M *hídrico*

D

electric flux density
densidad ^F *de flujo* ^M *eléctrico*

P

polarization
polarización ^F

α

polarizability
polarizabilidad ^F

Magnetism
Magnetismo ^M

P

effective power
potencia ^F *efectiva*

B

magnetic flux density
densidad ^F *de flujo* ^M *magnético*

J

magnetic polarization
polarización ^F *magnética*

ϵ

permittivity
permitividad ^F

M

magnetization
magnetización ^F

Φ

magnetic flux
flujo ^M *magnético*

C

electric capacity
capacidad ^F *eléctrica*

S

elastance
elastancia ^F

L

inductance
inductancia ^F

H

magnetic field strength
fuerza ^F *de campo* ^M *magnético*

S

apparent power
potencia ^F *aparente*

m

magnetic moment
momento ^M *magnético*

Atomic and molecular quantities
Cantidades F atómicas y moleculares

n

amount of substance
cantidad F de sustancia F

V_m

molar volume
volumen M molar

M

molar mass
masa F molar

M_r

relative molar mass
masa F molecular relativa

A_r

relative atomic mass
masa F atómica relativa

Nuclear physics
Física F nuclear

σ

effect cross section
sección F eficaz

A

activity
actividad F

τ

mean lifetime
vida F media

λ

disintegration constant
constante F de desintegración F

D

absorbed dose
dosis F absorbida

H

equivalent dose
dosis F equivalente

$T_{1/2}$

half-life
período M de semidesintegración F

J

ion dose
dosis F iónica

Radiometry
Radiometría F

H

radiant exposure
exposición F radiante

I

radiant intensity
intensidad F radiante

Φ

radiant flux
flujo M radiante

Q

radiant energy
energía F radiante

L

radiance
radiancia F

M

radiant exitance
emitancia F radiante

E

irradiance
irradiancia F

MATHEMATICS *MATEMÁTICA* F
Mathematical symbols *Símbolos F matemáticos*

l

length
longitud F

b

width
anchura F

h

height
altura F

σ

thickness
espesor M

r

radius
radio M

d

diameter
diámetro M

s

distance
longitud F lineal

A

area
área F

S

cross-sectional area
área F transversal

V

volume
volumen M

Ω

space angle
ángulo M espacial

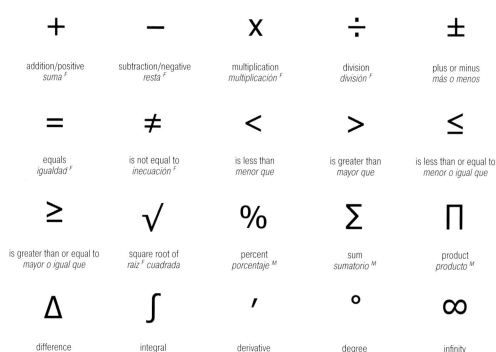

+	−	X	÷	±
addition/positive *suma* [F]	subtraction/negative *resta* [F]	multiplication *multiplicación* [F]	division *división* [F]	plus or minus *más o menos*

=	≠	<	>	≤
equals *igualdad* [F]	is not equal to *inecuación* [F]	is less than *menor que*	is greater than *mayor que*	is less than or equal to *menor o igual que*

≥	√	%	Σ	∏
is greater than or equal to *mayor o igual que*	square root of *raíz* [F] *cuadrada*	percent *porcentaje* [M]	sum *sumatorio* [M]	product *producto* [M]

Δ	∫	′	°	∞
difference *diferencia* [F]	integral *integral* [F]	derivative *diferencial* [M]	degree *grado* [M]	infinity *inifinito* [M]

∠	∟	⊥	‖	⌀
acute angle *ángulo* [M] *agudo* [M]	right angle *ángulo* [M] *recto*	is perpendicular to *perpendicular* [F]	is parallel to *paralelo* [M]	diameter *diámetro* [M]

∪	∩	∅	∈	⊂
union of two sets *unión* [F] *de dos conjuntos* [M]	intersection of two sets *intersección* [F] *de dos conjuntos* [M]	empty set *conjunto* [M] *vacío*	is an element of *pertenece a*	is included in/is a subset of *está contenido en*

∀	∃	ℕ	ℤ	ℚ
universal quantification *cuantificador* [M] *universal*	existential quantification *cuantificador* [M] *existencial*	natural numbers *número* [M] *natural*	integers *número* [M] *entero*	rational numbers *número* [M] *racional*

$\mathbb{A}$

algebraic numbers
número ^M algebraico

$\mathbb{R}$

real numbers
número ^M real

$\mathbb{C}$

complex numbers
número ^M complejo

$\mathbb{H}$

quaternions
cuaternión ^M

π

pi
pi ^M

simple fraction
fracción ^F ordinaria

numerator
numerador ^M

fraction bar
barra ^F de fracción ^F

$$\frac{3}{4}$$

denominator
denominador ^M

e

Euler's number
número ^M de Euler

φ

golden ratio
proporción ^F áurea

i

imaginary number
número ^M imaginario

Roman numerals *Numeración* ^F *romana*

I

one
uno ^M

II

two
dos ^M

III

three
tres ^M

IV

four
cuatro ^M

V

five
cinco ^M

VI

six
seis ^M

VII

seven
siete ^M

VIII

eight
ocho ^M

IX

nine
nueve ^M

X

ten
diez ^M

XX

twenty
veinte ^M

XXX

thirty
treinta ^M

XL

forty
cuarenta ^M

L

fifty
cincuenta ^M

LX

sixty
sesenta ^M

XC

ninety
noventa ^M

C

one hundred
cien ^M

D

five hundred
quinientos ^M

M

one thousand
mil ^M

Circle
Círculo M

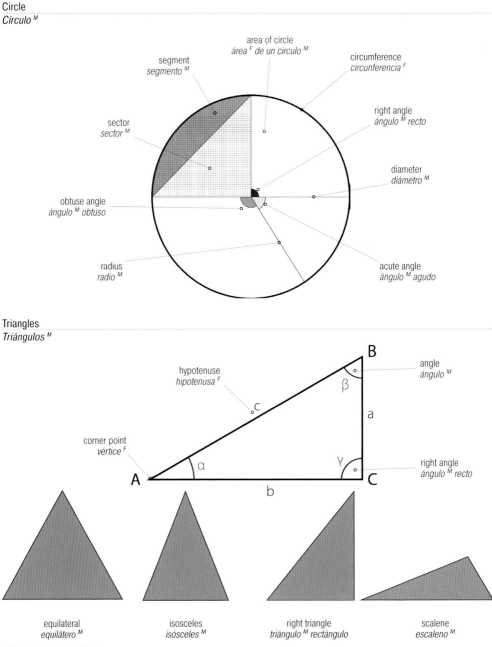

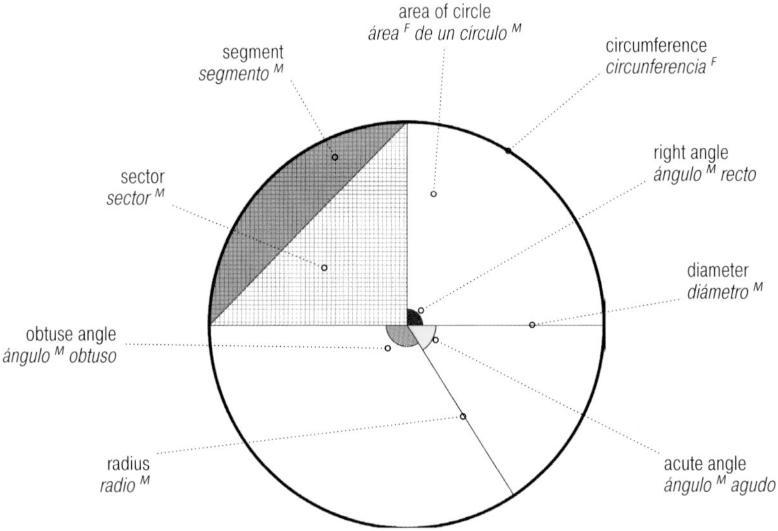
area of circle
área F *de un círculo* M
segment
segmento M
circumference
circunferencia F
right angle
ángulo M *recto*
sector
sector M
diameter
diámetro M
obtuse angle
ángulo M *obtuso*
radius
radio M
acute angle
ángulo M *agudo*

Triangles
Triángulos M

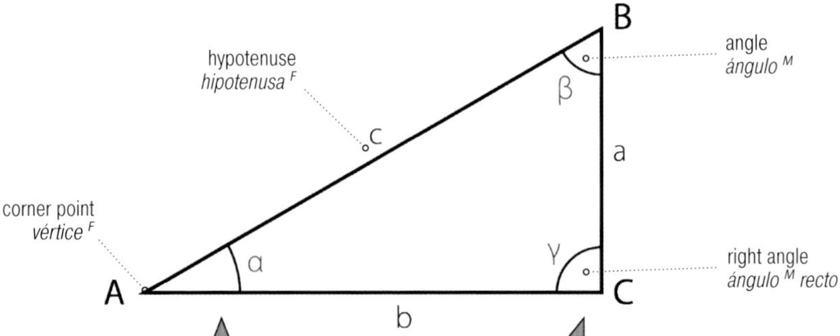
B
angle
ángulo M
hypotenuse
hipotenusa F
β
c
a
corner point
vértice F
α
γ
right angle
ángulo M *recto*
A
C
b

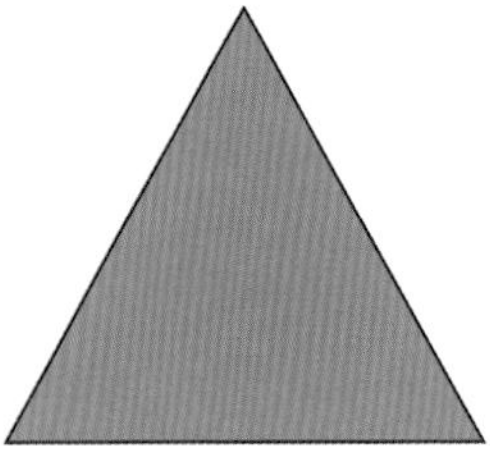

equilateral
equilátero M

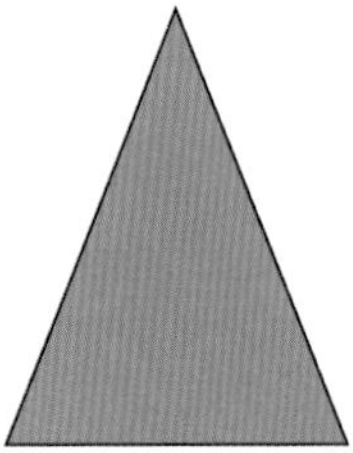

isosceles
isósceles M

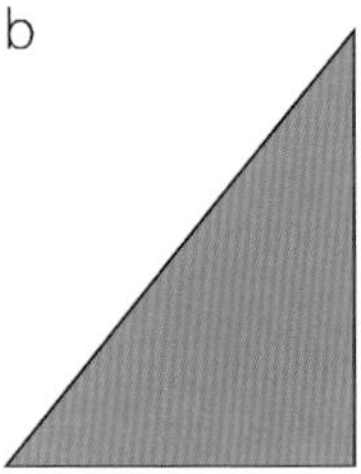

right triangle
triángulo M *rectángulo*

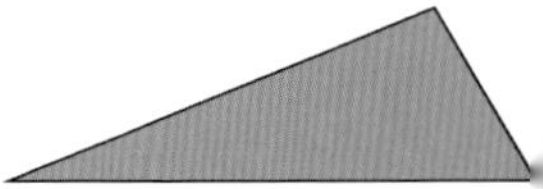

scalene
escaleno M

Polygons
Polígonos ^M

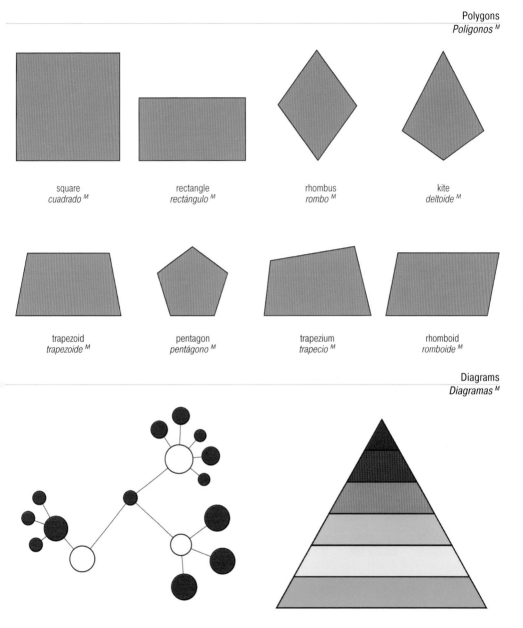

square
cuadrado ^M

rectangle
rectángulo ^M

rhombus
rombo ^M

kite
deltoide ^M

trapezoid
trapezoide ^M

pentagon
pentágono ^M

trapezium
trapecio ^M

rhomboid
romboide ^M

Diagrams
Diagramas ^M

cluster diagram
diagrama ^M *de racimo* ^M

pyramid diagram
diagrama ^M *ternario*

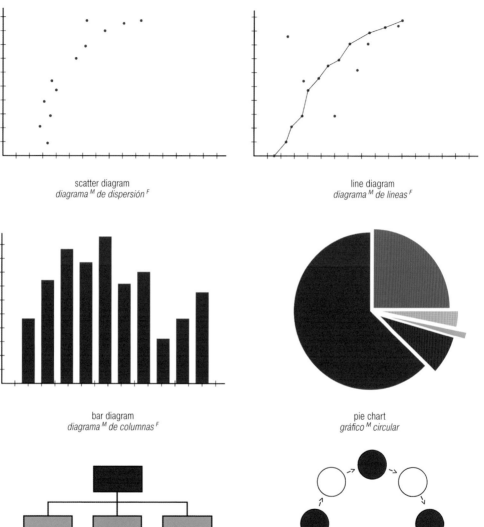

scatter diagram
diagrama M de dispersión F

line diagram
diagrama M de líneas F

bar diagram
diagrama M de columnas F

pie chart
gráfico M circular

tree diagram
diagrama M de árbol M

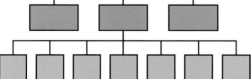

cycle diagram
diagrama M de ciclos M

Solids
Sólidos M

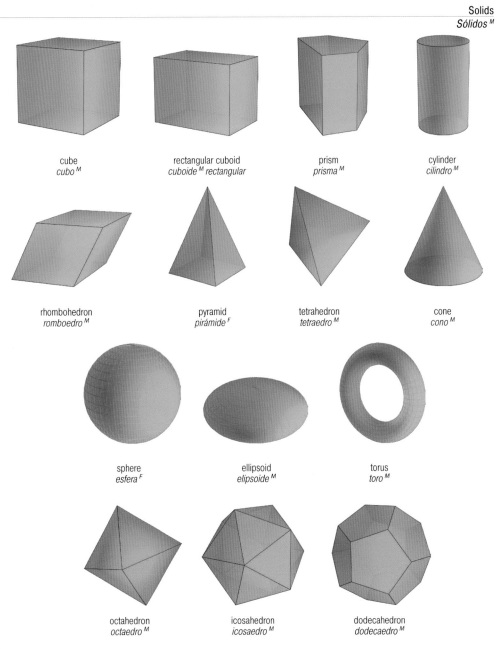

cube
cubo M

rectangular cuboid
cuboide M *rectangular*

prism
prisma M

cylinder
cilindro M

rhombohedron
romboedro M

pyramid
pirámide F

tetrahedron
tetraedro M

cone
cono M

sphere
esfera F

ellipsoid
elipsoide M

torus
toro M

octahedron
octaedro M

icosahedron
icosaedro M

dodecahedron
dodecaedro M

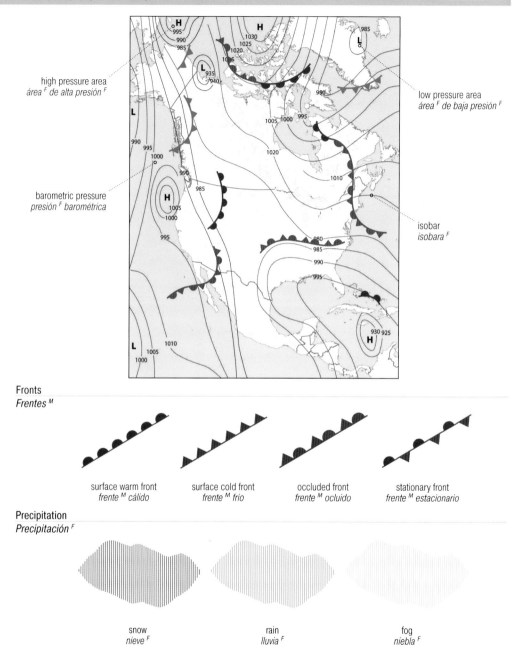

high pressure area
área F *de alta presión* F

low pressure area
área F *de baja presión* F

barometric pressure
presión F *barométrica*

isobar
isobara F

Fronts
Frentes M

surface warm front
frente M *cálido*

surface cold front
frente M *frío*

occluded front
frente M *ocluido*

stationary front
frente M *estacionario*

Precipitation
Precipitación F

snow
nieve F

rain
lluvia F

fog
niebla F

station model
modelo M *de estación* M

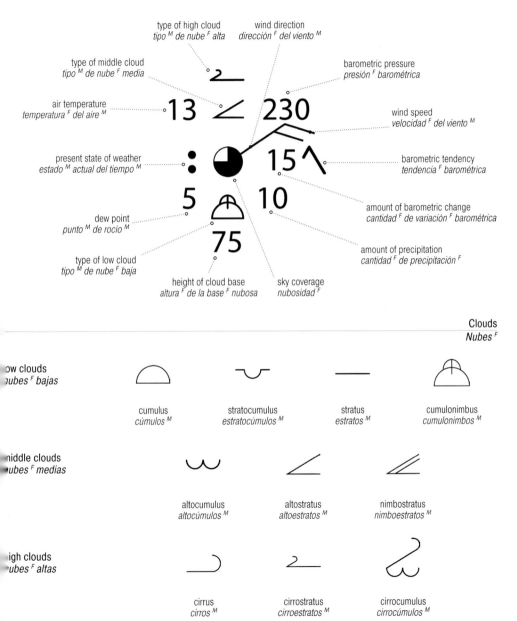

type of high cloud
tipo M *de nube* F *alta*

wind direction
dirección F *del viento* M

type of middle cloud
tipo M *de nube* F *media*

barometric pressure
presión F *barométrica*

air temperature
temperatura F *del aire* M

wind speed
velocidad F *del viento* M

present state of weather
estado M *actual del tiempo* M

barometric tendency
tendencia F *barométrica*

dew point
punto M *de rocío* M

amount of barometric change
cantidad F *de variación* F *barométrica*

type of low cloud
tipo M *de nube* F *baja*

amount of precipitation
cantidad F *de precipitación* F

height of cloud base
altura F *de la base* F *nubosa*

sky coverage
nubosidad F

Clouds
Nubes F

ow clouds
ubes F bajas

cumulus
cúmulos M

stratocumulus
estratocúmulos M

stratus
estratos M

cumulonimbus
cumulonimbos M

middle clouds
ubes F medias

altocumulus
altocúmulos M

altostratus
altoestratos M

nimbostratus
nimboestratos M

igh clouds
ubes F altas

cirrus
cirros M

cirrostratus
cirroestratos M

cirrocumulus
cirrocúmulos M

Precipitation
Precipitación [F]

light intermittent rain
lluvia [F] *leve intermitente*

moderate intermittent rain
lluvia [F] *moderada intermitente*

heavy intermittent rain
lluvia [F] *fuerte intermitente*

freezing rain
lluvia [F] *helada*

light intermittent drizzle
llovizna [F] *leve intermitente*

moderate intermittent drizzle
llovizna [F] *moderada intermitente*

thick intermittent drizzle
llovizna [F] *fuerte intermitente*

freezing drizzle
llovizna [F] *helada*

sleet
aguanieve [F]

ice crystals
cristales [M] *de hielo* [M]

intermittent light snow
nevada [F] *leve intermitente*

continuous moderate snow
nevada [F] *moderada continua*

intermittent heavy snow
nevada [F] *fuerte intermitente*

graupel (soft hail)
granizo [M] *suave*

haze
calima [F]

sandstorm or dust storm
tormenta [F] *de polvo* [M]
o arena [F]

well-developed dust or sand whirl
remolino [M] *de polvo* [M]

drifting snow, low
ventisca [F] *de nieve* [F] *leve*

drifting snow, high
ventisca [F] *de nieve* [F] *intensa*

fog
niebla [F]

lightning visible, no thunder heard
relámpago [M] *visible, sin sonido* [M]
de truenos [M]

thunderstorm
tormenta [F]

shower of rain and snow, mixed
chubasco [M] *de aguanieve* [F]

snow shower
nevada [F]

rain shower
chubasco [M]

funnel clouds or tornadoes
nubes [F] *embudos o tornados* [M]

hurricane
huracán [M]

Sky coverage
Nubosidad [F]

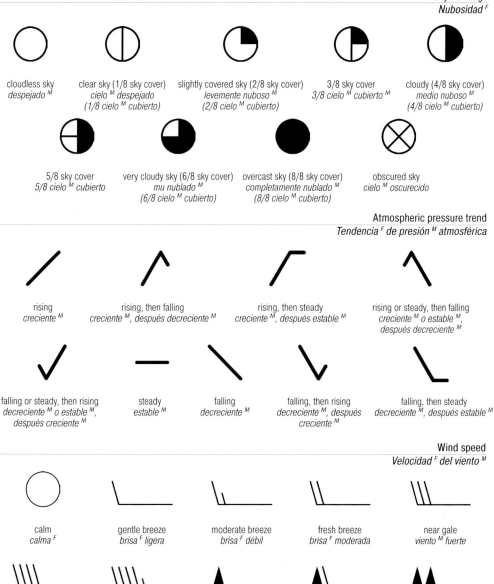

cloudless sky
despejado [M]

clear sky (1/8 sky cover)
cielo [M] *despejado*
(1/8 cielo [M] *cubierto)*

slightly covered sky (2/8 sky cover)
levemente nuboso [M]
(2/8 cielo [M] *cubierto)*

3/8 sky cover
3/8 cielo [M] *cubierto* [M]

cloudy (4/8 sky cover)
medio nuboso [M]
(4/8 cielo [M] *cubierto)*

5/8 sky cover
5/8 cielo [M] *cubierto*

very cloudy sky (6/8 sky cover)
mu nublado [M]
(6/8 cielo [M] *cubierto)*

overcast sky (8/8 sky cover)
completamente nublado [M]
(8/8 cielo [M] *cubierto)*

obscured sky
cielo [M] *oscurecido*

Atmospheric pressure trend
Tendencia [F] *de presión* [M] *atmosférica*

rising
creciente [M]

rising, then falling
creciente [M]*, después decreciente* [M]

rising, then steady
creciente [M]*, después estable* [M]

rising or steady, then falling
creciente [M] *o estable* [M]*,*
después decreciente [M]

falling or steady, then rising
decreciente [M] *o estable* [M]*,*
después creciente [M]

steady
estable [M]

falling
decreciente [M]

falling, then rising
decreciente [M]*, después*
creciente [M]

falling, then steady
decreciente [M]*, después estable* [M]

Wind speed
Velocidad [F] *del viento* [M]

calm
calma [F]

gentle breeze
brisa [F] *ligera*

moderate breeze
brisa [F] *débil*

fresh breeze
brisa [F] *moderada*

near gale
viento [M] *fuerte*

gale
viento [M] *tormentoso*

severe gale
tormenta [F]

storm
tormenta [F] *intensa*

violent storm
tormenta [F] *huracanada*

hurricane
huracán [M]

subtractive colors
colores ᴹ *sustractivos*

additive colors
colores ᴹ *aditivos*

magenta
magenta ᴹ

red
rojo ᴹ

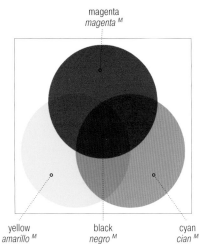

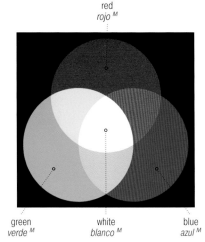

yellow
amarillo ᴹ

black
negro ᴹ

cyan
cian ᴹ

green
verde ᴹ

white
blanco ᴹ

blue
azul ᴹ

Color contrasts *Contrastes* ᴹ *de color* ᴹ

contrast of hue
contraste ᴹ *del tono* ᴹ

simultaneous contrast
contraste ᴹ *simultáneo*

light-dark contrast
contraste ᴹ *claro/oscuro*

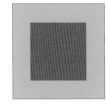

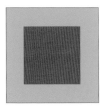

saturation contrast
contraste ᴹ *de saturación* ᶠ

warm-cool contrast
contraste ᴹ *cálido/frío*

quantity contrast
contraste ᴹ *cuantitativo*

complementary contrast
contraste ᴹ *complementario*

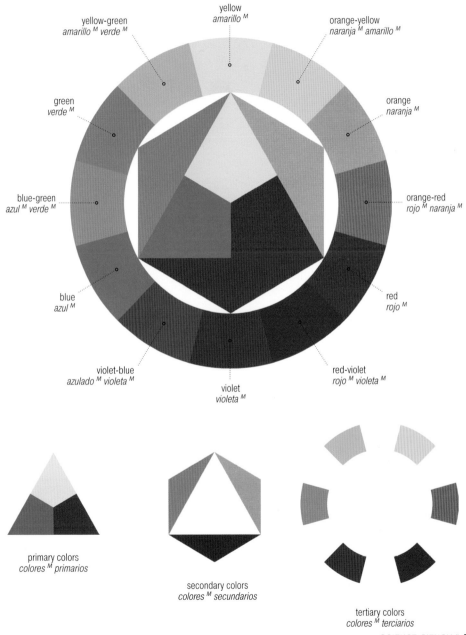

yellow
amarillo [M]

yellow-green
amarillo [M] *verde* [M]

orange-yellow
naranja [M] *amarillo* [M]

green
verde [M]

orange
naranja [M]

blue-green
azul [M] *verde* [M]

orange-red
rojo [M] *naranja* [M]

blue
azul [M]

red
rojo [M]

violet-blue
azulado [M] *violeta* [M]

red-violet
rojo [M] *violeta* [M]

violet
violeta [M]

primary colors
colores [M] *primarios*

secondary colors
colores [M] *secundarios*

tertiary colors
colores [M] *terciarios*

flask on stand
matraz M con soporte M

round-bottom flask
matraz M

liquid
líquido M

stand
soporte M

crucible with cover
crisol M con tapa F

flask with glass tubes
matraz M con tubos de vidrio M

fractional distillation kit
equipo M de destilación F fraccionada

heating mantle
manta F calefactora

universal heater
calentador M universal

liquid
líquido M

mantle
elemento M calorífico

power button
botón M de encendido M

laboratory flask
matraz M

heat control knob
perilla F de control M de temperatura F

desiccator
desecador M

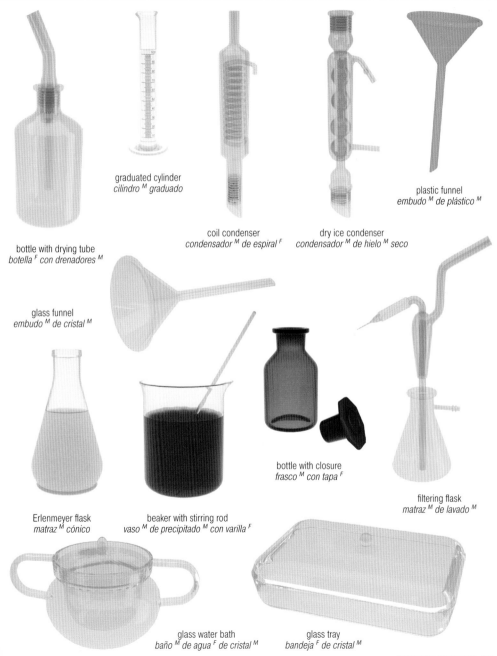

graduated cylinder
cilindro ᴹ *graduado*

plastic funnel
embudo ᴹ *de plástico* ᴹ

coil condenser
condensador ᴹ *de espiral* ᶠ

dry ice condenser
condensador ᴹ *de hielo* ᴹ *seco*

bottle with drying tube
botella ᶠ *con drenadores* ᴹ

glass funnel
embudo ᴹ *de cristal* ᴹ

bottle with closure
frasco ᴹ *con tapa* ᶠ

filtering flask
matraz ᴹ *de lavado* ᴹ

Erlenmeyer flask
matraz ᴹ *cónico*

beaker with stirring rod
vaso ᴹ *de precipitado* ᴹ *con varilla* ᶠ

glass water bath
baño ᴹ *de agua* ᶠ *de cristal* ᴹ

glass tray
bandeja ᶠ *de cristal* ᴹ

ring stand with clamps
base F *de anillos* M *con abrazaderas* F

separatory funnel
pera F *de decantación* M

barrel
barril M

electronic pipette
pipeta F *electrónica*

filter funnel
embudo M *de filtración* F

test tube with stopper
tubo M *de ensayo* M *con tapón* M

test tube on stand
tubo M *de ensayo* M *en
soporte* M

beaker with handle
jarra F *con asa* F

wash bottle
botella F *de lavado* M

beaker
vaso M *de precipitado* M

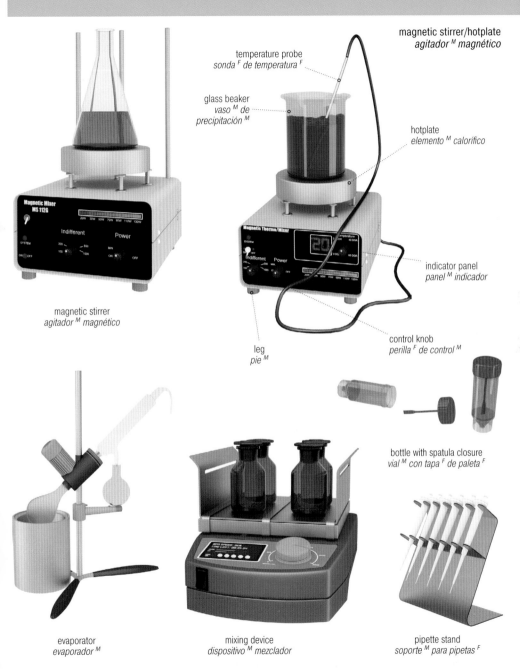

magnetic stirrer/hotplate
agitador **M** *magnético*

temperature probe
sonda **F** *de temperatura* **F**

glass beaker
vaso **M** *de precipitación* **M**

hotplate
elemento **M** *calorífico*

Magnetic Mixer
MS 112G

20W 30W 50W 70W 90W 110W 130W

Indifferent   Power

SYSTEM
ON OFF   MIN   ON OFF

Magnetic Thermo/Mixer

indicator panel
panel **M** *indicador*

control knob
perilla **F** *de control* **M**

magnetic stirrer
agitador **M** *magnético*

leg
pie **M**

bottle with spatula closure
vial **M** *con tapa* **F** *de paleta* **F**

evaporator
evaporador **M**

mixing device
dispositivo **M** *mezclador*

pipette stand
soporte **M** *para pipetas* **F**

fume hood
campana ^F *de humos* ^M

note stand
atril ^M

laminar flow unit
cabina ^F *de flujo* ^M *laminar*

spatula
espátula ^F

mobile base cabinet
armario ^M *móvil*

flask support ring
anillo ^M *de soporte* ^M *para matraz* ^M

steam autoclave
autoclave ^M *a vapor* ^M

electric water bath
baño ^M *María* ^F *eléctrico*

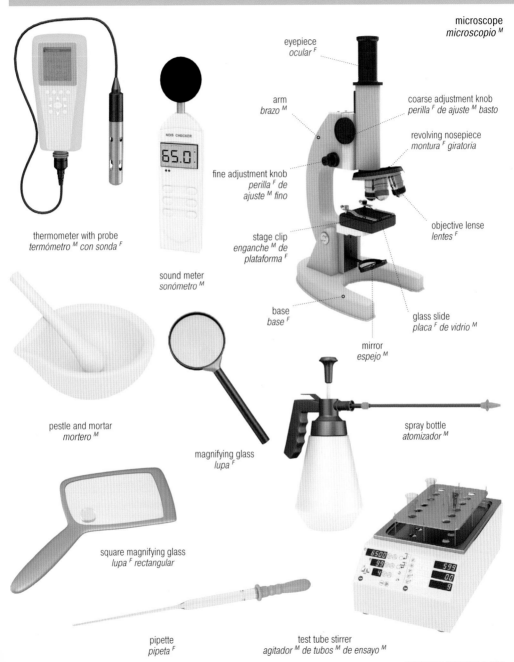

microscope
microscopio ᴹ

eyepiece
ocular ᶠ

arm
brazo ᴹ

coarse adjustment knob
perilla ᶠ de ajuste ᴹ basto

revolving nosepiece
montura ᶠ giratoria

fine adjustment knob
perilla ᶠ de ajuste ᴹ fino

objective lense
lentes ᶠ

stage clip
enganche ᴹ de plataforma ᶠ

base
base ᶠ

glass slide
placa ᶠ de vidrio ᴹ

mirror
espejo ᴹ

thermometer with probe
termómetro ᴹ con sonda ᶠ

sound meter
sonómetro ᴹ

pestle and mortar
mortero ᴹ

magnifying glass
lupa ᶠ

spray bottle
atomizador ᴹ

square magnifying glass
lupa ᶠ rectangular

pipette
pipeta ᶠ

test tube stirrer
agitador ᴹ de tubos ᴹ de ensayo ᴹ

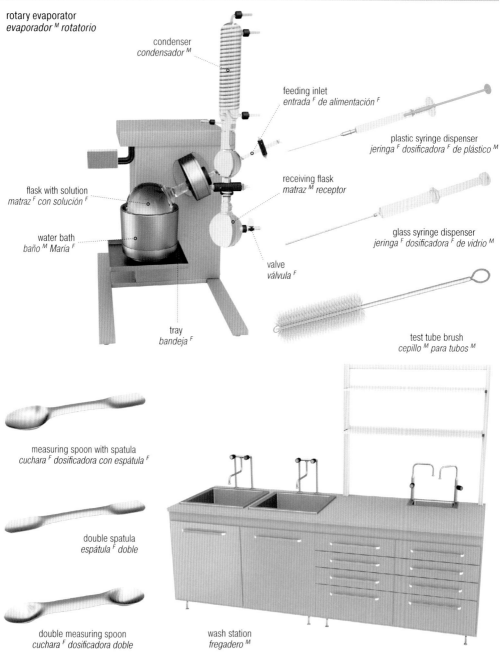

rotary evaporator
evaporador ^M rotatorio

condenser
condensador ^M

feeding inlet
entrada ^F de alimentación ^F

plastic syringe dispenser
jeringa ^F dosificadora ^F de plástico ^M

flask with solution
matraz ^F con solución ^F

receiving flask
matraz ^M receptor

glass syringe dispenser
jeringa ^F dosificadora ^F de vidrio ^M

water bath
baño ^M María ^F

valve
válvula ^F

tray
bandeja ^F

test tube brush
cepillo ^M para tubos ^M

measuring spoon with spatula
cuchara ^F dosificadora con espátula ^F

double spatula
espátula ^F doble

double measuring spoon
cuchara ^F dosificadora doble

wash station
fregadero ^M

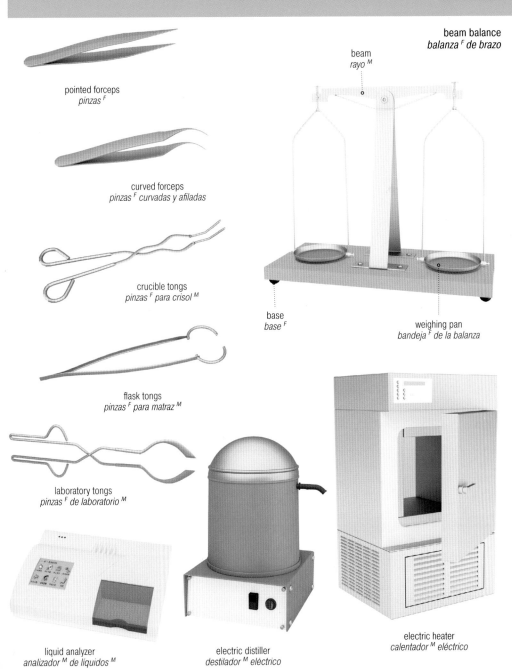

beam balance
balanza ᶠ de brazo

beam
rayo ᴹ

pointed forceps
pinzas ᶠ

curved forceps
pinzas ᶠ curvadas y afiladas

crucible tongs
pinzas ᶠ para crisol ᴹ

base
base ᶠ

weighing pan
bandeja ᶠ de la balanza

flask tongs
pinzas ᶠ para matraz ᴹ

laboratory tongs
pinzas ᶠ de laboratorio ᴹ

electric heater
calentador ᴹ eléctrico

liquid analyzer
analizador ᴹ de líquidos ᴹ

electric distiller
destilador ᴹ eléctrico

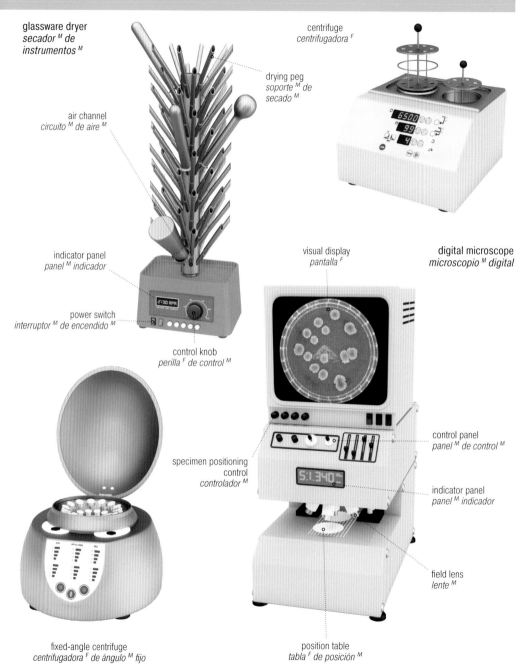

glassware dryer
secador ^M *de*
instrumentos ^M

centrifuge
centrifugadora ^F

drying peg
soporte ^M *de*
secado ^M

air channel
circuito ^M *de aire* ^M

visual display
pantalla ^F

digital microscope
microscopio ^M *digital*

indicator panel
panel ^M *indicador*

power switch
interruptor ^M *de encendido* ^M

control knob
perilla ^F *de control* ^M

control panel
panel ^M *de control* ^M

specimen positioning
control
controlador ^M

indicator panel
panel ^M *indicador*

field lens
lente ^M

fixed-angle centrifuge
centrifugadora ^F *de ángulo* ^M *fijo*

position table
tabla ^F *de posición* ^M

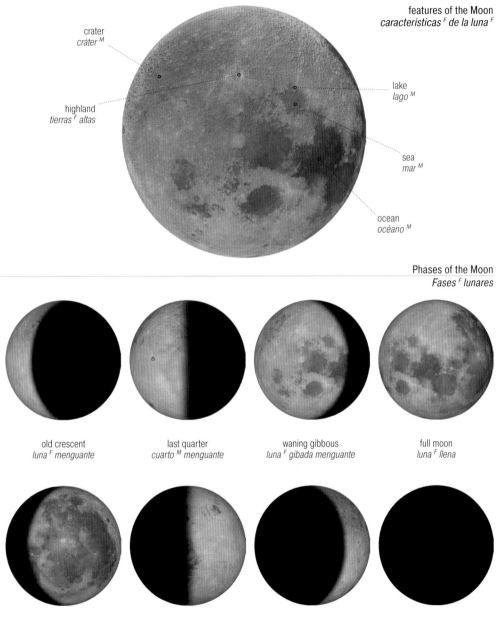

features of the Moon
características F de la luna F

crater
cráter M

highland
tierras F altas

lake
lago M

sea
mar M

ocean
océano M

Phases of the Moon
Fases F lunares

old crescent
luna F menguante

last quarter
cuarto M menguante

waning gibbous
luna F gibada menguante

full moon
luna F llena

waxing gibbous
luna F gibada creciente

first quarter
cuarto M creciente

new crescent
luna F nueva visible

new moon
luna F nueva

solar system
sistema ^M *solar*

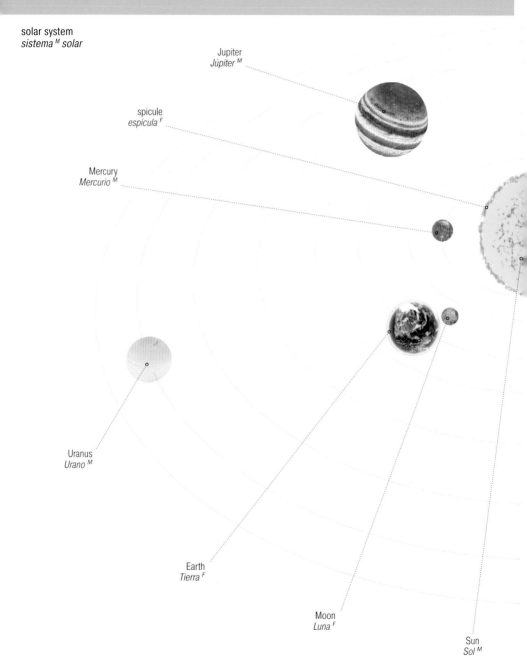

Jupiter
Júpiter ^M

spicule
espicula ^F

Mercury
Mercurio ^M

Uranus
Urano ^M

Earth
Tierra ^F

Moon
Luna ^F

Sun
Sol ^M

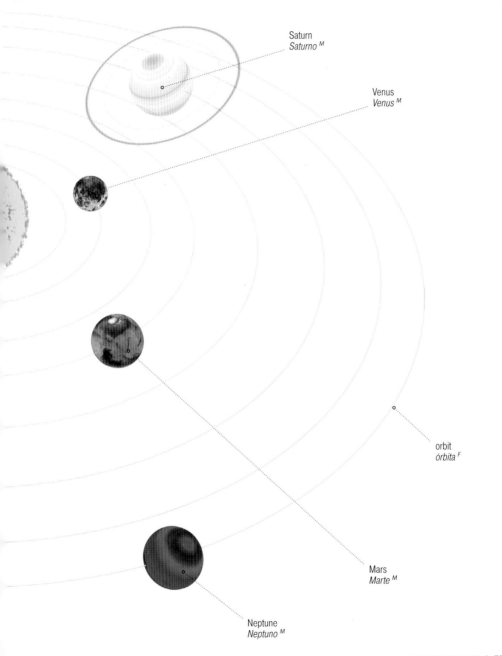

Saturn
Saturno ^M

Venus
Venus ^M

orbit
órbita ^F

Mars
Marte ^M

Neptune
Neptuno ^M

seasons of the year
estaciones del año ᶠ

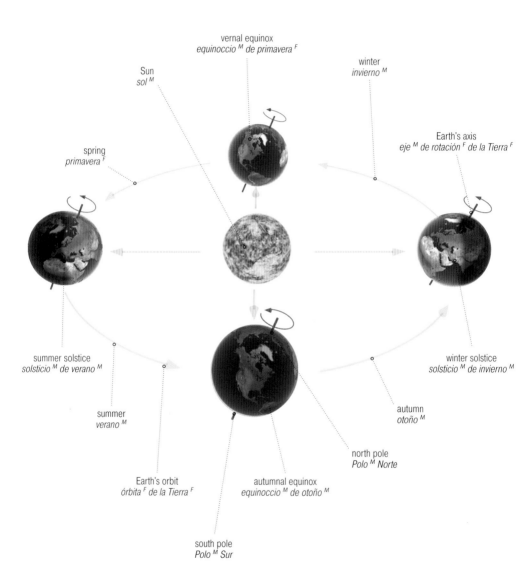

vernal equinox
equinoccio ᴹ *de primavera* ᶠ

Sun
sol ᴹ

winter
invierno ᴹ

Earth's axis
eje ᴹ *de rotación* ᶠ *de la Tierra* ᶠ

spring
primavera ᶠ

summer solstice
solsticio ᴹ *de verano* ᴹ

winter solstice
solsticio ᴹ *de invierno* ᴹ

summer
verano ᴹ

autumn
otoño ᴹ

north pole
Polo ᴹ *Norte*

Earth's orbit
órbita ᶠ *de la Tierra* ᶠ

autumnal equinox
equinoccio ᴹ *de otoño* ᴹ

south pole
Polo ᴹ *Sur*

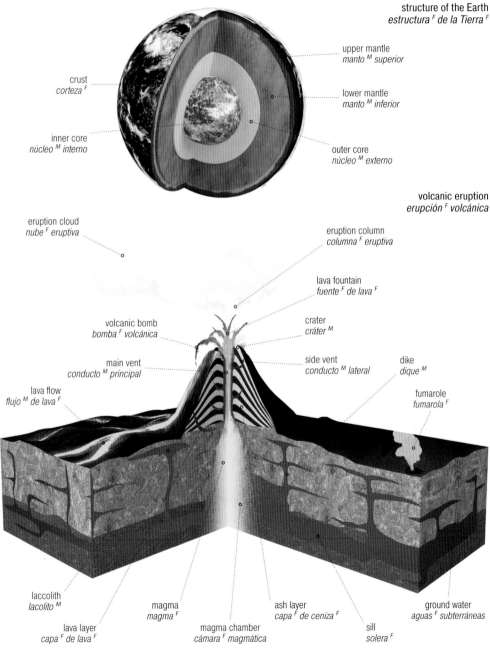

structure of the Earth
estructura F *de la Tierra* F

upper mantle
manto M *superior*

lower mantle
manto M *inferior*

crust
corteza F

inner core
núcleo M *interno*

outer core
núcleo M *externo*

volcanic eruption
erupción F *volcánica*

eruption cloud
nube F *eruptiva*

eruption column
columna F *eruptiva*

lava fountain
fuente F *de lava* F

volcanic bomb
bomba F *volcánica*

crater
cráter M

main vent
conducto M *principal*

side vent
conducto M *lateral*

dike
dique M

lava flow
flujo M *de lava* F

fumarole
fumarola F

laccolith
lacolito M

magma
magma F

ash layer
capa F *de ceniza* F

ground water
aguas F *subterráneas*

lava layer
capa F *de lava* F

magma chamber
cámara F *magmática*

sill
solera F

radio telescope
radiotelescopio M

receiver
receptor M

steerable parabolic reflector
reflector M *parabólico orientable*

parabolic reflector
reflector M *parabólico*

support structure
estructura F *de soporte* M

rotating track
eje M *rotatorio*

circular track
eje M *circular*

laboratory
laboratorio M

observatory
observatorio M

rotating dome
cúpula F *rotatoria*

dome shutter
escotilla F

door
puerta F

telescope
telescopio M

finderscope
mira F *del telescopio* M

dew shield
protector M *de rocío* M

eyepiece
ocular M

focusing knob
perilla F *de enfoque* M

main tube
tubo M *principal*

cradle
agarre M

azimuth fine adjustment
ajuste M *de azimut* M

counterweight
contrapeso M

altitude fine adjustment
ajuste M *de altitud* F

tripod
trípode M

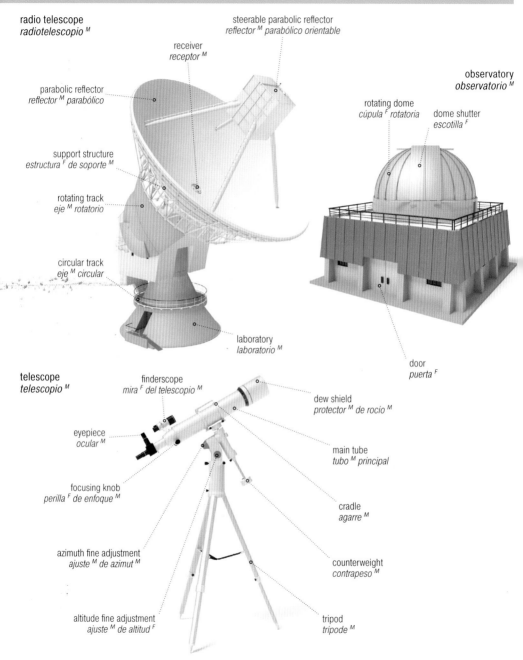

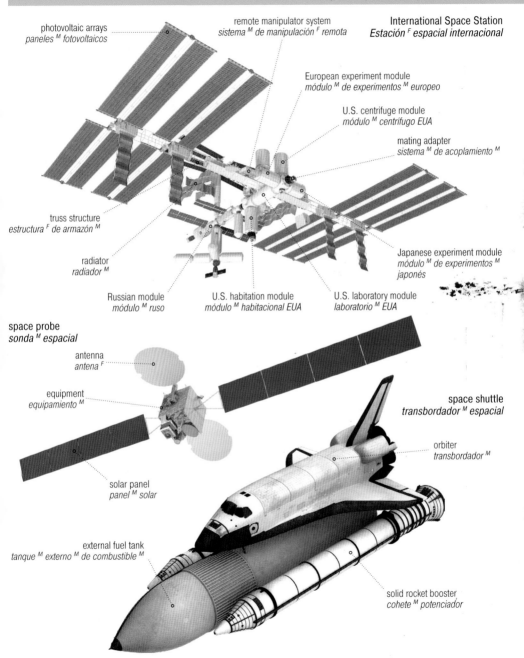

photovoltaic arrays
paneles M fotovoltaicos

remote manipulator system
sistema M de manipulación F remota

International Space Station
Estación F espacial internacional

European experiment module
módulo M de experimentos M europeo

U.S. centrifuge module
módulo M centrífugo EUA

mating adapter
sistema M de acoplamiento M

truss structure
estructura F de armazón M

radiator
radiador M

Russian module
módulo M ruso

U.S. habitation module
módulo M habitacional EUA

U.S. laboratory module
laboratorio M EUA

Japanese experiment module
módulo M de experimentos M japonés

space probe
sonda M espacial

antenna
antena F

equipment
equipamiento M

space shuttle
transbordador M espacial

orbiter
transbordador M

solar panel
panel M solar

external fuel tank
tanque M externo M de combustible M

solid rocket booster
cohete M potenciador

Moon landing
aterrizaje ^F *lunar*

lunar rover
vehículo ^M *de exploración* ^F *lunar*

landing module
módulo ^M *de aterrizaje*

Earth
Tierra ^F

crater
cráter ^M

surface of the Moon
superficie ^F *lunar*

astronaut
astronauta ^M

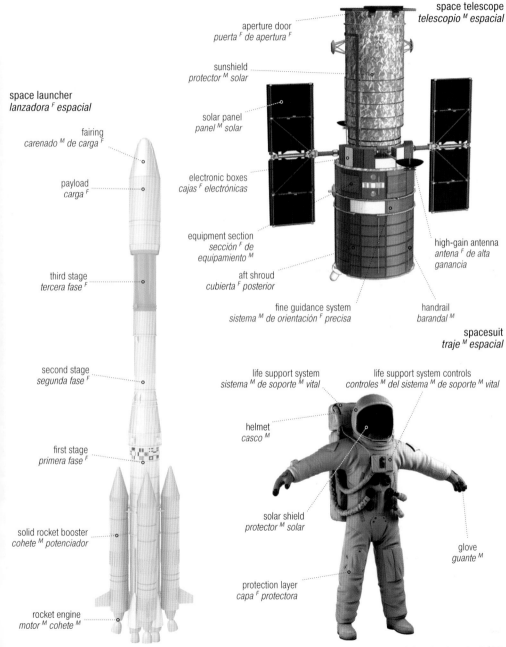

space telescope
telescopio [M] *espacial*

aperture door
puerta [F] *de apertura* [F]

sunshield
protector [M] *solar*

space launcher
lanzadora [F] *espacial*

solar panel
panel [M] *solar*

fairing
carenado [M] *de carga* [F]

payload
carga [F]

electronic boxes
cajas [F] *electrónicas*

equipment section
sección [F] *de
equipamiento* [M]

third stage
tercera fase [F]

high-gain antenna
antena [F] *de alta
ganancia*

aft shroud
cubierta [F] *posterior*

second stage
segunda fase [F]

fine guidance system
sistema [M] *de orientación* [F] *precisa*

handrail
barandal [M]

spacesuit
traje [M] *espacial*

life support system
sistema [M] *de soporte* [M] *vital*

life support system controls
controles [M] *del sistema* [M] *de soporte* [M] *vital*

helmet
casco [M]

first stage
primera fase [F]

solid rocket booster
cohete [M] *potenciador*

solar shield
protector [M] *solar*

glove
guante [M]

rocket engine
motor [M] *cohete* [M]

protection layer
capa [F] *protectora*

ENERGY AND INDUSTRY

INDUSTRIA Y ENERGÍA

solar panel
panel M solar

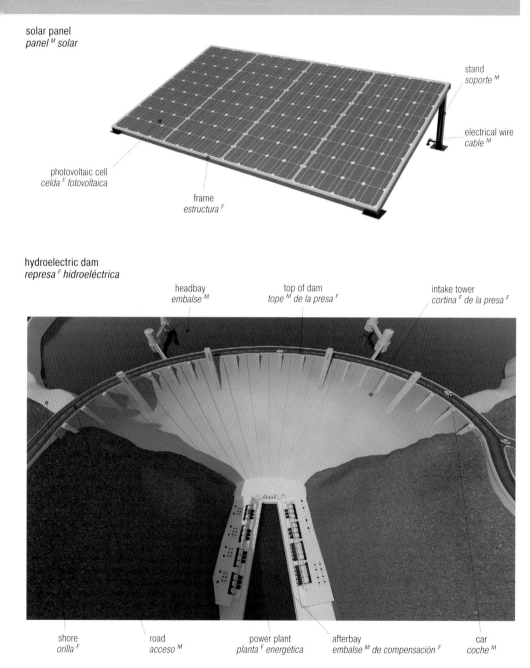

stand
soporte M

electrical wire
cable M

photovoltaic cell
celda F fotovoltaica

frame
estructura F

hydroelectric dam
represa F hidroeléctrica

headbay
embalse M

top of dam
tope M de la presa F

intake tower
cortina F de la presa F

shore
orilla F

road
acceso M

power plant
planta F energética

afterbay
embalse M de compensación F

car
coche M

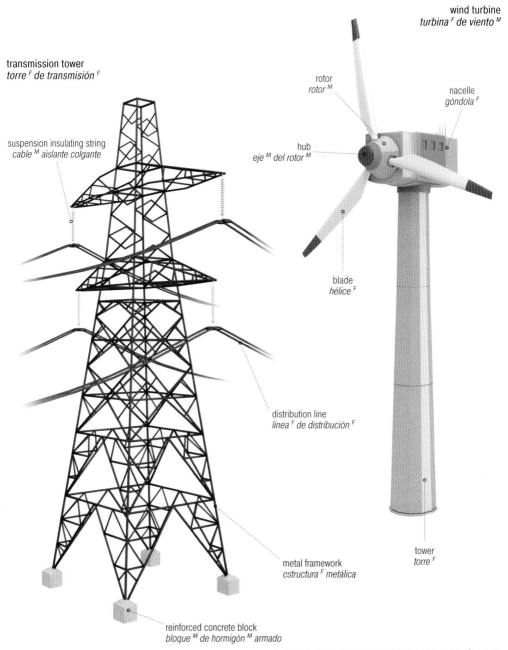

wind turbine
turbina ᶠ de viento ᴹ

transmission tower
torre ᶠ de transmisión ᶠ

rotor
rotor ᴹ

nacelle
góndola ᶠ

suspension insulating string
cable ᴹ aislante colgante

hub
eje ᴹ del rotor ᴹ

blade
hélice ᶠ

distribution line
línea ᶠ de distribución ᶠ

metal framework
estructura ᶠ metálica

tower
torre ᶠ

reinforced concrete block
bloque ᴹ de hormigón ᴹ armado

nuclear power plant
planta [F] *de energía* [F] *nuclear*

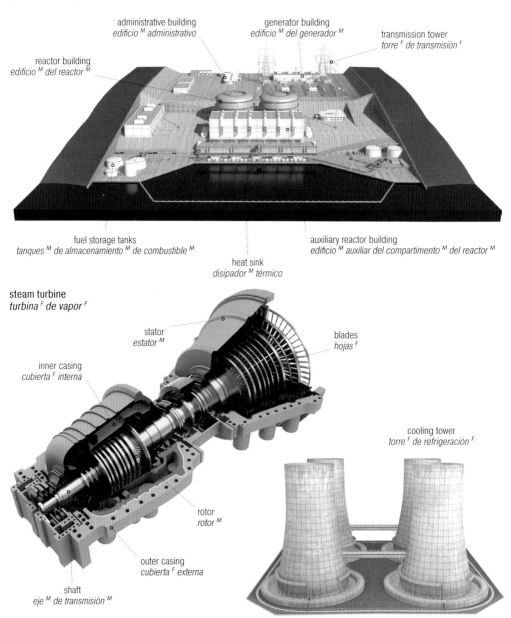

administrative building
edificio [M] *administrativo*

generator building
edificio [M] *del generador* [M]

transmission tower
torre [F] *de transmisión* [F]

reactor building
edificio [M] *del reactor* [M]

fuel storage tanks
tanques [M] *de almacenamiento* [M] *de combustible* [M]

heat sink
disipador [M] *térmico*

auxiliary reactor building
edificio [M] *auxiliar del compartimento* [M] *del reactor* [M]

steam turbine
turbina [F] *de vapor* [F]

stator
estator [M]

blades
hojas [F]

inner casing
cubierta [F] *interna*

cooling tower
torre [F] *de refrigeración* [F]

rotor
rotor [M]

outer casing
cubierta [F] *externa*

shaft
eje [M] *de transmisión* [M]

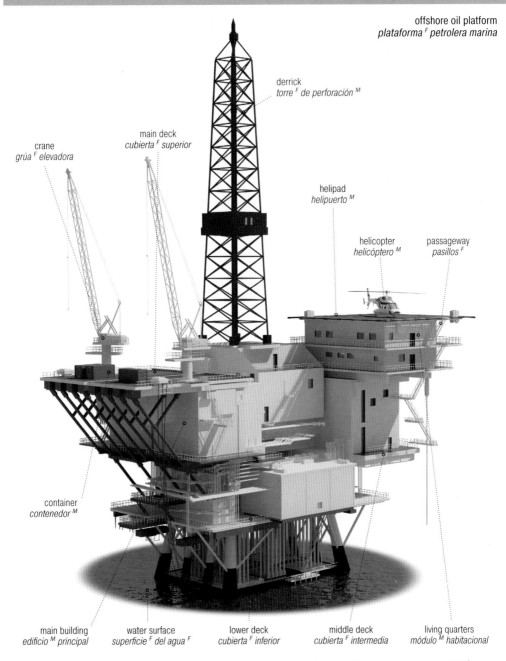

offshore oil platform
plataforma ᶠ *petrolera marina*

derrick
torre ᶠ *de perforación* ᴹ

main deck
cubierta ᶠ *superior*

crane
grúa ᶠ *elevadora*

helipad
helipuerto ᴹ

helicopter
helicóptero ᴹ

passageway
pasillos ᶠ

container
contenedor ᴹ

main building
edificio ᴹ *principal*

water surface
superficie ᶠ *del agua* ᶠ

lower deck
cubierta ᶠ *inferior*

middle deck
cubierta ᶠ *intermedia*

living quarters
módulo ᴹ *habitacional*

oil tank farm
patio ^M *de tanques* ^M *de petróleo* ^M

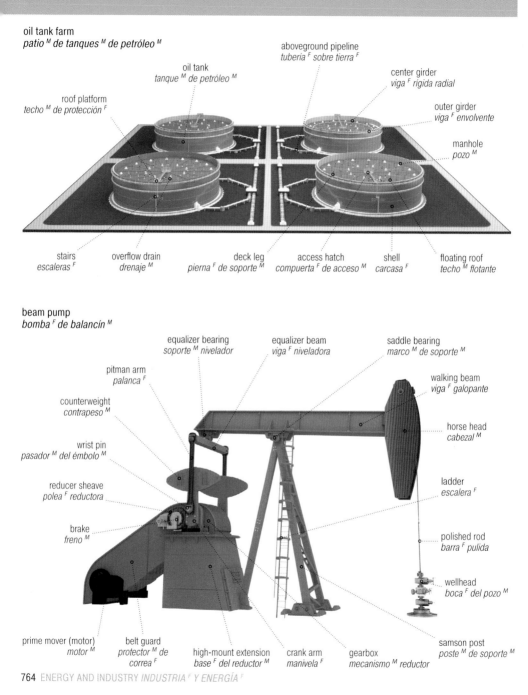

aboveground pipeline
tubería ^F *sobre tierra* ^F

oil tank
tanque ^M *de petróleo* ^M

center girder
viga ^F *rígida radial*

roof platform
techo ^M *de protección* ^F

outer girder
viga ^F *envolvente*

manhole
pozo ^M

stairs
escaleras ^F

overflow drain
drenaje ^M

deck leg
pierna ^F *de soporte* ^M

access hatch
compuerta ^F *de acceso* ^M

shell
carcasa ^F

floating roof
techo ^M *flotante*

beam pump
bomba ^F *de balancín* ^M

equalizer bearing
soporte ^M *nivelador*

equalizer beam
viga ^F *niveladora*

saddle bearing
marco ^M *de soporte* ^M

pitman arm
palanca ^F

walking beam
viga ^F *galopante*

counterweight
contrapeso ^M

horse head
cabezal ^M

wrist pin
pasador ^M *del émbolo* ^M

reducer sheave
polea ^F *reductora*

ladder
escalera ^F

brake
freno ^M

polished rod
barra ^F *pulida*

wellhead
boca ^F *del pozo* ^M

prime mover (motor)
motor ^M

belt guard
protector ^M *de correa* ^F

high-mount extension
base ^F *del reductor* ^M

crank arm
manivela ^F

gearbox
mecanismo ^M *reductor*

samson post
poste ^M *de soporte* ^M

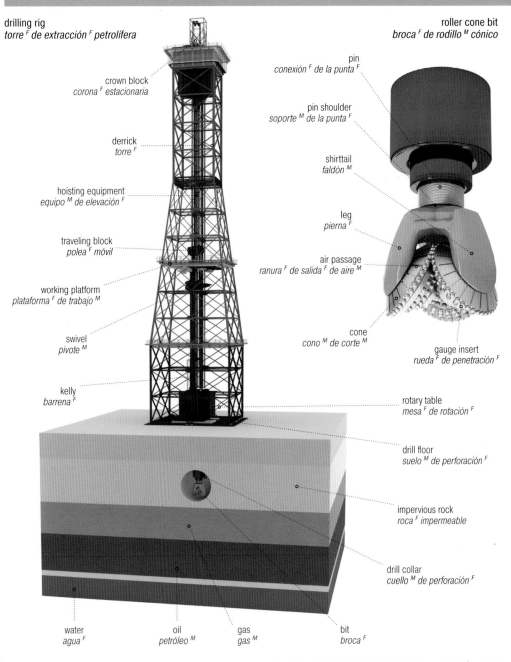

drilling rig
torre ^F de extracción ^F petrolífera

roller cone bit
broca ^F de rodillo ^M cónico

crown block
corona ^F estacionaria

pin
conexión ^F de la punta ^F

pin shoulder
soporte ^M de la punta ^F

derrick
torre ^F

shirttail
faldón ^M

hoisting equipment
equipo ^M de elevación ^F

leg
pierna ^F

traveling block
polea ^F móvil

air passage
ranura ^F de salida ^F de aire ^M

working platform
plataforma ^F de trabajo ^M

swivel
pivote ^M

cone
cono ^M de corte ^F

kelly
barrena ^F

gauge insert
rueda ^F de penetración ^F

rotary table
mesa ^F de rotación ^F

drill floor
suelo ^M de perforación ^F

impervious rock
roca ^F impermeable

drill collar
cuello ^M de perforación ^F

water
agua ^F

oil
petróleo ^M

gas
gas ^M

bit
broca ^F

oil and gas field
campo ^{M} *petrolero y de gas* ^{M}

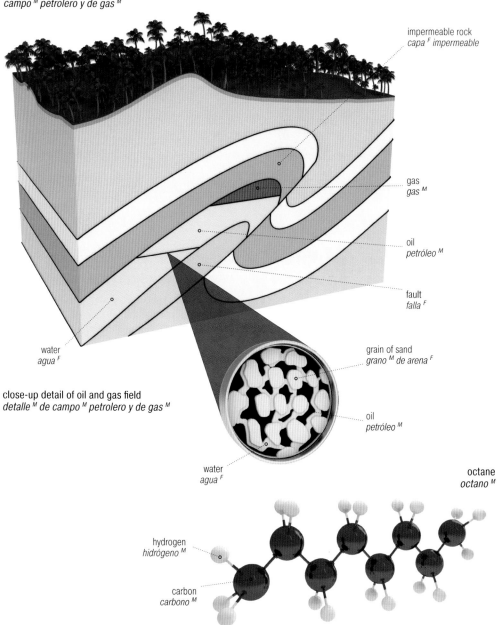

impermeable rock
capa ^{F} *impermeable*

gas
gas ^{M}

oil
petróleo ^{M}

fault
falla ^{F}

water
agua ^{F}

close-up detail of oil and gas field
detalle ^{M} *de campo* ^{M} *petrolero y de gas* ^{M}

grain of sand
grano ^{M} *de arena* ^{F}

oil
petróleo ^{M}

water
agua ^{F}

octane
octano ^{M}

hydrogen
hidrógeno ^{M}

carbon
carbono ^{M}

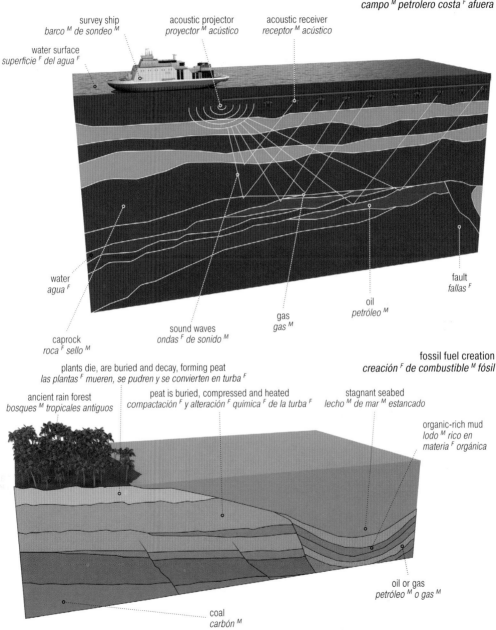

offshore oil field
campo ^M petrolero costa ^F afuera

survey ship
barco ^M de sondeo ^M

acoustic projector
proyector ^M acústico

acoustic receiver
receptor ^M acústico

water surface
superficie ^F del agua ^F

water
agua ^F

fault
fallas ^F

caprock
roca ^F sello ^M

sound waves
ondas ^F de sonido ^M

gas
gas ^M

oil
petróleo ^M

fossil fuel creation
creación ^F de combustible ^M fósil

plants die, are buried and decay, forming peat
las plantas ^F mueren, se pudren y se convierten en turba ^F

ancient rain forest
bosques ^M tropicales antiguos

peat is buried, compressed and heated
compactación ^F y alteración ^F química ^F de la turba ^F

stagnant seabed
lecho ^M de mar ^M estancado

organic-rich mud
lodo ^M rico en materia ^F orgánica

oil or gas
petróleo ^M o gas ^M

coal
carbón ^M

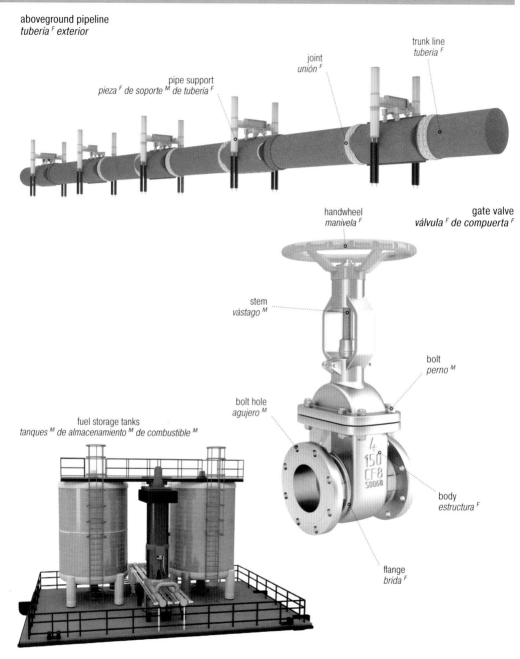

aboveground pipeline
tubería ᶠ exterior

trunk line
tubería ᶠ

joint
unión ᶠ

pipe support
pieza ᶠ de soporte ᴹ de tubería ᶠ

handwheel
manivela ᶠ

gate valve
válvula ᶠ de compuerta ᶠ

stem
vástago ᴹ

bolt
perno ᴹ

bolt hole
agujero ᴹ

fuel storage tanks
tanques ᴹ de almacenamiento ᴹ de combustible ᴹ

body
estructura ᶠ

flange
brida ᶠ

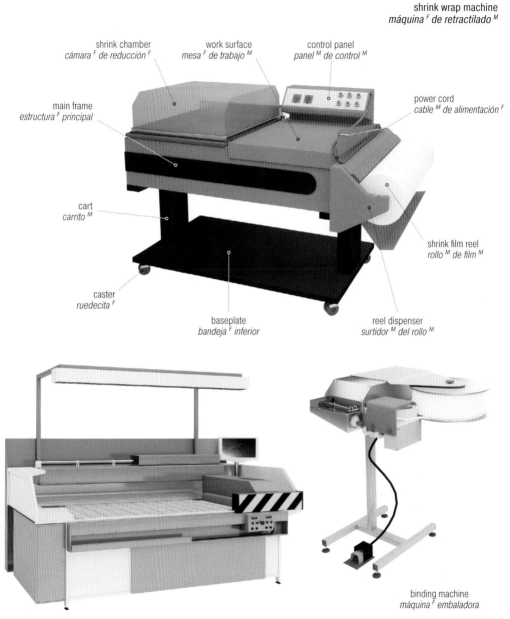

shrink wrap machine
máquina F de retractilado M

shrink chamber
cámara F de reducción F

work surface
mesa F de trabajo M

control panel
panel M de control M

main frame
estructura F principal

power cord
cable M de alimentación F

cart
carrito M

shrink film reel
rollo M de film M

caster
ruedecita F

baseplate
bandeja F inferior

reel dispenser
surtidor M del rollo M

fabric-cutting machine
máquina F de corte M de telas F

binding machine
máquina F embaladora

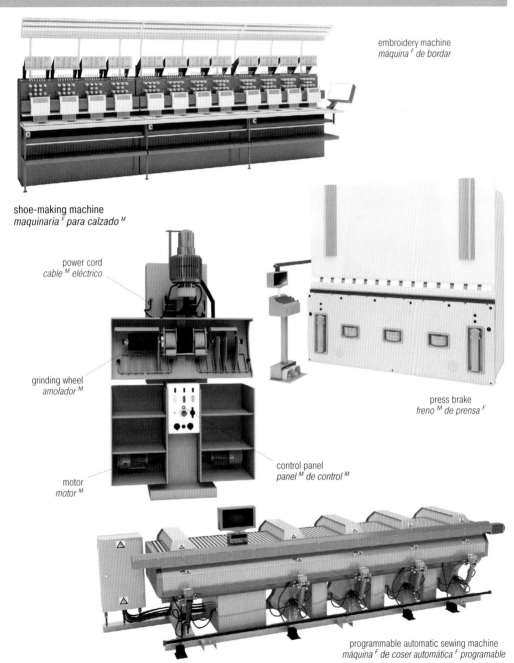

embroidery machine
máquina ᶠ de bordar

shoe-making machine
maquinaria ᶠ para calzado ᴹ

power cord
cable ᴹ eléctrico

grinding wheel
amolador ᴹ

motor
motor ᴹ

press brake
freno ᴹ de prensa ᶠ

control panel
panel ᴹ de control ᴹ

programmable automatic sewing machine
máquina ᶠ de coser automática ᶠ programable

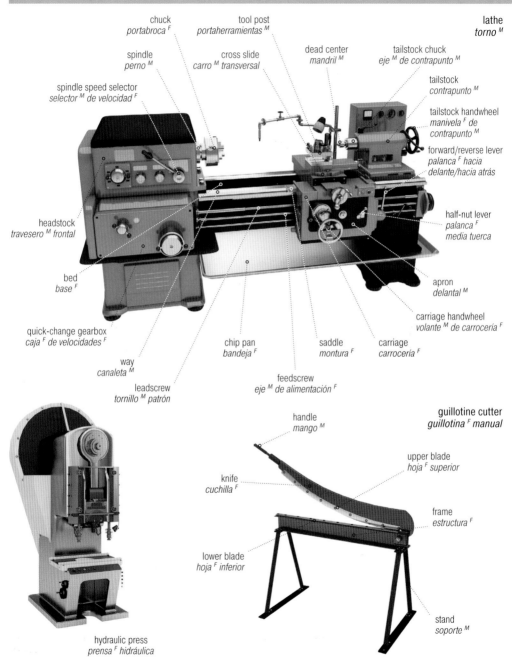

chuck
portabroca ^F

tool post
portaherramientas ^M

lathe
torno ^M

spindle
perno ^M

cross slide
carro ^M transversal

dead center
mandril ^M

tailstock chuck
eje ^M de contrapunto ^M

spindle speed selector
selector ^M de velocidad ^F

tailstock
contrapunto ^M

tailstock handwheel
manivela ^F de
contrapunto ^M

forward/reverse lever
palanca ^F hacia
delante/hacia atrás

half-nut lever
palanca ^F
media tuerca

headstock
travesero ^M frontal

bed
base ^F

apron
delantal ^M

quick-change gearbox
caja ^F de velocidades ^F

carriage handwheel
volante ^M de carrocería ^F

way
canaleta ^M

chip pan
bandeja ^F

saddle
montura ^F

carriage
carrocería ^F

leadscrew
tornillo ^M patrón

feedscrew
eje ^M de alimentación ^F

handle
mango ^M

guillotine cutter
guillotina ^F manual

knife
cuchilla ^F

upper blade
hoja ^F superior

frame
estructura ^F

lower blade
hoja ^F inferior

stand
soporte ^M

hydraulic press
prensa ^F hidráulica

milling machine
máquina ^F *de fresado* ^M

spindle
husillo ^M

control panel
panel ^M *de control* ^M

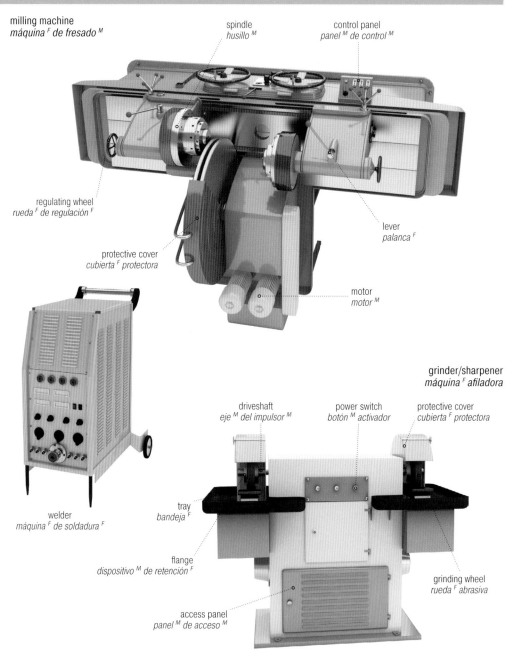

regulating wheel
rueda ^F *de regulación* ^F

lever
palanca ^F

protective cover
cubierta ^F *protectora*

motor
motor ^M

grinder/sharpener
máquina ^F *afiladora*

driveshaft
eje ^M *del impulsor* ^M

power switch
botón ^M *activador*

protective cover
cubierta ^F *protectora*

tray
bandeja ^F

welder
máquina ^F *de soldadura* ^F

flange
dispositivo ^M *de retención* ^F

grinding wheel
rueda ^F *abrasiva*

access panel
panel ^M *de acceso* ^M

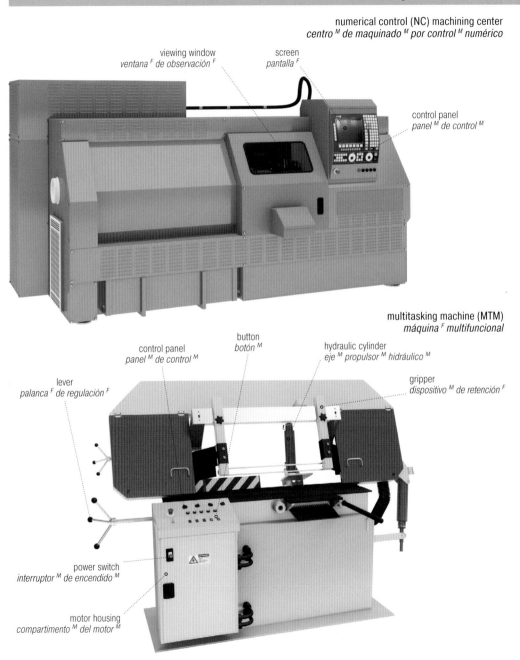

numerical control (NC) machining center
centro ^M *de maquinado* ^M *por control* ^M *numérico*

viewing window
ventana ^F *de observación* ^F

screen
pantalla ^F

control panel
panel ^M *de control* ^M

multitasking machine (MTM)
máquina ^F *multifuncional*

button
botón ^M

control panel
panel ^M *de control* ^M

hydraulic cylinder
eje ^M *propulsor* ^M *hidráulico* ^M

lever
palanca ^F *de regulación* ^F

gripper
dispositivo ^M *de retención* ^F

power switch
interruptor ^M *de encendido* ^M

motor housing
compartimento ^M *del motor* ^M

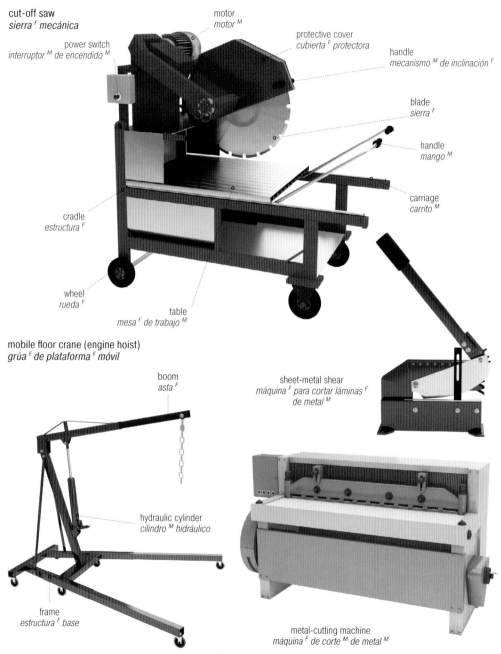

cut-off saw
sierra ꟳ mecánica

motor
motor ᴹ

power switch
interruptor ᴹ de encendido ᴹ

protective cover
cubierta ꟳ protectora

handle
mecanismo ᴹ de inclinación ꟳ

blade
sierra ꟳ

handle
mango ᴹ

carriage
carrito ᴹ

cradle
estructura ꟳ

wheel
rueda ꟳ

table
mesa ꟳ de trabajo ᴹ

mobile floor crane (engine hoist)
grúa ꟳ de plataforma ꟳ móvil

boom
asta ꟳ

sheet-metal shear
máquina ꟳ para cortar láminas ꟳ de metal ᴹ

hydraulic cylinder
cilindro ᴹ hidráulico

frame
estructura ꟳ base

metal-cutting machine
máquina ꟳ de corte ᴹ de metal ᴹ

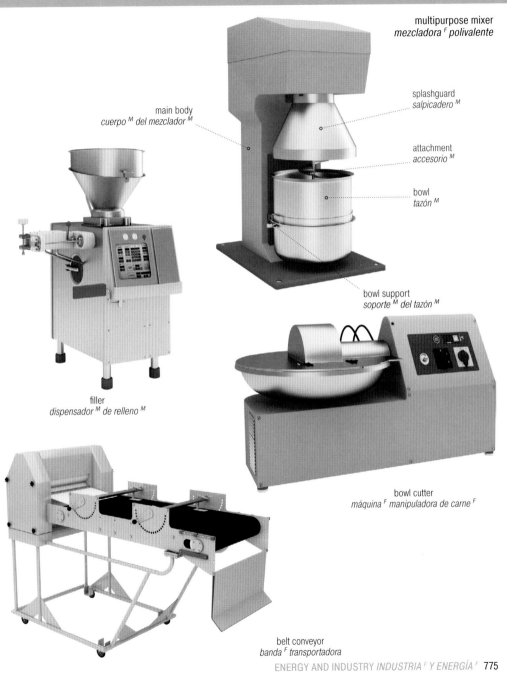

multipurpose mixer
mezcladora ^F polivalente

splashguard
salpicadero ^M

main body
cuerpo ^M del mezclador ^M

attachment
accesorio ^M

bowl
tazón ^M

bowl support
soporte ^M del tazón ^M

filler
dispensador ^M de relleno ^M

bowl cutter
máquina ^F manipuladora de carne ^F

belt conveyor
banda ^F transportadora

part of conveyor system
parte ^F *de cinta* ^F *transportadora*

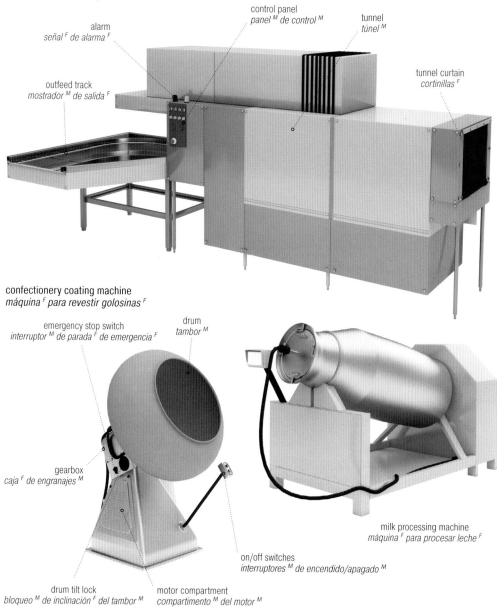

alarm
señal ^F *de alarma* ^F

control panel
panel ^M *de control* ^M

tunnel
túnel ^M

outfeed track
mostrador ^M *de salida* ^F

tunnel curtain
cortinillas ^F

confectionery coating machine
máquina ^F *para revestir golosinas* ^F

emergency stop switch
interruptor ^M *de parada* ^F *de emergencia* ^F

drum
tambor ^M

gearbox
caja ^F *de engranajes* ^M

milk processing machine
máquina ^F *para procesar leche* ^F

on/off switches
interruptores ^M *de encendido/apagado* ^M

drum tilt lock
bloqueo ^M *de inclinación* ^F *del tambor* ^M

motor compartment
compartimento ^M *del motor* ^M

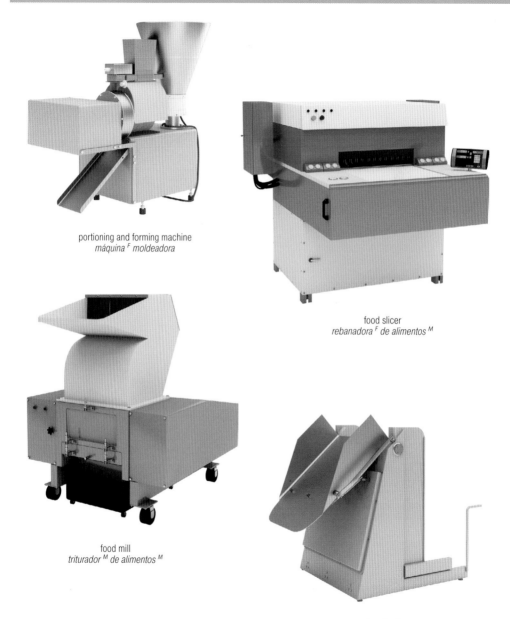

portioning and forming machine
máquina [F] *moldeadora*

food slicer
rebanadora [F] *de alimentos* [M]

food mill
triturador [M] *de alimentos* [M]

conveyor system feeder
alimentador [M] *de banda* [F] *de transporte* [M]

rib
refuerzo ^M

hard hat
casco ^M *de seguridad* ^F

peak
visera ^F

face shield
protector de cara ^M

suspension
cinta ^F *para la cabeza* ^F

earplugs
tapones ^M

ear protectors
protectores ^M *para el oído* ^M

safety boots
botas ^F *de seguridad* ^F

toe guard
protector para los dedos ^M *de los pies* ^M

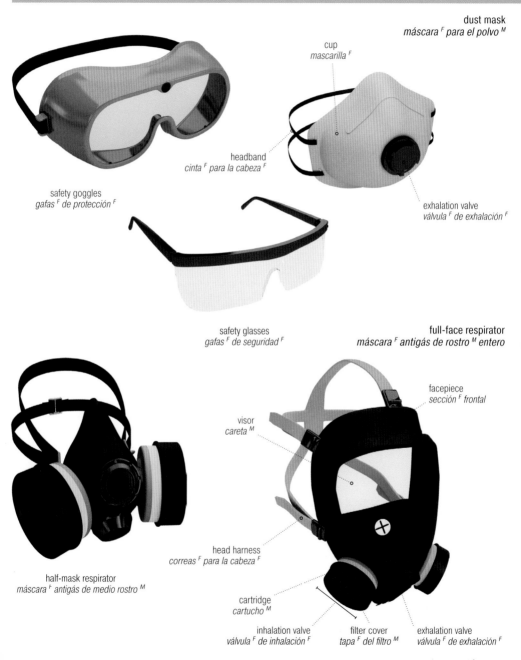

dust mask
máscara **F** *para el polvo* **M**

cup
mascarilla **F**

headband
cinta **F** *para la cabeza* **F**

safety goggles
gafas **F** *de protección* **F**

exhalation valve
válvula **F** *de exhalación* **F**

safety glasses
gafas **F** *de seguridad* **F**

full-face respirator
máscara **F** *antigás de rostro* **M** *entero*

facepiece
sección **F** *frontal*

visor
careta **M**

head harness
correas **F** *para la cabeza* **F**

half-mask respirator
máscara **F** *antigás de medio rostro* **M**

cartridge
cartucho **M**

inhalation valve
válvula **F** *de inhalación* **F**

filter cover
tapa **F** *del filtro* **M**

exhalation valve
válvula **F** *de exhalación* **F**

ENGLISH INDEX

T

ÍNDICE ESPAÑOL